THE
HARVARD CLASSICS

Registered Edition

◆

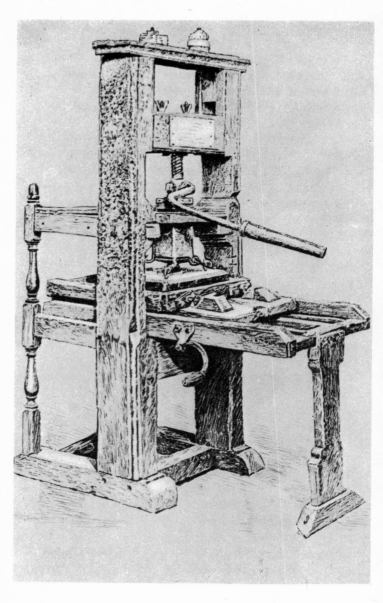

Printing Press at which Franklin worked in Watts's
Printing Office, London, in 1725 —Page 44

THE HARVARD CLASSICS
EDITED BY CHARLES W. ELIOT, LL.D.

The Autobiography *of* Benjamin Franklin

The Journal *of* John Woolman

Fruits of Solitude
William Penn

With *Introductions and* Notes

P. F. Collier & Son Corporation
NEW YORK

MANUFACTURED IN U. S. A.

CONTENTS

INTRODUCTORY NOTE

BENJAMIN FRANKLIN was born in Milk Street, Boston, on January 6 (January 17, new style), 1706. His father, Josiah Franklin, was a tallow chandler who married twice, and of his seventeen children Benjamin was the youngest son. His schooling ended at ten, and at twelve he was bound apprentice to his brother James, a printer, who published the *New England Courant*. To this journal he became a contributor, and later was for a time its nominal editor. But the brothers quarreled, and Benjamin ran away, going first to New York, and thence to Philadelphia, where he arrived in October, 1723. He soon obtained work as a printer, but after a few months he was induced by Governor Keith to go to London, where, finding Keith's promises empty, he again worked as a compositor till he was brought back to Philadelphia by a merchant named Denman, who gave him a position in his business. On Denman's death he returned to his former trade, and shortly set up a printing house of his own from which he published *The Pennsylvania Gazette*, to which he contributed many essays, and which he made a medium for agitating a variety of local reforms. In 1732 he began to issue his famous *Poor Richard's Almanac,* for the enrichment of which he borrowed or composed those pithy utterances of worldly wisdom which are the basis of a large part of his popular reputation. In 1758, the year in which he ceased writing for the Almanac, he printed in it "Father Abraham's Sermon," now regarded as the most famous piece of literature produced in Colonial America.

Meantime Franklin was concerning himself more and more with public affairs. He set forth a scheme for an Academy, which was taken up later and finally developed into the University of Pennsylvania; and he founded an "American Philosophical Society" for the purpose of enabling scientific men to communicate their discoveries to one another. He himself had already begun his electrical researches, which, with other scientific inquiries, he carried on in the intervals of money-making and politics to the end of his life. In 1748 he sold his business in order to get leisure for study, having now acquired comparative wealth; and in a few years he had made discoveries that gave him a reputation with the learned throughout Europe. In politics he proved very able both as an administrator and as a controversialist; but his record as an office-holder is stained by the use he made of his position to advance his relatives. His most notable service in home politics was his reform of the postal system;

but his fame as a statesman rests chiefly on his services in connection with the relations of the Colonies with Great Britain, and later with France. In 1757 he was sent to England to protest against the influence of the Penns in the government of the colony, and for five years he remained there, striving to enlighten the people and the ministry of England as to Colonial conditions. On his return to America he played an honorable part in the Paxton affair, through which he lost his seat in the Assembly; but in 1764 he was again despatched to England as agent for the colony, this time to petition the King to resume the government from the hands of the proprietors. In London he actively opposed the proposed Stamp Act, but lost the credit for this and much of his popularity through his securing for a friend the office of stamp agent in America. Even his effective work in helping to obtain the repeal of the act left him still a suspect; but he continued his efforts to present the case for the Colonies as the troubles thickened toward the crisis of the Revolution. In 1767 he crossed to France, where he was received with honor; but before his return home in 1775 he lost his position as postmaster through his share in divulging to Massachusetts the famous letter of Hutchinson and Oliver. On his arrival in Philadelphia he was chosen a member of the Continental Congress, and in 1777 he was despatched to France as commissioner for the United States. Here he remained till 1785, the favorite of French society; and with such success did he conduct the affairs of his country that when he finally returned he received a place only second to that of Washington as the champion of American independence. He died on April 17, 1790.

The first five chapters of the Autobiography were composed in England in 1771, continued in 1784–5, and again in 1788, at which date he brought it down to 1757. After a most extraordinary series of adventures, the original form of the manuscript was finally printed by Mr. John Bigelow, and is here reproduced in recognition of its value as a picture of one of the most notable personalities of Colonial times, and of its acknowledged rank as one of the great autobiographies of the world.

BENJAMIN FRANKLIN
HIS AUTOBIOGRAPHY
1706–1757

TWYFORD, *at the Bishop of St. Asaph's*,[1] 1771.

DEAR SON: I have ever had pleasure in obtaining any little anecdotes of my ancestors. You may remember the inquiries I made among the remains of my relations when you were with me in England, and the journey I undertook for that purpose. Imagining it may be equally agreeable to[2] you to know the circumstances of my life, many of which you are yet unacquainted with, and expecting the enjoyment of a week's uninterrupted leisure in my present country retirement, I sit down to write them for you. To which I have besides some other inducements. Having emerged from the poverty and obscurity in which I was born and bred, to a state of affluence and some degree of reputation in the world, and having gone so far through life with a considerable share of felicity, the conducing means I made use of, which with the blessing of God so well succeeded, my posterity may like to know, as they may find some of them suitable to their own situations, and therefore fit to be imitated.

That felicity, when I reflected on it, has induced me sometimes to say, that were it offered to my choice, I should have no objection to a repetition of the same life from its beginning, only asking the advantages authors have in a second edition to correct some faults of the first. So I might, besides correcting the faults, change some sinister accidents and events of it for others more favorable. But though this were denied, I should still accept the offer. Since such a repetition is not to be expected, the next thing most like living

---

[1] The country-seat of Bishop Shipley, the good bishop, as Dr. Franklin used to style him.—B.

[2] After the words "agreeable to" the words "some of" were interlined and afterward effaced.—B.

one's life over again seems to be a recollection of that life, and to make that recollection as durable as possible by putting it down in writing.

Hereby, too, I shall indulge the inclination so natural in old men, to be talking of themselves and their own past actions; and I shall indulge it without being tiresome to others, who, through respect to age, might conceive themselves obliged to give me a hearing, since this may be read or not as any one pleases. And, lastly (I may as well confess it, since my denial of it will be believed by nobody), perhaps I shall a good deal gratify my own *vanity*. Indeed, I scarce ever heard or saw the introductory words, *"Without vanity I may say,"* &c., but some vain thing immediately followed. Most people dislike vanity in others, whatever share they have of it themselves; but I give it fair quarter wherever I meet with it, being persuaded that it is often productive of good to the possessor, and to others that are within his sphere of action; and therefore, in many cases, it would not be altogether absurd if a man were to thank God for his vanity among the other comforts of life.

And now I speak of thanking God, I desire with all humility to acknowledge that I owe the mentioned happiness of my past life to His kind providence, which lead me to the means I used and gave them success. My belief of this induces me to *hope,* though I must not *presume,* that the same goodness will still be exercised toward me, in continuing that happiness, or enabling me to bear a fatal reverse, which I may experience as others have done: the complexion of my future fortune being known to Him only in whose power it is to bless to us even our afflictions.

The notes one of my uncles (who had the same kind of curiosity in collecting family anecdotes) once put into my hands, furnished me with several particulars relating to our ancestors. From these notes I learned that the family had lived in the same village, Ecton, in Northamptonshire, for three hundred years, and how much longer he knew not (perhaps from the time when the name of Franklin, that before was the name of an order of people, was assumed by them as a surname when others took surnames all over the kingdom), on a freehold of about thirty acres, aided by the smith's business, which had continued in the family till his time, the eldest son being always bred to that business; a custom which he and my father followed as to their eldest sons. When I searched the registers at Ecton, I found an account of their births, marriages and burials from the year 1555 only, there being no registers kept in that parish at any time preceding. By that register I perceived that I was the youngest son of the youngest son for five generations back. My grandfather Thomas, who was born in 1598, lived at Ecton till he grew too old to follow business longer, when he went to live with his son John, a dyer at Banbury, in Oxfordshire, with whom my father served an apprenticeship. There my grandfather died and lies buried. We saw his gravestone in 1758. His eldest son Thomas lived in the house at Ecton, and left it with the land to his only child, a daughter, who, with her husband, one Fisher, of Wellingborough, sold it to Mr. Isted, now lord of the manor there. My grandfather had four sons that grew up, viz.: Thomas, John, Benjamin and Josiah. I will give you what account I can of them, at this distance from my papers, and if these are not lost in my absence, you will among them find many more particulars.

Thomas was bred a smith under his father; but, being ingenious, and encouraged in learning (as all my brothers were) by an Esquire Palmer, then the principal gentleman in that parish, he qualified himself for the business of scrivener; became a considerable man in the county; was a chief mover of all public-spirited undertakings for the county or town of Northampton, and his own village, of which many instances were related of him; and much taken notice of and patronized by the then Lord Halifax. He died in 1702, January 6, old style, just four years to a day before I was born. The account we received of his life and character from some old people at Ecton, I remember, struck you as something extraordinary, from its similarity to what you knew of mine. "Had he died on the same day," you said, "one might have supposed a transmigration."

John was bred a dyer, I believe of woolens. Benjamin was bred a silk dyer, serving an apprenticeship at London. He was an ingenious man. I remember him well, for when I was a boy he came over to my father in Boston, and lived in the house with us some years. He lived to a great age. His grandson, Samuel Franklin, now lives in Boston. He left behind him two quarto volumes, MS.,

of his own poetry, consisting of little occasional pieces addressed to
his friends and relations, of which the following, sent to me, is a
specimen.[3] He had formed a short-hand of his own, which he
taught me, but, never practising it, I have now forgot it. I was
named after this uncle, there being a particular affection between
him and my father. He was very pious, a great attender of sermons
of the best preachers, which he took down in his short-hand, and
had with him many volumes of them. He was also much of a
politician; too much, perhaps, for his station. There fell lately into
my hands, in London, a collection he had made of all the principal
pamphlets, relating to public affairs, from 1641 to 1717; many of
the volumes are wanting as appears by the numbering, but there
still remain eight volumes in folio, and twenty-four in quarto and
in octavo. A dealer in old books met with them, and knowing me
by my sometimes buying of him, he brought them to me. It seems
my uncle must have left them here, when he went to America,
which was about fifty years since. There are many of his notes in
the margins.

This obscure family of ours was early in the Reformation, and
continued Protestants through the reign of Queen Mary, when
they were sometimes in danger of trouble on account of their zeal
against popery. They had got an English Bible, and to conceal
and secure it, it was fastened open with tapes under and within
the cover of a joint-stool. When my great-great-grandfather read
it to his family, he turned up the joint-stool upon his knees, turning
over the leaves then under the tapes. One of the children stood at
the door to give notice if he saw the apparitor coming, who was
an officer of the spiritual court. In that case the stool was turned
down again upon its feet, when the Bible remained concealed under
it as before. This anecdote I had from my uncle Benjamin. The
family continued all of the Church of England till about the end
of Charles the Second's reign, when some of the ministers that had
been outed for non-conformity holding conventicles in Northamptonshire, Benjamin and Josiah adhered to them, and so continued

---

[3] Here follow in the margin the words, in brackets, "here insert it," but the poetry
is not given. Mr. Sparks informs us (Life of Franklin, p. 6) that these volumes had
been preserved, and were in possession of Mrs. Emmons, of Boston, great-grand-
daughter of their author.

all their lives: the rest of the family remained with the Episcopal Church.

Josiah, my father, married young, and carried his wife with three children into New England, about 1682. The conventicles having been forbidden by law, and frequently disturbed, induced some considerable men of his acquaintance to remove to that country, and he was prevailed with to accompany them thither, where they expected to enjoy their mode of religion with freedom. By the same wife he had four children more born there, and by a second wife ten more, in all seventeen; of which I remember thirteen sitting at one time at his table, who all grew up to be men and women, and married; I was the youngest son, and the youngest child but two, and was born in Boston, New England. My mother, the second wife, was Abiah Folger, daughter of Peter Folger, one of the first settlers of New England, of whom honorable mention is made by Cotton Mather, in his church history of that country, entitled Magnalia Christi Americana, as *a godly, learned Englishman,* if I remember the words rightly. I have heard that he wrote sundry small occasional pieces, but only one of them was printed, which I saw now many years since. It was written in 1675, in the home-spun verse of that time and people, and addressed to those then concerned in the government there. It was in favor of liberty of conscience, and in behalf of the Baptists, Quakers, and other sectaries that had been under persecution, ascribing the Indian wars, and other distresses that had befallen the country, to that persecution, as so many judgments of God to punish so heinous an offense, and exhorting a repeal of those uncharitable laws. The whole appeared to me as written with a good deal of decent plainness and manly freedom. The six concluding lines I remember, though I have forgotten the two first of the stanza; but the purport of them was, that his censures proceeded from good-will, and, therefore, he would be known to be the author.

> "Because to be a libeller (says he)
> I hate it with my heart;
> From Sherburne town, where now I dwell
> My name I do put here;
> Without offense your real friend,
> It is Peter Folgier."

My elder brothers were all put apprentices to different trades. I was put to the grammar-school at eight years of age, my father intending to devote me, as the tithe of his sons, to the service of the Church. My early readiness in learning to read (which must have been very early, as I do not remember when I could not read), and the opinion of all his friends, that I should certainly make a good scholar, encouraged him in this purpose of his. My uncle Benjamin, too, approved of it, and proposed to give me all his short-hand volumes of sermons, I suppose as a stock to set up with, if I would learn his character. I continued, however, at the grammar-school not quite one year, though in that time I had risen gradually from the middle of the class of that year to be the head of it, and farther was removed into the next class above it, in order to go with that into the third at the end of the year. But my father, in the meantime, from a view of the expense of a college education, which having so large a family he could not well afford, and the mean living many so educated were afterwards able to obtain—reasons that he gave to his friends in my hearing—altered his first intention, took me from the grammar-school, and sent me to a school for writing and arithmetic, kept by a then famous man, Mr. George Brownell, very successful in his profession generally, and that by mild, encouraging methods. Under him I acquired fair writing pretty soon, but I failed in the arithmetic, and made no progress in it. At ten years old I was taken home to assist my father in his business, which was that of a tallow-chandler and sope-boiler; a business he was not bred to, but had assumed on his arrival in New England, and on finding his dying trade would not maintain his family, being in little request. Accordingly, I was employed in cutting wick for the candles, filling the dipping mold and the molds for cast candles, attending the shop, going of errands, etc.

I disliked the trade, and had a strong inclination for the sea, but my father declared against it; however, living near the water, I was much in and about it, learnt early to swim well, and to manage boats; and when in a boat or canoe with other boys, I was commonly allowed to govern, especially in any case of difficulty; and upon other occasions I was generally a leader among the boys, and sometimes led them into scrapes, of which I will mention one instance, as it shows an early projecting public spirit, tho' not then justly conducted.

There was a salt-marsh that bounded part of the mill-pond, on the edge of which, at high water, we used to stand to fish for minnows. By much trampling, we had made it a mere quagmire. My proposal was to build a wharff there fit for us to stand upon, and I showed my comrades a large heap of stones, which were intended for a new house near the marsh, and which would very well suit our purpose. Accordingly, in the evening, when the workmen were gone, I assembled a number of my play-fellows, and working with them diligently like so many emmets, sometimes two or three to a stone, we brought them all away and built our little wharff. The next morning the workmen were surprised at missing the stones, which were found in our wharff. Inquiry was made after the removers; we were discovered and complained of; several of us were corrected by our fathers; and though I pleaded the usefulness of the work, mine convinced me that nothing was useful which was not honest.

I think you may like to know something of his person and character. He had an excellent constitution of body, was of middle stature, but well set, and very strong; he was ingenious, could draw prettily, was skilled a little in music, and had a clear pleasing voice, so that when he played psalm tunes on his violin and sung withal, as he sometimes did in an evening after the business of the day was over, it was extremely agreeable to hear. He had a mechanical genius too, and, on occasion, was very handy in the use of other tradesmen's tools; but his great excellence lay in a sound understanding and solid judgment in prudential matters, both in private and publick affairs. In the latter, indeed, he was never employed, the numerous family he had to educate and the straitness of his circumstances keeping him close to his trade; but I remember well his being frequently visited by leading people, who consulted him for his opinion in affairs of the town or of the church he belonged to, and showed a good deal of respect for his judgment and advice: he was also much consulted by private persons about their affairs when any difficulty occurred, and frequently chosen an arbitrator between contending parties.

At his table he liked to have, as often as he could, some sensible friend or neighbor to converse with, and always took care to start some ingenious or useful topic for discourse, which might tend to improve the minds of his children. By this means he turned our attention to what was good, just, and prudent in the conduct of life; and little or no notice was ever taken of what related to the victuals on the table, whether it was well or ill dressed, in or out of season, of good or bad flavor, preferable or inferior to this or that other thing of the kind, so that I was bro't up in such a perfect inattention to those matters as to be quite indifferent what kind of food was set before me, and so unobservant of it, that to this day if I am asked I can scarce tell a few hours after dinner what I dined upon. This has been a convenience to me in travelling, where my companions have been sometimes very unhappy for want of a suitable gratification of their more delicate, because better instructed, tastes and appetites.

My mother had likewise an excellent constitution: she suckled all her ten children. I never knew either my father or mother to have any sickness but that of which they dy'd, he at 89, and she at 85 years of age. They lie buried together at Boston, where I some years since placed a marble over their grave, with this inscription:

JOSIAH FRANKLIN,
and
ABIAH his wife,
lie here interred.
They lived lovingly together in wedlock
fifty-five years.
Without an estate, or any gainful employment,
By constant labor and industry,
with God's blessing,
They maintained a large family
comfortably,
and brought up thirteen children
and seven grandchildren
reputably.
From this instance, reader,
Be encouraged to diligence in thy calling,
And distrust not Providence.
He was a pious and prudent man;
She, a discreet and virtuous woman.

Their youngest son,
In filial regard to their memory,
Places this stone.
J. F. born 1655, died 1744, Ætat 89.
A. F. born 1667, died 1752, —— 85.

By my rambling digressions I perceive myself to be grown old. I us'd to write more methodically. But one does not dress for private company as for a publick ball. 'Tis perhaps only negligence.

To return: I continued thus employed in my father's business for two years, that is, till I was twelve years old; and my brother John, who was bred to that business, having left my father, married, and set up for himself at Rhode Island, there was all appearance that I was destined to supply his place, and become a tallow-chandler. But my dislike to the trade continuing, my father was under apprehensions that if he did not find one for me more agreeable, I should break away and get to sea, as his son Josiah had done, to his great vexation. He therefore sometimes took me to walk with him, and see joiners, bricklayers, turners, braziers, etc., at their work, that he might observe my inclination, and endeavor to fix it on some trade or other on land. It has ever since been a pleasure to me to see good workmen handle their tools; and it has been useful to me, having learnt so much by it as to be able to do little jobs myself in my house when a workman could not readily be got, and to construct little machines for my experiments, while the intention of making the experiment was fresh and warm in my mind. My father at last fixed upon the cutler's trade, and my uncle Benjamin's son Samuel, who was bred to that business in London, being about that time established in Boston, I was sent to be with him some time on liking. But his expectations of a fee with me displeasing my father, I was taken home again.

From a child I was fond of reading, and all the little money that came into my hands was ever laid out in books. Pleased with the Pilgrim's Progress, my first collection was of John Bunyan's works in separate little volumes. I afterward sold them to enable me to buy R. Burton's Historical Collections; they were small chapmen's books, and cheap, 40 or 50 in all. My father's little library consisted chiefly of books in polemic divinity, most of which I read, and have since often regretted that, at a time when I had such a thirst for knowledge, more proper books had not fallen in my way, since it was now resolved I should not be a clergyman. Plutarch's Lives there was in which I read abundantly, and I still think that time spent to great advantage. There was also a book of De Foe's, called an Essay on Projects, and another of Dr. Mather's, called Essays to do Good, which perhaps gave me a turn of thinking that had an influence on some of the principal future events of my life.

This bookish inclination at length determined my father to make me a printer, though he had already one son (James) of that profession. In 1717 my brother James returned from England with a press and letters to set up his business in Boston. I liked it much better than that of my father, but still had a hankering for the sea. To prevent the apprehended effect of such an inclination, my father was impatient to have me bound to my brother. I stood out some time, but at last was persuaded, and signed the indentures when I was yet but twelve years old. I was to serve as an apprentice till I was twenty-one years of age, only I was to be allowed journeyman's wages during the last year. In a little time I made great proficiency in the business, and became a useful hand to my brother. I now had access to better books. An acquaintance with the apprentices of booksellers enabled me sometimes to borrow a small one, which I was careful to return soon and clean. Often I sat up in my room reading the greatest part of the night, when the book was borrowed in the evening and to be returned early in the morning, lest it should be missed or wanted.

And after some time an ingenious tradesman, Mr. Matthew Adams, who had a pretty collection of books, and who frequented our printing-house, took notice of me, invited me to his library, and very kindly lent me such books as I chose to read. I now took a fancy to poetry, and made some little pieces; my brother, thinking it might turn to account, encouraged me, and put me on composing occasional ballads. One was called The Lighthouse Tragedy, and contained an account of the drowning of Captain Worthilake, with his two daughters: the other was a sailor's song, on the taking of Teach (or Blackbeard) the pirate. They were wretched stuff, in the Grub-street-ballad style; and when they were printed he sent me about the town to sell them. The first sold wonderfully, the event being recent, having made a great noise. This flattered my vanity; but my father discouraged me by ridiculing my performances, and telling me verse-makers were generally beggars. So I escaped being a poet, most probably a very bad one; but as prose writing had been of great use to me in the course of my life, and was a principal means of my advancement, I shall tell you how, in such a situation, I acquired what little ability I have in that way.

There was another bookish lad in the town, John Collins by name, with whom I was intimately acquainted. We sometimes disputed, and very fond we were of argument, and very desirous of confuting one another, which disputatious turn, by the way, is apt to become a very bad habit, making people often extremely disagreeable in company by the contradiction that is necessary to bring it into practice; and thence, besides souring and spoiling the conversation, is productive of disgusts and, perhaps enmities where you may have occasion for friendship. I had caught it by reading my father's books of dispute about religion. Persons of good sense, I have since observed, seldom fall into it, except lawyers, university men, and men of all sorts that have been bred at Edinborough.

A question was once, somehow or other, started between Collins and me, of the propriety of educating the female sex in learning, and their abilities for study. He was of opinion that it was improper, and that they were naturally unequal to it. I took the contrary side, perhaps a little for dispute's sake. He was naturally more eloquent, had a ready plenty of words; and sometimes, as I thought, bore me down more by his fluency than by the strength of his reasons. As we parted without settling the point, and were not to see one another again for some time, I sat down to put my arguments in writing, which I copied fair and sent to him. He answered, and I replied. Three or four letters of a side had passed, when my father happened to find my papers and read them. Without entering into the discussion, he took occasion to talk to me about the manner of my writing; observed that, though I had the advantage of my antagonist in correct spelling and pointing (which I ow'd to the printing-house), I fell far short in elegance of expression, in method and in perspicuity, of which he convinced me by several instances.

I saw the justice of his remark, and thence grew more attentive to the manner in writing, and determined to endeavor at improvement.

About this time I met with an odd volume of the *Spectator*. It was the third. I had never before seen any of them. I bought it, read it over and over, and was much delighted with it. I thought the writing excellent, and wished, if possible, to imitate it. With this view I took some of the papers, and, making short hints of the sentiment in each sentence, laid them by a few days, and then, without looking at the book, try'd to compleat the papers again, by expressing each hinted sentiment at length, and as fully as it had been expressed before, in any suitable words that should come to hand. Then I compared my *Spectator* with the original, discovered some of my faults, and corrected them. But I found I wanted a stock of words, or a readiness in recollecting and using them, which I thought I should have acquired before that time if I had gone on making verses; since the continual occasion for words of the same import, but of different length, to suit the measure, or of different sound for the rhyme, would have laid me under a constant necessity of searching for variety, and also have tended to fix that variety in my mind, and make me master of it. Therefore I took some of the tales and turned them into verse; and, after a time, when I had pretty well forgotten the prose, turned them back again. I also sometimes jumbled my collections of hints into confusion, and after some weeks endeavored to reduce them into the best order, before I began to form the full sentences and compleat the paper. This was to teach me method in the arrangement of thoughts. By comparing my work afterwards with the original, I discovered many faults and amended them; but I sometimes had the pleasure of fancying that, in certain particulars of small import, I had been lucky enough to improve the method or the language, and this encouraged me to think I might possibly in time come to be a tolerable English writer, of which I was extremely ambitious. My time for these exercises and for reading was at night, after work or before it began in the morning, or on Sundays, when I contrived to be in the printing-house alone, evading as much as I could the common attendance on public worship which my father used to exact on me when I was under his care, and which indeed I still thought a duty, though I could not, as it seemed to me, afford time to practise it.

When about 16 years of age I happened to meet with a book, written by one Tryon, recommending a vegetable diet. I determined to go into it. My brother, being yet unmarried, did not keep house, but boarded himself and his apprentices in another family. My refusing to eat flesh occasioned an inconveniency, and I was frequently chid for my singularity. I made myself acquainted with Tryon's manner of preparing some of his dishes, such as boiling potatoes or rice, making hasty pudding, and a few others, and then proposed to my brother, that if he would give me, weekly, half the money he paid for my board, I would board myself. He instantly agreed to it, and I presently found that I could save half what he paid me. This was an additional fund for buying books. But I had another advantage in it. My brother and the rest going from the printing-house to their meals, I remained there alone, and, despatching presently my light repast, which often was no more than a bisket or a slice of bread, a handful of raisins or a tart from the pastry-cook's, and a glass of water, had the rest of the time till their return for study, in which I made the greater progress, from that greater clearness of head and quicker apprehension which usually attend temperance in eating and drinking.

And now it was that, being on some occasion made asham'd of my ignorance in figures, which I had twice failed in learning when at school, I took Cocker's book of Arithmetick, and went through the whole by myself with great ease. I also read Seller's and Shermy's books of Navigation, and became acquainted with the little geometry they contain; but never proceeded far in that science. And I read about this time Locke *On Human Understanding,* and the *Art of Thinking,* by Messrs. du Port Royal.

While I was intent on improving my language, I met with an English grammar (I think it was Greenwood's), at the end of which there were two little sketches of the arts of rhetoric and logic, the latter finishing with a specimen of a dispute in the Socratic method; and soon after I procur'd Xenophon's Memorable Things of Socrates, wherein there are many instances of the same method.

I was charm'd with it, adopted it, dropt my abrupt contradiction and positive argumentation, and put on the humble inquirer and doubter. And being then, from reading Shaftesbury and Collins, become a real doubter in many points of our religious doctrine, I found this method safest for myself and very embarrassing to those against whom I used it; therefore I took a delight in it, practis'd it continually, and grew very artful and expert in drawing people, even of superior knowledge, into concessions, the consequences of which they did not foresee, entangling them in difficulties out of which they could not extricate themselves, and so obtaining victories that neither myself nor my cause always deserved. I continu'd this method some few years, but gradually left it, retaining only the habit of expressing myself in terms of modest diffidence; never using, when I advanced any thing that may possibly be disputed, the words *certainly, undoubtedly,* or any others that give the air of positiveness to an opinion; but rather say, I conceive or apprehend a thing to be so and so; it appears to me, or *I should think it so or so,* for such and such reasons; or *I imagine it to be so;* or *it is so, if I am not mistaken.* This habit, I believe, has been of great advantage to me when I have had occasion to inculcate my opinions, and persuade men into measures that I have been from time to time engag'd in promoting; and, as the chief ends of conversation are to *inform* or to be *informed,* to *please* or to *persuade,* I wish well-meaning, sensible men would not lessen their power of doing good by a positive, assuming manner, that seldom fails to disgust, tends to create opposition, and to defeat every one of those purposes for which speech was given to us, to wit, giving or receiving information or pleasure. For, if you would inform, a positive and dogmatical manner in advancing your sentiments may provoke contradiction and prevent a candid attention. If you wish information and improvement from the knowledge of others, and yet at the same time express yourself as firmly fix'd in your present opinions, modest, sensible men, who do not love disputation, will probably leave you undisturbed in the possession of your error. And by such a manner, you can seldom hope to recommend yourself in *pleasing* your hearers, or to persuade those whose concurrence you desire. Pope says, judiciously:

"Men should be taught as if you taught them not,
And things unknown propos'd as things forgot;"

farther recommending to us

"To speak, tho' sure, with seeming diffidence."

And he might have coupled with this line that which he has coupled
with another, I think, less properly,

"For want of modesty is want of sense."

If you ask, Why less properly? I must repeat the lines,

"Immodest words admit of no defense,
For want of modesty is want of sense."

Now, is not *want of sense* (where a man is so unfortunate as to
want it) some apology for his *want of modesty?* and would not
the lines stand more justly thus?

"Immodest words admit *but* this defense,
That want of modesty is want of sense."

This, however, I should submit to better judgments.

My brother had, in 1720 or 1721, begun to print a newspaper. It
was the second that appeared in America, and was called the New
England Courant. The only one before it was the Boston News-
Letter. I remember his being dissuaded by some of his friends from
the undertaking, as not likely to succeed, one newspaper being, in
their judgment, enough for America. At this time (1771) there
are not less than five-and-twenty. He went on, however, with the
undertaking, and after having worked in composing the types and
printing off the sheets, I was employed to carry the papers thro' the
streets to the customers.

He had some ingenious men among his friends, who amus'd
themselves by writing little pieces for this paper, which gain'd it
credit and made it more in demand, and these gentlemen often
visited us. Hearing their conversations, and their accounts of the
approbation their papers were received with, I was excited to try
my hand among them; but, being still a boy, and suspecting that
my brother would object to printing anything of mine in his paper
if he knew it to be mine, I contrived to disguise my hand, and,

writing an anonymous paper, I put it in at night under the door of the printing-house. It was found in the morning, and communicated to his writing friends when they call'd in as usual. They read it, commented on it in my hearing, and I had the exquisite pleasure of finding it met with their approbation, and that, in their different guesses at the author, none were named but men of some character among us for learning and ingenuity. I suppose now that I was rather lucky in my judges, and that perhaps they were not really so very good ones as I then esteem'd them.

Encourag'd, however, by this, I wrote and convey'd in the same way to the press several more papers which were equally approv'd; and I kept my secret till my small fund of sense for such performances was pretty well exhausted, and then I discovered it, when I began to be considered a little more by my brother's acquaintance, and in a manner that did not quite please him, as he thought, probably with reason, that it tended to make me too vain. And, perhaps, this might be one occasion of the differences that we began to have about this time. Though a brother, he considered himself as my master, and me as his apprentice, and accordingly, expected the same services from me as he would from another, while I thought he demean'd me too much in some he requir'd of me, who from a brother expected more indulgence. Our disputes were often brought before our father, and I fancy I was either generally in the right, or else a better pleader, because the judgment was generally in my favor. But my brother was passionate, and had often beaten me, which I took extreamly amiss; and, thinking my apprenticeship very tedious, I was continually wishing for some opportunity of shortening it, which at length offered in a manner unexpected.[4]

One of the pieces in our newspaper on some political point, which I have now forgotten, gave offense to the Assembly. He was taken up, censur'd, and imprison'd for a month, by the speaker's warrant, I suppose, because he would not discover his author. I too was taken up and examin'd before the council; but, tho' I did not give them any satisfaction, they content'd themselves with admonishing

---

[4] I fancy his harsh and tyrannical treatment of me might be a means of impressing me with that aversion to arbitrary power that has stuck to me through my whole life.

me, and dismissed me, considering me, perhaps, as an apprentice, who was bound to keep his master's secrets.

During my brother's confinement, which I resented a good deal, notwithstanding our private differences, I had the management of the paper; and I made bold to give our rulers some rubs in it, which my brother took very kindly, while others began to consider me in an unfavorable light, as a young genius that had a turn for libelling and satyr. My brother's discharge was accompany'd with an order of the House (a very odd one), that *"James Franklin should no longer print the paper called the New England Courant."*

There was a consultation held in our printing-house among his friends, what he should do in this case. Some proposed to evade the order by changing the name of the paper; but my brother, seeing inconveniences in that, it was finally concluded on as a better way, to let it be printed for the future under the name of BENJAMIN FRANKLIN; and to avoid the censure of the Assembly, that might fall on him as still printing it by his apprentice, the contrivance was that my old indenture should be return'd to me, with a full discharge on the back of it, to be shown on occasion, but to secure to him the benefit of my service, I was to sign new indentures for the remainder of the term, which were to be kept private. A very flimsy scheme it was; however, it was immediately executed, and the paper went on accordingly, under my name for several months.

At length, a fresh difference arising between my brother and me, I took upon me to assert my freedom, presuming that he would not venture to produce the new indentures. It was not fair in me to take this advantage, and this I therefore reckon one of the first errata of my life; but the unfairness of it weighed little with me, when under the impressions of resentment for the blows his passion too often urged him to bestow upon me, though he was otherwise not an ill-natur'd man: perhaps I was too saucy and provoking.

When he found I would leave him, he took care to prevent my getting employment in any other printing-house of the town, by going round and speaking to every master, who accordingly refus'd to give me work. I then thought of going to New York, as the nearest place where there was a printer; and I was rather inclin'd to leave Boston when I reflected that I had already made myself a little obnoxious to the governing party, and, from the arbitrary proceedings of the Assembly in my brother's case, it was likely I might, if I stay'd, soon bring myself into scrapes; and farther, that my indiscrete disputations about religion began to make me pointed at with horror by good people as an infidel or atheist. I determin'd on the point, but my father now siding with my brother, I was sensible that, if I attempted to go openly, means would be used to prevent me. My friend Collins, therefore, undertook to manage a little for me. He agreed with the captain of a New York sloop for my passage, under the notion of my being a young acquaintance of his, that had got a naughty girl with child, whose friends would compel me to marry her, and therefore I could not appear or come away publicly. So I sold some of my books to raise a little money, was taken on board privately, and as we had a fair wind, in three days I found myself in New York, near 300 miles from home, a boy of but 17, without the least recommendation to, or knowledge of any person in the place, and with very little money in my pocket.

My inclinations for the sea were by this time worne out, or I might now have gratify'd them. But, having a trade, and supposing myself a pretty good workman, I offer'd my service to the printer in the place, old Mr. William Bradford, who had been the first printer in Pennsylvania, but removed from thence upon the quarrel of George Keith. He could give me no employment, having little to do, and help enough already; but says he, "My son at Philadelphia has lately lost his principal hand, Aquila Rose, by death; if you go thither, I believe he may employ you." Philadelphia was a hundred miles further; I set out, however, in a boat for Amboy, leaving my chest and things to follow me round by sea.

In crossing the bay, we met with a squall that tore our rotten sails to pieces, prevented our getting into the Kill, and drove us upon Long Island. In our way, a drunken Dutchman, who was a passenger too, fell overboard; when he was sinking, I reached through the water to his shock pate, and drew him up, so that we got him in again. His ducking sobered him a little, and he went to sleep, taking first out of his pocket a book, which he desir'd I would dry for him. It proved to be my old favorite author, Bunyan's Pilgrim's Progress, in Dutch, finely printed on good paper, with copper cuts, a dress better than I had ever seen it wear in its own language. I have since found that it has been translated into most of the languages of Europe, and suppose it has been more generally read than any other book, except perhaps the Bible. Honest John was the first that I know of who mix'd narration and dialogue; a method of writing very engaging to the reader, who in the most interesting parts finds himself, as it were, brought into the company and present at the discourse. De Foe in his Cruso, his Moll Flanders, Religious Courtship, Family Instructor, and other pieces, has imitated it with success; and Richardson has done the same in his Pamela, etc.

When we drew near the island, we found it was at a place where there could be no landing, there being a great surff on the stony beach. So we dropt anchor, and swung round towards the shore. Some people came down to the water edge and hallow'd to us, as we did to them; but the wind was so high, and the surff so loud, that we could not hear so as to understand each other. There were canoes on the shore, and we made signs, and hallow'd that they should fetch us; but they either did not understand us, or thought it impracticable, so they went away, and night coming on, we had no remedy but to wait till the wind should abate; and, in the meantime, the boatman and I concluded to sleep, if we could; and so crowded into the scuttle, with the Dutchman, who was still wet, and the spray beating over the head of our boat, leak'd thro' to us, so that we were soon almost as wet as he. In this manner we lay all night, with very little rest; but, the wind abating the next day, we made a shift to reach Amboy before night, having been thirty hours on the water, without victuals, or any drink but a bottle of filthy rum, and the water we sail'd on being salt.

In the evening I found myself very feverish, and went in to bed; but, having read somewhere that cold water drank plentifully was good for a fever, I follow'd the prescription, sweat plentiful most of the night, my fever left me, and in the morning, crossing the ferry, I proceeded on my journey on foot, having fifty miles to Burlington, where I was told I should find boats that would carry me the rest of the way to Philadelphia.

It rained very hard all the day; I was thoroughly soak'd, and by noon a good deal tired; so I stopt at a poor inn, where I staid all night, beginning now to wish that I had never left home. I cut so miserable a figure, too, that I found, by the questions ask'd me, I was suspected to be some runaway servant, and in danger of being taken up on that suspicion. However, I proceeded the next day, and got in the evening to an inn, within eight or ten miles of Burlington, kept by one Dr. Brown. He entered into conversation with me while I took some refreshment, and, finding I had read a little, became very sociable and friendly. Our acquaintance continu'd as long as he liv'd. He had been, I imagine, an itinerant doctor, for there was no town in England, or country in Europe, of which he could not give a very particular account. He had some letters, and was ingenious, but much of an unbeliever, and wickedly undertook, some years after, to travestie the Bible in doggrel verse, as Cotton had done Virgil. By this means he set many of the facts in a very ridiculous light, and might have hurt weak minds if his work had been published; but it never was.

At his house I lay that night, and the next morning reach'd Burlington, but had the mortification to find that the regular boats were gone a little before my coming, and no other expected to go before Tuesday, this being Saturday; wherefore I returned to an old woman in the town, of whom I had bought gingerbread to eat on the water, and ask'd her advice. She invited me to lodge at her house till a passage by water should offer; and being tired with my foot travelling, I accepted the invitation. She understanding I was a printer, would have had me stay at that town and follow my business, being ignorant of the stock necessary to begin with. She was very hospitable, gave me a dinner of ox-cheek with great good will, accepting only a pot of ale in return; and I thought myself fixed till Tuesday should come. However, walking in the evening by the side of the river, a boat came by, which I found was going towards Philadelphia, with several people in her. They took me in, and, as there was no wind, we row'd all the way; and about midnight, not having yet seen the city, some of the company were confident we must have passed it, and would row no farther; the others knew not where we were; so we put toward the shore, got into a creek, landed near an old fence, with the rails of which we made a fire, the night being cold, in October, and there we remained till daylight. Then one of the company knew the place to be Cooper's Creek, a little above Philadelphia, which we saw as soon as we got out of the creek, and arriv'd there about eight or nine o'clock on the Sunday morning, and landed at the Market-street wharf.

I have been the more particular in this description of my journey, and shall be so of my first entry into that city, that you may in your mind compare such unlikely beginnings with the figure I have since made there. I was in my working dress, my best cloaths being to come round by sea. I was dirty from my journey; my pockets were stuff'd out with shirts and stockings, and I knew no soul nor where to look for lodging. I was fatigued with travelling, rowing, and want of rest, I was very hungry; and my whole stock of cash consisted of a Dutch dollar, and about a shilling in copper. The latter I gave the people of the boat for my passage, who at first refus'd it, on account of my rowing; but I insisted on their taking it. A man being sometimes more generous when he has but a little money than when he has plenty, perhaps thro' fear of being thought to have but little.

Then I walked up the street, gazing about till near the market-house I met a boy with bread. I had made many a meal on bread, and, inquiring where he got it, I went immediately to the baker's he directed me to, in Second-street, and ask'd for bisket, intending such as we had in Boston; but they, it seems, were not made in Philadelphia. Then I asked for a three-penny loaf, and was told they had none such. So not considering or knowing the difference of money, and the greater cheapness nor the names of his bread, I made him give me three-penny worth of any sort. He gave me, accordingly, three great puffy rolls. I was surpriz'd at the quantity, but took it, and, having no room in my pockets, walk'd off with a roll under each arm, and eating the other. Thus I went up Market-street as far as Fourth-street, passing by the door of Mr. Read, my future wife's father; when she, standing at the door, saw me, and thought I made, as I certainly did, a most awkward, ridiculous appearance. Then I turned and went down Chestnut-street and part of Walnut-street, eating my roll all the way, and, coming round, found myself again at Market-street wharf, near the boat I came in, to which I went for a draught of the river water; and, being filled with one of my rolls, gave the other two to a woman and her child that came down the river in the boat with us, and were waiting to go farther.

Thus refreshed, I walked again up the street, which by this time had many clean-dressed people in it, who were all walking the same way. I joined them, and thereby was led into the great meeting-house of the Quakers near the market. I sat down among them, and, after looking round awhile and hearing nothing said, being very drowsy thro' labor and want of rest the preceding night, I fell fast asleep, and continued so till the meeting broke up, when one was kind enough to rouse me. This was, therefore, the first house I was in, or slept in, in Philadelphia.

Walking down again toward the river, and, looking in the faces of people, I met a young Quaker man, whose countenance I lik'd, and, accosting him, requested he would tell me where a stranger could get lodging. We were then near the sign of the Three Mariners. "Here," says he, "is one place that entertains strangers, but it is not a reputable house; if thee wilt walk with me, I'll show thee a better." He brought me to the Crooked Billet in Water-street. Here I got a dinner; and, while I was eating it, several sly questions were asked me, as it seemed to be suspected from my youth and appearance, that I might be some runaway.

After dinner, my sleepiness return'd, and being shown to a bed, I lay down without undressing, and slept till six in the evening, was call'd to supper, went to bed again very early, and slept soundly till next morning. Then I made myself as tidy as I could, and went to Andrew Bradford the printer's. I found in the shop the old man his father, whom I had seen at New York, and who, travelling on horseback, had got to Philadelphia before me. He introduc'd me to his son, who receiv'd me civilly, gave me a breakfast, but told me he did not at present want a hand, being lately suppli'd with one; but there was another printer in town, lately set up, one Keimer, who, perhaps, might employ me; if not, I should be welcome to lodge at his house, and he would give me a little work to do now and then till fuller business should offer.

The old gentleman said he would go with me to the new printer;

and when we found him, "Neighbor," says Bradford, "I have brought to see you a young man of your business; perhaps you may want such a one." He ask'd me a few questions, put a composing stick in my hand to see how I work'd, and then said he would employ me soon, though he had just then nothing for me to do; and, taking old Bradford, whom he had never seen before, to be one of the town's people that had a good will for him, enter'd into a conversation on his present undertaking and prospects; while Bradford, not discovering that he was the other printer's father, on Keimer's saying he expected soon to get the greatest part of the business into his own hands, drew him on by artful questions, and starting little doubts, to explain all his views, what interests he reli'd on, and in what manner he intended to proceed. I, who stood by and heard all, saw immediately that one of them was a crafty old sophister, and the other a mere novice. Bradford left me with Keimer, who was greatly surpris'd when I told him who the old man was.

Keimer's printing-house, I found, consisted of an old shatter'd press, and one small, worn-out font of English which he was then using himself, composing an Elegy on Aquila Rose, before mentioned, an ingenious young man, of excellent character, much respected in the town, clerk of the Assembly, and a pretty poet. Keimer made verses too, but very indifferently. He could not be said to write them, for his manner was to compose them in the types directly out of his head. So there being no copy, but one pair of cases, and the Elegy likely to require all the letter, no one could help him. I endeavor'd to put his press (which he had not yet us'd, and of which he understood nothing) into order fit to be work'd with; and, promising to come and print off his Elegy as soon as he should have got it ready, I return'd to Bradford's, who gave me a little job to do for the present, and there I lodged and dieted. A few days after, Keimer sent for me to print off the Elegy. And now he had got another pair of cases, and a pamphlet to reprint, on which he set me to work.

These two printers I found poorly qualified for their business. Bradford had not been bred to it, and was very illiterate; and Keimer, tho' something of a scholar, was a mere compositor, knowing nothing of presswork. He had been one of the French prophets, and could act their enthusiastic agitations. At this time he did not profess any particular religion, but something of all on occasion; was very ignorant of the world, and had, as I afterward found, a good deal of the knave in his composition. He did not like my lodging at Bradford's while I work'd with him. He had a house, indeed, but without furniture, so he could not lodge me; but he got me a lodging at Mr. Read's, before mentioned, who was the owner of his house; and, my chest and clothes being come by this time, I made rather a more respectable appearance in the eyes of Miss Read than I had done when she first happen'd to see me eating my roll in the street.

I began now to have some acquaintance among the young people of the town, that were lovers of reading, with whom I spent my evenings very pleasantly; and gaining money by my industry and frugality, I lived very agreeably, forgetting Boston as much as I could, and not desiring that any there should know where I resided, except my friend Collins, who was in my secret, and kept it when I wrote to him. At length, an incident happened that sent me back again much sooner than I had intended. I had a brother-in-law, Robert Holmes, master of a sloop that traded between Boston and Delaware. He being at Newcastle, forty miles below Philadelphia, heard there of me, and wrote me a letter mentioning the concern of my friends in Boston at my abrupt departure, assuring me of their good will to me, and that every thing would be accommodated to my mind if I would return, to which he exhorted me very earnestly. I wrote an answer to his letter, thank'd him for his advice, but stated my reasons for quitting Boston fully and in such a light as to convince him I was not so wrong as he had apprehended.

Sir William Keith, governor of the province, was then at New-castle, and Captain Holmes, happening to be in company with him when my letter came to hand, spoke to him of me, and show'd him the letter. The governor read it, and seem'd surpris'd when he was told my age. He said I appear'd a young man of promising parts, and therefore should be encouraged; the printers at Philadelphia were wretched ones; and, if I would set up there, he made no doubt I should succeed; for his part, he would procure me the public business, and do me every other service in his power. This my brother-in-law afterwards told me in Boston, but I knew as yet nothing of it; when, one day, Keimer and I being at work together near the window, we saw the governor and another gentleman (which proved to be Colonel French, of Newcastle), finely dress'd, come directly across the street to our house, and heard them at the door.

Keimer ran down immediately, thinking it a visit to him; but the governor inquir'd for me, came up, and with a condescension of politeness I had been quite unus'd to, made me many compliments, desired to be acquainted with me, blam'd me kindly for not having made myself known to him when I first came to the place, and would have me away with him to the tavern, where he was going with Colonel French to taste, as he said, some excellent Madeira. I was not a little surprised, and Keimer star'd like a pig poison'd. I went, however, with the governor and Colonel French to a tavern, at the corner of Third-street, and over the Madeira he propos'd my setting up my business, laid before me the probabilities of success, and both he and Colonel French assur'd me I should have their interest and influence in procuring the public business of both governments. On my doubting whether my father would assist me in it, Sir William said he would give me a letter to him, in which he would state the advantages, and he did not doubt of prevailing with him. So it was concluded I should return to Boston in the first vessel, with the governor's letter recommending me to my father. In the mean time the intention was to be kept a secret, and I went on working with Keimer as usual, the governor sending for me now and then to dine with him, a very great honor I thought it, and conversing with me in the most affable, familiar, and friendly manner imaginable.

About the end of April, 1724, a little vessel offer'd for Boston. I took leave of Keimer as going to see my friends. The governor gave me an ample letter, saying many flattering things of me to my father, and strongly recommending the project of my setting up at Philadelphia as a thing that must make my fortune. We struck on a shoal in going down the bay, and sprung a leak; we had a blustering time at sea, and were oblig'd to pump almost continually, at which I took my turn. We arriv'd safe, however, at Boston in about a fortnight. I had been absent seven months, and my friends had heard nothing of me; for my br. Holmes was not yet return'd, ,and had not written about me. My unexpected appearance surpriz'd the family; all were, however, very glad to see me, and made me welcome, except my brother. I went to see him at his printing-house. I was better dress'd than ever while in his service, having a genteel new suit from head to foot, a watch, and my pockets lin'd with near five pounds sterling in silver. He receiv'd me not very frankly, look'd me all over, and turn'd to his work again.

The journeymen were inquisitive where I had been, what sort of a country it was, and how I lik'd it. I prais'd it much, the happy life I led in it, expressing strongly my intention of returning to it; and, one of them asking what kind of money we had there, I produc'd a handful of silver, and spread it before them, which was a kind of raree-show they had not been us'd to, paper being the money of Boston. Then I took an opportunity of letting them see my watch; and, lastly (my brother still grum and sullen), I gave them a piece of eight to drink, and took my leave. This visit of mine offended him extreamly; for, when my mother some time after spoke to him of a reconciliation, and of her wishes to see us on good terms together, and that we might live for the future as brothers, he said I had insulted him in such a manner before his people that he could never forget or forgive it. In this, however, he was mistaken.

My father received the governor's letter with some apparent surprise, but said little of it to me for some days, when Capt. Holmes returning he showed it to him, ask'd him if he knew Keith, and what kind of man he was; adding his opinion that he must be of small discretion to think of setting a boy up in business who wanted yet three years of being at man's estate. Holmes said what he could in favor of the project, but my father was clear in the impropriety of it, and at last gave a flat denial to it. Then he wrote a civil letter to Sir William, thanking him for the patronage he had so kindly offered me, but declining to assist me as yet in setting up, I being, in his opinion, too young to be trusted with the management of a business so important, and for which the preparation must be so expensive.

My friend and companion Collins, who was a clerk in the post-office, pleas'd with the account I gave him of my new country, determined to go thither also; and, while I waited for my father's determination, he set out before me by land to Rhode Island, leaving his books, which were a pretty collection of mathematicks and natural philosophy, to come with mine and me to New York, where he propos'd to wait for me.

My father, tho' he did not approve Sir William's proposition, was yet pleas'd that I had been able to obtain so advantageous a character from a person of such note where I had resided, and that I had been so industrious and careful as to equip myself so handsomely in so short a time; therefore, seeing no prospect of an accommodation between my brother and me, he gave his consent to my returning again to Philadelphia, advis'd me to behave respectfully to the people there, endeavor to obtain the general esteem, and avoid lampooning and libeling, to which he thought I had too much inclination; telling me, that by steady industry and a prudent parsimony I might save enough by the time I was one-and-twenty to set me up; and that, if I came near the matter, he would help me out with the rest. This was all I could obtain, except some small gifts as tokens of his and my mother's love, when I embark'd again for New York, now with their approbation and their blessing.

The sloop putting in at Newport, Rhode Island, I visited my brother John, who had been married and settled there some years. He received me very affectionately, for he always lov'd me. A friend of his, one Vernon, having some money due to him in Pensilvania, about thirty-five pounds currency, desired I would receive it for him, and keep it till I had his directions what to remit it in. Accordingly, he gave me an order. This afterwards occasion'd me a good deal of uneasiness.

At Newport we took in a number of passengers for New York, among which were two young women, companions, and a grave, sensible, matron-like Quaker woman, with her attendants. I had shown an obliging readiness to do her some little services, which impress'd her I suppose with a degree of good will toward me; therefore, when she saw a daily growing familiarity between me and the two young women, which they appear'd to encourage, she took me aside, and said: "Young man, I am concern'd for thee as thou has no friend with thee, and seems not to know much of the world, or of the snares youth is expos'd to; depend upon it, those are very bad women; I can see it in all their actions; and if thee art not upon thy guard, they will draw thee into some danger; they are strangers to thee, and I advise thee, in a friendly concern for thy welfare, to have no acquaintance with them." As I seem'd at first not to think so ill of them as she did, she mentioned some things she had observ'd and heard that had escap'd my notice, but now convinc'd me she was right. I thank'd her for her kind advice, and promis'd to follow it. When we arriv'd at New York, they told me where they liv'd, and invited me to come and see them; but I avoided it, and it was well I did; for the next day the captain miss'd a silver spoon and some other things, that had been taken out of his cabbin, and, knowing that these were a couple of strumpets, he got a warrant to search their lodgings, found the stolen goods, and had the thieves punish'd. So, tho' we had escap'd a sunken rock, which we scrap'd upon in the passage, I thought this escape of rather more importance to me.

At New York I found my friend Collins, who had arriv'd there some time before me. We had been intimate from children, and had read the same books together; but he had the advantage of more time for reading and studying, and a wonderful genius for mathematical learning, in which he far outstript me. While I liv'd in Boston most of my hours of leisure for conversation were spent with him, and he continu'd a sober as well as an industrious lad; was much respected for his learning by several of the clergy and other gentlemen, and seemed to promise making a good figure in life. But, during my absence, he had acquir'd a habit of sotting with brandy; and I found by his own account, and what I heard from others, that he had been drunk every day since his arrival at New York, and behav'd very oddly. He had gam'd, too, and lost his money, so that I was oblig'd to discharge his lodgings, and defray his expenses to and at Philadelphia, which prov'd extremely inconvenient to me.

The then governor of New York, Burnet (son of Bishop Burnet), hearing from the captain that a young man, one of his passengers, had a great many books, desir'd he would bring me to see him. I waited upon him accordingly, and should have taken Collins with me but that he was not sober. The gov'r. treated me with great civility, show'd me his library, which was a very large one, and we had a good deal of conversation about books and authors. This was the second governor who had done me the honor to take notice of me; which, to a poor boy like me, was very pleasing.

We proceeded to Philadelphia. I received on the way Vernon's money, without which we could hardly have finish'd our journey. Collins wished to be employ'd in some counting-house; but, whether they discover'd his dramming by his breath, or by his behaviour, tho' he had some recommendations, he met with no success in any application, and continu'd lodging and boarding at the same house with me, and at my expense. Knowing I had that money of Vernon's, he was continually borrowing of me, still promising repayment as soon as he should be in business. At length he had got so much of it that I was distress'd to think what I should do in case of being call'd on to remit it.

His drinking continu'd, about which we sometimes quarrell'd; for, when a little intoxicated, he was very fractious. Once, in a boat on the Delaware with some other young men, he refused to row in his turn. "I will be row'd home," says he. "We will not row you," says I. "You must, or stay all night on the water," says he, "just as you please." The others said, "Let us row; what signifies it?" But, my mind being soured with his other conduct, I continu'd to refuse. So he swore he would make me row, or throw me overboard; and coming along, stepping on the thwarts, toward me, when he came up and struck at me, I clapped my hand under his crutch, and, rising, pitched him head-foremost into the river. I knew he was a good swimmer, and so was under little concern about him; but before he could get round to lay hold of the boat, we had with a few strokes pull'd her out of his reach; and ever when he drew near the boat, we ask'd if he would row, striking a few strokes to slide her away from him. He was ready to die with vexation, and obstinately would not promise to row. However, seeing him at last beginning to tire, we lifted him in and brought him home dripping wet in the evening. We hardly exchang'd a civil word afterwards, and a West India captain, who had a commission to procure a tutor for the sons of a gentleman at Barbadoes, happening to meet with him, agreed to carry him thither. He left me then, promising to remit me the first money he should receive in order to discharge the debt; but I never heard of him after.

The breaking into this money of Vernon's was one of the first great errata of my life; and this affair show'd that my father was not much out in his judgment when he suppos'd me too young to manage business of importance. But Sir William, on reading his letter, said he was too prudent. There was great difference in persons; and discretion did not always accompany years, nor was youth always without it. "And since he will not set you up," says he, "I will do it myself. Give me an inventory of the things necessary to be had from England, and I will send for them. You shall repay me when you are able; I am resolv'd to have a good printer here, and I am sure you must succeed." This was spoken with such an appearance of cordiality, that I had not the least doubt of his meaning what he said. I had hitherto kept the proposition of my setting up, a secret in Philadelphia, and I still kept it. Had it been known that I depended on the governor, probably some friend, that knew him better, would have advis'd me not to rely on him, as I afterwards heard it as his known character to be liberal of promises which he never meant to keep. Yet, unsolicited as he was by me, how could I think his generous offers insincere? I believ'd him one of the best men in the world.

I presented him an inventory of a little print'g-house, amounting by my computation to about one hundred pounds sterling. He lik'd it, but ask'd me if my being on the spot in England to chuse the types, and see that every thing was good of the kind, might not be of some advantage. "Then," says he, "when there, you may make acquaintances, and establish correspondences in the bookselling and stationery way." I agreed that this might be advantageous. "Then," says he, "get yourself ready to go with Annis;" which was the annual ship, and the only one at that time usually passing between London and Philadelphia. But it would be some months before Annis sail'd, so I continu'd working with Keimer, fretting about the money Collins had got from me, and in daily apprehensions of being call'd upon by Vernon, which, however, did not happen for some years after.

I believe I have omitted mentioning that, in my first voyage from Boston, being becalm'd off Block Island, our people set about catching cod, and hauled up a great many. Hitherto I had stuck to my resolution of not eating animal food, and on this occasion consider'd, with my master Tryon, the taking every fish as a kind of unprovoked murder, since none of them had, or ever could do us any injury that might justify the slaughter. All this seemed very reasonable. But I had formerly been a great lover of fish, and, when this came hot out of the frying-pan, it smelt admirably well. I balanc'd some time between principle and inclination, till I recollected that, when the fish were opened, I saw smaller fish taken out of their stomachs; then thought I, "If you eat one another, I don't see why we mayn't eat you." So I din'd upon cod very heartily, and continued to eat with other people, returning only now and then occasionally to a vegetable diet. So convenient a thing it is to be a *reasonable creature,* since it enables one to find or make a reason for everything one has a mind to do.

Keimer and I liv'd on a pretty good familiar footing, and agreed tolerably well, for he suspected nothing of my setting up. He retained a great deal of his old enthusiasms and lov'd argumentation. We therefore had many disputations. I used to work him so with my Socratic method, and had trepann'd him so often by questions apparently so distant from any point we had in hand, and yet by degrees lead to the point, and brought him into difficulties and contradictions, that at last he grew ridiculously cautious, and would hardly answer me the most common question, without asking first, *"What do you intend to infer from that?"* However, it gave him so high an opinion of my abilities in the confuting way, that he seriously proposed my being his colleague in a project he had of setting up a new sect. He was to preach the doctrines, and I was to confound all opponents. When he came to explain with me upon the doctrines, I found several conundrums which I objected to, unless I might have my way a little too, and introduce some of mine.

Keimer wore his beard at full length, because somewhere in the Mosaic law it is said, *"Thou shalt not mar the corners of thy beard."* He likewise kept the Seventh day, Sabbath; and these two points were essentials with him. I dislik'd both; but agreed to admit them upon condition of his adopting the doctrine of using no animal food. "I doubt," said he, "my constitution will not bear that." I assur'd him it would, and that he would be the better for it. He was usually a great glutton, and I promised myself some diversion in half starving him. He agreed to try the practice, if I would keep him company. I did so, and we held it for three months. We had our victuals dress'd, and brought to us regularly by a woman in the neighborhood, who had from me a list of forty dishes to be prepar'd for us at different times, in all which there was neither fish, flesh, nor fowl, and the whim suited me the better at this time from the cheapness of it, not costing us above eighteenpence sterling each per week. I have since kept several Lents most strictly, leaving the common diet for that, and that for the common, abruptly, without the least inconvenience, so that I think there is little in the advice of making those changes by easy gradations. I went on pleasantly, but poor Keimer suffered grievously, tired of the project, long'd for the flesh-pots of Egypt, and order'd a roast pig. He invited me and two women friends to dine with him; but, it being brought too soon upon table, he could not resist the temptation, and ate the whole before we came.

I had made some courtship during this time to Miss Read. I had a great respect and affection for her, and had some reason to believe she had the same for me; but, as I was about to take a long voyage, and we were both very young, only a little above eighteen, it was thought most prudent by her mother to prevent our going too far at present, as a marriage, if it was to take place, would be more convenient after my return, when I should be, as I expected, set up in my business. Perhaps, too, she thought my expectations not so well founded as I imagined them to be.

My chief acquaintances at this time were Charles Osborne, Joseph Watson, and James Ralph, all lovers of reading. The two first were clerks to an eminent scrivener or conveyancer in the town, Charles Brogden; the other was clerk to a merchant. Watson was a pious, sensible young man, of great integrity; the others rather more lax in their principles of religion, particularly Ralph, who, as well as Collins, had been unsettled by me, for which they both made me suffer. Osborne was sensible, candid, frank; sincere and affectionate to his friends; but, in literary matters, too fond of criticising. Ralph was ingenious, genteel in his manners, and extremely eloquent; I think I never knew a prettier talker. Both of them great admirers of poetry, and began to try their hands in little pieces. Many pleasant walks we four had together on Sundays into the woods, near Schuylkill, where we read to one another, and conferr'd on what we read.

Ralph was inclin'd to pursue the study of poetry, not doubting but he might become eminent in it, and make his fortune by it, alleging that the best poets must, when they first began to write, make as many faults as he did. Osborne dissuaded him, assur'd him he had no genius for poetry, and advis'd him to think of nothing beyond the business he was bred to; that, in the mercantile way, tho' he had no stock, he might, by his diligence and punctuality, recommend himself to employment as a factor, and in time acquire wherewith to trade on his own account. I approv'd the amusing one's self with poetry now and then, so far as to improve one's language, but no farther.

On this it was propos'd that we should each of us, at our next meeting, produce a piece of our own composing, in order to improve by our mutual observations, criticisms, and corrections. As language and expression were what we had in view, we excluded all considerations of invention by agreeing that the task should be a version of the eighteenth Psalm, which describes the descent of a Deity. When the time of our meeting drew nigh, Ralph called on me first, and let me know his piece was ready. I told him I had been busy, and, having little inclination, had done nothing. He then show'd me his piece for my opinion, and I much approv'd it, as it appear'd to me to have great merit. "Now," says he, "Osborne never will allow the least merit in any thing of mine, but makes 1000 criticisms out of mere envy. He is not so jealous of you; I wish, therefore, you would take this piece, and produce it as yours; I will pretend not to have had time, and so produce nothing. We shall then see what he will say to it." It was agreed, and I immediately transcrib'd it, that it might appear in my own hand.

We met; Watson's performance was read; there were some beauties in it, but many defects. Osborne's was read; it was much better; Ralph did it justice; remarked some faults, but applauded the beauties. He himself had nothing to produce. I was backward; seemed desirous of being excused; had not had sufficient time to correct, etc.; but no excuse could be admitted; produce I must. It was read and repeated; Watson and Osborne gave up the contest, and join'd in applauding it. Ralph only made some criticisms, and propos'd some amendments; but I defended my text. Osborne was against Ralph, and told him he was no better a critic than poet, so he dropt the argument. As they two went home together, Osborne expressed himself still more strongly in favor of what he thought my production; having restrain'd himself before, as he said, lest I should think it flattery. "But who would have imagin'd," said he, "that Franklin had been capable of such a performance; such painting, such force, such fire! He has even improv'd the original. In his common conversation he seems to have no choice of words; he hesitates and blunders; and yet, good God! how he writes!" When we next met, Ralph discovered the trick we had plaid him, and Osborne was a little laught at.

This transaction fixed Ralph in his resolution of becoming a poet. I did all I could to dissuade him from it, but he continued scribbling verses till *Pope* cured him. He became, however, a pretty good prose writer. More of him hereafter. But, as I may not have occasion again to mention the other two, I shall just remark here, that Watson died in my arms a few years after, much lamented, being the best of our set. Osborne went to the West Indies, where he became an eminent lawyer and made money, but died young. He and I had made a serious agreement, that the one who happen'd first to die should, if possible, make a friendly visit to the other, and acquaint him how he found things in that separate state. But he never fulfill'd his promise.

The governor, seeming to like my company, had me frequently to his house, and his setting me up was always mention'd as a fixed thing. I was to take with me letters recommendatory to a number of his friends, besides the letter of credit to furnish me with the necessary money for purchasing the press and types, paper, etc. For these letters I was appointed to call at different times, when they were to be ready, but a future time was still named. Thus he went on till the ship, whose departure too had been several times postponed, was on the point of sailing. Then, when I call'd to take my leave and receive the letters, his secretary, Dr. Bard, came out to me and said the governor was extremely busy in writing, but would be down at Newcastle before the ship, and there the letters would be delivered to me.

Ralph, though married, and having one child, had determined to accompany me in this voyage. It was thought he intended to establish a correspondence, and obtain goods to sell on commission; but I found afterwards, that, thro' some discontent with his wife's relations, he purposed to leave her on their hands, and never return again. Having taken leave of my friends, and interchang'd some promises with Miss Read, I left Philadelphia in the ship, which anchor'd at Newcastle. The governor was there; but when I went to his lodging, the secretary came to me from him with the civillest message in the world, that he could not then see me, being engaged in business of the utmost importance, but should send the letters to me on board, wish'd me heartily a good voyage and a speedy return, etc. I returned on board a little puzzled, but still not doubting.

Mr. Andrew Hamilton, a famous lawyer of Philadelphia, had taken passage in the same ship for himself and son, and with Mr. Denham, a Quaker merchant, and Messrs. Onion and Russel, masters of an iron work in Maryland, had engag'd the great cabin; so that Ralph and I were forced to take up with a berth in the steerage, and none on board knowing us, were considered as ordinary persons. But Mr. Hamilton and his son (it was James, since governor) return'd from Newcastle to Philadelphia, the father being recall'd by a great fee to plead for a seized ship; and, just before we sail'd, Colonel French coming on board, and showing me great respect, I was more taken notice of, and, with my friend Ralph, invited by the other gentlemen to come into the cabin, there being now room. Accordingly, we remov'd thither.

Understanding that Colonel French had brought on board the governor's despatches, I ask'd the captain for those letters that were to be under my care. He said all were put into the bag together and he could not then come at them; but, before we landed in England, I should have an opportunity of picking them out; so I was satisfied for the present, and we proceeded on our voyage. We had a sociable company in the cabin, and lived uncommonly well, having the addition of all Mr. Hamilton's stores, who had laid in plentifully. In this passage Mr. Denham contracted a friendship for me that continued during his life. The voyage was otherwise not a pleasant one, as we had a great deal of bad weather.

When we came into the Channel, the captain kept his word with me, and gave me an opportunity of examining the bag for the governor's letters. I found none upon which my name was put as under my care. I picked out six or seven, that, by the handwriting, I thought might be the promised letters, especially as one of them was directed to Basket, the king's printer, and another to some stationer. We arriv'd in London the 24th of December, 1724. I waited upon the stationer, who came first in my way, delivering the letter as from Governor Keith. "I don't know such a person," says he; but, opening the letter, "O! this is from Riddlesden. I have lately found him to be a compleat rascal, and I will have nothing to do with him, nor receive any letters from him." So, putting the letter into my hand, he turn'd on his heel and left me to serve some customer. I was surprized to find these were not the governor's letters; and, after recollecting and comparing circumstances, I began to doubt his sincerity. I found my friend Denham, and opened the whole affair to him. He let me into Keith's character; told me there was not the least probability that he had written any letters for me; that no one, who knew him, had the smallest dependence on him; and he laught at the notion of the governor's giving me a letter of credit, having, as he said, no credit to give. On my expressing some concern about what I should do, he advised me to endeavor getting some employment in the way of my business. "Among the printers here," said he, "you will improve yourself, and when you return to America, you will set up to greater advantage."

We both of us happen'd to know, as well as the stationer, that Riddlesden, the attorney, was a very knave. He had half ruin'd Miss Read's father by persuading him to be bound for him. By this letter it appear'd there was a secret scheme on foot to the prejudice of Hamilton (suppos'd to be then coming over with us); and that Keith was concerned in it with Riddlesden. Denham, who was a friend of Hamilton's thought he ought to be acquainted with it; so, when he arriv'd in England, which was soon after, partly from resentment and ill-will to Keith and Riddlesden, and partly from good-will to him, I waited on him, and gave him the letter. He thank'd me cordially, the information being of importance to him; and from that time he became my friend, greatly to my advantage afterwards on many occasions.

But what shall we think of a governor's playing such pitiful tricks, and imposing so grossly on a poor ignorant boy! It was a habit he had acquired. He wish'd to please everybody; and, having little to give, he gave expectations. He was otherwise an ingenious, sensible man, a pretty good writer, and a good governor for the people, tho' not for his constituents, the proprietaries, whose instructions he sometimes disregarded. Several of our best laws were of his planning and passed during his administration.

Ralph and I were inseparable companions. We took lodgings together in Little Britain at three shillings and sixpence a week— as much as we could then afford. He found some relations, but they were poor, and unable to assist him. He now let me know his intentions of remaining in London, and that he never meant to return to Philadelphia. He had brought no money with him, the whole he could muster having been expended in paying his passage. I had fifteen pistoles; so he borrowed occasionally of me to subsist, while he was looking out for business. He first endeavored to get into the playhouse, believing himself qualify'd for an actor; but Wilkes, to whom he apply'd, advis'd him candidly not to think of that employment, as it was impossible he should succeed in it. Then he propos'd to Roberts, a publisher in Paternoster Row, to write for him a weekly paper like the Spectator, on certain conditions, which Roberts did not approve. Then he endeavored to get employment as a hackney writer, to copy for the stationers and lawyers about the Temple, but could find no vacancy.

I immediately got into work at Palmer's, then a famous printing-house in Bartholomew Close, and here I continu'd near a year. I was pretty diligent, but spent with Ralph a good deal of my earnings in going to plays and other places of amusement. We had together consumed all my pistoles, and now just rubbed on from hand to mouth. He seem'd quite to forget his wife and child, and I, by degrees, my engagements with Miss Read, to whom I never wrote more than one letter, and that was to let her know I was not likely soon to return. This was another of the great errata of my life, which I should wish to correct if I were to live it over again. In fact, by our expenses, I was constantly kept unable to pay my passage.

At Palmer's I was employed in composing for the second edition of Wollaston's "Religion of Nature." Some of his reasonings not appearing to me well founded, I wrote a little metaphysical piece in which I made remarks on them. It was entitled "A Dissertation on Liberty and Necessity, Pleasure and Pain." I inscribed it to my friend Ralph; I printed a small number. It occasion'd my being more consider'd by Mr. Palmer as a young man of some ingenuity, tho' he seriously expostulated with me upon the principles of my pamphlet, which to him appear'd abominable. My printing this pamphlet was another erratum. While I lodg'd in Little Britain, I made an acquaintance with one Wilcox, a bookseller, whose shop was at the next door. He had an immense collection of second-hand books. Circulating libraries were not then in use; but we agreed that, on certain reasonable terms, which I have now forgotten, I might take, read, and return any of his books. This I esteem'd a great advantage, and I made as much use of it as I could.

My pamphlet by some means falling into the hands of one Lyons, a surgeon, author of a book entitled "The Infallibility of Human Judgment," it occasioned an acquaintance between us. He took great notice of me, called on me often to converse on those subjects, carried me to the Horns, a pale alehouse in —— Lane, Cheapside, and introduced me to Dr. Mandeville, author of the "Fable of the

Bees," who had a club there, of which he was the soul, being a most facetious, entertaining companion. Lyons, too, introduced me to Dr. Pemberton, at Batson's Coffee-house, who promis'd to give me an opportunity, some time or other, of seeing Sir Isaac Newton, of which I was extreamly desirous; but this never happened.

I had brought over a few curiosities, among which the principal was a purse made of the asbestos, which purifies by fire. Sir Hans Sloane heard of it, came to see me, and invited me to his house in Bloomsbury Square, where he show'd me all his curiosities, and persuaded me to let him add that to the number, for which he paid me handsomely.

In our house there lodg'd a young woman, a milliner, who, I think, had a shop in the Cloisters. She had been genteelly bred, was sensible and lively, and of most pleasing conversation. Ralph read plays to her in the evenings, they grew intimate, she took another lodging, and he followed her. They liv'd together some time; but, he being still out of business, and her income not sufficient to maintain them with her child, he took a resolution of going from London, to try for a country school, which he thought himself well qualified to undertake, as he wrote an excellent hand, and was a master of arithmetic and accounts. This, however, he deemed a business below him, and confident of future better fortune, when he should be unwilling to have it known that he once was so meanly employed, he changed his name, and did me the honor to assume mine; for I soon after had a letter from him, acquainting me that he was settled in a small village (in Berkshire, I think it was, where he taught reading and writing to ten or a dozen boys, at sixpence each per week), recommending Mrs. T—— to my care, and desiring me to write to him, directing for Mr. Franklin, schoolmaster, at such a place.

He continued to write frequently, sending me large specimens of an epic poem which he was then composing, and desiring my remarks and corrections. These I gave him from time to time, but endeavor'd rather to discourage his proceeding. One of Young's Satires was then just published. I copy'd and sent him a great part of it, which set in a strong light the folly of pursuing the Muses with any hope of advancement by them. All was in vain; sheets of the poem continued to come by every post. In the mean time, Mrs. T——, having on his account lost her friends and business, was often in distresses, and us'd to send for me, and borrow what I could spare to help her out of them. I grew fond of her company, and, being at that time under no religious restraint, and presuming upon my importance to her, I attempted familiarities (another erratum) which she repuls'd with a proper resentment, and acquainted him with my behaviour. This made a breach between us; and, when he returned again to London, he let me know he thought I had cancell'd all the obligations he had been under to me. So I found I was never to expect his repaying me what I lent to him, or advanc'd for him. This, however, was not then of much consequence, as he was totally unable; and in the loss of his friendship I found myself relieved from a burthen. I now began to think of getting a little money beforehand, and, expecting better work, I left Palmer's to work at Watts's, near Lincoln's Inn Fields, a still greater printing-house. Here I continued all the rest of my stay in London.

At my first admission into this printing-house I took to working at press, imagining I felt a want of the bodily exercise I had been us'd to in America, where presswork is mix'd with composing. I drank only water; the other workmen, near fifty in number, were great guzzlers of beer. On occasion, I carried up and down stairs a large form of types in each hand, when others carried but one in both hands. They wondered to see, from this and several instances, that the *Water-American,* as they called me, was *stronger* than themselves, who drank *strong* beer! We had an alehouse boy who attended always in the house to supply the workmen. My companion at the press drank every day a pint before breakfast, a pint at breakfast with his bread and cheese, a pint between breakfast and dinner, a pint at dinner, a pint in the afternoon about six o'clock, and another when he had done his day's work. I thought it a detestable custom; but it was necessary, he suppos'd, to drink *strong* beer, that he might be *strong* to labor. I endeavored to convince him that the bodily strength afforded by beer could only be in proportion to the grain or flour of the barley dissolved in the water of which it was made; that there was more flour in a pennyworth of bread; and therefore, if he would eat that with a pint of water, it would give him more strength than a quart of beer. He drank on, however, and had four or five shillings to pay out of his wages every Saturday night for that muddling liquor; an expense I was free from. And thus these poor devils keep themselves always under.

Watts, after some weeks, desiring to have me in the composing-room, I left the pressmen; a new bien venu or sum for drink, being five shillings, was demanded of me by the compositors. I thought it an imposition, as I had paid below; the master thought so too, and forbad my paying it. I stood out two or three weeks, was accordingly considered as an excommunicate, and had so many little pieces of private mischief done me, by mixing my sorts, transposing my pages, breaking my matter, etc., etc., if I were ever so little out of the room, and all ascribed to the chappel ghost, which they said ever haunted those not regularly admitted, that, notwithstanding the master's protection, I found myself oblig'd to comply and pay the money, convinc'd of the folly of being on ill terms with those one is to live with continually.

I was now on a fair footing with them, and soon acquir'd considerable influence. I propos'd some reasonable alterations in their chappel[5] laws, and carried them against all opposition. From my example, a great part of them left their muddling breakfast of beer, and bread, and cheese, finding they could with me be suppli'd from a neighboring house with a large porringer of hot water-gruel, sprinkled with pepper, crumbl'd with bread and a bit of butter in it, for the price of a pint of beer, viz., three half-pence. This was a more comfortable as well as cheaper breakfast, and kept their heads clearer. Those who continued sotting with beer all day, were often, by not paying, out of credit at the alehouse, and us'd to make interest with me to get beer; their *light,* as they phrased it, *being out.* I watch'd the pay-table on Saturday night, and collected what I stood engag'd for them, having to pay sometimes near thirty shillings a

[5] "A printing-house is always called a chapel by the workmen, the origin of which appears to have been that printing was first carried on in England in an ancient chapel converted into a printing-house, and the title has been preserved by tradition. The bien venu among the printers answers to the terms entrance and footing among mechanics; thus a journeyman, on entering a printing-house, was accustomed to pay one or more gallons of beer for the good of the chapel: this custom was falling into disuse thirty years ago; it is very properly rejected entirely in the United States."— W. T. F.

week on their account. This, and my being esteem'd a pretty good *riggite,* that is, a jocular verbal satirist, supported my consequence in the society. My constant attendance (I never making a St. Monday) recommended me to the master; and my uncommon quickness at composing occasioned my being put upon all work of dispatch, which was generally better paid. So I went on now very agreeably.

My lodging in Little Britain being too remote, I found another in Duke-street, opposite to the Romish Chapel. It was two pair of stairs backwards, at an Italian warehouse. A widow lady kept the house; she had a daughter, and a maid servant, and a journeyman who attended the warehouse, but lodg'd abroad. After sending to inquire my character at the house where I last lodg'd she agreed to take me in at the same rate, 3s. 6d. per week; cheaper, as she said, from the protection she expected in having a man lodge in the house. She was a widow, an elderly woman; had been bred a Protestant, being a clergyman's daughter, but was converted to the Catholic religion by her husband, whose memory she much revered; had lived much among people of distinction, and knew a thousand anecdotes of them as far back as the times of Charles the Second. She was lame in her knees with the gout, and, therefore, seldom stirred out of her room, so sometimes wanted company; and hers was so highly amusing to me, that I was sure to spend an evening with her whenever she desired it. Our supper was only half an anchovy each, on a very little strip of bread and butter, and half a pint of ale between us; but the entertainment was in her conversation. My always keeping good hours, and giving little trouble in the family, made her unwilling to part with me; so that, when I talk'd of a lodging I had heard of, nearer my business, for two shillings a week, which, intent as I now was on saving money, made some difference, she bid me not think of it, for she would abate me two shillings a week for the future; so I remained with her at one shilling and sixpence as long as I staid in London.

In a garret of her house there lived a maiden lady of seventy, in the most retired manner, of whom my landlady gave me this account: that she was a Roman Catholic, had been sent abroad when young, and lodg'd in a nunnery with an intent of becoming a nun; but, the country not agreeing with her, she returned to England, where, there being no nunnery, she had vow'd to lead the life of a nun, as near as might be done in those circumstances. Accordingly, she had given all her estate to charitable uses, reserving only twelve pounds a year to live on, and out of this sum she still gave a great deal in charity, living herself on water-gruel only, and using no fire but to boil it. She had lived many years in that garret, being permitted to remain there gratis by successive Catholic tenants of the house below, as they deemed it a blessing to have her there. A priest visited her to confess her every day. "I have ask'd her," says my landlady, "how she, as she liv'd, could possibly find so much employment for a confessor?" "Oh," said she, "it is impossible to avoid *vain thoughts.*" I was permitted once to visit her. She was chearful and polite, and convers'd pleasantly. The room was clean, but had no other furniture than a matras, a table with a crucifix and book, a stool which she gave me to sit on, and a picture over the chimney of Saint Veronica displaying her handkerchief, with the miraculous figure of Christ's bleeding face on it, which she explained to me with great seriousness. She look'd pale, but was never sick; and I give it as another instance on how small an income life and health may be supported.

At Watts's printing-house I contracted an acquaintance with an ingenious young man, one Wygate, who, having wealthy relations, had been better educated than most printers; was a tolerable Latinist, spoke French, and lov'd reading. I taught him and a friend of his to swim at twice going into the river, and they soon became good swimmers. They introduc'd me to some gentlemen from the country, who went to Chelsea by water to see the College and Don Saltero's curiosities. In our return, at the request of the company, whose curiosity Wygate had excited, I stripped and leaped into the river, and swam from near Chelsea to Blackfryar's, performing on the way many feats of activity, both upon and under water, that surpris'd and pleas'd those to whom they were novelties.

I had from a child been ever delighted with this exercise, had studied and practis'd all Thevenot's motions and positions, added some of my own, aiming at the graceful and easy as well as the useful. All these I took this occasion of exhibiting to the company, and was much flatter'd by their admiration; and Wygate, who was desirous of becoming a master, grew more and more attach'd to me on that account, as well as from the similarity of our studies. He at length proposed to me travelling all over Europe together, supporting ourselves everywhere by working at our business. I was once inclined to it; but, mentioning it to my good friend Mr. Denham, with whom I often spent an hour when I had leisure, he dissuaded me from it, advising me to think only of returning to Pennsilvania, which he was now about to do.

I must record one trait of this good man's character. He had formerly been in business at Bristol, but failed in debt to a number of people, compounded and went to America. There, by a close application to business as a merchant, he acquir'd a plentiful fortune in a few years. Returning to England in the ship with me, he invited his old creditors to an entertainment, at which he thank'd them for the easy composition they had favored him with, and, when they expected nothing but the treat, every man at the first remove found under his plate an order on a banker for the full amount of the unpaid remainder with interest.

He now told me he was about to return to Philadelphia, and should carry over a great quantity of goods in order to open a store there. He propos'd to take me over as his clerk, to keep his books, in which he would instruct me, copy his letters, and attend the store. He added that, as soon as I should be acquainted with mercantile business, he would promote me by sending me with a cargo of flour and bread, etc., to the West Indies, and procure me commissions from others which would be profitable; and, if I manag'd well, would establish me handsomely. The thing pleas'd me; for I was grown tired of London, remembered with pleasure the happy months I had spent in Pennsylvania, and wish'd again to see it; therefore I immediately agreed on the terms of fifty pounds a year, Pennsylvania money; less, indeed, than my present gettings as a compositor, but affording a better prospect.

I now took leave of printing, as I thought, for ever, and was daily employed in my new business, going about with Mr. Denham among the tradesmen to purchase various articles, and seeing them pack'd up, doing errands, calling upon workmen to dispatch, etc.; and, when all was on board, I had a few days' leisure. On one of these days, I was, to my surprise, sent for by a great man I knew only by name, a Sir William Wyndham, and I waited upon him. He had heard by some means or other of my swimming from Chelsea to Blackfriar's, and of my teaching Wygate and another young man to swim in a few hours. He had two sons, about to set out on their travels; he wish'd to have them first taught swimming, and proposed to gratify me handsomely if I would teach them. They were not yet come to town, and my stay was uncertain, so I could not undertake it; but, from this incident, I thought it likely that, if I were to remain in England and open a swimming-school, I might get a good deal of money; and it struck me so strongly, that, had the overture been sooner made me, probably I should not so soon have returned to America. After many years, you and I had something of more importance to do with one of these sons of Sir William Wyndham, become Earl of Egremont, which I shall mention in its place.

Thus I spent about eighteen months in London; most part of the time I work'd hard at my business, and spent but little upon myself except in seeing plays and in books. My friend Ralph had kept me poor; he owed me about twenty-seven pounds, which I was now never likely to receive; a great sum out of my small earnings! I lov'd him, notwithstanding, for he had many amiable qualities. I had by no means improv'd my fortune; but I had picked up some very ingenious acquaintance, whose conversation was of great advantage to me; and I had read considerably.

We sail'd from Gravesend on the 23d of July, 1726. For the incidents of the voyage, I refer you to my Journal, where you will find them all minutely related. Perhaps the most important part of that journal is the *plan*[6] to be found in it, which I formed at sea, for regulating my future conduct in life. It is the more remarkable, as being formed when I was so young, and yet being pretty faithfully adhered to quite thro' to old age.

We landed in Philadelphia on the 11th of October, where I found sundry alterations. Keith was no longer governor, being superseded by Major Gordon. I met him walking the streets as a common citizen. He seem'd a little asham'd at seeing me, but pass'd without

[6] The "Journal" was printed by Sparks, from a copy made at Reading in 1787. But it does not contain the *Plan*.—ED.

saying anything. I should have been as much asham'd at seeing Miss Read, had not her friends, despairing with reason of my return after the receipt of my letter, persuaded her to marry another, one Rogers, a potter, which was done in my absence. With him, however, she was never happy, and soon parted from him, refusing to cohabit with him or bear his name, it being now said that he had another wife. He was a worthless fellow, tho' an excellent workman, which was the temptation to her friends. He got into debt, ran away in 1727 or 1728, went to the West Indies, and died there. Keimer had got a better house, a shop well supply'd with stationery, plenty of new types, a number of hands, tho' none good, and seem'd to have a great deal of business.

Mr. Denham took a store in Water-street, where we open'd our goods; I attended the business diligently, studied accounts, and grew, in a little time, expert at selling. We lodg'd and boarded together; he counsell'd me as a father, having a sincere regard for me. I respected and lov'd him, and we might have gone on together very happy; but, in the beginning of February, 1726-7, when I had just pass'd my twenty-first year, we both were taken ill. My distemper was a pleurisy, which very nearly carried me off. I suffered a good deal, gave up the point in my own mind, and was rather disappointed when I found myself recovering, regretting, in some degree, that I must now, some time or other, have all that disagreeable work to do over again. I forget what his distemper was; it held him a long time, and at length carried him off. He left me a small legacy in a nuncupative will, as a token of his kindness for me, and he left me once more to the wide world; for the store was taken into the care of his executors, and my employment under him ended.

My brother-in-law, Holmes, being now at Philadelphia, advised my return to my business; and Keimer tempted me, with an offer of large wages by the year, to come and take the management of his printing-house, that he might better attend his stationer's shop. I had heard a bad character of him in London from his wife and her friends, and was not fond of having any more to do with him. I tri'd for farther employment as a merchant's clerk; but, not readily meeting with any, I clos'd again with Keimer. I found in his house these hands: Hugh Meredith, a Welsh Pensilvanian, thirty years of age, bred to country work; honest, sensible, had a great deal of solid observation, was something of a reader, but given to drink. Stephen Potts, a young countryman of full age, bred to the same, of uncommon natural parts, and great wit and humor, but a little idle. These he had agreed with at extream low wages per week, to be rais'd a shilling every three months, as they would deserve by improving in their business; and the expectation of these high wages, to come on hereafter, was what he had drawn them in with. Meredith was to work at press, Potts at book-binding, which he, by agreement, was to teach them, though he knew neither one nor t'other. John ———, a wild Irishman, brought up to no business, whose service, for four years, Keimer had purchased from the captain of a ship; he, too, was to be made a pressman. George Webb, an Oxford scholar, whose time for four years he had likewise bought, intending him for a compositor, of whom more presently; and David Harry, a country boy, whom he had taken apprentice.

I soon perceiv'd that the intention of engaging me at wages so much higher than he had been us'd to give, was, to have these raw, cheap hands form'd thro' me; and, as soon as I had instructed them, then they being all articled to him, he should be able to do without me. I went on, however, very cheerfully, put his printing-house in order, which had been in great confusion, and brought his hands by degrees to mind their business and to do it better.

It was an odd thing to find an Oxford scholar in the situation of a bought servant. He was not more than eighteen years of age, and gave me this account of himself; that he was born in Gloucester, educated at a grammar-school there, had been distinguish'd among the scholars for some apparent superiority in performing his part, when they exhibited plays; belong'd to the Witty Club there, and had written some pieces in prose and verse, which were printed in the Gloucester newspapers; thence he was sent to Oxford; where he continued about a year, but not well satisfi'd, wishing of all things to see London, and become a player. At length, receiving his quarterly allowance of fifteen guineas, instead of discharging his debts he walk'd out of town, hid his gown in a furze bush, and footed it to London, where, having no friend to advise him, he fell into bad company, soon spent his guineas, found no means of being introduc'd among the players, grew necessitous, pawn'd his cloaths, and wanted bread. Walking the street very hungry, and not knowing what to do with himself, a crimp's bill was put into his hand, offering immediate entertainment and encouragement to such as would bind themselves to serve in America. He went directly, sign'd the indentures, was put into the ship, and came over, never writing a line to acquaint his friends what was become of him. He was lively, witty, good-natur'd, and a pleasant companion, but idle, thoughtless, and imprudent to the last degree.

John, the Irishman, soon ran away; with the rest I began to live very agreeably, for they all respected me the more, as they found Keimer incapable of instructing them, and that from me they learned something daily. We never worked on Saturday, that being Keimer's Sabbath, so I had two days for reading. My acquaintance with ingenious people in the town increased. Keimer himself treated me with great civility and apparent regard, and nothing now made me uneasy but my debt to Vernon, which I was yet unable to pay, being hitherto but a poor œconomist. He, however, kindly made no demand of it.

Our printing-house often wanted sorts, and there was no letter-founder in America; I had seen types cast at James's in London, but without much attention to the manner; however, I now contrived a mould, made use of the letters we had as puncheons, struck the matrices in lead, and thus supply'd in a pretty tolerable way all deficiencies. I also engrav'd several things on occasion; I made the ink; I was warehouseman, and everything, and, in short, quite a factotum.

But, however serviceable I might be, I found that my services became every day of less importance, as the other hands improv'd in the business; and, when Keimer paid my second quarter's wages, he let me know that he felt them too heavy, and thought I should make an abatement. He grew by degrees less civil, put on more of the master, frequently found fault, was captious, and seem'd ready for an outbreaking. I went on, nevertheless, with a good deal of patience, thinking that his encumber'd circumstances were partly the cause. At length a trifle snapt our connections; for, a great noise happening near the court-house, I put my head out of the window to see what was the matter. Keimer, being in the street, look'd up and saw me, call'd out to me in a loud voice and angry tone to mind my business, adding some reproachful words, that nettled me the more for their publicity, all the neighbors who were looking out on the same occasion being witnesses how I was treated. He came up immediately into the printing-house, continu'd the quarrel, high words pass'd on both sides, he gave me the quarter's warning we had stipulated, expressing a wish that he had not been oblig'd to so long a warning. I told him his wish was unnecessary, for I would leave him that instant; and so, taking my hat, walk'd out of doors, desiring Meredith, whom I saw below, to take care of some things I left, and bring them to my lodgings.

Meredith came accordingly in the evening, when we talked my affair over. He had conceiv'd a great regard for me, and was very unwilling that I should leave the house while he remain'd in it. He dissuaded me from returning to my native country, which I began to think of; he reminded me that Keimer was in debt for all he possess'd; that his creditors began to be uneasy; that he kept his shop miserably, sold often without profit for ready money, and often trusted without keeping accounts; that he must therefore fail, which would make a vacancy I might profit of. I objected my want of money. He then let me know that his father had a high opinion of me, and, from some discourse that had pass'd between them, he was sure would advance money to set us up, if I would enter into partnership with him. "My time," says he, "will be out with Keimer in the spring; by that time we may have our press and types in from London. I am sensible I am no workman; if you like it, your skill in the business shall be set against the stock I furnish, and we will share the profits equally."

The proposal was agreeable, and I consented; his father was in town and approv'd of it; the more as he saw I had great influence with his son, had prevail'd on him to abstain long from dram-drinking, and he hop'd might break him off that wretched habit entirely, when we came to be so closely connected. I gave an inventory to the father, who carry'd it to a merchant; the things were sent for, the secret was to be kept till they should arrive, and in the mean time I was to get work, if I could, at the other printing-house. But

I found no vacancy there, and so remain'd idle a few days, when Keimer, on a prospect of being employ'd to print some paper money in New Jersey, which would require cuts and various types that I only could supply, and apprehending Bradford might engage me and get the jobb from him, sent me a very civil message, that old friends should not part for a few words, the effect of sudden passion, and wishing me to return. Meredith persuaded me to comply, as it would give more opportunity for his improvement under my daily instructions; so I return'd, and we went on more smoothly than for some time before. The New Jersey jobb was obtain'd, I contriv'd a copperplate press for it, the first that had been seen in the country; I cut several ornaments and checks for the bills. We went together to Burlington, where I executed the whole to satisfaction; and he received so large a sum for the work as to be enabled thereby to keep his head much longer above water.

At Burlington I made an acquaintance with many principal people of the province. Several of them had been appointed by the Assembly a committee to attend the press, and take care that no more bills were printed than the law directed. They were therefore, by turns, constantly with us, and generally he who attended, brought with him a friend or two for company. My mind having been much more improv'd by reading than Keimer's, I suppose it was for that reason my conversation seem'd to be more valu'd. They had me to their houses, introduced me to their friends, and show'd me much civility; while he, tho' the master, was a little neglected. In truth, he was an odd fish; ignorant of common life, fond of rudely opposing receiv'd opinions, slovenly to extreme dirtiness, enthusiastic in some points of religion, and a little knavish withal.

We continu'd there near three months; and by that time I could reckon among my acquired friends, Judge Allen, Samuel Bustill, the secretary of the Province, Isaac Pearson, Joseph Cooper, and several of the Smiths, members of Assembly, and Isaac Decow, the surveyor-general. The latter was a shrewd, sagacious old man, who told me that he began for himself, when young, by wheeling clay for the brickmakers, learned to write after he was of age, carri'd the chain for surveyors, who taught him surveying, and he had now by his industry, acquir'd a good estate; and says he, "I foresee that you will soon work this man out of business, and make a fortune in it at Philadelphia." He had not then the least intimation of my intention to set up there or anywhere. These friends were afterwards of great use to me, as I occasionally was to some of them. They all continued their regard for me as long as they lived.

Before I enter upon my public appearance in business, it may be well to let you know the then state of my mind with regard to my principles and morals, that you may see how far those influenc'd the future events of my life. My parents had early given me religious impressions, and brought me through my childhood piously in the Dissenting way. But I was scarce fifteen, when, after doubting by turns of several points, as I found them disputed in the different books I read, I began to doubt of Revelation itself. Some books against Deism fell into my hands; they were said to be the substance of sermons preached at Boyle's Lectures. It happened that they wrought an effect on me quite contrary to what was intended by them; for the arguments of the Deists, which were quoted to be refuted, appeared to me much stronger than the refutations; in short, I soon became a thorough Deist. My arguments perverted some others, particularly Collins and Ralph; but, each of them having afterwards wrong'd me greatly without the least compunction, and recollecting Keith's conduct towards me (who was another free-thinker), and my own towards Vernon and Miss Read, which at times gave me great trouble, I began to suspect that this doctrine, tho' it might be true, was not very useful. My London pamphlet, which had for its motto these lines of Dryden:

> "Whatever is, is right. Though purblind man
> Sees but a part o' the chain, the nearest link:
> His eyes not carrying to the equal beam,
> That poises all above;"

and from the attributes of God, his infinite wisdom, goodness and power, concluded that nothing could possibly be wrong in the world, and that vice and virtue were empty distinctions, no such things existing, appear'd now not so clever a performance as I once thought it; and I doubted whether some error had not insinuated itself unperceiv'd into my argument, so as to infect all that follow'd, as is common in metaphysical reasonings.

I grew convinc'd that *truth, sincerity* and *integrity* in dealings between man and man were of the utmost importance to the felicity of life; and I form'd written resolutions, which still remain in my journal book, to practice them ever while I lived. Revelation had indeed no weight with me, as such; but I entertain'd an opinion that, though certain actions might not be bad *because* they were forbidden by it, or good *because* it commanded them, yet probably these actions might be forbidden *because* they were bad for us, or commanded *because* they were beneficial to us, in their own natures, all the circumstances of things considered. And this persuasion, with the kind hand of Providence, or some guardian angel, or accidental favorable circumstances and situations, or all together, preserved me, thro' this dangerous time of youth, and the hazardous situations I was sometimes in among strangers, remote from the eye and advice of my father, without any willful gross immorality or injustice, that might have been expected from my want of religion. I say willful, because the instances I have mentioned had something of *necessity* in them, from my youth, inexperience, and the knavery of others. I had therefore a tolerable character to begin the world with; I valued it properly, and determin'd to preserve it.

We had not been long return'd to Philadelphia before the new types arriv'd from London. We settled with Keimer, and left him by his consent before he heard of it. We found a house to hire near the market, and took it. To lessen the rent, which was then but twenty-four pounds a year, tho' I have since known it to let for seventy, we took in Thomas Godfrey, a glazier, and his family, who were to pay a considerable part of it to us, and we to board with them. We had scarce opened our letters and put our press in order, before George House, an acquaintance of mine, brought a countryman to us, whom he had met in the street inquiring for a printer. All our cash was now expended in the variety of particulars we had been obliged to procure, and this countryman's five shillings, being our first-fruits, and coming so seasonably, gave me more pleasure than any crown I have since earned; and the gratitude I felt toward House has made me often more ready than perhaps I should otherwise have been to assist young beginners.

There are croakers in every country, always boding its ruin. Such a one then lived in Philadelphia; a person of note, an elderly man, with a wise look and a very grave manner of speaking; his name was Samuel Mickle. This gentleman, a stranger to me, stopt one day at my door, and asked me if I was the young man who had lately opened a new printing-house. Being answered in the affirmative, he said he was sorry for me, because it was an expensive undertaking, and the expense would be lost; for Philadelphia was a sinking place, the people already half-bankrupts, or near being so; all appearances to the contrary, such as new buildings and the rise of rents, being to his certain knowledge fallacious; for they were, in fact, among the things that would soon ruin us. And he gave me such a detail of misfortunes now existing, or that were soon to exist, that he left me half melancholy. Had I known him before I engaged in this business, probably I never should have done it. This man continued to live in this decaying place, and to declaim in the same strain, refusing for many years to buy a house there, because all was going to destruction; and at last I had the pleasure of seeing him give five times as much for one as he might have bought it for when he first began his croaking.

I should have mentioned before, that, in the autumn of the preceding year, I had form'd most of my ingenious acquaintance into a club of mutual improvement, which we called the Junto; we met on Friday evenings. The rules that I drew up required that every member, in his turn, should produce one or more queries on any point of Morals, Politics, or Natural Philosophy, to be discuss'd by the company; and once in three months produce and read an essay of his own writing, on any subject he pleased. Our debates were to be under the direction of a president, and to be conducted in the sincere spirit of inquiry after truth, without fondness for dispute, or desire of victory; and, to prevent warmth, all expressions of positiveness in opinions, or direct contradiction, were after some time made contraband, and prohibited under small pecuniary penalties.

The first members were Joseph Breintnal, a copyer of deeds for the scriveners, a good-natur'd, friendly, middle-ag'd man, a great lover of poetry, reading all he could meet with, and writing some that was tolerable; very ingenious in many little Nicknackeries, and of sensible conversation.

Thomas Godfrey, a self-taught mathematician, great in his way, and afterward inventor of what is now called Hadley's Quadrant. But he knew little out of his way, and was not a pleasing companion; as, like most great mathematicians I have met with, he expected universal precision in everything said, or was for ever denying or distinguishing upon trifles, to the disturbance of all conversation. He soon left us.

Nicholas Scull, a surveyor, afterwards surveyor-general, who lov'd books, and sometimes made a few verses.

William Parsons, bred a shoemaker, but loving reading, had acquir'd a considerable share of mathematics, which he first studied with a view to astrology, that he afterwards laught at it. He also became surveyor-general.

William Maugridge, a joiner, a most exquisite mechanic, and a solid, sensible man.

Hugh Meredith, Stephen Potts, and George Webb I have characteriz'd before.

Robert Grace, a young gentleman of some fortune, generous, lively, and witty; a lover of punning and of his friends.

And William Coleman, then a merchant's clerk, about my age, who had the coolest, clearest head, the best heart, and the exactest morals of almost any man I ever met with. He became afterwards a merchant of great note, and one of our provincial judges. Our friendship continued without interruption to his death, upward of forty years; and the club continued almost as long, and was the best school of philosophy, morality, and politics that then existed in the province; for our queries, which were read the week preceding their discussion, put us upon reading with attention upon the several subjects, that we might speak more to the purpose; and here, too, we acquired better habits of conversation, every thing being studied in our rules which might prevent our disgusting each other. From hence the long continuance of the club, which I shall have frequent occasion to speak further of hereafter.

But my giving this account of it here is to show something of the interest I had, every one of these exerting themselves in recommending business to us. Breintnal particularly procur'd us from the Quakers the printing forty sheets of their history, the rest being to be done by Keimer; and upon this we work'd exceedingly hard, for the price was low. It was a folio, pro patria size, in pica, with long primer notes. I compos'd of it a sheet a day, and Meredith worked it off at press; it was often eleven at night, and sometimes later, before I had finished my distribution for the next day's work, for the little jobbs sent in by our other friends now and then put us back. But so determin'd I was to continue doing a sheet a day of the folio, that one night, when, having impos'd my forms, I thought my day's work over, one of them by accident was broken, and two pages reduced to pi, I immediately distributed and compos'd it over again before I went to bed; and this industry, visible to our neighbors, began to give us character and credit; particularly, I was told, that mention being made of the new printing-office at the merchants' Every-night club, the general opinion was that it must fail, there being already two printers in the place, Keimer and Bradford; but Dr. Baird (whom you and I saw many years after at his native place, St. Andrew's in Scotland) gave a contrary opinion: "For the industry of that Franklin," says he, "is superior to any thing I ever saw of the kind; I see him still at work when I go home from club, and he is at work again before his neighbors are out of bed." This struck the rest, and we soon after had offers from one of them to supply us with stationery; but as yet we did not chuse to engage in shop business.

I mention this industry the more particularly and the more freely, tho' it seems to be talking in my own praise, that those of my posterity, who shall read it, may know the use of that virtue, when they see its effects in my favour throughout this relation.

George Webb, who had found a female friend that lent him wherewith to purchase his time of Keimer, now came to offer himself as a journeyman to us. We could not then employ him; but I foolishly let him know as a secret that I soon intended to begin a newspaper, and might then have work for him. My hopes of success, as I told him, were founded on this, that the then only newspaper, printed by Bradford, was a paltry thing, wretchedly manag'd, no way entertaining, and yet was profitable to him; I therefore thought a good paper would scarcely fail of good encouragement. I requested Webb not to mention it; but he told it to Keimer, who immediately, to be beforehand with me, published proposals for printing one himself, on which Webb was to be employ'd. I resented this; and, to counteract them, as I could not yet begin our paper, I wrote several pieces of entertainment for Bradford's paper, under the title of the BUSY BODY, which Breintnal continu'd some months. By this means the attention of the publick was fixed on that paper, and Keimer's proposals, which we burlesqu'd and ridicul'd, were disregarded. He began his paper, however, and, after carrying it on three quarters of a year, with at most only ninety subscribers, he offered it to me for a trifle; and I, having been ready some time to go on with it, took it in hand directly; and it prov'd in a few years extremely profitable to me.

I perceive that I am apt to speak in the singular number, though our partnership still continu'd; the reason may be that, in fact, the whole management of the business lay upon me. Meredith was no compositor, a poor pressman, and seldom sober. My friends lamented my connection with him, but I was to make the best of it.

Our first papers made a quite different appearance from any before in the province; a better type, and better printed; but some spirited remarks of my writing, on the dispute then going on between Governor Burnet and the Massachusetts Assembly, struck the principal people, occasioned the paper and the manager of it to be much talk'd of, and in a few weeks brought them all to be our subscribers.

Their example was follow'd by many, and our number went on growing continually. This was one of the first good effects of my having learnt a little to scribble; another was, that the leading men, seeing a newspaper now in the hands of one who could also handle a pen, thought it convenient to oblige and encourage me. Bradford still printed the votes, and laws, and other publick business. He had printed an address of the House to the governor, in a coarse, blundering manner, we reprinted it elegantly and correctly, and sent one to every member. They were sensible of the difference: it strengthened the hands of our friends in the House, and they voted us their printers for the year ensuing.

Among my friends in the House I must not forget Mr. Hamilton, before mentioned, who was then returned from England, and had a seat in it. He interested himself for me strongly in that instance, as he did in many others afterward, continuing his patronage till his death.[7]

Mr. Vernon, about this time, put me in mind of the debt I ow'd him, but did not press me. I wrote him an ingenuous letter of acknowledgment, crav'd his forbearance a little longer, which he allow'd me, and as soon as I was able, I paid the principal with interest, and many thanks; so that erratum was in some degree corrected.

But now another difficulty came upon me which I had never the least reason to expect. Mr. Meredith's father, who was to have paid for our printing-house, according to the expectations given me, was able to advance only one hundred pounds currency, which had been paid; and a hundred more was due to the merchant, who grew impatient, and su'd us all. We gave bail, but saw that, if the money could not be rais'd in time, the suit must soon come to a judgment and execution, and our hopeful prospects must, with us, be ruined, as the press and letters must be sold for payment, perhaps at half price.

In this distress two true friends, whose kindness I have never forgotten, nor ever shall forget while I can remember any thing, came to me separately, unknown to each other, and, without any application from me, offering each of them to advance me all the money that should be necessary to enable me to take the whole business upon myself, if that should be practicable; but they did not like my continuing the partnership with Meredith, who, as they said, was often seen drunk in the streets, and playing at low games in ale-houses, much to our discredit. These two friends were William Coleman and Robert Grace. I told them I could not propose a separation while any prospect remain'd of the Merediths' fulfilling their part of our agreement, because I thought myself under great obligations to them for what they had done, and would do if they could; but, if they finally fail'd in their performance, and our partnership must be dissolv'd, I should then think myself at liberty to accept the assistance of my friends.

Thus the matter rested for some time, when I said to my partner,

[7] I got his son once £500.—[*Marg. note.*]

"Perhaps your father is dissatisfied at the part you have undertaken in this affair of ours, and is unwilling to advance for you and me what he would for you alone. If that is the case, tell me, and I will resign the whole to you, and go about my business." "No," said he, "my father has really been disappointed, and is really unable; and I am unwilling to distress him farther. I see this is a business I am not fit for. I was bred a farmer, and it was a folly in me to come to town, and put myself, at thirty years of age, an apprentice to learn a new trade. Many of our Welsh people are going to settle in North Carolina, where land is cheap. I am inclin'd to go with them, and follow my old employment. You may find friends to assist you. If you will take the debts of the company upon you; return to my father the hundred pound he has advanced; pay my little personal debts, and give me thirty pounds and a new saddle, I will relinquish the partnership, and leave the whole in your hands." I agreed to this proposal: it was drawn up in writing, sign'd, and seal'd immediately. I gave him what he demanded, and he went soon after to Carolina, from whence he sent me next year two long letters, containing the best account that had been given of that country, the climate, the soil, husbandry, etc., for in those matters he was very judicious. I printed them in the papers, and they gave great satisfaction to the publick.

As soon as he was gone, I recurr'd to my two friends; and because I would not give an unkind preference to either, I took half of what each had offered and I wanted of one, and half of the other; paid off the company's debts, and went on with the business in my own name, advertising that the partnership was dissolved. I think this was in or about the year 1729.

About this time there was a cry among the people for more paper money, only fifteen thousand pounds being extant in the province, and that soon to be sunk. The wealthy inhabitants oppos'd any addition, being against all paper currency, from an apprehension that it would depreciate, as it had done in New England, to the prejudice of all creditors. We had discuss'd this point in our Junto, where I was on the side of an addition, being persuaded that the first small sum struck in 1723 had done much good by increasing the trade, employment, and number of inhabitants in the province, since I now saw all the old houses inhabited, and many new ones building: whereas I remembered well, that when I first walk'd about the streets of Philadelphia, eating my roll, I saw most of the houses in Walnut-street, between Second and Front streets, with bills on their doors, "To be let"; and many likewise in Chestnut-street and other streets, which made me then think the inhabitants of the city were deserting it one after another.

Our debates possess'd me so fully of the subject, that I wrote and printed an anonymous pamphlet on it, entitled "*The Nature and Necessity of a Paper Currency.*" It was well receiv'd by the common people in general; but the rich men dislik'd it, for it increas'd and strengthen'd the clamor for more money, and they happening to have no writers among them that were able to answer it, their opposition slacken'd, and the point was carried by a majority in the House. My friends there, who conceiv'd I had been of some service, thought fit to reward me my employing me in printing the money; a very profitable jobb and a great help to me. This was another advantage gain'd by my being able to write.

The utility of this currency became by time and experience so evident as never afterwards to be much disputed; so that it grew soon to fifty-five thousand pounds, and in 1739 to eighty thousand pounds, since which it arose during war to upwards of three hundred and fifty thousand pounds trade, building, and inhabitants all the while increasing, tho' I now think there are limits beyond which the quantity may be hurtful.

I soon after obtain'd, thro' my friend Hamilton, the printing of the Newcastle paper money, another profitable jobb as I then thought it; small things appearing great to those in small circumstances; and these, to me, were really great advantages, as they were great encouragements. He procured for me, also, the printing of the laws and votes of that government, which continu'd in my hands as long as I follow'd the business.

I now open'd a little stationer's shop. I had in it blanks of all sorts, the correctest that ever appear'd among us, being assisted in that by my friend Breintnal. I had also paper, parchment, chapmen's books, etc. One Whitemash, a compositor I had known in London, an excellent workman, now came to me, and work'd with me constantly and diligently; and I took an apprentice, the son of Aquila Rose.

I began now gradually to pay off the debt I was under for the printing-house. In order to secure my credit and character as a tradesman, I took care not only to be in *reality* industrious and frugal, but to avoid all appearances to the contrary. I drest plainly; I was seen at no places of idle diversion. I never went out a fishing or shooting; a book, indeed, sometimes debauch'd me from my work, but that was seldom, snug, and gave no scandal; and, to show that I was not above my business, I sometimes brought home the paper I purchas'd at the stores thro' the streets on a wheelbarrow. Thus being esteem'd an industrious, thriving young man, and paying duly for what I bought, the merchants who imported stationery solicited my custom; others proposed supplying me with books, and I went on swimmingly. In the mean time, Keimer's credit and business declining daily, he was at last forc'd to sell his printing-house to satisfy his creditors. He went to Barbadoes, and there lived some years in very poor circumstances.

His apprentice, David Harry, whom I had instructed while I work'd with him, set up in his place at Philadelphia, having bought his materials. I was at first apprehensive of a powerful rival in Harry, as his friends were very able, and had a good deal of interest. I therefore propos'd a partnership to him, which he, fortunately for me, rejected with scorn. He was very proud, dress'd like a gentleman, liv'd expensively, took much diversion and pleasure abroad, ran in debt, and neglected his business; upon which, all business left him; and, finding nothing to do, he followed Keimer to Barbadoes, taking the printing-house with him. There this apprentice employ'd his former master as a journeyman; they quarrel'd often; Harry went continually behindhand, and at length was forc'd to sell his types and return to his country work in Pensilvania. The person that bought them employ'd Keimer to use them, but in a few years he died.

There remained now no competitor with me at Philadelphia but the old one, Bradford; who was rich and easy, did a little printing now and then by straggling hands, but was not very anxious about the business. However, as he kept the post-office, it was imagined he had better opportunities of obtaining news; his paper was thought a better distributer of advertisements than mine, and therefore had many more, which was a profitable thing to him, and a disadvantage to me; for, tho' I did indeed receive and send papers by the post, yet the publick opinion was otherwise, for what I did send was by bribing the riders, who took them privately, Bradford being unkind enough to forbid it, which occasion'd some resentment on my part; and I thought so meanly of him for it, that, when I afterward came into his situation, I took care never to imitate it.

I had hitherto continu'd to board with Godfrey, who lived in part of my house with his wife and children, and had one side of the shop for his glazier's business, tho' he worked little, being always absorbed in his mathematics. Mrs. Godfrey projected a match for me with a relation's daughter, took opportunities of bringing us often together, till a serious courtship on my part ensu'd, the girl being in herself very deserving. The old folks encourag'd me by continual invitations to supper, and by leaving us together, till at length it was time to explain. Mrs. Godfrey manag'd our little treaty. I let her know that I expected as much money with their daughter as would pay off my remaining debt for the printing-house, which I believe was not then above a hundred pounds. She brought me word they had no such sum to spare; I said they might mortgage their house in the loan-office. The answer to this, after some days, was, that they did not approve the match; that, on inquiry of Bradford, they had been inform'd the printing business was not a profitable one; the types would soon be worn out, and more wanted; that S. Keimer and D. Harry had failed one after the other, and I should probably soon follow them; and, therefore, I was forbidden the house, and the daughter shut up.

Whether this was a real change of sentiment or only artifice, on a supposition of our being too far engaged in affection to retract, and therefore that we should steal a marriage, which would leave them at liberty to give or withhold what they pleas'd, I know not; but I suspected the latter, resented it, and went no more. Mrs. Godfrey brought me afterward some more favorable accounts of their disposition, and would have drawn me on again; but I declared absolutely my resolution to have nothing more to do with that family.

This was resented by the Godfreys; we differ'd, and they removed, leaving me the whole house, and I resolved to take no more inmates.

But this affair having turned my thoughts to marriage, I look'd round me and made overtures of acquaintance in other places; but soon found that, the business of a printer being generally thought a poor one, I was not to expect money with a wife, unless with such a one as I should not otherwise think agreeable. In the mean time, that hard-to-be-governed passion of youth hurried me frequently into intrigues with low women that fell in my way, which were attended with some expense and great inconvenience, besides a continual risque to my health by a distemper which of all things I dreaded, though by great good luck I escaped it. A friendly correspondence as neighbors and old acquaintances had continued between me and Mrs. Read's family, who all had a regard for me from the time of my first lodging in their house. I was often invited there and consulted in their affairs, wherein I sometimes was of service. I piti'd poor Miss Read's unfortunate situation, who was generally dejected, seldom cheerful, and avoided company. I considered my giddiness and inconstancy when in London as in a great degree the cause of her unhappiness, tho' the mother was good enough to think the fault more her own than mine, as she had prevented our marrying before I went thither, and persuaded the other match in my absence. Our mutual affection was revived, but there were now great objections to our union. The match was indeed looked upon as invalid, a preceding wife being said to be living in England; but this could not easily be prov'd, because of the distance; and, tho' there was a report of his death, it was not certain. Then, tho' it should be true, he had left many debts, which his successor might be call'd upon to pay. We ventured, however, over all these difficulties, and I took her to wife, September 1st, 1730. None of the inconveniences happened that we had apprehended; she proved a good and faithful helpmate, assisted me much by attending the shop; we throve together, and have ever mutually endeavored to make each other happy. Thus I corrected that great *erratum* as well as I could.

About this time, our club meeting, not at a tavern, but in a little room of Mr. Grace's, set apart for that purpose, a proposition was made by me, that, since our books were often referr'd to in our disquisitions upon the queries, it might be convenient to us to have them altogether where we met, that upon occasion they might be consulted; and by thus clubbing our books to a common library, we should, while we lik'd to keep them together, have each of us the advantage of using the books of all the other members, which would be nearly as beneficial as if each owned the whole. It was lik'd and agreed to, and we fill'd one end of the room with such books as we could best spare. The number was not so great as we expected; and tho' they had been of great use, yet some inconveniences occurring for want of due care of them, the collection, after about a year, was separated, and each took his books home again.

And now I set on foot my first project of a public nature, that for a subscription library. I drew up the proposals, got them put into form by our great scrivener, Brockden, and, by the help of my friends in the Junto, procured fifty subscribers of forty shillings each to begin with, and ten shillings a year for fifty years, the term our company was to continue. We afterwards obtain'd a charter, the company being increased to one hundred: this was the mother of all the North American subscription libraries, now so numerous. It is become a great thing itself, and continually increasing. These libraries have improved the general conversation of the Americans, made the common tradesmen and farmers as intelligent as most gentlemen from other countries, and perhaps have contributed in some degree to the stand so generally made throughout the colonies in defense of their privileges.

Memo. Thus far was written with the intention express'd in the beginning and therefore contains several little family anecdotes of no importance to others. What follows was written many years after in compliance with the advice contain'd in these letters, and accordingly intended for the public. The affairs of the Revolution occasion'd the interruption.

Letter from Mr. Abel James, with Notes of my Life
(received in Paris).

"MY DEAR AND HONORED FRIEND: I have often been desirous of writing to thee, but could not be reconciled to the thought that the letter might fall into the hands of the British, lest some printer or busy-body should publish some part of the contents, and give our friend pain, and myself censure.

"Some time since there fell into my hands, to my great joy, about twenty-three sheets in thy own handwriting, containing an account of the parentage and life of thyself, directed to thy son, ending in the year 1730, with which there were notes, likewise in thy writing; a copy of which I inclose, in hopes it may be a means, if thou continued it up to a later period, that the first and latter part may be put together; and if it is not yet continued, I hope thee will not delay it. Life is uncertain, as the preacher tells us; and what will the world say if kind, humane, and benevolent Ben. Franklin should leave his friends and the world deprived of so pleasing and profitable a work; a work which would be useful and entertaining not only to a few, but to millions? The influence writings under that class have on the minds of youth is very great, and has nowhere appeared to me so plain, as in our public friend's journals. It almost insensibly leads the youth into the resolution of endeavoring to become as good and eminent as the journalist. Should thine, for instance, when published (and I think it could not fail of it), lead the youth to equal the industry and temperance of thy early youth, what a blessing with that class would such a work be! I know of no character living, nor many of them put together, who has so much in his power as thyself to promote a greater spirit of industry and early attention to business, frugality, and temperance with the American youth. Not that I think the work would have no other merit and use in the world, far from it; but the first is of such vast importance that I know nothing that can equal it."

68

The foregoing letter and the minutes accompanying it being shown to a friend, I received from him the following:

Letter from Mr. Benjamin Vaughan.

"Paris, *January* 31, 1783.

"My Dearest Sir: When I had read over your sheets of minutes of the principal incidents of your life, recovered for you by your Quaker acquaintance, I told you I would send you a letter expressing my reasons why I thought it would be useful to complete and publish it as he desired. Various concerns have for some time past prevented this letter being written, and I do not know whether it was worth any expectation; happening to be at leisure, however, at present, I shall by writing, at least interest and instruct myself; but as the terms I am inclined to use may tend to offend a person of your manners, I shall only tell you how I would address any other person, who was as good and as great as yourself, but less diffident. I would say to him, Sir, I solicit the history of your life from the following motives: Your history is so remarkable, that if you do not give it, somebody else will certainly give it; and perhaps so as nearly to do as much harm, as your own management of the thing might do good. It will moreover present a table of the internal circumstances of your country, which will very much tend to invite to it settlers of virtuous and manly minds. And considering the eagerness with which such information is sought by them, and the extent of your reputation, I do not know of a more efficacious advertisement than your biography would give. All that has happened to you is also connected with the detail of the manners and situation of a rising people; and in this respect I do not think that the writings of Cæsar and Tacitus can be more interesting to a true judge of human nature and society. But these, sir, are small reasons, in my opinion, compared with the chance which your life will give for the forming of future great men; and in conjunction with your Art of Virtue (which you design to publish) of improving the features of private character, and consequently of aiding all happiness, both public and domestic. The two works I allude to, sir, will in particular give a noble rule and example of self-education. School and other education constantly proceed upon false principles, and show a clumsy apparatus pointed at a false mark; but your apparatus is simple, and the mark a true one; and while parents and young persons are left destitute of other just means of estimating and becoming prepared for a reasonable course in life, your discovery that the thing is in many a man's private power, will be invaluable! Influence upon the private character, late in life, is not only an influence late in life, but a weak influence. It is in youth that we plant our chief habits and prejudices; it is in youth that we take our party as to profession, pursuits and matrimony. In youth, therefore, the turn is given; in youth the education even of the next generation is given; in youth the private and public character is determined; and the term of life extending but from youth to age, life ought to begin well from youth, and more especially before we take our party as to our principal objects. But your biography will not merely teach self-education, but the education of a wise man; and the wisest man will receive lights and improve his progress, by seeing detailed the conduct of another wise man. And why are weaker men to be deprived of such helps, when we see our race has been blundering on in the dark, almost without a guide in this particular, from the farthest trace of time? Show then, sir, how much is to be done, both to sons and fathers; and invite all wise men to become like yourself, and other men to become wise. When we see how cruel statesmen and warriors can be to the human race, and how absurd distinguished men can be to their acquaintance, it will be instructive to observe the instances multiply of pacific, acquiescing manners; and to find how compatible it is to be great and domestic, enviable and yet good-humored.

"The little private incidents which you will also have to relate, will have considerable use, as we want, above all things, rules of prudence in ordinary affairs; and it will be curious to see how you have acted in these. It will be so far a sort of key to life, and explain many things that all men ought to have once explained to them, to give them a chance of becoming wise by foresight. The nearest thing to having experience of one's own, is to have other people's affairs brought before us in a shape that is interesting; this is sure to happen from your pen; our affairs and management will have an air of simplicity or importance that will not fail to strike; and I am convinced you have conducted them with as much originality as if you had been conducting discussions in politics or philosophy; and what more worthy of experiments and system (its importance and its errors considered) than human life?

"Some men have been virtuous blindly, others have speculated fantastically, and others have been shrewd to bad purposes; but you, sir, I am sure, will give under your hand, nothing but what is at the same moment, wise, practical and good. Your account of yourself (for I suppose the parallel I am drawing for Dr. Franklin, will hold not only in point of character, but of private history) will show that you are ashamed of no origin; a thing the more important, as you prove how little necessary all origin is to happiness, virtue, or greatness. As no end likewise happens without a means, so we shall find, sir, that even you yourself framed a plan by which you became considerable; but at the same time we may see that though the event is flattering, the means are as simple as wisdom could make them; that is, depending upon nature, virtue, thought and habit. Another thing demonstrated will be the propriety of every man's waiting for his time for appearing upon the stage of the world. Our sensations being very much fixed to the moment, we are apt to forget that more moments are to follow the first, and consequently that man should arrange his conduct so as to suit the whole of a life. Your attribution appears to have been applied to your life, and the passing moments of it have been enlivened with content and enjoyment, instead of being tormented with foolish impatience or regrets. Such a conduct is easy for those who make virtue and themselves in countenance by examples of other truly great men, of whom patience is so often the characteristic. Your Quaker correspondent, sir (for here again I will suppose the subject of my letter resembling Dr. Franklin), praised your frugality, diligence and temperance, which he considered as a pattern for all youth; but it is singular that he should have forgotten your modesty and your disinterestedness, without which you never could have waited for your advancement, or found your situation in the mean time comfortable; which is a strong lesson to show the poverty of glory and the importance of regulating our minds. If this correspondent had known the nature of your reputation as well as I do, he would have said, Your former writings and measures would secure attention to your Biography, and Art of Virtue; and your Biography and Art of Virtue, in return, would secure attention to them. This is an advantage attendant upon a various character, and which brings all that belongs to it into greater play; and it is the more useful, as perhaps more persons are at a loss for the means of improving their minds and characters, than they are for the time or the inclination to do it. But there is one concluding reflection, sir, that will shew the use of your life as a mere piece of biography. This style of writing seems a little gone out of vogue, and yet it is a very useful one; and your specimen of it may be particularly serviceable, as it will make a subject of comparison with the lives of various public cutthroats and intriguers, and with absurd monastic self-tormentors or vain literary triflers. If it encourages more writings of the same kind with your own, and induces more men to spend lives fit to be written, it will be worth all Plutarch's Lives put together. But being tired of figuring to myself a character of which every feature suits only one man in the world, without giving him the praise of it, I shall end my letter, my dear Dr. Franklin, with a personal application to your proper self. I am earnestly desirous, then, my dear sir, that you should let the world into the traits of your genuine character, as civil broils may otherwise tend to disguise or traduce it. Considering your great age, the caution of your character, and your peculiar style of thinking, it is not likely that any one besides yourself can be sufficiently master of the facts of your life, or the intentions of your mind. Besides all this, the immense revolution of the present period, will necessarily turn our attention towards the author of it, and when virtuous principles have been pretended in it, it will be highly important to shew that such have really influenced; and, as your own character will be the principal one to receive a scrutiny, it is proper (even for its effects upon your vast and rising country, as well as upon England and upon Europe) that it should stand respectable and eternal. For the furtherance of human happiness, I have always maintained that it is necessary to prove that man is not even at present a vicious and detestable animal; and still more to prove that good management may greatly amend him; and it is for much the same reason, that I am anxious to see the opinion established, that there are fair characters existing among the individuals of the race; for the moment that all men, without exception, shall be conceived abandoned, good people will cease efforts deemed to be hopeless, and perhaps think of taking their share in the scramble of life, or at least of making it comfortable principally for themselves. Take then, my dear sir, this work most speedily into hand: shew yourself good as you are good; temperate as you are temperate; and above all things, prove yourself as one, who from your infancy have loved justice, liberty and concord, in a way that has made it natural and consistent for you to have acted, as we have seen you act in the last seventeen years of your life. Let Englishmen be made not only to respect, but even to love you. When they think well of individuals in your native country, they will go nearer to thinking well of your country; and when your countrymen see themselves well thought of by Englishmen, they will go nearer to thinking well of England. Extend your views even further; do not stop at those who speak the English tongue, but after having settled so many points in nature and politics, think of bettering the whole race of men. As I have not read any part of the life in question, but know only the character that lived it, I write somewhat at hazard. I am sure, however, that the life and the treatise I allude to (on the Art of Virtue) will necessarily fulfil the chief of my expectations; and still more so if you take up the measure of suiting these performances to the several views above stated. Should they even prove unsuccessful in all that a sanguine admirer of yours hopes from them, you will at least have framed pieces to interest the human mind; and whoever gives a feeling of pleasure that is innocent to man, has added so much to the fair side of a life otherwise too much darkened by anxiety and too much injured by pain. In the hope, therefore, that you will listen to the prayer addressed to you in this letter, I beg to subscribe myself, my dearest sir, etc., etc.,

"Signed, BENJ. VAUGHAN."

Continuation of the Account of my Life, begun at Passy, near Paris, 1784.

It is some time since I receiv'd the above letters, but I have been too busy till now to think of complying with the request they contain. It might, too, be much better done if I were at home among my papers, which would aid my memory, and help to ascertain dates; but my return being uncertain, and having just now a little leisure, I will endeavor to recollect and write what I can; if I live to get home, it may there be corrected and improv'd.

Not having any copy here of what is already written, I know not whether an account is given of the means I used to establish the Philadelphia public library, which, from a small beginning, is now become so considerable, though I remember to have come down to near the time of that transaction (1730). I will therefore begin here with an account of it, which may be struck out if found to have been already given.

At the time I establish'd myself in Pennsylvania, there was not a good bookseller's shop in any of the colonies to the southward of Boston. In New York and Philad'a the printers were indeed stationers; they sold only paper, etc., almanacs, ballads, and a few common school-books. Those who lov'd reading were oblig'd to send for their books from England; the members of the Junto had each a few. We had left the alehouse, where we first met, and hired a room to hold our club in. I propos'd that we should all of us bring our books to that room, where they would not only be ready to consult in our conferences, but become a common benefit, each of us being at liberty to borrow such as he wish'd to read at home. This was accordingly done, and for some time contented us.

Finding the advantage of this little collection, I propos'd to render the benefit from books more common, by commencing a public subscription library. I drew a sketch of the plan and rules that would be necessary, and got a skilful conveyancer, Mr. Charles Brockden, to put the whole in form of articles of agreement to be subscribed, by which each subscriber engag'd to pay a certain sum down for the first purchase of books, and an annual contribution for increasing them. So few were the readers at that time in Philadelphia, and the majority of us so poor, that I was not able, with great industry, to find more than fifty persons, mostly young tradesmen, willing to pay down for this purpose forty shillings each, and ten shillings per annum. On this little fund we began. The books were imported; the library was opened one day in the week for lending to the subscribers, on their promissory notes to pay double the value if not duly returned. The institution soon manifested its utility, was imitated by other towns, and in other provinces. The libraries were augmented by donations; reading became fashionable; and our people, having no publick amusements to divert their attention from study, became better acquainted with books, and in a few years were observ'd by strangers to be better instructed and more intelligent than people of the same rank generally are in other countries.

When we were about to sign the above-mentioned articles, which were to be binding upon us, our heirs, etc., for fifty years, Mr. Brockden, the scrivener, said to us, "You are young men, but it is scarcely probable that any of you will live to see the expiration of the term fix'd in the instrument." A number of us, however, are yet living; but the instrument was after a few years rendered null by a charter that incorporated and gave perpetuity to the company.

The objections and reluctances I met with in soliciting the subscriptions, made me soon feel the impropriety of presenting one's self as the proposer of any useful project, that might be suppos'd to raise one's reputation in the smallest degree above that of one's neighbors, when one has need of their assistance to accomplish that project. I therefore put myself as much as I could out of sight, and stated it as a scheme of a *number of friends,* who had requested me to go about and propose it to such as they thought lovers of reading. In this way my affair went on more smoothly, and I ever after practis'd it on such occasions; and, from my frequent successes, can heartily recommend it. The present little sacrifice of your vanity will afterwards be amply repaid. If it remains a while uncertain to whom the merit belongs, some one more vain than yourself will be encouraged to claim it, and then even envy will be disposed to do you justice by plucking those assumed feathers, and restoring them to their right owner.

This library afforded me the means of improvement by constant study, for which I set apart an hour or two each day, and thus repair'd in some degree the loss of the learned education my father once intended for me. Reading was the only amusement I allow'd myself. I spent no time in taverns, games, or frolicks of any kind; and my industry in my business continu'd as indefatigable as it was necessary. I was indebted for my printing-house; I had a young family coming on to be educated, and I had to contend with for business two printers, who were established in the place before me. My circumstances, however, grew daily easier. My original habits of frugality continuing, and my father having, among his instructions to me when a boy, frequently repeated a proverb of Solomon, "Seest thou a man diligent in his calling, he shall stand before kings, he shall not stand before mean men," I from thence considered industry as a means of obtaining wealth and distinction, which encourag'd me, tho' I did not think that I should ever literally *stand before kings,* which, however, has since happened; for I have stood before *five,* and even had the honor of sitting down with one, the King of Denmark, to dinner.

We have an English proverb that says, *"He that would thrive, must ask his wife."* It was lucky for me that I had one as much dispos'd to industry and frugality as myself. She assisted me cheerfully in my business, folding and stitching pamphlets, tending shop, purchasing old linen rags for the papermakers, etc., etc. We kept no idle servants, our table was plain and simple, our furniture of the cheapest. For instance, my breakfast was a long time bread and milk (no tea), and I ate it out of a twopenny earthen porringer, with a pewter spoon. But mark how luxury will enter families, and make a progress, in spite of principle: being call'd one morning to breakfast, I found it in a China bowl, with a spoon of silver! They had been bought for me without my knowledge by my wife, and had cost her the enormous sum of three-and-twenty shillings, for which she had no other excuse or apology to make, but that she thought *her* husband deserv'd a silver spoon and China bowl as well as any of his neighbors. This was the first appearance of plate and China in our house, which afterward, in a course of years, as our wealth increas'd, augmented gradually to several hundred pounds in value.

I had been religiously educated as a Presbyterian; and tho' some of the dogmas of that persuasion, such as *the eternal decrees of God, election, reprobation, etc.,* appeared to me unintelligible, others doubtful, and I early absented myself from the public assemblies of the sect, Sunday being my studying day, I never was without some religious principles. I never doubted, for instance, the existence of the Deity; that he made the world, and govern'd it by his Providence; that the most acceptable service of God was the doing good to man; that our souls are immortal; and that all crime will be punished, and virtue rewarded, either here or hereafter. These I esteem'd the essentials of every religion; and, being to be found in all the religions we had in our country, I respected them all, tho' with different degrees of respect, as I found them more or less mix'd with other articles, which, without any tendency to inspire, promote, or confirm morality, serv'd principally to divide us, and make us unfriendly to one another. This respect to all, with an opinion that the worst had some good effects, induc'd me to avoid all discourse that might tend to lessen the good opinion another might have of his own religion; and as our province increas'd in people, and new places of worship were continually wanted, and generally erected by voluntary contributions, my mite for such purpose, whatever might be the sect, was never refused.

Tho' I seldom attended any public worship, I had still an opinion of its propriety, and of its utility when rightly conducted, and I regularly paid my annual subscription for the support of the only Presbyterian minister or meeting we had in Philadelphia. He us'd to visit me sometimes as a friend, and admonish me to attend his administrations, and I was now and then prevail'd on to do so, once for five Sundays successively. Had he been in my opinion a good preacher, perhaps I might have continued, notwithstanding the occasion I had for the Sunday's leisure in my course of study; but his discourses were chiefly either polemic arguments, or explications of the peculiar doctrines of our sect, and were all to me very dry, uninteresting, and unedifying, since not a single moral principle was inculcated or enforc'd, their aim seeming to be rather to make us Presbyterians than good citizens.

At length he took for his text that verse of the fourth chapter of Philippians, *"Finally, brethren, whatsoever things are true, honest, just, pure, lovely, or of good report, if there be any virtue, or any praise, think on these things."* And I imagin'd, in a sermon on such a text, we could not miss of having some morality. But he confin'd himself to five points only, as meant by the apostle, viz.: 1. Keeping holy the Sabbath day. 2. Being diligent in reading the holy Scriptures. 3. Attending duly the publick worship. 4. Partaking of the Sacrament. 5. Paying a due respect to God's ministers. These might be all good things; but, as they were not the kind of good things that I expected from that text, I despaired of ever meeting with them from any other, was disgusted, and attended his preaching no more. I had some years before compos'd a little Liturgy, or form of prayer, for my own private use (viz., in 1728), entitled, *Articles of Belief and Acts of Religion.* I return'd to the use of this, and went no more to the public assemblies. My conduct might be blameable, but I leave it, without attempting further to excuse it; my present purpose being to relate facts, and not to make apologies for them.

It was about this time I conceiv'd the bold and arduous project of arriving at moral perfection. I wish'd to live without committing any fault at any time; I would conquer all that either natural inclination, custom, or company might lead me into. As I knew, or thought I knew, what was right and wrong, I did not see why I might not always do the one and avoid the other. But I soon found I had undertaken a task of more difficulty than I had imagined. While my care was employ'd in guarding against one fault, I was often surprised by another; habit took the advantage of inattention; inclination was sometimes too strong for reason. I concluded, at length, that the mere speculative conviction that it was our interest to be completely virtuous, was not sufficient to prevent our slipping; and that the contrary habits must be broken, and good ones acquired and established, before we can have any dependence on a steady, uniform rectitude of conduct. For this purpose I therefore contrived the following method.

In the various enumerations of the moral virtues I had met with in my reading, I found the catalogue more or less numerous, as different writers included more or fewer ideas under the same name. Temperance, for example, was by some confined to eating and drinking, while by others it was extended to mean the moderating every other pleasure, appetite, inclination, or passion, bodily or mental, even to our avarice and ambition. I propos'd to myself, for the sake of clearness, to use rather more names, with fewer ideas annex'd to each, than a few names with more ideas; and I included under thirteen names of virtues all that at that time occurr'd to me as necessary or desirable, and annexed to each a short precept, which fully express'd the extent I gave to its meaning.

These names of virtues, with their precepts, were:

1. TEMPERANCE.

Eat not to dullness; drink not to elevation.

2. SILENCE.

Speak not but what may benefit others or yourself; avoid trifling conversation.

3. ORDER.

Let all your things have their places; let each part of your business have its time.

4. RESOLUTION.

Resolve to perform what you ought; perform without fail what you resolve.

5. FRUGALITY.

Make no expense but to do good to others or yourself; *i. e.,* waste nothing.

6. INDUSTRY.

Lose no time; be always employ'd in something useful; cut off all unnecessary actions.

7. SINCERITY.

Use no hurtful deceit; think innocently and justly, and, if you speak, speak accordingly.

8. JUSTICE.

Wrong none by doing injuries, or omitting the benefits that are your duty.

9. MODERATION.

Avoid extreams; forbear resenting injuries so much as you think they deserve.

10. Cleanliness.

Tolerate no uncleanliness in body, cloaths, or habitation.

11. Tranquillity.

Be not disturbed at trifles, or at accidents common or unavoidable.

12. Chastity.

Rarely use venery but for health or offspring, never to dulness, weakness, or the injury of your own or another's peace or reputation.

13. Humility.

Imitate Jesus and Socrates.

My intention being to acquire the *habitude* of all these virtues, I judg'd it would be well not to distract my attention by attempting the whole at once, but to fix it on one of them at a time; and, when I should be master of that, then to proceed to another, and so on, till I should have gone thro' the thirteen; and, as the previous acquisition of some might facilitate the acquisition of certain others, I arrang'd them with that view, as they stand above. Temperance first, as it tends to procure that coolness and clearness of head, which is so necessary where constant vigilance was to be kept up, and guard maintained against the unremitting attraction of ancient habits, and the force of perpetual temptations. This being acquir'd and establish'd, Silence would be more easy; and my desire being to gain knowledge at the same time that I improv'd in virtue, and considering that in conversation it was obtain'd rather by the use of the ears than of the tongue, and therefore wishing to break a habit I was getting into of prattling, punning, and joking, which only made me acceptable to trifling company, I gave *Silence* the second place. This and the next, *Order,* I expected would allow me more time for attending to my project and my studies. *Resolution,* once become habitual, would keep me firm in my endeavors to obtain all the subsequent virtues; *Frugality* and Industry freeing me from my remaining debt, and producing affluence and independence, would make more easy the practice of Sincerity and Justice, etc., etc. Conceiving then, that, agreeably to the advice of Pythagoras in his Golden Verses, daily examination would be necessary, I contrived the following method for conducting that examination.

I made a little book, in which I allotted a page for each of the virtues. I rul'd each page with red ink, so as to have seven columns, one for each day of the week, marking each column with a letter for the day. I cross'd these columns with thirteen red lines, marking the beginning of each line with the first letter of one of the virtues, on which line, and in its proper column, I might mark, by a little black spot, every fault I found upon examination to have been committed respecting that virtue upon that day.

Form of the pages.

TEMPERANCE.						
EAT NOT TO DULNESS; DRINK NOT TO ELEVATION.						
	S.	M.	T.	W.	T.	F.	S.
T.							
S.	•	•		•		•	
O.	• •	•	•		•	•	•
R.			•			•	
F.		•			•		
I.			•				
S.							
J.							
M.							
C.							
T.							
C.							
H.							

I determined to give a week's strict attention to each of the virtues successively. Thus, in the first week, my great guard was to avoid every the least offence against *Temperance,* leaving the other virtues to their ordinary chance, only marking every evening the faults of the day. Thus, if in the first week I could keep my first line, marked T, clear of spots, I suppos'd the habit of that virtue so much strengthen'd, and its opposite weaken'd, that I might venture extending my attention to include the next, and for the following week keep both lines clear of spots. Proceeding thus to the last, I could go thro' a course compleat in thirteen weeks, and four courses in a year. And like him who, having a garden to weed, does not attempt to eradicate all the bad herbs at once, which would exceed his reach and his strength, but works on one of the beds at a time, and, having accomplish'd the first, proceeds to a second, so I should have, I hoped, the encouraging pleasure of seeing on my pages the progress I made in virtue, by clearing successively my lines of their spots, till in the end, by a number of courses, I should be happy in viewing a clean book, after a thirteen weeks' daily examination.

This my little book had for its motto these lines from Addison's *Cato:*

> "Here will I hold. If there's a power above us
> (And that there is, all nature cries aloud
> Thro' all her works), He must delight in virtue;
> And that which he delights in must be happy."

Another from Cicero,

"O vitæ Philosophia dux! O virtutum indagatrix expultrixque vitiorum! Unus dies, bene et ex præceptis tuis actus, peccanti immortalitati est anteponendus."

Another from the Proverbs of Solomon, speaking of wisdom or virtue:

"Length of days is in her right hand, and in her left hand riches and honour. Her ways are ways of pleasantness, and all her paths are peace." iii. 16, 17.

And conceiving God to be the fountain of wisdom, I thought it right and necessary to solicit his assistance for obtaining it; to this end I formed the following little prayer, which was prefix'd to my tables of examination, for daily use.

"O powerful Goodness! bountiful Father! merciful Guide! Increase in me that wisdom which discovers my truest interest. Strengthen my reso-

lutions to perform what that wisdom dictates. Accept my kind offices to thy other children as the only return in my power for thy continual favors to me."

I used also sometimes a little prayer which I took from Thomson's Poems, viz.:

"Father of light and life, thou Good Supreme!
O teach me what is good; teach me Thyself!
Save me from folly, vanity, and vice,
From every low pursuit; and fill my soul
With knowledge, conscious peace, and virtue pure;
Sacred, substantial, never-fading bliss!"

The precept of *Order* requiring that *every part of my business should have its allotted time,* one page in my little book contain'd the following scheme of employment for the twenty-four hours of a natural day:

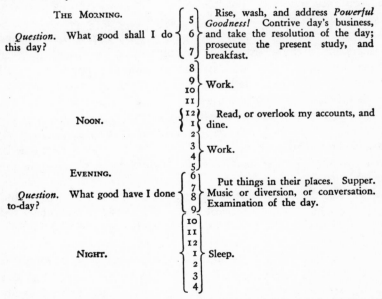

THE MORNING.	5	Rise, wash, and address *Powerful Goodness!* Contrive day's business, and take the resolution of the day; prosecute the present study, and breakfast.
Question. What good shall I do this day?	6	
	7	
	8	
	9	Work.
	10	
	11	
NOON.	12	Read, or overlook my accounts, and dine.
	1	
	2	
	3	Work.
	4	
	5	
EVENING.	6	
Question. What good have I done to-day?	7	Put things in their places. Supper. Music or diversion, or conversation. Examination of the day.
	8	
	9	
	10	
	11	
	12	
NIGHT.	1	Sleep.
	2	
	3	
	4	

I enter'd upon the execution of this plan for self-examination, and continu'd it with occasional intermissions for some time. I was surpris'd to find myself so much fuller of faults than I had imagined;

but I had the satisfaction of seeing them diminish. To avoid the trouble of renewing now and then my little book, which, by scraping out the marks on the paper of old faults to make room for new ones in a new course, became full of holes, I transferr'd my tables and precepts to the ivory leaves of a memorandum book, on which the lines were drawn with red ink, that made a durable stain, and on those lines I mark'd my faults with a black-lead pencil, which marks I could easily wipe out with a wet sponge. After a while I went thro' one course only in a year, and afterward only one in several years, till at length I omitted them entirely, being employ'd in voyages and business abroad, with a multiplicity of affairs that interfered; but I always carried my little book with me.

My scheme of ORDER gave me the most trouble; and I found that, tho' it might be practicable where a man's business was such as to leave him the disposition of his time, that of a journeyman printer, for instance, it was not possible to be exactly observed by a master, who must mix with the world, and often receive people of business at their own hours. *Order,* too, with regard to places for things, papers, etc., I found extreamly difficult to acquire. I had not been early accustomed to it, and, having an exceeding good memory, I was not so sensible of the inconvenience attending want of method. This article, therefore, cost me so much painful attention, and my faults in it vexed me so much, and I made so little progress in amendment, and had such frequent relapses, that I was almost ready to give up the attempt, and content myself with a faulty character in that respect, like the man who, in buying an ax of a smith, my neighbour, desired to have the whole of its surface as bright as the edge. The smith consented to grind it bright for him if he would turn the wheel; he turn'd, while the smith press'd the broad face of the ax hard and heavily on the stone, which made the turning of it very fatiguing. The man came every now and then from the wheel to see how the work went on, and at length would take his ax as it was, without farther grinding. "No," said the smith, "turn on, turn on; we shall have it bright by-and-by; as yet, it is only speckled." "Yes," said the man, *"but I think I like a speckled ax best."* And I believe this may have been the case with many, who, having, for want of some such means as I employ'd, found the difficulty of obtaining good and breaking bad habits in other points of vice and virtue, have given up the struggle, and concluded that *"a speckled ax was best"*; for something, that pretended to be reason, was every now and then suggesting to me that such extream nicety as I exacted of myself might be a kind of foppery in morals, which, if it were known, would make me ridiculous; that a perfect character might be attended with the inconvenience of being envied and hated; and that a benevolent man should allow a few faults in himself, to keep his friends in countenance.

In truth, I found myself incorrigible with respect to Order; and now I am grown old, and my memory bad, I feel very sensibly the want of it. But, on the whole, tho' I never arrived at the perfection I had been so ambitious of obtaining, but fell far short of it, yet I was, by the endeavour, a better and a happier man than I otherwise should have been if I had not attempted it; as those who aim at perfect writing by imitating the engraved copies, tho' they never reach the wish'd-for excellence of those copies, their hand is mended by the endeavor, and is tolerable while it continues fair and legible.

It may be well my posterity should be informed that to this little artifice, with the blessing of God, their ancestor ow'd the constant felicity of his life, down to his 79th year, in which this is written. What reverses may attend the remainder is in the hand of Providence; but, if they arrive, the reflection on past happiness enjoy'd ought to help his bearing them with more resignation. To Temperance he ascribes his long-continued health, and what is still left to him of a good constitution; to Industry and Frugality, the early easiness of his circumstances and acquisition of his fortune, with all that knowledge that enabled him to be a useful citizen, and obtained for him some degree of reputation among the learned; to Sincerity and Justice, the confidence of his country, and the honorable employs it conferred upon him; and to the joint influence of the whole mass of the virtues, even in the imperfect state he was able to acquire them, all that evenness of temper, and that cheerfulness in conversation, which makes his company still sought for, and agreeable even to his younger acquaintance. I hope, therefore, that some of my descendants may follow the example and reap the benefit.

It will be remark'd that, tho' my scheme was not wholly without religion, there was in it no mark of any of the distinguishing tenets of any particular sect. I had purposely avoided them; for, being fully persuaded of the utility and excellency of my method, and that it might be serviceable to people in all religions, and intending some time or other to publish it, I would not have any thing in it that should prejudice any one, of any sect, against it. I purposed writing a little comment on each virtue, in which I would have shown the advantages of possessing it, and the mischiefs attending its opposite vice; and I should have called my book THE ART OF VIRTUE,[8] because it would have shown the means and manner of obtaining virtue, which would have distinguished it from the mere exhortation to be good, that does not instruct and indicate the means, but is like the apostle's man of verbal charity, who only without showing to the naked and hungry how or where they might get clothes or victuals, exhorted them to be fed and clothed.— James ii. 15, 16.

But it so happened that my intention of writing and publishing this comment was never fulfilled. I did, indeed, from time to time, put down short hints of the sentiments, reasonings, etc., to be made use of in it, some of which I have still by me; but the necessary close attention to private business in the earlier part of my life, and public business since, have occasioned my postponing it; for, it being connected in my mind with *a great and extensive project,* that required the whole man to execute, and which an unforeseen succession of employs prevented my attending to, it has hitherto remain'd unfinish'd.

In this piece it was my design to explain and enforce this doctrine, that vicious actions are not hurtful because they are forbidden, but forbidden because they are hurtful, the nature of man alone considered; that it was, therefore, every one's interest to be virtuous who wish'd to be happy even in this world; and I should, from this circumstance (there being always in the world a number of rich merchants, nobility, states, and princes, who have need of honest instruments for the management of their affairs, and such being so rare), have endeavored to convince young persons that no qualities

[8] Nothing so likely to make a man's fortune as virtue.—[*Marg. note.*]

were so likely to make a poor man's fortune as those of probity and integrity.

My list of virtues contain'd at first but twelve; but a Quaker friend having kindly informed me that I was generally thought proud; that my pride show'd itself frequently in conversation; that I was not content with being in the right when discussing any point, but was overbearing, and rather insolent, of which he convinc'd me by mentioning several instances; I determined endeavouring to cure myself, if I could, of this vice or folly among the rest, and I added *Humility* to my list, giving an extensive meaning to the word.

I cannot boast of much success in acquiring the *reality* of this virtue, but I had a good deal with regard to the *appearance* of it. I made it a rule to forbear all direct contradiction to the sentiments of others, and all positive assertion of my own. I even forbid myself, agreeably to the old laws of our Junto, the use of every word or expression in the language that imported a fix'd opinion, such as *certainly, undoubtedly,* etc., and I adopted, instead of them, *I conceive, I apprehend,* or *I imagine* a thing to be so or so; or it *so appears to me at present.* When another asserted something that I thought an error, I deny'd myself the pleasure of contradicting him abruptly, and of showing immediately some absurdity in his proposition; and in answering I began by observing that in certain cases or circumstances his opinion would be right, but in the present case there *appear'd* or *seem'd* to me some difference, etc. I soon found the advantage of this change in my manner; the conversations I engag'd in went on more pleasantly. The modest way in which I propos'd my opinions procur'd them a readier reception and less contradiction; I had less mortification when I was found to be in the wrong, and I more easily prevail'd with others to give up their mistakes and join with me when I happened to be in the right.

And this mode, which I at first put on with some violence to natural inclination, became at length so easy, and so habitual to me, that perhaps for these fifty years past no one has ever heard a dogmatical expression escape me. And to this habit (after my character of integrity) I think it principally owing that I had early so much weight with my fellow-citizens when I proposed new institutions, or alterations in the old, and so much influence in public councils when I became a member; for I was but a bad speaker, never eloquent, subject to much hesitation in my choice of words, hardly correct in language, and yet I generally carried my points.

In reality, there is, perhaps, no one of our natural passions so hard to subdue as *pride*. Disguise it, struggle with it, beat it down, stifle it, mortify it as much as one pleases, it is still alive, and will every now and then peep out and show itself; you will see it, perhaps, often in this history; for, even if I could conceive that I had compleatly overcome it, I should probably be proud of my humility.

[Thus far written at Passy, 1784.]

["I am now about to write at home, August, 1788, but can not have the help expected from my papers, many of them being lost in the war. I have, however, found the following."][9]

HAVING mentioned *a great and extensive project* which I had conceiv'd, it seems proper that some account should be here given of that project and its object. Its first rise in my mind appears in the following little paper, accidentally preserv'd, viz.:

Observations on my reading history, in Library, May 19th, 1731.

"That the great affairs of the world, the wars, revolutions, etc., are carried on and affected by parties.

"That the view of these parties is their present general interest, or what they take to be such.

"That the different views of these different parties occasion all confusion.

"That while a party is carrying on a general design, each man has his particular private interest in view.

"That as soon as a party has gain'd its general point, each member becomes intent upon his particular interest; which, thwarting others, breaks that party into divisions, and occasions more confusion.

"That few in public affairs act from a meer view of the good of their country, whatever they may pretend; and, tho' their actings bring real good to their country, yet men primarily considered that their own and their country's interest was united, and did not act from a principle of benevolence.

"That fewer still, in public affairs, act with a view to the good of mankind.

"There seems to me at present to be great occasion for raising a United Party for Virtue, by forming the virtuous and good men of all nations into a regular body, to be govern'd by suitable good and wise rules, which good and wise men may probably be more

9 This is a marginal memorandum.—B.

unanimous in their obedience to, than common people are to common laws.

"I at present think that whoever attempts this aright, and is well qualified, can not fail of pleasing God, and of meeting with success. B. F."

Revolving this project in my mind, as to be undertaken hereafter, when my circumstances should afford me the necessary leisure, I put down from time to time, on pieces of paper, such thoughts as occurr'd to me respecting it. Most of these are lost; but I find one purporting to be the substance of an intended creed, containing, as I thought, the essentials of every known religion, and being free of every thing that might shock the professors of any religion. It is express'd in these words, viz.:

"That there is one God, who made all things.

"That he governs the world by his providence.

"That he ought to be worshiped by adoration, prayer, and thanksgiving.

"But that the most acceptable service of God is doing good to man.

"That the soul is immortal.

"And that God will certainly reward virtue and punish vice, either here or hereafter."[10]

My ideas at that time were, that the sect should be begun and spread at first among young and single men only; that each person to be initiated should not only declare his assent to such creed, but should have exercised himself with the thirteen weeks' examination and practice of the virtues, as in the before-mention'd model; that the existence of such a society should be kept a secret, till it was become considerable, to prevent solicitations for the admission of improper persons, but that the members should each of them search among his acquaintance for ingenuous, well-disposed youths, to whom, with prudent caution, the scheme should be gradually communicated; that the members should engage to afford their advice, assistance, and support to each other in promoting one another's interests, business, and advancement in life; that, for distinction,

[10] In the Middle Ages, Franklin, if such a phenomenon as Franklin were possible in the Middle Ages, would probably have been the founder of a monastic order.—B.

we should be call'd *The Society of the Free and Easy:* free, as being, by the general practice and habit of the virtues, free from the dominion of vice; and particularly by the practice of industry and frugality, free from debt, which exposes a man to confinement, and a species of slavery to his creditors.

This is as much as I can now recollect of the project, except that I communicated it in part to two young men, who adopted it with some enthusiasm; but my then narrow circumstances, and the necessity I was under of sticking close to my business, occasion'd my postponing the further prosecution of it at that time; and my multifarious occupations, public and private, induc'd me to continue postponing, so that it has been omitted till I have no longer strength or activity left sufficient for such an enterprise; tho' I am still of opinion that it was a practicable scheme, and might have been very useful, by forming a great number of good citizens; and I was not discourag'd by the seeming magnitude of the undertaking, as I have always thought that one man of tolerable abilities may work great changes, and accomplish great affairs among mankind, if he first forms a good plan, and, cutting off all amusements or other employments that would divert his attention, makes the execution of that same plan his sole study and business.

In 1732 I first publish'd my Almanack, under the name of *Richard Saunders;* it was continu'd by me about twenty-five years, commonly call'd *Poor Richard's Almanac.* I endeavor'd to make it both entertaining and useful, and it accordingly came to be in such demand, that I reap'd considerable profit from it, vending annually near ten thousand. And observing that it was generally read, scarce any neighborhood in the province being without it, I consider'd it as a proper vehicle for conveying instruction among the common people, who bought scarcely any other books; I therefore filled all the little spaces that occurr'd between the remarkable days in the calendar with proverbial sentences, chiefly such as inculcated industry and frugality, as the means of procuring wealth, and thereby securing virtue; it being more difficult for a man in want, to act always honestly, as, to use here one of those proverbs, *it is hard for an empty sack to stand upright.*

These proverbs, which contained the wisdom of many ages and

nations, I assembled and form'd into a connected discourse prefix'd to the Almanack of 1757, as the harangue of a wise old man to the people attending an auction. The bringing all these scatter'd counsels thus into a focus enabled them to make greater impression. The piece, being universally approved, was copied in all the newspapers of the Continent; reprinted in Britain on a broad side, to be stuck up in houses; two translations were made of it in French, and great numbers bought by the clergy and gentry, to distribute gratis among their poor parishioners and tenants. In Pennsylvania, as it discouraged useless expense in foreign superfluities, some thought it had its share of influence in producing that growing plenty of money which was observable for several years after its publication.

I considered my newspaper, also, as another means of communicating instruction, and in that view frequently reprinted in it extracts from the Spectator, and other moral writers; and sometimes publish'd little pieces of my own, which had been first compos'd for reading in our Junto. Of these are a Socratic dialogue, tending to prove that, whatever might be his parts and abilities, a vicious man could not properly be called a man of sense; and a discourse on self-denial, showing that virtue was not secure till its practice became a habitude, and was free from the opposition of contrary inclinations. These may be found in the papers about the beginning of 1735.

In the conduct of my newspaper, I carefully excluded all libelling and personal abuse, which is of late years become so disgraceful to our country. Whenever I was solicited to insert anything of that kind, and the writers pleaded, as they generally did, the liberty of the press, and that a newspaper was like a stage-coach, in which any one who would pay had a right to a place, my answer was, that I would print the piece separately if desired, and the author might have as many copies as he pleased to distribute himself, but that I would not take upon me to spread his detraction; and that, having contracted with my subscribers to furnish them with what might be either useful or entertaining, I could not fill their papers with private altercation, in which they had no concern, without doing them manifest injustice. Now, many of our printers make no scruple of gratifying the malice of individuals by false accusations of the fairest characters among ourselves, augmenting animosity even to the producing of duels; and are, moreover, so indiscreet as to print scurrilous reflections on the government of neighboring states, and even on the conduct of our best national allies, which may be attended with the most pernicious consequences. These things I mention as a caution to young printers, and that they may be encouraged not to pollute their presses and disgrace their profession by such infamous practices, but refuse steadily, as they may see by my example that such a course of conduct will not, on the whole, be injurious to their interests.

In 1733 I sent one of my journeymen to Charleston, South Carolina, where a printer was wanting. I furnish'd him with a press and letters, on an agreement of partnership, by which I was to receive one-third of the profits of the business, paying one-third of the expense. He was a man of learning, and honest but ignorant in matters of account; and, tho' he sometimes made me remittances, I could get no account from him, nor any satisfactory state of our partnership while he lived. On his decease, the business was continued by his widow, who, being born and bred in Holland, where, as I have been inform'd, the knowledge of accounts makes a part of female education, she not only sent me as clear a state as she could find of the transactions past, but continued to account with the greatest regularity and exactness every quarter afterwards, and managed the business with such success, that she not only brought up reputably a family of children, but, at the expiration of the term, was able to purchase of me the printing-house, and establish her son in it.

I mention this affair chiefly for the sake of recommending that branch of education for our young females, as likely to be of more use to them and their children, in case of widowhood, than either music or dancing, by preserving them from losses by imposition of crafty men, and enabling them to continue, perhaps, a profitable mercantile house, with establish'd correspondence, till a son is grown up fit to undertake and go on with it, to the lasting advantage and enriching of the family.

About the year 1734 there arrived among us from Ireland a young

Presbyterian preacher, named Hemphill, who delivered with a good voice, and apparently extempore, most excellent discourses, which drew together considerable numbers of different persuasion, who join'd in admiring them. Among the rest, I became one of his constant hearers, his sermons pleasing me, as they had little of the dogmatical kind, but inculcated strongly the practice of virtue, or what in the religious stile are called good works. Those, however, of our congregation, who considered themselves as orthodox Presbyterians, disapprov'd his doctrine, and were join'd by most of the old clergy, who arraign'd him of heterodoxy before the synod, in order to have him silenc'd. I became his zealous partisan, and contributed all I could to raise a party in his favour, and we combated for him a while with some hopes of success. There was much scribbling pro and con upon the occasion; and finding that, tho' an elegant preacher, he was but a poor writer, I lent him my pen and wrote for him two or three pamphlets, and one piece in the Gazette of April, 1735. Those pamphlets, as is generally the case with controversial writings, tho' eagerly read at the time, were soon out of vogue, and I question whether a single copy of them now exists.

During the contest an unlucky occurrence hurt his cause exceedingly. One of our adversaries having heard him preach a sermon that was much admired, thought he had somewhere read the sermon before, or at least a part of it. On search he found that part quoted at length, in one of the British Reviews, from a discourse of Dr. Foster's. This detection gave many of our party disgust, who accordingly abandoned his cause, and occasion'd our more speedy discomfiture in the synod. I stuck by him, however, as I rather approv'd his giving us good sermons compos'd by others, than bad ones of his own manufacture, tho' the latter was the practice of our common teachers. He afterward acknowledg'd to me that none of those he preach'd were his own; adding, that his memory was such as enabled him to retain and repeat any sermon after one reading only. On our defeat, he left us in search elsewhere of better fortune, and I quitted the congregation, never joining it after, tho' I continu'd many years my subscription for the support of its ministers.

I had begun in 1733 to study languages; I soon made myself so much a master of the French as to be able to read the books with ease. I then undertook the Italian. An acquaintance, who was also learning it, us'd often to tempt me to play chess with him. Finding this took up too much of the time I had to spare for study, I at length refus'd to play any more, unless on this condition, that the victor in every game should have a right to impose a task, either in parts of the grammar to be got by heart, or in translations, etc., which tasks the vanquish'd was to perform upon honour, before our next meeting. As we play'd pretty equally, we thus beat one another into that language. I afterwards with a little painstaking, acquir'd as much of the Spanish as to read their books also.

I have already mention'd that I had only one year's instruction in a Latin school, and that when very young, after which I neglected that language entirely. But, when I had attained an acquaintance with the French, Italian, and Spanish, I was surpriz'd to find, on looking over a Latin Testament, that I understood so much more of that language than I had imagined, which encouraged me to apply myself again to the study of it, and I met with more success, as those preceding languages had greatly smooth'd my way.

From these circumstances, I have thought that there is some inconsistency in our common mode of teaching languages. We are told that it is proper to begin first with the Latin, and, having acquir'd that, it will be more easy to attain those modern languages which are deriv'd from it; and yet we do not begin with the Greek, in order more easily to acquire the Latin. It is true that, if you can clamber and get to the top of a staircase without using the steps, you will more easily gain them in descending; but certainly, if you begin with the lowest you will with more ease ascend to the top; and I would therefore offer it to the consideration of those who superintend the education of our youth, whether, since many of those who begin with the Latin quit the same after spending some years without having made any great proficiency, and what they have learnt becomes almost useless, so that their time has been lost, it would not have been better to have begun with the French, proceeding to the Italian, etc.; for, tho', after spending the same time, they should quit the study of languages and never arrive at the Latin, they would, however, have acquired another tongue or two, that, being in modern use, might be serviceable to them in common life.

After ten years' absence from Boston, and having become easy in my circumstances, I made a journey thither to visit my relations, which I could not sooner well afford. In returning, I call'd at Newport to see my brother, then settled there with his printing-house. Our former differences were forgotten, and our meeting was very cordial and affectionate. He was fast declining in his health, and requested of me that, in case of his death, which he apprehended not far distant, I would take home his son, then but ten years of age, and bring him up to the printing business. This I accordingly perform'd, sending him a few years to school before I took him into the office. His mother carried on the business till he was grown up, when I assisted him with an assortment of new types, those of his father being in a manner worn out. Thus it was that I made my brother ample amends for the service I had depriv'd him of by leaving him so early.

In 1736 I lost one of my sons, a fine boy of four years old, by the small-pox, taken in the common way. I long regretted bitterly, and still regret that I had not given it to him by inoculation. This I mention for the sake of parents who omit that operation, on the supposition that they should never forgive themselves if a child died under it; my example showing that the regret may be the same either way, and that, therefore, the safer should be chosen.

Our club, the Junto, was found so useful, and afforded such satisfaction to the members, that several were desirous of introducing their friends, which could not well be done without exceeding what we had settled as a convenient number, viz., twelve. We had from the beginning made it a rule to keep our institution a secret, which was pretty well observ'd; the intention was to avoid applications, of improper persons for admittance, some of whom, perhaps, we might find it difficult to refuse. I was one of those who were against any addition to our number, but, instead of it, made in writing a proposal, that every member separately should endeavor to form a subordinate club, with the same rules respecting queries, etc., and without informing them of the connection with the Junto. The advantages proposed were, the improvement of so many more young citizens by the use of our institutions; our better acquaintance with the general sentiments of the inhabitants on any occasion, as the Junto member might propose what queries we should desire, and was to report to the Junto what pass'd in his separate club; the promotion of our particular interests in business by more extensive recommendation, and the increase of our influence in public affairs, and our power of doing good by spreading thro' the several clubs the sentiments of the Junto.

The project was approv'd, and every member undertook to form his club, but they did not all succeed. Five or six only were compleated, which were called by different names, as the Vine, the Union, the Band, etc. They were useful to themselves, and afforded us a good deal of amusement, information, and instruction, besides answering, in some considerable degree, our views of influencing the public opinion on particular occasions, of which I shall give some instances in course of time as they happened.

My first promotion was my being chosen, in 1736, clerk of the General Assembly. The choice was made that year without opposition; but the year following, when I was again propos'd (the choice, like that of the members, being annual), a new member made a long speech against me, in order to favour some other candidate. I was, however, chosen, which was the more agreeable to me, as, besides the pay for the immediate service as clerk, the place gave me a better opportunity of keeping up an interest among the members, which secur'd to me the business of printing the votes, laws, paper money, and other occasional jobbs for the public, that, on the whole, were very profitable.

I therefore did not like the opposition of this new member, who was a gentleman of fortune and education, with talents that were likely to give him, in time, great influence in the House, which, indeed, afterwards happened. I did not, however, aim at gaining his favour by paying any servile respect to him, but, after some time, took this other method. Having heard that he had in his library a certain very scarce and curious book, I wrote a note to him, expressing my desire of perusing that book, and requesting he would do me the favour of lending it to me for a few days. He sent it immediately, and I return'd it in about a week with another note, expressing strongly my sense of the favour. When we next met in the House, he spoke to me (which he had never done before), and with great civility; and he ever after manifested a readiness to serve me on all occasions, so that we became great friends, and our friendship continued to his death. This is another instance of the truth of an old maxim I had learned, which says, *"He that has once done you a kindness will be more ready to do you another, than he whom you yourself have obliged."* And it shows how much more profitable it is prudently to remove, than to resent, return, and continue inimical proceedings.

In 1737, Colonel Spotswood, late governor of Virginia, and then postmaster-general, being dissatisfied with the conduct of his deputy at Philadelphia, respecting some negligence in rendering, and inexactitude of his accounts, took from him the commission and offered it to me. I accepted it readily, and found it of great advantage; for, tho' the salary was small, it facilitated the correspondence that improv'd my newspaper, increas'd the number demanded, as well as the advertisements to be inserted, so that it came to afford me a considerable income. My old competitor's newspaper declin'd proportionably, and I was satisfy'd without retaliating his refusal, while postmaster, to permit my papers being carried by the riders. Thus he suffer'd greatly from his neglect in due accounting; and I mention it as a lesson to those young men who may be employ'd in managing affairs for others, that they should always render accounts, and make remittances, with great clearness and punctuality. The character of observing such a conduct is the most powerful of all recommendations to new employments and increase of business.

I began now to turn my thoughts a little to public affairs, beginning, however, with small matters. The city watch was one of the first things that I conceiv'd to want regulation. It was managed by the constables of the respective wards in turn; the constable warned a number of housekeepers to attend him for the night. Those who chose never to attend paid him six shillings a year to be excus'd, which was suppos'd to be for hiring substitutes, but was, in reality, much more than was necessary for that purpose, and made the constableship a place of profit; and the constable, for a little drink, often got such ragamuffins about him as a watch, that respectable housekeepers did not choose to mix with. Walking the rounds, too, was often neglected, and most of the nights spent in tippling. I thereupon wrote a paper to be read in Junto, representing these irregularities, but insisting more particularly on the inequality of this six-shilling tax of the constables, respecting the circumstances of those who paid it, since a poor widow housekeeper, all whose property to be guarded by the watch did not perhaps exceed the value of fifty pounds, paid as much as the wealthiest merchant, who had thousands of pounds' worth of goods in his stores.

On the whole, I proposed as a more effectual watch, the hiring of proper men to serve constantly in that business; and as a more equitable way of supporting the charge the levying a tax that should be proportion'd to the property. This idea, being approv'd by the Junto, was communicated to the other clubs, but as arising in each of them; and though the plan was not immediately carried into execution, yet, by preparing the minds of people for the change, it paved the way for the law obtained a few years after, when the members of our clubs were grown into more influence.

About this time I wrote a paper (first to be read in Junto, but it was afterward publish'd) on the different accidents and carelessnesses by which houses were set on fire, with cautions against them, and means proposed of avoiding them. This was much spoken of as a useful piece, and gave rise to a project, which soon followed it, of forming a company for the more ready extinguishing of fires, and mutual assistance in removing and securing the goods when in danger. Associates in this scheme were presently found, amounting to thirty. Our articles of agreement oblig'd every member to keep always in good order, and fit for use, a certain number of leather buckets, with strong bags and baskets (for packing and transporting of goods), which were to be brought to every fire; and we agreed to meet once a month and spend a social evening together, in discoursing and communicating such ideas as occurred to us upon the subject of fires, as might be useful in our conduct on such occasions.

The utility of this institution soon appeared, and many more desiring to be admitted than we thought convenient for one company, they were advised to form another, which was accordingly done; and this went on, one new company being formed after another, till they became so numerous as to include most of the inhabitants who were men of property; and now, at the time of my writing this, tho' upward of fifty years since its establishment, that which I first formed, called the Union Fire Company, still subsists and flourishes, tho' the first members are all deceas'd but myself and one, who is older by a year than I am. The small fines that have been paid by members for absence at the monthly meetings have been apply'd to the purchase of fire-engines, ladders, fire-hooks, and other useful implements for each company, so that I question whether there is a city in the world better provided with the means of putting a stop to beginning conflagrations; and, in fact, since these institutions, the city has never lost by fire more than one or two houses at a time, and the flames have often been extinguished before the house in which they began has been half consumed.

In 1739 arrived among us from Ireland the Reverend Mr. White-field, who had made himself remarkable there as an itinerant preacher. He was at first permitted to preach in some of our churches; but the clergy, taking a dislike to him, soon refus'd him their pulpits, and he was oblig'd to preach in the fields. The multitudes of all sects and denominations that attended his sermons were enormous, and it was matter of speculation to me, who was one of the number, to observe the extraordinary influence of his oratory on his hearers, and how much they admir'd and respected him, notwithstanding his common abuse of them, by assuring them that they were naturally *half beasts and half devils*. It was wonderful to see the change soon made in the manners of our inhabitants. From being thoughtless or indifferent about religion, it seem'd as if all the world were growing religious, so that one could not walk thro' the town in an evening without hearing psalms sung in different families of every street.

And it being found inconvenient to assemble in the open air, subject to its inclemencies, the building of a house to meet in was no sooner propos'd, and persons appointed to receive contributions, but sufficient sums were soon receiv'd to procure the ground and erect the building, which was one hundred feet long and seventy broad, about the size of Westminster Hall; and the work was carried on with such spirit as to be finished in a much shorter time than could have been expected. Both house and ground were vested in trustees, expressly for the use of any preacher of any religious persuasion who might desire to say something to the people at Philadelphia; the design in building not being to accommodate any particular sect, but the inhabitants in general; so that even if the Mufti of Constantinople were to send a missionary to preach Mohammedanism to us, he would find a pulpit at his service.

Mr. Whitefield, in leaving us, went preaching all the way thro' the colonies to Georgia. The settlement of that province had lately been begun, but, instead of being made with hardy, industrious husbandmen, accustomed to labor, the only people fit for such an enterprise, it was with families of broken shop-keepers and other insolvent debtors, many of indolent and idle habits, taken out of the jails, who, being set down in the woods, unqualified for clearing land, and unable to endure the hardships of a new settlement, perished in numbers, leaving many helpless children unprovided for. The sight of their miserable situation inspir'd the benevolent heart of Mr. Whitefield with the idea of building an Orphan House there, in which they might be supported and educated. Returning northward, he preach'd up this charity, and made large collections, for his eloquence had a wonderful power over the hearts and purses of his hearers, of which I myself was an instance.

I did not disapprove of the design, but, as Georgia was then destitute of materials and workmen, and it was proposed to send them from Philadelphia at a great expense, I thought it would have been better to have built the house here, and brought the children to it. This I advis'd; but he was resolute in his first project, rejected my counsel, and I therefore refus'd to contribute. I happened soon after to attend one of his sermons, in the course of which I perceived he intended to finish with a collection, and I silently resolved he should get nothing from me. I had in my pocket a handful of copper money, three or four silver dollars, and five pistoles in gold.

As he proceeded I began to soften, and concluded to give the coppers. Another stroke of his oratory made me asham'd of that, and determin'd me to give the silver; and he finish'd so admirably, that I empty'd my pocket wholly into the collector's dish, gold and all. At this sermon there was also one of our club, who, being of my sentiments respecting the building in Georgia, and suspecting a collection might be intended, had, by precaution, emptied his pockets before he came from home. Towards the conclusion of the discourse, however, he felt a strong desire to give, and apply'd to a neighbour, who stood near him, to borrow some money for the purpose. The application was unfortunately [made] to perhaps the only man in the company who had the firmness not to be affected by the preacher. His answer was, *"At any other time, Friend Hopkinson, I would lend to thee freely; but not now, for thee seems to be out of thy right senses."*

Some of Mr. Whitefield's enemies affected to suppose that he would apply these collections to his own private emolument; but I who was intimately acquainted with him (being employed in printing his Sermons and Journals, etc.), never had the least suspicion of his integrity, but am to this day decidedly of opinion that he was in all his conduct a perfectly *honest man;* and methinks my testimony in his favour ought to have the more weight, as we had no religious connection. He us'd, indeed, sometimes to pray for my conversion, but never had the satisfaction of believing that his prayers were heard. Ours was a mere civil friendship, sincere on both sides, and lasted to his death.

The following instance will show something of the terms on which we stood. Upon one of his arrivals from England at Boston, he wrote to me that he should come soon to Philadelphia, but knew not where he could lodge when there, as he understood his old friend and host, Mr. Benezet, was removed to Germantown. My answer was, "You know my house; if you can make shift with its scanty accommodations, you will be most heartily welcome." He reply'd, that if I made that kind offer for Christ's sake, I should not miss of a reward. And I returned, *"Don't let me be mistaken; it was not for Christ's sake, but for your sake."* One of our common acquaintance jocosely remark'd, that, knowing it to be the custom of the saints, when they received any favour, to shift the burden of the obligation from off their own shoulders, and place it in heaven, I had contriv'd to fix it on earth.

The last time I saw Mr. Whitefield was in London, when he consulted me about his Orphan House concern, and his purpose of appropriating it to the establishment of a college.

He had a loud and clear voice, and articulated his words and sentences so perfectly, that he might be heard and understood at a great distance, especially as his auditories, however numerous, observ'd the most exact silence. He preach'd one evening from the top of the Court-house steps, which are in the middle of Market-street, and on the west side of Second-street, which crosses it at right angles. Both streets were fill'd with his hearers to a considerable distance. Being among the hindmost in Market-street, I had the curiosity to learn how far he could be heard, by retiring backwards down the street towards the river; and I found his voice distinct till I came near Front-street, when some noise in that street obscur'd it. Imagining then a semicircle, of which my distance should be the radius, and that it were fill'd with auditors, to each of whom I allow'd two square feet, I computed that he might well be heard by more than thirty thousand. This reconcil'd me to the newspaper accounts of his having preach'd to twenty-five thousand people in the fields, and to the antient histories of generals haranguing whole armies, of which I had sometimes doubted.

By hearing him often, I came to distinguish easily between sermons newly compos'd, and those which he had often preach'd in the course of his travels. His delivery of the latter was so improv'd by frequent repetitions that every accent, every emphasis, every modulation of voice, was so perfectly well turn'd and well plac'd, that, without being interested in the subject, one could not help being pleas'd with the discourse; a pleasure of much the same kind with that receiv'd from an excellent piece of musick. This is an advantage itinerant preachers have over those who are stationary, as the latter can not well improve their delivery of a sermon by so many rehearsals.

His writing and printing from time to time gave great advantage to his enemies; unguarded expressions, and even erroneous opinions, delivered in preaching, might have been afterwards explain'd or qualifi'd by supposing others that might have accompani'd them, or they might have been deny'd; but *litera scripta manet*. Critics attack'd his writings violently, and with so much appearance of reason as to diminish the number of his votaries and prevent their encrease; so that I am of opinion if he had never written any thing, he would have left behind him a much more numerous and important sect, and his reputation might in that case have been still growing, even after his death, as there being nothing of his writing on which to found a censure and give him a lower character, his proselytes would be left at liberty to feign for him as great a variety of excellence as their enthusiastic admiration might wish him to have possessed.

My business was now continually augmenting, and my circumstances growing daily easier, my newspaper having become very profitable, as being for a time almost the only one in this and the neighbouring provinces. I experienced, too, the truth of the observation, *"that after getting the first hundred pound, it is more easy to get the second,"* money itself being of a prolific nature.

The partnership at Carolina having succeeded, I was encourag'd to engage in others, and to promote several of my workmen, who had behaved well, by establishing them with printing-houses in different colonies, on the same terms with that in Carolina. Most of them did well, being enabled at the end of our term, six years, to purchase the types of me and go on working for themselves, by which means several families were raised. Partnerships often finish in quarrels; but I was happy in this, that mine were all carried on and ended amicably, owing, I think, a good deal to the precaution of having very explicitly settled, in our articles, every thing to be done by or expected from each partner, so that there was nothing to dispute, which precaution I would therefore recommend to all who enter into partnerships; for, whatever esteem partners may have for, and confidence in each other at the time of the contract, little jealousies and disgusts may arise, with ideas of inequality in the care and burden of the business, etc., which are attended often with breach of friendship and of the connection, perhaps with lawsuits and other disagreeable consequences.

I had, on the whole, abundant reason to be satisfied with my being established in Pennsylvania. There were, however, two things that I regretted, there being no provision for defense, nor for a compleat education of youth; no militia, nor any college. I therefore, in 1743, drew up a proposal for establishing an academy; and at that time, thinking the Reverend Mr. Peters, who was out of employ, a fit person to superintend such an institution, I communicated the project to him; but he, having more profitable views in the service of the proprietaries, which succeeded, declin'd the undertaking; and, not knowing another at that time suitable for such a trust, I let the scheme lie a while dormant. I succeeded better the next year, 1744, in proposing and establishing a Philosophical Society. The paper I wrote for that purpose will be found among my writings, when collected.

With respect to defense, Spain having been several years at war against Great Britain, and being at length join'd by France, which brought us into great danger; and the laboured and long-continued endeavour of our governor, Thomas, to prevail with our Quaker Assembly to pass a militia law, and make other provisions for the security of the province, having proved abortive, I determined to try what might be done by a voluntary association of the people. To promote this, I first wrote and published a pamphlet, entitled PLAIN TRUTH, in which I stated our defenceless situation in strong lights, with the necessity of union and discipline for our defense, and promis'd to propose in a few days an association, to be generally signed for that purpose. The pamphlet had a sudden and surprising effect. I was call'd upon for the instrument of association, and having settled the draft of it with a few friends, I appointed a meeting of the citizens in the large building before mentioned. The house was pretty full; I had prepared a number of printed copies, and provided pens and ink dispers'd all over the room. I harangued them a little on the subject, read the paper, and explained it, and then distributed the copies, which were eagerly signed, not the least objection being made.

When the company separated, and the papers were collected, we found about twelve hundred hands; and, other copies being dispersed in the country, the subscribers amounted at length to upward of ten thousand. These all furnished themselves as soon as they could with arms, formed themselves into companies and regiments, chose their own officers, and met every week to be instructed in the manual exercise, and other parts of military discipline. The women, by subscriptions among themselves, provided silk colors, which they presented to the companies, painted with different devices and mottos, which I supplied.

The officers of the companies composing the Philadelphia regiment, being met, chose me for their colonel; but, conceiving myself unfit, I declin'd that station, and recommended Mr. Lawrence, a fine person, and man of influence, who was accordingly appointed. I then propos'd a lottery to defray the expense of building a battery below the town, and furnishing it with cannon. It filled expeditiously, and the battery was soon erected, the merlons being fram'd of logs and fill'd with earth. We bought some old cannon from Boston, but, these not being sufficient, we wrote to England for more, soliciting, at the same time, our proprietaries for some assistance, tho' without much expectation of obtaining it.

Meanwhile, Colonel Lawrence, William Allen, Abram Taylor, Esqr., and myself were sent to New York by the associators, commission'd to borrow some cannon of Governor Clinton. He at first refus'd us peremptorily; but at dinner with his council, where there was great drinking of Madeira wine, as the custom of that place then was, he softened by degrees, and said he would lend us six. After a few more bumpers he advanc'd to ten; and at length he very good-naturedly conceded eighteen. They were fine cannon, eighteen-pounders, with their carriages, which we soon transported and mounted on our battery, where the associators kept a nightly guard while the war lasted, and among the rest I regularly took my turn of duty there as a common soldier.

My activity in these operations was agreeable to the governor and council; they took me into confidence, and I was consulted by them in every measure wherein their concurrence was thought useful to the association. Calling in the aid of religion, I propos'd to them the proclaiming a fast, to promote reformation, and implore the blessing of Heaven on our undertaking. They embrac'd the motion; but, as it was the first fast ever thought of in the province, the secretary had no precedent from which to draw the proclamation. My education in New England, where a fast is proclaimed every year, was here of some advantage: I drew it in the accustomed stile, it was translated into German, printed in both languages, and divulg'd thro' the province. This gave the clergy of the different sects an opportunity of influencing their congregations to join in the association, and it would probably have been general among all but Quakers if the peace had not soon interven'd.

It was thought by some of my friends that, by my activity in these affairs, I should offend that sect, and thereby lose my interest in the Assembly of the province, where they formed a great majority. A young gentleman who had likewise some friends in the House, and wished to succeed me as their clerk, acquainted me that it was decided to displace me at the next election; and he, therefore, in good will, advis'd me to resign, as more consistent with my honour than being turn'd out. My answer to him was, that I had read or heard of some public man who made it a rule never to ask for an office, and never to refuse one when offer'd to him. "I approve," says I, "of his rule, and will practice it with a small addition; I shall never *ask*, never *refuse*, nor ever *resign* an office. If they will have my office of clerk to dispose of to another, they shall take it from me. I will not, by giving it up, lose my right of some time or other making reprisals on my adversaries." I heard, however, no more of this; I was chosen again unanimously as usual at the next election. Possibly, as they dislik'd my late intimacy with the members of council, who had join'd the governors in all the disputes about military preparations, with which the House had long been harass'd, they might have been pleas'd if I would voluntarily have left them; but they did not care to displace me on account merely of my zeal for the association, and they could not well give another reason.

Indeed I had some cause to believe that the defense of the country was not disagreeable to any of them, provided they were not requir'd to assist in it. And I found that a much greater number of them than I could have imagined, tho' against offensive war, were clearly for the defensive. Many pamphlets *pro* and *con* were publish'd on the subject, and some by good Quakers, in favour of defense, which I believe convinc'd most of their younger people.

A transaction in our fire company gave me some insight into their prevailing sentiments. It had been propos'd that we should encourage the scheme for building a battery by laying out the present stock, then about sixty pounds, in tickets of the lottery. By our rules, no money could be dispos'd of till the next meeting after the proposal. The company consisted of thirty members, of which twenty-two were Quakers, and eight only of other persuasions. We eight punctually attended the meeting; but, tho' we thought that some of the Quakers would join us, we were by no means sure of a majority. Only one Quaker, Mr. James Morris, appear'd to oppose the measure. He expressed much sorrow that it had ever been propos'd, as he said *Friends* were all against it, and it would create such discord as might break up the company. We told him that we saw no reason for that; we were the minority, and if *Friends* were against the measure, and outvoted us, we must and should, agreeably to the usage of all societies, submit. When the hour for business arriv'd it was mov'd to put the vote; he allow'd we might then do it by the rules, but, as he could assure us that a number of members intended to be present for the purpose of opposing it, it would be but candid to allow a little time for their appearing.

While we were disputing this, a waiter came to tell me two gentlemen below desir'd to speak with me. I went down, and found they were two of our Quaker members. They told me there were eight of them assembled at a tavern just by; that they were determin'd to come and vote with us if there should be occasion, which they hop'd would not be the case, and desir'd we would not call for their assistance if we could do without it, as their voting for such a measure might embroil them with their elders and friends. Being thus secure of a majority, I went up, and after a little seeming hesitation, agreed to a delay of another hour. This Mr. Morris allow'd to be extreamly fair. Not one of his opposing friends appear'd, at which he express'd great surprize; and, at the expiration of the hour, we carry'd the resolution eight to one; and as, of the twenty-two Quakers, eight were ready to vote with us, and thirteen, by their absence, manifested that they were not inclin'd to oppose the measure, I afterward estimated the proportion of

Quakers sincerely against defense as one to twenty-one only; for these were all regular members of that society, and in good reputation among them, and had due notice of what was propos'd at that meeting.

The honorable and learned Mr. Logan, who had always been of that sect, was one who wrote an address to them, declaring his approbation of defensive war, and supporting his opinion by many strong arguments. He put into my hands sixty pounds to be laid out in lottery tickets for the battery, with directions to apply what prizes might be drawn wholly to that service. He told me the following anecdote of his old master, William Penn, respecting defense. He came over from England, when a young man, with that proprietary, and as his secretary. It was war-time, and their ship was chas'd by an armed vessel, suppos'd to be an enemy. Their captain prepar'd for defense; but told William Penn, and his company of Quakers, that he did not expect their assistance, and they might retire into the cabin, which they did, except James Logan, who chose to stay upon deck, and was quarter'd to a gun. The suppos'd enemy prov'd a friend, so there was no fighting; but when the secretary went down to communicate the intelligence, William Penn rebuk'd him severely for staying upon deck, and undertaking to assist in defending the vessel, contrary to the principles of *Friends,* especially as it had not been required by the captain. This reproof, being before all the company, piqu'd the secretary, who answer'd, *"I being thy servant, why did thee not order me to come down? But thee was willing enough that I should stay and help to fight the ship when thee thought there was danger."*

My being many years in the Assembly, the majority of which were constantly Quakers, gave me frequent opportunities of seeing the embarrassment given them by their principle against war, whenever application was made to them, by order of the crown, to grant aids for military purposes. They were unwilling to offend government, on the one hand, by a direct refusal; and their friends, the body of the Quakers, on the other, by a compliance contrary to their principles; hence a variety of evasions to avoid complying, and modes of disguising the compliance when it became unavoidable. The common mode at last was, to grant money under the phrase of its being *"for the king's use,"* and never to inquire how it was applied.

But, if the demand was not directly from the crown, that phrase was found not so proper, and some other was to be invented. As, when powder was wanting (I think it was for the garrison at Louisburg), and the government of New England solicited a grant of some from Pennsilvania, which was much urg'd on the House by Governor Thomas, they could not grant money to buy powder, because that was an ingredient of war; but they voted an aid to New England of three thousand pounds, to be put into the hands of the governor, and appropriated it for the purchasing of bread, flour, wheat, or *other grain.* Some of the council, desirous of giving the House still further embarrassment, advis'd the governor not to accept provision, as not being the thing he had demanded; but he reply'd, "I shall take the money, for I understand very well their meaning; other grain is gunpowder," which he accordingly bought, and they never objected to it.[11]

It was in allusion to this fact that, when in our fire company we feared the success of our proposal in favour of the lottery, and I had said to my friend Mr. Syng, one of our members, "If we fail, let us move the purchase of a fire-engine with the money; the Quakers can have no objection to that; and then, if you nominate me and I you as a committee for that purpose, we will buy a great gun, which is certainly a *fire-engine.*" "I see," says he, "you have improv'd by being so long in the Assembly; your equivocal project would be just a match for their wheat or *other grain.*"

These embarrassments that the Quakers suffer'd from having establish'd and published it as one of their principles that no kind of war was lawful, and which, being once published, they could not afterwards, however they might change their minds, easily get rid of, reminds me of what I think a more prudent conduct in another sect among us, that of the Dunkers. I was acquainted with one of its founders, Michael Welfare, soon after it appear'd. He complain'd to me that they were grievously calumniated by the zealots of other persuasions, and charg'd with abominable principles and practices, to which they were utter strangers. I told him

11 See the votes.—[*Marg. note.*]

this had always been the case with new sects, and that, to put a stop to such abuse, I imagin'd it might be well to publish the articles of their belief, and the rules of their discipline. He said that it had been propos'd among them, but not agreed to, for this reason: "When we were first drawn together as a society," says he, "it had pleased God to enlighten our minds so far as to see that some doctrines, which we once esteemed truths, were errors; and that others, which we had esteemed errors, were real truths. From time to time He has been pleased to afford us farther light, and our principles have been improving, and our errors diminishing. Now we are not sure that we are arrived at the end of this progression, and at the perfection of spiritual or theological knowledge; and we fear that, if we should once print our confession of faith, we should feel ourselves as if bound and confin'd by it, and perhaps be unwilling to receive farther improvement, and our successors still more so, as conceiving what we their elders and founders had done, to be something sacred, never to be departed from."

This modesty in a sect is perhaps a singular instance in the history of mankind, every other sect supposing itself in possession of all truth, and that those who differ are so far in the wrong; like a man traveling in foggy weather, those at some distance before him on the road he sees wrapped up in the fog, as well as those behind him, and also the people in the fields on each side, but near him all appears clear, tho' in truth he is as much in the fog as any of them. To avoid this kind of embarrassment, the Quakers have of late years been gradually declining the public service in the Assembly and in the magistracy, choosing rather to quit their power than their principle.

In order of time, I should have mentioned before, that having, in 1742, invented an open stove for the better warming of rooms, and at the same time saving fuel, as the fresh air admitted was warmed in entering, I made a present of the model to Mr. Robert Grace, one of my early friends, who, having an iron-furnace, found the casting of the plates for these stoves a profitable thing, as they were growing in demand. To promote that demand, I wrote and published a pamphlet, entitled *"An Account of the new-invented Pennsylvania Fireplaces; wherein their Construction and Manner of Operation is particularly explained; their Advantages above every other Method of warming Rooms demonstrated; and all Objections that have been raised against the Use of them answered and obviated,"* etc. This pamphlet had a good effect. Gov'r. Thomas was so pleas'd with the construction of this stove, as described in it, that he offered to give me a patent for the sole vending of them for a term of years; but I declin'd it from a principle which has ever weighed with me on such occasions, viz., *That, as we enjoy great advantages from the inventions of others, we should be glad of an opportunity to serve others by any invention of ours; and this we should do freely and generously.*

An ironmonger in London however, assuming a good deal of my pamphlet, and working it up into his own, and making some small changes in the machine, which rather hurt its operation, got a patent for it there, and made, as I was told, a little fortune by it. And this is not the only instance of patents taken out for my inventions by others, tho' not always with the same success, which I never contested, as having no desire of profiting by patents myself. and hating disputes. The use of these fireplaces in very many houses, both of this and the neighbouring colonies, has been, and is, a great saving of wood to the inhabitants.

Peace being concluded, and the association business therefore at an end, I turn'd my thoughts again to the affair of establishing an academy. The first step I took was to associate in the design a number of active friends, of whom the Junto furnished a good part; the next was to write and publish a pamphlet, entitled *Proposals Relating to the Education of Youth in Pennsylvania.* This I distributed among the principal inhabitants gratis; and as soon as I could suppose their minds a little prepared by the perusal of it, I set on foot a subscription for opening and supporting an academy; it was to be paid in quotas yearly for five years; by so dividing it, I judg'd the subscription might be larger, and I believe it was so, amounting to no less, if I remember right, than five thousand pounds.

In the introduction to these proposals, I stated their publication, not as an act of mine, but of some *publick-spirited gentlemen,* avoiding as much as I could, according to my usual rule, the presenting myself to the publick as the author of any scheme for their benefit.

The subscribers, to carry the project into immediate execution, chose out of their number twenty-four trustees, and appointed Mr. Francis, then attorney-general, and myself to draw up constitutions for the government of the academy; which being done and signed, a house was hired, masters engag'd, and the schools opened, I think, in the same year, 1749.

The scholars increasing fast, the house was soon found too small, and we were looking out for a piece of ground, properly situated, with intention to build, when Providence threw into our way a large house ready built, which, with a few alterations, might well serve our purpose. This was the building before mentioned, erected by the hearers of Mr. Whitefield, and was obtained for us in the following manner.

It is to be noted that the contributions to this building being made by people of different sects, care was taken in the nomination of trustees, in whom the building and ground was to be vested, that a predominancy should not be given to any sect, lest in time that predominancy might be a means of appropriating the whole to the use of such sect, contrary to the original intention. It was therefore that one of each sect was appointed, viz., one Church-of-England man, one Presbyterian, one Baptist, one Moravian, etc., those, in case of vacancy by death, were to fill it by election from among the contributors. The Moravian happen'd not to please his colleagues, and on his death they resolved to have no other of that sect. The difficulty then was, how to avoid having two of some other sect, by means of the new choice.

Several persons were named, and for that reason not agreed to. At length one mention'd me, with the observation that I was merely an honest man, and of no sect at all, which prevail'd with them to chuse me. The enthusiasm which existed when the house was built had long since abated, and its trustees had not been able to procure fresh contributions for paying the ground-rent, and discharging some other debts the building had occasion'd, which embarrass'd them greatly. Being now a member of both setts of trustees, that for the building and that for the Academy, I had a good opportunity of negotiating with both, and brought them finally to an agreement, by which the trustees for the building were to cede it to those of the academy, the latter undertaking to discharge the debt, to keep for ever open in the building a large hall for occasional preachers, according to the original intention, and maintain a freeschool for the instruction of poor children. Writings were accordingly drawn, and on paying the debts the trustees of the academy were put in possession of the premises; and by dividing the great and lofty hall into stories, and different rooms above and below for the several schools, and purchasing some additional ground, the whole was soon made fit for our purpose, and the scholars remov'd into the building. The care and trouble of agreeing with the workmen, purchasing materials, and superintending the work, fell upon me; and I went thro' it the more cheerfully, as it did not then interfere with my private business, having the year before taken a very able, industrious, and honest partner, Mr. David Hall, with whose character I was well acquainted, as he had work'd for me four years. He took off my hands all care of the printing-office, paying me punctually my share of the profits. This partnership continued eighteen years, successfully for us both.

The trustees of the academy, after a while, were incorporated by a charter from the governor; their funds were increas'd by contributions in Britain and grants of land from the proprietaries, to which the Assembly has since made considerable addition; and thus was established the present University of Philadelphia. I have been continued one of its trustees from the beginning, now near forty years, and have had the very great pleasure of seeing a number of the youth who have receiv'd their education in it, distinguish'd by their improv'd abilities, serviceable in public stations, and ornaments to their country.

When I disengaged myself, as above mentioned, from private business, I flatter'd myself that, by the sufficient tho' moderate fortune I had acquir'd, I had secured leisure during the rest of my life for philosophical studies and amusements. I purchased all Dr. Spence's apparatus, who had come from England to lecture here, and I proceeded in my electrical experiments with great alacrity; but the publick, now considering me as a man of leisure, laid hold of me for their purposes, every part of our civil government, and almost at the same time, imposing some duty upon me. The governor put me into the commission of the peace; the corporation of the city chose me of the common council, and soon after an alderman; and the citizens at large chose me a burgess to represent them in Assembly. This latter station was the more agreeable to me, as I was at length tired with sitting there to hear debates, in which, as clerk, I could take no part, and which were often so unentertaining that I was induc'd to amuse myself with making magic squares or circles, or any thing to avoid weariness; and I conceiv'd my becoming a member would enlarge my power of doing good. I would not, however, insinuate that my ambition was not flatter'd by all these promotions; it certainly was; for, considering my low beginning, they were great things to me; and they were still more pleasing, as being so many spontaneous testimonies of the public good opinion, and by me entirely unsolicited.

The office of justice of the peace I try'd a little, by attending a few courts, and sitting on the bench to hear causes; but finding that more knowledge of the common law than I possess'd was necessary to act in that station with credit, I gradually withdrew from it, excusing myself by my being oblig'd to attend the higher duties of a legislator in the Assembly. My election to this trust was repeated every year for ten years, without my ever asking any elector for his vote, or signifying, either directly or indirectly, any desire of being chosen. On taking my seat in the House, my son was appointed their clerk.

The year following, a treaty being to be held with the Indians at Carlisle, the governor sent a message to the House, proposing that they should nominate some of their members, to be join'd with some members of council, as commissioners for that purpose.[12] The House named the speaker (Mr. Norris) and myself; and, being commission'd, we went to Carlisle, and met the Indians accordingly.

As those people are extreamly apt to get drunk, and, when so, are very quarrelsome and disorderly, we strictly forbad the selling any liquor to them; and when they complain'd of this restriction, we told them that if they would continue sober during the treaty, we would give them plenty of rum when business was over. They promis'd this, and they kept their promise, because they could get

[12] See the votes to have this more correctly.—[*Marg. note.*]

no liquor, and the treaty was conducted very orderly, and concluded to mutual satisfaction. They then claim'd and receiv'd the rum; this was in the afternoon; they were near one hundred men, women, and children, and were lodg'd in temporary cabins, built in the form of a square, just without the town. In the evening, hearing a great noise among them, the commissioners walk'd out to see what was the matter. We found they had made a great bonfire in the middle of the square; they were all drunk, men and women, quarreling and fighting. Their dark-colour'd bodies, half naked, seen only by the gloomy light of the bonfire, running after and beating one another with firebrands, accompanied by their horrid yellings, form'd a scene the most resembling our ideas of hell that could well be imagin'd; there was no appeasing the tumult, and we retired to our lodging. At midnight a number of them came thundering at our door, demanding more rum, of which we took no notice.

The next day, sensible they had misbehav'd in giving us that disturbance, they sent three of their old counselors to make their apology. The orator acknowledg'd the fault, but laid it upon the rum; and then endeavored to excuse the rum by saying, *"The Great Spirit, who made all things, made every thing for some use, and whatever use he design'd any thing for, that use it should always be put to. Now, when he made rum, he said 'Let this be for the Indians to get drunk with,' and it must be so."* And, indeed, if it be the design of Providence to extirpate these savages in order to make room for cultivators of the earth, it seems not improbable that rum may be the appointed means. It has already annihilated all the tribes who formerly inhabited the sea-coast.

In 1751, Dr. Thomas Bond, a particular friend of mine, conceived the idea of establishing a hospital in Philadelphia (a very beneficent design, which has been ascrib'd to me, but was originally his), for the reception and cure of poor sick persons, whether inhabitants of the province or strangers. He was zealous and active in endeavouring to procure subscriptions for it, but the proposal being a novelty in America, and at first not well understood, he met with but small success.

At length he came to me with the compliment that he found there was no such thing as carrying a public-spirited project through without my being concern'd in it. "For," says he, "I am often ask'd by those to whom I propose subscribing, Have you consulted Franklin upon this business? And what does he think of it? And when I tell them that I have not (supposing it rather out of your line), they do not subscribe, but say they will consider of it." I enquired into the nature and probable utility of his scheme, and receiving from him a very satisfactory explanation, I not only subscrib'd to it myself, but engag'd heartily in the design of procuring subscriptions from others. Previously, however, to the solicitation, I endeavoured to prepare the minds of the people by writing on the subject in the newspapers, which was my usual custom in such cases, but which he had omitted.

The subscriptions afterwards were more free and generous; but, beginning to flag, I saw they would be insufficient without some assistance from the Assembly, and therefore propos'd to petition for it, which was done. The country members did not at first relish the project; they objected that it could only be serviceable to the city, and therefore the citizens alone should be at the expense of it; and they doubted whether the citizens themselves generally approv'd of it. My allegation on the contrary, that it met with such approbation as to leave no doubt of our being able to raise two thousand pounds by voluntary donations, they considered as a most extravagant supposition, and utterly impossible.

On this I form'd my plan; and asking leave to bring in a bill for incorporating the contributors according to the prayer of their petition, and granting them a blank sum of money, which leave was obtained chiefly on the consideration that the House could throw the bill out if they did not like it, I drew it so as to make the important clause a conditional one, viz., "And be it enacted, by the authority aforesaid, that when the said contributors shall have met and chosen their managers and treasurer, *and shall have raised by their contributions a capital stock of* —— *value* (the yearly interest of which is to be applied to the accommodating of the sick poor in the said hospital, free of charge for diet, attendance, advice, and medicines), *and shall make the same appear to the satisfaction of the speaker of the Assembly for the time being,* that *then* it shall and may be lawful for the said speaker, and he is hereby required, to sign an order on the provincial treasurer for the payment of two thousand pounds, in two yearly payments, to the treasurer of the said hospital, to be applied to the founding, building and finishing of the same."

This condition carried the bill through; for the members, who had oppos'd the grant, and now conceiv'd they might have the credit of being charitable without the expence, agreed to its passage; and then, in soliciting subscriptions among the people, we urg'd the conditional promise of the law as an additional motive to give, since every man's donation would be doubled; thus the clause work'd both ways. The subscriptions accordingly soon exceeded the requisite sum, and we claim'd and receiv'd the public gift, which enabled us to carry the design into execution. A convenient and handsome building was soon erected; the institution has by constant experience been found useful, and flourishes to this day; and I do not remember any of my political manœuvres, the success of which gave me at the time more pleasure, or wherein, after thinking of it, I more easily excus'd myself for having made some use of cunning.

It was about this time that another projector, the Rev. Gilbert Tennent, came to me with a request that I would assist him in procuring a subscription for erecting a new meeting-house. It was to be for the use of a congregation he had gathered among the Presbyterians, who were originally disciples of Mr. Whitefield. Unwilling to make myself disagreeable to my fellow-citizens by too frequently soliciting their contributions, I absolutely refus'd. He then desired I would furnish him with a list of the names of persons I knew by experience to be generous and public-spirited. I thought it would be unbecoming in me, after their kind compliance with my solicitations, to mark them out to be worried by other beggars, and therefore refus'd also to give such a list. He then desir'd I would at least give him my advice. "That I will readily do," said I; "and, in the first place, I advise you to apply to all those whom you know will give something; next, to those whom you are uncertain whether they will give any thing or not, and show them the list of those who have given; and, lastly, do not neglect those who you are sure will give nothing, for in some of them you may be mistaken." He laugh'd and thank'd me, and said he would take my advice. He did so, for he ask'd of *everybody,* and he obtained a much larger sum than he expected, with which he erected the capacious and very elegant meeting-house that stands in Arch-street.

Our city, tho' laid out with a beautiful regularity, the streets large, strait, and crossing each other at right angles, had the disgrace of suffering those streets to remain long unpav'd, and in wet weather the wheels of heavy carriages plough'd them into a quagmire, so that it was difficult to cross them; and in dry weather the dust was offensive. I had liv'd near what was call'd the Jersey Market, and saw with pain the inhabitants wading in mud while purchasing their provisions. A strip of ground down the middle of that market was at length pav'd with brick, so that, being once in the market, they had firm footing, but were often over shoes in dirt to get there. By talking and writing on the subject, I was at length instrumental in getting the street pav'd with stone between the market and the brick'd foot-pavement, that was on each side next the houses. This, for some time, gave an easy access to the market dry-shod; but, the rest of the street not being pav'd, whenever a carriage came out of the mud upon this pavement, it shook off and left its dirt upon it, and it was soon cover'd with mire, which was not remov'd, the city as yet having no scavengers.

After some inquiry I found a poor industrious man, who was willing to undertake keeping the pavement clean, by sweeping it twice a week, carrying off the dirt from before all the neighbours' doors, for the sum of sixpence per month, to be paid by each house. I then wrote and printed a paper setting forth the advantages to the neighbourhood that might be obtain'd by this small expense; the greater ease in keeping our houses clean, so much dirt not being brought in by people's feet; the benefit to the shops by more custom, etc., etc., as buyers could more easily get at them; and by not having, in windy weather, the dust blown in upon their goods, etc., etc. I sent one of these papers to each house, and in a day or two went round to see who would subscribe an agreement to pay these sixpences; it was unanimously sign'd, and for a time well executed. All the inhabitants of the city were delighted with the cleanliness of the pavement that surrounded the market, it being a convenience to all, and this rais'd a general desire to have all the streets paved, and made the people more willing to submit to a tax for that purpose.

After some time I drew a bill for paving the city, and brought it into the Assembly. It was just before I went to England, in 1757, and did not pass till I was gone,[13] and then with an alteration in the mode of assessment, which I thought not for the better, but with an additional provision for lighting as well as paving the streets, which was a great improvement. It was by a private person, the late Mr. John Clifton, his giving a sample of the utility of lamps, by placing one at his door, that the people were first impress'd with the idea of enlighting all the city. The honour of this public benefit has also been ascrib'd to me, but it belongs truly to that gentleman. I did but follow his example, and have only some merit to claim respecting the form of our lamps, as differing from the globe lamps we were at first supply'd with from London. Those we found inconvenient in these respects: they admitted no air below; the smoke, therefore, did not readily go out above, but circulated in the globe, lodg'd on its inside, and soon obstructed the light they were intended to afford; giving, besides, the daily trouble of wiping them clean; and an accidental stroke on one of them would demolish it, and render it totally useless. I therefore suggested the composing them of four flat panes, with a long funnel above to draw up the smoke, and crevices admitting air below, to facilitate the ascent of the smoke; by this means they were kept clean, and did not grow dark in a few hours, as the London lamps do, but continu'd bright till morning, and an accidental stroke would generally break but a single pane, easily repair'd.

I have sometimes wonder'd that the Londoners did not, from the effect holes in the bottom of the globe lamps us'd at Vauxhall have in keeping them clean, learn to have such holes in their street lamps. But, these holes being made for another purpose, viz., to communicate flame more suddenly to the wick by a little flax hanging down thro' them, the other use, of letting in air, seems not to have been thought of; and therefore, after the lamps have been lit a few hours, the streets of London are very poorly illuminated.

The mention of these improvements puts me in mind of one I propos'd, when in London, to Dr. Fothergill, who was among the best men I have known, and a great promoter of useful projects. I had observ'd that the streets, when dry, were never swept, and the

13 See votes

light dust carried away; but it was suffer'd to accumulate till wet weather reduc'd it to mud, and then, after lying some days so deep on the pavement that there was no crossing but in paths kept clean by poor people with brooms, it was with great labour rak'd together and thrown up into carts open above, the sides of' which suffer'd some of the slush at every jolt on the pavement to shake out and fall, sometimes to the annoyance of foot-passengers. The reason given for not sweeping the dusty streets was, that the dust would fly into the windows of shops and houses.

An accidental occurrence had instructed me how much sweeping might be done in a little time. I found at my door in Craven-street, one morning, a poor woman sweeping my pavement with a birch broom; she appeared very pale and feeble, as just come out of a fit of sickness. I ask'd who employ'd her to sweep there; she said, "Nobody, but I am very poor and in distress, and I sweeps before gentle-folkses doors, and hopes they will give me something." I bid her sweep the whole street clean, and I would give her a shilling; this was at nine o'clock; at 12 she came for the shilling. From the slowness I saw at first in her working, I could scarce believe that the work was done so soon, and sent my servant to examine it, who reported that the whole street was swept perfectly clean, and all the dust plac'd in the gutter, which was in the middle; and the next rain wash'd it quite away, so that the pavement and even the kennel were perfectly clean.

I then judg'd that, if that feeble woman could sweep such a street in three hours, a strong, active man might have done it in half the time. And here let me remark the convenience of having but one gutter in such a narrow street, running down its middle, instead of two, one on each side, near the footway; for where all the rain that falls on a street runs from the sides and meets in the middle, it forms there a current strong enough to wash away all the mud it meets with; but when divided into two channels, it is often too weak to cleanse either, and only makes the mud it finds more fluid, so that the wheels of carriages and feet of horses throw and dash it upon the foot-pavement, which is thereby rendered foul and slippery, and sometimes splash it upon those who are walking. My proposal, communicated to the good doctor, was as follows:

"For the more effectual cleaning and keeping clean the streets of London and Westminster, it is proposed that the several watchmen be contracted with to have the dust swept up in dry seasons, and the mud rak'd up at other times, each in the several streets and lanes of his round; that they be furnish'd with brooms and other proper instruments for these purposes, to be kept at their respective stands, ready to furnish the poor people they may employ in the service.

"That in the dry summer months the dust be all swept up into heaps at proper distances, before the shops and windows of houses are usually opened, when the scavengers, with close-covered carts, shall also carry it all away.

"That the mud, when rak'd up, be not left in heaps to be spread abroad again by the wheels of carriages and trampling of horses, but that the scavengers be provided with bodies of carts, not plac'd high upon wheels, but low upon sliders, with lattice bottoms, which, being cover'd with straw, will retain the mud thrown into them, and permit the water to drain from it, whereby it will become much lighter, water making the greatest part of its weight; these bodies of carts to be plac'd at convenient distances, and the mud brought to them in wheel-barrows; they remaining where plac'd till the mud is drain'd, and then horses brought to draw them away."

I have since had doubts of the practicability of the latter part of this proposal, on account of the narrowness of some streets, and the difficulty of placing the draining-sleds so as not to encumber too much the passage; but I am still of opinion that the former, requiring the dust to be swept up and carry'd away before the shops are open, is very practicable in the summer, when the days are long; for, in walking thro' the Strand and Fleet-street one morning at seven o'clock, I observ'd there was not one shop open, tho' it had been daylight and the sun up above three hours; the inhabitants of London chusing voluntarily to live much by candle-light, and sleep by sunshine, and yet often complain, a little absurdly, of the duty on candles and the high price of tallow.

Some may think these trifling matters not worth minding or relating; but when they consider that tho' dust blown into the eyes of a single person, or into a single shop on a windy day, is but of small importance, yet the great number of the instances in a populous city, and its frequent repetitions give it weight and consequence, perhaps they will not censure very severely those who bestow some attention to affairs of this seemingly low nature. Human felicity is produc'd not so much by great pieces of good fortune that seldom happen, as by little advantages that occur every day. Thus, if you teach a poor young man to shave himself, and keep his razor in order, you may contribute more to the happiness of his life than in giving him a thousand guineas. The money may be soon spent, the regret only remaining of having foolishly consumed it; but in the other case, he escapes the frequent vexation of waiting for barbers, and of their sometimes dirty fingers, offensive breaths, and dull razors; he shaves when most convenient to him, and enjoys daily the pleasure of its being done with a good instrument. With these sentiments I have hazarded the few preceding pages, hoping they may afford hints which some time or other may be useful to a city I love, having lived many years in it very happily, and perhaps to some of our towns in America.

Having been for some time employed by the postmaster-general of America as his comptroller in regulating several offices, and bringing the officers to account, I was, upon his death in 1753, appointed, jointly with Mr. William Hunter, to succeed him, by a commission from the postmaster-general in England. The American office never had hitherto paid any thing to that of Britain. We were to have six hundred pounds a year between us, if we could make that sum out of the profits of the office. To do this, a variety of improvements were necessary; some of these were inevitably at first expensive, so that in the first four years the office became above nine hundred pounds in debt to us. But it soon after began to repay us; and before I was displac'd by a freak of the ministers, of which I shall speak hereafter, we had brought it to yield *three times* as much clear revenue to the crown as the postoffice of Ireland. Since that imprudent transaction, they have receiv'd from it—not one farthing!

The business of the postoffice occasion'd my taking a journey this year to New England, where the College of Cambridge, of their own motion, presented me with the degree of Master of Arts. Yale College, in Connecticut, had before made me a similar compliment. Thus, without studying in any college, I came to partake of their honours. They were conferr'd in consideration of my improvements and discoveries in the electric branch of natural philosophy.

In 1754, war with France being again apprehended, a congress of commissioners from the different colonies was, by an order of the Lords of Trade, to be assembled at Albany, there to confer with the chiefs of the Six Nations concerning the means of defending both their country and ours. Governor Hamilton, having receiv'd this order, acquainted the House with it, requesting they would furnish proper presents for the Indians, to be given on this occasion; and naming the speaker (Mr. Norris) and myself to join Mr. Thomas Penn and Mr. Secretary Peters as commissioners to act for Pennsylvania. The House approv'd the nomination, and provided the goods for the present, and tho' they did not much like treating out of the provinces; and we met the other commissioners at Albany about the middle of June.

In our way thither, I projected and drew a plan for the union of all the colonies under one government, so far as might be necessary for defense, and other important general purposes. As we pass'd thro' New York, I had there shown my project to Mr. James Alexander and Mr. Kennedy, two gentlemen of great knowledge in public affairs, and, being fortified by their approbation, I ventur'd to lay it before the Congress. It then appeared that several of the commissioners had form'd plans of the same kind. A previous question was first taken, whether a union should be established, which pass'd in the affirmative unanimously. A committee was then appointed, one member from each colony, to consider the several plans and report. Mine happen'd to be preferr'd, and, with a few amendments, was accordingly reported.

By this plan the general government was to be administered by a president-general, appointed and supported by the crown, and a grand council was to be chosen by the representatives of the people of the several colonies, met in their respective assemblies. The debates upon it in Congress went on daily, hand in hand with the Indian business. Many objections and difficulties were started, but at length they were all overcome, and the plan was unanimously agreed to, and copies ordered to be transmitted to the Board of Trade and to the assemblies of the several provinces. Its fate was singular: the assemblies did not adopt it, as they all thought there was too much *prerogative* in it, and in England it was judg'd to have too much of the *democratic*.

The Board of Trade therefore did not approve of it, nor recommend it for the approbation of his majesty; but another scheme was form'd, supposed to answer the same purpose better, whereby the governors of the provinces, with some members of their respective councils, were to meet and order the raising of troops, building of forts, etc., and to draw on the treasury of Great Britain for the expense, which was afterwards to be refunded by an act of Parliament laying a tax on America. My plan, with my reasons in support of it, is to be found among my political papers that are printed.

Being the winter following in Boston, I had much conversation with Governor Shirley upon both the plans. Part of what passed between us on the occasion may also be seen among those papers. The different and contrary reasons of dislike to my plan makes me suspect that it was really the true medium; and I am still of opinion it would have been happy for both sides the water if it had been adopted. The colonies, so united, would have been sufficiently strong to have defended themselves; there would then have been no need of troops from England; of course, the subsequent pretence for taxing America, and the bloody contest it occasioned, would have been avoided. But such mistakes are not new; history is full of the errors of states and princes.

> "Look round the habitable world, how few
> Know their own good, or, knowing it, pursue!"

Those who govern, having much business on their hands, do not generally like to take the trouble of considering and carrying into execution new projects. The best public measures are therefore seldom *adopted from previous wisdom, but forc'd by the occasion.*

The Governor of Pennsylvania, in sending it down to the Assembly, express'd his approbation of the plan, "as appearing to him to be drawn up with great clearness and strength of judgment, and therefore recommended it as well worthy of their closest and most serious attention." The House, however, by the management of a certain member, took it up when I happen'd to be absent, which I thought not very fair, and reprobated it without paying any attention to it at all, to my no small mortification.

In my journey to Boston this year, I met at New York with our new governor, Mr. Morris, just arriv'd there from England, with whom I had been before intimately acquainted. He brought a commission to supersede Mr. Hamilton, who, tir'd with the disputes his proprietary instructions subjected him to, had resign'd. Mr. Morris ask'd me if I thought he must expect as uncomfortable an administration. I said, "No; you may, on the contrary, have a very comfortable one, if you will only take care not to enter into any dispute with the Assembly." "My dear friend," says he, pleasantly, "how can you advise my avoiding disputes? You know I love disputing; it is one of my greatest pleasures; however, to show the regard I have for your counsel, I promise you I will, if possible, avoid them." He had some reason for loving to dispute, being eloquent, an acute sophister, and, therefore, generally successful in argumentative conversation. He had been brought up to it from a boy, his father, as I have heard, accustoming his children to dispute with one another for his diversion, while sitting at table after dinner; but I think the practice was not wise; for, in the course of my observation, these disputing, contradicting, and confuting people are generally unfortunate in their affairs. They get victory sometimes, but they never get good will, which would be of more use to them. We parted, he going to Philadelphia, and I to Boston.

In returning, I met at New York with the votes of the Assembly, by which it appear'd that, notwithstanding his promise to me, he and the House were already in high contention; and it was a continual battle between them as long as he retain'd the government. I had my share of it; for, as soon as I got back to my seat in the Assembly, I was put on every committee for answering his speeches and messages, and by the committees always desired to make the drafts. Our answers, as well as his messages, were often tart, and sometimes indecently abusive; and, as he knew I wrote for the Assembly, one might have imagined that, when we met, we could hardly avoid cutting throats; but he was so good-natur'd a man that no personal difference between him and me was occasion'd by the contest, and we often din'd together.

One afternoon, in the height of this public quarrel, we met in the street. "Franklin," says he, "you must go home with me and spend the evening; I am to have some company that you will like;" and, taking me by the arm, he led me to his house. In gay conversation over our wine, after supper, he told us, jokingly, that he much admir'd the idea of Sancho Panza, who, when it was proposed to give him a government, requested it might be a government of *blacks,* as then, if he could not agree with his people, he might sell them. One of his friends, who sat next to me, says, "Franklin, why do you continue to side with these damn'd Quakers? Had not you better sell them? The proprietor would give you a good price." "The governor," says I, "has not yet *blacked* them enough." He, indeed, had labored hard to blacken the Assembly in all his messages, but they wip'd off his coloring as fast as he laid it on, and plac'd it, in return, thick upon his own face; so that, finding he was likely to be negrofied himself, he, as well as Mr. Hamilton, grew tir'd of the contest, and quitted the government.

[14]These public quarrels were all at bottom owing to the proprietaries, our hereditary governors, who, when any expense was to be incurred for the defense of their province, with incredible meanness instructed their deputies to pass no act for levying the necessary taxes, unless their vast estates were in the same act expressly excused; and they had even taken bonds of these deputies to observe such instructions. The Assemblies for three years held out against this injustice, tho' constrained to bend at last. At length Captain Denny, who was Governor Morris's successor, ventured to disobey those instructions; how that was brought about I shall show hereafter.

But I am got forward too fast with my story: there are still some transactions to be mention'd that happened during the administration of Governor Morris.

War being in a manner commenced with France, the government of Massachusetts Bay projected an attack upon Crown Point, and sent Mr. Quincy to Pennsylvania, and Mr. Pownall, afterward Governor Pownall, to New York, to solicit assistance. As I was in the Assembly, knew its temper, and was Mr. Quincy's countryman, he

[14] My acts in Morris's time, military, etc.—[*Marg. note.*]

appli'd to me for my influence and assistance. I dictated his address to them, which was well receiv'd. They voted an aid of ten thousand pounds, to be laid out in provisions. But the governor refusing his assent to their bill (which included this with other sums granted for the use of the crown), unless a clause were inserted exempting the proprietary estate from bearing any part of the tax that would be necessary, the Assembly, tho' very desirous of making their grant to New England effectual, were at a loss how to accomplish it. Mr. Quincy labored hard with the governor to obtain his assent, but he was obstinate.

I then suggested a method of doing the business without the governor, by orders on the trustees of the Loan Office, which, by law, the Assembly had the right of drawing. There was, indeed, little or no money at that time in the office, and therefore I propos'd that the orders should be payable in a year, and to bear an interest of five per cent. With these orders I suppos'd the provisions might easily be purchas'd. The Assembly, with very little hesitation, adopted the proposal. The orders were immediately printed, and I was one of the committee directed to sign and dispose of them. The fund for paying them was the interest of all the paper currency then extant in the province upon loan, together with the revenue arising from the excise, which being known to be more than sufficient, they obtain'd instant credit, and were not only receiv'd in payment for the provisions, but many money'd people, who had cash lying by them, vested it in those orders, which they found advantageous, as they bore interest while upon hand, and might on any occasion be used as money; so that they were eagerly all bought up, and in a few weeks none of them were to be seen. Thus this important affair was by my means compleated. My Quincy return'd thanks to the Assembly in a handsome memorial, went home highly pleas'd with the success of his embassy, and ever after bore for me the most cordial and affectionate friendship.

The British government, not chusing to permit the union of the colonies as propos'd at Albany, and to trust that union with their defense, lest they should thereby grow too military, and feel their own strength, suspicions and jealousies at this time being entertain'd of them, sent over General Braddock with two regiments of regular

English troops for that purpose. He landed at Alexandria, in Virginia, and thence march'd to Frederictown, in Maryland, where he halted for carriages. Our Assembly apprehending, from some information, that he had conceived violent prejudices against them, as averse to the service, wish'd me to wait upon him, not as from them, but as postmaster-general, under the guise of proposing to settle with him the mode of conducting with most celerity and certainty the despatches between him and the governors of the several provinces, with whom he must necessarily have continual correspondence, and of which they propos'd to pay the expense. My son accompanied me on this journey.

We found the general at Frederictown, waiting impatiently for the return of those he had sent thro' the back parts of Maryland and Virginia to collect waggons. I stayed with him several days, din'd with him daily, and had full opportunity of removing all his prejudices, by the information of what the Assembly had before his arrival actually done, and were still willing to do, to facilitate his operations. When I was about to depart, the returns of waggons to be obtained were brought in, by which it appear'd that they amounted only to twenty-five, and not all of those were in serviceable condition. The general and all the officers were surpris'd, declar'd the expedition was then at an end, being impossible, and exclaim'd against the ministers for ignorantly landing them in a country destitute of the means of conveying their stores, baggage, etc., not less than one hundred and fifty waggons being necessary.

I happened to say I thought it was a pity they had not been landed rather in Pennsylvania, as in that country almost every farmer had his waggon. The general eagerly laid hold of my words, and said, "Then you, sir, who are a man of interest there, can probably procure them for us; and I beg you will undertake it." I ask'd what terms were to be offer'd the owners of the waggons; and I was desir'd to put on paper the terms that appeared to me necessary. This I did, and they were agreed to, and a commission and instructions accordingly prepar'd immediately. What those terms were will appear in the advertisement I publish'd as soon as I arriv'd at Lancaster, which being, from the great and sudden effect it produc'd, a piece of some curiosity, I shall insert it at length, as follows:

"ADVERTISEMENT.

"LANCASTER, *April 26,* 1755.

"Whereas, one hundred and fifty waggons, with four horses to each waggon, and fifteen hundred saddle or pack horses, are wanted for the service of his majesty's forces now about to rendezvous at Will's Creek, and his excellency General Braddock having been pleased to empower me to contract for the hire of the same, I hereby give notice that I shall attend for that purpose at Lancaster from this day to next Wednesday evening, and at York from next Thursday morning till Friday evening, where I shall be ready to agree for waggons and teams, or single horses, on the following terms, viz.: 1. That there shall be paid for each waggon, with four good horses and a driver, fifteen shillings per diem; and for each able horse with a pack-saddle, or other saddle and furniture, two shillings per diem; and for each able horse without a saddle, eighteen pence per diem. 2. That the pay commence from the time of their joining the forces at Will's Creek, which must be on or before the 20th of May ensuing, and that a reasonable allowance be paid over and above for the time necessary for their travelling to Will's Creek and home again after their discharge. 3. Each waggon and team, and every saddle or pack horse, is to be valued by indifferent persons chosen between me and the owner; and in case of the loss of any waggon, team, or other horse in the service, the price according to such valuation is to be allowed and paid. 4. Seven days' pay is to be advanced and paid in hand by me to the owner of each waggon and team, or horse, at the time of contracting, if required, and the remainder to be paid by General Braddock, or by the paymaster of the army, at the time of their discharge, or from time to time, as it shall be demanded. 5. No drivers of waggons, or persons taking care of the hired horses, are on any account to be called upon to do the duty of soldiers, or be otherwise employed than in conducting or taking care of their carriages or horses. 6. All oats, Indian corn, or other forage that waggons or horses bring to the camp, more than is necessary for the subsistence of the horses, is to be taken for the use of the army, and a reasonable price paid for the same.

"Note.—My son, William Franklin, is empowered to enter into like contracts with any person in Cumberland county.

"B. FRANKLIN."

"To the inhabitants of the Counties of Lancaster, York and Cumberland.

"Friends and Countrymen,

"Being occasionally at the camp at Frederic a few days since, I found the general and officers extremely exasperated on account of their not being supplied with horses and carriages, which had been expected from this province, as most able to furnish them; but, through the dissensions between our governor and Assembly, money had not been provided, nor any steps taken for that purpose.

"It was proposed to send an armed force immediately into these counties, to seize as many of the best carriages and horses as should be wanted, and compel as many persons into the service as would be necessary to drive and take care of them.

"I apprehended that the progress of British soldiers through these counties on such an occasion, especially considering the temper they are in, and their resentment against us, would be attended with many and great inconveniences to the inhabitants, and therefore more willingly took the trouble of trying first what might be done by fair and equitable means. The people of these back counties have lately complained to the Assembly that a sufficient currency was wanting; you have an opportunity of receiving and dividing among you a very considerable sum; for, if the service of this expedition should continue, as it is more than probable it will, for one hundred and twenty days, the hire of these waggons and horses will amount to upward of thirty thousand pounds, which will be paid you in silver and gold of the king's money.

"The service will be light and easy, for the army will scarce march above twelve miles per day, and the waggons and baggage-horses, as they carry those things that are absolutely necessary to the welfare of the army, must march with the army, and no faster; and are, for the army's sake, always placed where they can be most secure, whether in a march or in a camp.

"If you are really, as I believe you are, good and loyal subjects to his majesty, you may now do a most acceptable service, and make it easy to yourselves; for three or four of such as can not separately spare from the business of their plantations a waggon and four horses and a driver, may do it together, one furnishing the waggon, another one or two horses, and another the driver, and divide the pay proportionately between you; but if you do not this service to your king and country voluntarily, when such good pay and reasonable terms are offered to you, your loyalty will be strongly suspected. The king's business must be done; so many brave troops, come so far for your defense, must not stand idle through your backwardness to do what may be reasonably expected from you; waggons and horses must be had; violent measures will probably be used, and you will be left to seek for a recompense where you can find it, and your case, perhaps, be little pitied or regarded.

"I have no particular interest in this affair, as, except the satisfaction of endeavoring to do good, I shall have only my labour for my pains. If this method of obtaining the waggons and horses is not likely to succeed, I am obliged to send word to the general in fourteen days; and I suppose Sir John St. Clair, the hussar, with a body of soldiers, will immediately enter the province for the purpose, which I shall be sorry to hear, because I am very sincerely and truly your friend and well-wisher,   B. FRANKLIN."

I received of the general about eight hundred pounds, to be disbursed in advance-money to the waggon owners, etc.; but that sum being insufficient, I advanc'd upward of two hundred pounds more, and in two weeks the one hundred and fifty waggons, with two hundred and fifty-nine carrying horses, were on their march for the camp. The advertisement promised payment according to the valuation, in case any waggon or horse should be lost. The owners, however, alleging they did not know General Braddock, or what dependence might be had on his promise, insisted on my bond for the performance, which I accordingly gave them.

While I was at the camp, supping one evening with the officers of Colonel Dunbar's regiment, he represented to me his concern for the subalterns, who, he said, were generally not in affluence, and could ill afford, in this dear country, to lay in the stores that might be necessary in so long a march, thro' a wilderness, where nothing was to be purchas'd. I commiserated their case, and resolved to endeavor procuring them some relief. I said nothing, however, to him of my intention, but wrote the next morning to the committee of the Assembly, who had the disposition of some public money, warmly recommending the case of these officers to their consideration, and proposing that a present should be sent them of necessaries and refreshments. My son, who had some experience of a camp life, and of its wants, drew up a list for me, which I enclos'd in my letter. The committee approv'd, and used such diligence that, conducted by my son, the stores arrived at the camp as soon as the waggons. They consisted of twenty parcels, each containing

6 lbs. loaf sugar.	1 Gloucester cheese.
6 lbs. good Muscovado do.	1 kegg containing 20 lbs. good butter.
1 lb. good green tea.	
1 lb. good bohea do.	2 doz. old Madeira wine.
6 lbs. good ground coffee.	2 gallons Jamaica spirits.
6 lbs. chocolate.	1 bottle flour of mustard.
1-2 cwt. best white biscuit.	2 well-cur'd hams.
1-2 lb. pepper.	1-2 dozen dry'd tongues.
1 quart best white wine vinegar.	6 lbs. rice.
	6 lbs. raisins.

These twenty parcels, well pack'd, were placed on as many horses, each parcel, with the horse, being intended as a present for one officer. They were very thankfully receiv'd, and the kindness acknowledg'd by letters to me from the colonels of both regiments, in the most grateful terms. The general, too, was highly satisfied with my conduct in procuring him the waggons, etc., and readily paid my account of disbursements, thanking me repeatedly, and requesting my farther assistance in sending provisions after him. I undertook this also, and was busily employ'd in it till we heard of his defeat, advancing for the service of my own money, upwards of one thousand pounds sterling, of which I sent him an account. It came to his hands, luckily for me, a few days before the battle, and he return'd me immediately an order on the paymaster for the round sum of one thousand pounds, leaving the remainder to the next account.

I consider this payment as good luck, having never been able to obtain that remainder, of which more hereafter.

This general was, I think, a brave man, and might probably have made a figure as a good officer in some European war. But he had too much self-confidence, too high an opinion of the validity of regular troops, and too mean a one of both Americans and Indians. George Croghan, our Indian interpreter, join'd him on his march with one hundred of those people, who might have been of great use to his army as guides, scouts, etc., if he had treated them kindly; but he slighted and neglected them, and they gradually left him.

In conversation with him one day, he was giving me some account of his intended progress. "After taking Fort Duquesne," says he, "I am to proceed to Niagara; and, having taken that, to Frontenac, if the season will allow time; and I suppose it will, for Duquesne can hardly detain me above three or four days; and then I see nothing that can obstruct my march to Niagara." Having before revolv'd in my mind the long line his army must make in their march by a very narrow road, to be cut for them thro' the woods and bushes, and also what I had read of a former defeat of fifteen hundred French, who invaded the Iroquois country, I had conceiv'd some doubts and some fears for the event of the campaign. But I ventur'd only to say, "To be sure, sir, if you arrive well before Duquesne, with these fine troops, so well provided with artillery, that place not yet compleatly fortified, and as we hear with no very strong garrison, can probably make but a short resistance. The only danger I apprehend of obstruction to your march is from ambuscades of Indians, who, by constant practice, are dexterous in laying and executing them; and the slender line, near four miles long, which your army must make, may expose it to be attack'd by surprise in its flanks, and to be cut like a thread into several pieces, which, from their distance, can not come up in time to support each other."

He smil'd at my ignorance, and reply'd, "These savages may, indeed, be a formidable enemy to your raw American militia, but upon the king's regular and disciplin'd troops, sir, it is impossible they should make any impression." I was conscious of an impropriety in my disputing with a military man in matters of his profession, and said no more. The enemy, however, did not take the advantage of his army which I apprehended its long line of march expos'd it to, but let it advance without interruption till within nine miles of the place; and then, when more in a body (for it had just passed a river, where the front had halted till all were come over), and in a more open part of the woods than any it had pass'd, attack'd its advanced guard by a heavy fire from behind trees and bushes, which was the first intelligence the general had of an enemy's being near him. This guard being disordered, the general hurried the troops up to their assistance, which was done in great confusion, thro' waggons, baggage, and cattle; and presently the fire came upon their flank: the officers, being on horseback, were more easily distinguish'd, pick'd out as marks, and fell very fast; and the soldiers were crowded together in a huddle, having or hearing no orders, and standing to be shot at till two-thirds of them were killed; and then, being seiz'd with a panick, the whole fled with precipitation.

The waggoners took each a horse out of his team and scamper'd; their example was immediately followed by others; so that all the waggons, provisions, artillery, and stores were left to the enemy. The general, being wounded, was brought off with difficulty; his secretary, Mr. Shirley, was killed by his side; and out of eighty-six officers, sixty-three were killed or wounded, and seven hundred and fourteen men killed out of eleven hundred. These eleven hundred had been picked men from the whole army; the rest had been left behind with Colonel Dunbar, who was to follow with the heavier part of the stores, provisions, and baggage. The flyers, not being pursu'd, arriv'd at Dunbar's camp, and the panick they brought with them instantly seiz'd him and all his people; and, tho' he had now above one thousand men, and the enemy who had beaten Braddock did not at most exceed four hundred Indians and French together, instead of proceeding, and endeavoring to recover some of the lost honour, he ordered all the stores, ammunition, etc., to be destroy'd, that he might have more horses to assist his flight towards the settlements, and less lumber to remove. He was there met with requests from the governors of Virginia, Maryland, and Pennsylvania, that he would post his troops on the frontiers, so as to afford some protection to the inhabitants; but he continu'd his hasty march thro' all the country, not thinking himself safe till he arriv'd at Philadelphia, where the inhabitants could protect him. This whole transaction gave us Americans the first suspicion that our exalted ideas of the prowess of British regulars had not been well founded.

In their first march, too, from their landing till they got beyond the settlements, they had plundered and stripped the inhabitants, totally ruining some poor families, besides insulting, abusing, and confining the people if they remonstrated. This was enough to put us out of conceit of such defenders, if we had really wanted any. How different was the conduct of our French friends in 1781, who, during a march thro' the most inhabited part of our country from Rhode Island to Virginia, near seven hundred miles, occasioned not the smallest complaint for the loss of a pig, a chicken, or even an apple.

Captain Orme, who was one of the general's aids-de-camp, and, being grievously wounded, was brought off with him, and continu'd with him to his death, which happen'd in a few days, told me that he was totally silent all the first day, and at night only said, *"Who would have thought it?"* That he was silent again the following day, saying only at last, *"We shall better know how to deal with them another time;"* and dy'd in a few minutes after.

The secretary's papers, with all the general's orders, instructions, and correspondence, falling into the enemy's hands, they selected and translated into French a number of the articles, which they printed, to prove the hostile intentions of the British court before the declaration of war. Among these I saw some letters of the general to the ministry, speaking highly of the great service I had rendered the army, and recommending me to their notice. David Hume, too, who was some years after secretary to Lord Hertford, when minister in France, and afterward to General Conway, when secretary of state, told me he had seen among the papers in that office, letters from Braddock highly recommending me. But, the expedition having been unfortunate, my service, it seems, was not thought of much value, for those recommendations were never of any use to me.

As to rewards from himself, I ask'd only one, which was, that he would give orders to his officers not to enlist any more of our bought

servants, and that he would discharge such as had been already enlisted. This he readily granted, and several were accordingly return'd to their masters, on my application. Dunbar, when the command devolv'd on him, was not so generous. He being at Philadelphia, on his retreat, or rather flight, I apply'd to him for the discharge
of the servants of three poor farmers of Lancaster county that he had
enlisted, reminding him of the late general's orders on that head.
He promised me that, if the masters would come to him at Trenton,
where he should be in a few days on his march to New York, he
would there deliver their men to them. They accordingly were at
the expense and trouble of going to Trenton, and there he refus'd to
perform his promise, to their great loss and disappointment.

As soon as the loss of the waggons and horses was generally
known, all the owners came upon me for the valuation which I had
given bond to pay. Their demands gave me a great deal of trouble,
my acquainting them that the money was ready in the paymaster's
hands, but that orders for paying it must first be obtained from General Shirley, and my assuring them that I had apply'd to that general by letter; but, he being at a distance, an answer could not soon
be receiv'd, and they must have patience, all this was not sufficient
to satisfy, and some began to sue me. General Shirley at length relieved me from this terrible situation by appointing commissioners to
examine the claims, and ordering payment. They amounted to near
twenty thousand pound, which to pay would have ruined me.

Before we had the news of this defeat, the two Doctors Bond came
to me with a subscription paper for raising money to defray the expense of a grand firework, which it was intended to exhibit at a rejoicing on receipt of the news of our taking Fort Duquesne. I looked
grave, and said it would, I thought, be time enough to prepare for
the rejoicing when we knew we should have occasion to rejoice.
They seem'd surpris'd that I did not immediately comply with their
proposal. "Why the d—l!" says one of them, "you surely don't suppose that the fort will not be taken?" "I don't know that it will not
be taken, but I know that the events of war are subject to great uncertainty." I gave them the reasons of my doubting; the subscription was dropt, and the projectors thereby missed the mortification
they would have undergone if the firework had been prepared. Dr.

Bond, on some other occasion afterward, said that he did not like Franklin's forebodings.

Governor Morris, who had continually worried the Assembly with message after message before the defeat of Braddock, to beat them into the making of acts to raise money for the defense of the province, without taxing, among others, the proprietary estates, and had rejected all their bills for not having such an exempting clause, now redoubled his attacks with more hope of success, the danger and necessity being greater. The Assembly, however, continu'd firm, believing they had justice on their side, and that it would be giving up an essential right if they suffered the governor to amend their money-bills. In one of the last, indeed, which was for granting fifty thousand pounds, his propos'd amendment was only of a single word. The bill expressed "that all estates, real and personal, were to be taxed, those of the proprietaries *not* excepted." His amendment was, for *not* read *only:* a small, but very material alteration. However, when the news of this disaster reached England, our friends there, whom we had taken care to furnish with all the Assembly's answers to the governor's messages, rais'd a clamor against the proprietaries for their meanness and injustice in giving their governor such instructions; some going so far as to say that, by obstructing the defense of their province, they forfeited their right to it. They were intimidated by this, and sent orders to their receiver-general to add five thousand pounds of their money to whatever sum might be given by the Assembly for such purpose.

This, being notified to the House, was accepted in lieu of their share of a general tax, and a new bill was form'd, with an exempting clause, which passed accordingly. By this act I was appointed one of the commissioners for disposing of the money, sixty thousand pounds. I had been active in modelling the bill and procuring its passage, and had, at the same time, drawn a bill for establishing and disciplining of a voluntary militia, which I carried thro' the House without much difficulty, as care was taken in it to leave the Quakers at their liberty. To promote the association necessary to form the militia, I wrote a dialogue,[15] stating and answering all the objections

[15] This dialogue and the militia act are in the "Gentleman's Magazine" for February and March, 1756.—[*Marg. note.*]

I could think of to such a militia, which was printed, and had, as I thought, great effect.

While the several companies in the city and country were forming and learning their exercise, the governor prevail'd with me to take charge of our North-western frontier, which was infested by the enemy, and provide for the defense of the inhabitants by raising troops and building a line of forts. I undertook this military business, tho' I did not conceive myself well qualified for it. He gave me a commission with full powers, and a parcel of blank commissions for officers, to be given to whom I thought fit. I had but little difficulty in raising men, having soon five hundred and sixty under my command. My son, who had in the preceding war been an officer in the army rais'd against Canada, was my aid-de-camp, and of great use to me. The Indians had burned Gnadenhut, a village settled by the Moravians, and massacred the inhabitants; but the place was thought a good situation for one of the forts.

In order to march thither, I assembled the companies at Bethlehem, the chief establishment of those people. I was surprised to find it in so good a posture of defense; the destruction of Gnadenhut had made them apprehend danger. The principal buildings were defended by a stockade; they had purchased a quantity of arms and ammunition from New York, and had even plac'd quantities of small paving stones between the windows of their high stone houses, for their women to throw down upon the heads of any Indians that should attempt to force into them. The armed brethren, too, kept watch, and reliev'd as methodically as in any garrison town. In conversation with the bishop, Spangenberg, I mention'd this my surprise; for, knowing they had obtained an act of Parliament exempting them from military duties in the colonies, I had suppos'd they were conscientiously scrupulous of bearing arms. He answer'd me that it was not one of their established principles, but that, at the time of their obtaining that act, it was thought to be a principle with many of their people. On this occasion, however, they, to their surprise, found it adopted by but a few. It seems they were either deceiv'd in themselves, or deceiv'd the Parliament; but common sense, aided by present danger, will sometimes be too strong for whimsical opinions.

It was the beginning of January when we set out upon this business of building forts. I sent one detachment toward the Minisink, with instructions to erect one for the security of that upper part of the country, and another to the lower part, with similar instructions; and I concluded to go myself with the rest of my force to Gnadenhut, where a fort was tho't more immediately necessary. The Moravians procur'd me five waggons for our tools, stores, baggage, etc.

Just before we left Bethlehem, eleven farmers, who had been driven from their plantations by the Indians, came to me requesting a supply of firearms, that they might go back and fetch off their cattle. I gave them each a gun with suitable ammunition. We had not march'd many miles before it began to rain, and it continued raining all day; there were no habitations on the road to shelter us, till we arriv'd near night at the house of a German, where, and in his barn, we were all huddled together, as wet as water could make us. It was well we were not attack'd in our march, for our arms were of the most ordinary sort, and our men could not keep their gun locks dry. The Indians are dextrous in contrivances for that purpose, which we had not. They met that day the eleven poor farmers above mentioned, and killed ten of them. The one who escap'd inform'd that his and his companions' guns would not go off, the priming being wet with the rain.

The next day being fair, we continu'd our march, and arriv'd at the desolated Gnadenhut. There was a saw-mill near, round which were left several piles of boards, with which we soon hutted ourselves; an operation the more necessary at that inclement season, as we had no tents. Our first work was to bury more effectually the dead we found there, who had been half interr'd by the country people.

The next morning our fort was plann'd and mark'd out, the circumference measuring four hundred and fifty-five feet, which would require as many palisades to be made of trees, one with another, of a foot diameter each. Our axes, of which we had seventy, were immediately set to work to cut down trees, and, our men being dextrous in the use of them, great despatch was made. Seeing the trees fall so fast, I had the curiosity to look at my watch when two men began to cut at a pine; in six minutes they had it upon the ground, and I found it of fourteen inches diameter. Each pine made three palisades of eighteen feet long, pointed at one end. While these were preparing, our other men dug a trench all round, of three feet deep, in which the palisades were to be planted; and, our waggons, the bodys being taken off, and the fore and hind wheels separated by taking out the pin which united the two parts of the perch, we had ten carriages, with two horses each, to bring the palisades from the woods to the spot. When they were set up, our carpenters built a stage of boards all round within, about six feet high, for the men to stand on when to fire thro' the loopholes. We had one swivel gun, which we mounted on one of the angles, and fir'd it as soon as fix'd, to let the Indians know, if any were within hearing, that we had such pieces; and thus our fort, if such a magnificent name may be given to so miserable a stockade, was finish'd in a week, though it rain'd so hard every other day that the men could not work.

This gave me occasion to observe, that, when men are employ'd, they are best content'd; for on the days they worked they were good-natur'd and cheerful, and, with the consciousness of having done a good day's work, they spent the evening jollily; but on our idle days they were mutinous and quarrelsome, finding fault with their pork, the bread, etc., and in continual ill-humor, which put me in mind of a sea-captain, whose rule it was to keep his men constantly at work; and, when his mate once told him that they had done every thing, and there was nothing further to employ them about, *"Oh," says he, "make them scour the anchor."*

This kind of fort, however contemptible, is a sufficient defense against Indians, who have no cannon. Finding ourselves now posted securely, and having a place to retreat to on occasion, we ventur'd out in parties to scour the adjacent country. We met with no Indians, but we found the places on the neighboring hills where they had lain to watch our proceedings. There was an art in their contrivance of those places, that seems worth mention. It being winter, a fire was necessary for them; but a common fire on the surface of the ground would by its light have discovered their position at a distance. They had therefore dug holes in the ground about three feet diameter, and somewhat deeper; we saw where they had with their hatchets cut off the charcoal from the sides of burnt logs lying in the woods. With these coals they had made small fires in the bottom of the holes, and we observ'd among the weeds and grass the prints of their bodies, made by their laying all round, with their legs hanging down in the holes to keep their feet warm, which, with them, is an essential point. This kind of fire, so manag'd, could not discover them, either by its light, flame, sparks, or even smoke: it appear'd that their number was not great, and it seems they saw we were too many to be attacked by them with prospect of advantage.

We had for our chaplain a zealous Presbyterian minister, Mr. Beatty, who complained to me that the men did not generally attend his prayers and exhortations. When they enlisted, they were promised, besides pay and provisions, a gill of rum a day, which was punctually serv'd out to them, half in the morning, and the other half in the evening; and I observ'd they were as punctual in attending to receive it; upon which I said to Mr. Beatty, "It is, perhaps, below the dignity of your profession to act as steward of the rum, but if you were to deal it out and only just after prayers, you would have them all about you." He liked the tho't, undertook the office, and, with the help of a few hands to measure out the liquor, executed it to satisfaction, and never were prayers more generally and more punctually attended; so that I thought this method preferable to the punishment inflicted by some military laws for non-attendance on divine service.

I had hardly finish'd this business, and got my fort well stor'd with provisions, when I receiv'd a letter from the governor, acquainting me that he had call'd the Assembly, and wished my attendance there, if the posture of affairs on the frontiers was such that my remaining there was no longer necessary. My friends, too, of the Assembly, pressing me by their letters to be, if possible, at the meeting, and my three intended forts being now compleated, and the inhabitants contented to remain on their farms under that protection, I resolved to return; the more willingly, as a New England officer, Colonel Clapham, experienced in Indian war, being on a visit to our establishment, consented to accept the command. I gave him a commission, and, parading the garrison, had it read before them, and introduc'd him to them as an officer who, from his skill in military affairs, was much more fit to command them than myself; and, giving them a little exhortation, took my leave. I was escorted as far as Bethlehem, where I rested a few days to recover from the fatigue I had undergone. The first night, being in a good bed, I could hardly sleep, it was so different from my hard lodging on the floor of our hut at Gnaden wrapt only in a blanket or two.

While at Bethlehem, I inquir'd a little into the practice of the Moravians: some of them had accompanied me, and all were very kind to me. I found they work'd for a common stock, eat at common tables, and slept in common dormitories, great numbers together. In the dormitories I observed loopholes, at certain distances all along just under the ceiling, which I thought judiciously placed for change of air. I was at their church, where I was entertain'd with good musick, the organ being accompanied with violins, hautboys, flutes, clarinets, etc. I understood that their sermons were not usually preached to mixed congregations of men, women, and children, as is our common practice, but that they assembled sometimes the married men, at other times their wives, then the young men, the young women, and the little children, each division by itself. The sermon I heard was to the latter, who came in and were plac'd in rows on benches; the boys under the conduct of a young man, their tutor, and the girls conducted by a young woman. The discourse seem'd well adapted to their capacities, and was deliver'd in a pleasing, familiar manner, coaxing them, as it were, to be good. They behav'd very orderly, but looked pale and unhealthy, which made me suspect they were kept too much within doors, or not allow'd sufficient exercise.

I inquir'd concerning the Moravian marriages, whether the report was true that they were by lot. I was told that lots were us'd only in particular cases; that generally, when a young man found himself dispos'd to marry, he inform'd the elders of his class, who consulted the elder ladies that govern'd the young women. As these elders of the different sexes were well acquainted with the tempers and dispositions of their respective pupils, they could best judge what matches were suitable, and their judgments were generally acquiesc'd in; but if, for example, it should happen that two or three young women were found to be equally proper for the young man, the lot was then recurred to. I objected, if the matches are not made by the mutual choice of the parties, some of them may chance to be very unhappy. "And so they may," answer'd my informer, "if you let the parties chuse for themselves;" which, indeed, I could not deny.

Being returned to Philadelphia, I found the association went on swimmingly, the inhabitants that were not Quakers having pretty generally come into it, formed themselves into companies, and chose their captains, lieutenants, and ensigns, according to the new law. Dr. B. visited me, and gave me an account of the pains he had taken to spread a general good liking to the law, and ascribed much to those endeavors. I had had the vanity to ascribe all to my *Dialogue;* however, not knowing but that he might be in the right, I let him enjoy his opinion, which I take to be generally the best way in such cases. The officers, meeting, chose me to be colonel of the regiment, which I this time accepted. I forget how many companies we had, but we paraded about twelve hundred well-looking men, with a company of artillery, who had been furnished with six brass field-pieces, which they had become so expert in the use of as to fire twelve times in a minute. The first time I reviewed my regiment they accompanied me to my house, and would salute me with some rounds fired before my door, which shook down and broke several glasses of my electrical apparatus. And my new honour proved not much less brittle; for all our commissions were soon after broken by a repeal of the law in England.

During this short time of my colonelship, being about to set out on a journey to Virginia, the officers of my regiment took it into their heads that it would be proper for them to escort me out of town, as far as the Lower Ferry. Just as I was getting on horseback they came to my door, between thirty and forty, mounted, and all in their uniforms. I had not been previously acquainted with the project, or I should have prevented it, being naturally averse to the assuming of state on any occasion; and I was a good deal chagrin'd at their appearance, as I could not avoid their accompanying me. What made it worse was, that, as soon as we began to move, they drew their swords and rode with them naked all the way. Somebody wrote an account of this to the proprietor, and it gave him great offense. No such honor had been paid him when in the province, nor to any of his governors; and he said it was only proper to princes of the blood royal, which may be true for aught I know, who was, and still am, ignorant of the etiquette in such cases.

This silly affair, however, greatly increased his rancour against me, which was before not a little, on account of my conduct in the Assembly respecting the exemption of his estate from taxation, which I had always oppos'd very warmly, and not without severe reflections on his meanness and injustice of contending for it. He accused me to the ministry as being the great obstacle to the king's service, preventing, by my influence in the House, the proper form of the bills for raising money, and he instanced this parade with my officers as a proof of my having an intention to take the government of the province out of his hands by force. He also applied to Sir Everard Fawkener, the postmaster-general, to deprive me of my office; but it had no other effect than to procure from Sir Everard a gentle admonition.

Notwithstanding the continual wrangle between the governor and the House, in which I, as a member, had so large a share, there still subsisted a civil intercourse between that gentleman and myself, and we never had any personal difference. I have sometimes since thought that his little or no resentment against me, for the answers it was known I drew up to his messages, might be the effect of professional habit, and that, being bred a lawyer, he might consider us both as merely advocates for contending clients in a suit, he for the proprietaries and I for the Assembly. He would, therefore, sometimes call in a friendly way to advise with me on difficult points, and sometimes, tho' not often, take my advice.

We acted in concert to supply Braddock's army with provisions; and, when the shocking news arrived of his defeat, the governor sent in haste for me, to consult with him on measures for preventing the desertion of the back counties. I forget now the advice I gave; but I think it was, that Dunbar should be written to, and prevail'd with, if possible, to post his troops on the frontiers for their protection, till, by re-enforcements from the colonies, he might be able to proceed on the expedition. And, after my return from the frontier, he would have had me undertake the conduct of such an expedition with provincial troops, for the reduction of Fort Duquesne. Dunbar and his men being otherwise employed; and he proposed to commission me as general. I had not so good an opinion of my military abilities as he profess'd to have, and I believe his professions must have exceeded his real sentiments; but probably he might think that my popularity would facilitate the raising of the men, and my influence in Assembly, the grant of money to pay them, and that, perhaps, without taxing the proprietary estate. Finding me not so forward to engage as he expected, the project was dropt, and he soon after left the government, being superseded by Captain Denny.

Before I proceed in relating the part I had in public affairs under this new governor's administration, it may not be amiss here to give some account of the rise and progress of my philosophical reputation.

In 1746, being at Boston, I met there with a Dr. Spence, who was lately arrived from Scotland, and show'd me some electric experiments. They were imperfectly perform'd, as he was not very expert; but, being on a subject quite new to me, they equally surpris'd and pleased me. Soon after my return to Philadelphia, our library company receiv'd from Mr. P. Collinson, Fellow of the Royal Society of London, a present of a glass tube, with some account of the use of it in making such experiments. I eagerly seized the opportunity of repeating what I had seen at Boston; and, by much practice, acquir'd great readiness in performing those, also, which we had an account of from England, adding a number of new ones. I say much practice, for my house was continually full, for some time, with people who came to see these new wonders.

To divide a little this incumbrance among my friends, I caused a number of similar tubes to be blown at our glass-house, with which they furnish'd themselves, so that we had at length several performers. Among these, the principal was Mr. Kinnersley, an ingenious neighbor, who, being out of business, I encouraged to undertake showing the experiments for money, and drew up for him two lectures, in which the experiments were rang'd in such order, and accompanied with such explanations in such method, as that the foregoing should assist in comprehending the following. He procur'd an elegant apparatus for the purpose, in which all the little machines that I had roughly made for myself were nicely form'd by instrument-makers. His lectures were well attended, and gave great satisfaction; and after some time he went thro' the colonies, exhibiting them in every capital town, and pick'd up some money. In the West India islands, indeed, it was with difficulty the experiments could be made, from the general moisture of the air.

Oblig'd as we were to Mr. Collinson for his present of the tube, etc., I thought it right he should be inform'd of our success in using it, and wrote him several letters containing accounts of our experiments. He got them read in the Royal Society, where they were not at first thought worth so much notice as to be printed in their Transactions. One paper, which I wrote for Mr. Kinnersley, on the sameness of lightning with electricity, I sent to Dr. Mitchel, an acquaintance of mine, and one of the members also of that society, who wrote me word that it had been read, but was laughed at by the connoisseurs. The papers, however, being shown to Dr. Fothergill, he thought them of too much value to be stifled, and advis'd the printing of them. Mr. Collinson then gave them to *Cave* for publication in his Gentleman's Magazine; but he chose to print them separately in a pamphlet, and Dr. Fothergill wrote the preface. Cave, it seems, judged rightly for his profit, for by the additions that arrived afterward they swell'd to a quarto volume, which has had five editions, and cost him nothing for copy-money.

It was, however, some time before those papers were much taken notice of in England. A copy of them happening to fall into the hands of the Count de Buffon, a philosopher deservedly of great reputation in France, and, indeed, all over Europe, he prevailed with M. Dalibard to translate them into French, and they were printed at Paris. The publication offended the Abbé Nollet, preceptor in Natural Philosophy to the royal family, and an able experimenter, who had form'd and publish'd a theory of electricity, which then had the general vogue. He could not at first believe that such a work came from America, and said it must have been fabricated by his enemies at Paris, to decry his system. Afterwards, having been assur'd that there really existed such a person as Franklin at Philadelphia, which he had doubted, he wrote and published a volume of Letters, chiefly address'd to me, defending his theory, and denying the verity of my experiments, and of the positions deduc'd from them.

I once purpos'd answering the abbé, and actually began the

answer; but, on consideration that my writings contain'd a description of experiments which any one might repeat and verify, and if not to be verifi'd, could not be defended; or of observations offer'd as conjectures, and not delivered dogmatically, therefore not laying me under any obligation to defend them; and reflecting that a dispute between two persons, writing in different languages, might be lengthened greatly by mistranslations, and thence misconceptions of one another's meaning, much of one of the abbé's letters being founded on an error in the translation. I concluded to let my papers shift for themselves, believing it was better to spend what time I could spare from public business in making new experiments, than in disputing about those already made. I therefore never answered M. Nollet, and the event gave me no cause to repent my silence; for my friend M. le Roy, of the Royal Academy of Sciences, took up my cause and refuted him; my book was translated into the Italian, German, and Latin languages; and the doctrine it contain'd was by degrees universally adopted by the philosophers of Europe, in preference to that of the abbé; so that he lived to see himself the last of his sect, except Monsieur B———, of Paris, his *élève* and immediate disciple.

What gave my book the more sudden and general celebrity, was the success of one of its proposed experiments, made by Messrs. Dalibard and De Lor at Marly, for drawing lightning from the clouds. This engag'd the public attention every where. M. de Lor, who had an apparatus for experimental philosophy, and lectur'd in that branch of science, undertook to repeat what he called the *Philadelphia Experiments;* and, after they were performed before the king and court, all the curious of Paris flocked to see them. I will not swell this narrative with an account of that capital experiment, nor of the infinite pleasure I receiv'd in the success of a similar one I made soon after with a kite at Philadelphia, as both are to be found in the histories of electricity.

Dr. Wright, an English physician, when at Paris, wrote to a friend, who was of the Royal Society, an account of the high esteem my experiments were in among the learned abroad, and of their wonder that my writings had been so little noticed in England. The society, on this, resum'd the consideration of the letters that had been read to them; and the celebrated Dr. Watson drew up a summary account of them, and of all I had afterwards sent to England on the subject, which he accompanied with some praise of the writer. This summary was then printed in their Transactions; and some members of the society in London, particularly the very ingenious Mr. Canton, having verified the experiment of procuring lightning from the clouds by a pointed rod, and acquainting them with the success, they soon made me more than amends for the slight with which they had before treated me. Without my having made any application for that honor, they chose me a member, and voted that I should be excus'd the customary payments, which would have amounted to twenty-five guineas; and ever since have given me their Transactions gratis. They also presented me with the gold medal of Sir Godfrey Copley for the year 1753, the delivery of which was accompanied by a very handsome speech of the president, Lord Macclesfield, wherein I was highly honoured.

Our new governor, Captain Denny, brought over for me the before-mentioned medal from the Royal Society, which he presented to me at an entertainment given him by the city. He accompanied it with very polite expressions of his esteem for me, having, as he said, been long acquainted with my character. After dinner, when the company, as was customary at that time, were engag'd in drinking, he took me aside into another room, and acquainted me that he had been advis'd by his friends in England to cultivate a friendship with me, as one who was capable of giving him the best advice, and of contributing most effectually to the making his administration easy; that he therefore desired of all things to have a good understanding with me, and he begg'd me to be assur'd of his readiness on all occasions to render me every service that might be in his power. He said much to me, also, of the proprietor's good disposition towards the province, and of the advantage it might be to us all, and to me in particular, if the opposition that had been so long continu'd to his measures was dropt, and harmony restor'd between him and the people; in effecting which, it was thought no one could be more serviceable than myself; and I might depend on adequate acknowledgments and recompenses, etc., etc. The drinkers, finding we did not return immediately to the table, sent us a decanter of Madeira, which the governor made liberal use of, and in proportion became more profuse of his solicitations and promises.

My answers were to this purpose: that my circumstances, thanks to God, were such as to make proprietary favours unnecessary to me; and that, being a member of the Assembly, I could not possibly accept of any; that, however, I had no personal enmity to the proprietary, and that, whenever the public measures he propos'd should appear to be for the good of the people, no one should espouse and forward them more zealously than myself; my past opposition having been founded on this, that the measures which had been urged were evidently intended to serve the proprietary interest, with great prejudice to that of the people; that I was much obliged to him (the governor) for his professions of regard to me, and that he might rely on every thing in my power to make his administration as easy as possible, hoping at the same time that he had not brought with him the same unfortunate instruction his predecessor had been hamper'd with.

On this he did not then explain himself; but when he afterwards came to do business with the Assembly, they appear'd again, the disputes were renewed, and I was as active as ever in the opposition, being the penman, first, of the request to have a communication of the instructions, and then of the remarks upon them, which may be found in the votes of the time, and in the Historical Review I afterward publish'd. But between us personally no enmity arose; we were often together; he was a man of letters, had seen much of the world, and was very entertaining and pleasing in conversation. He gave me the first information that my old friend Jas. Ralph was still alive; that he was esteem'd one of the best political writers in England; had been employ'd in the dispute between Prince Frederic and the king, and had obtain'd a pension of three hundred a year; that his reputation was indeed small as a poet, Pope having damned his poetry in the Dunciad; but his prose was thought as good as any man's.

[16]The Assembly finally finding the proprietary obstinately persisted in manacling their deputies with instructions inconsistent not only with the privileges of the people, but with the service of the

[16] The many unanimous resolves of the Assembly—what date?—[*Marg. note.*]

crown, resolv'd to petition the king against them, and appointed me their agent to go over to England, to present and support the petition. The House had sent up a bill to the governor, granting a sum of sixty thousand pounds for the king's use (ten thousand pounds of which was subjected to the orders of the then general, Lord Loudoun), which the governor absolutely refus'd to pass, in compliance with his instructions.

I had agreed with Captain Morris, of the paquet at New York, for my passage, and my stores were put on board, when Lord Loudoun arriv'd at Philadelphia, expressly, as he told me, to endeavor an accommodation between the governor and Assembly, that his majesty's service might not be obstructed by their dissensions. Accordingly, he desir'd the governor and myself to meet him, that he might hear what was to be said on both sides. We met and discuss'd the business. In behalf of the Assembly, I urg'd all the various arguments that may be found in the public papers of that time, which were of my writing, and are printed with the minutes of the Assembly; and the governor pleaded his instructions; the bond he had given to observe them, and his ruin if he disobey'd, yet seemed not unwilling to hazard himself if Lord Loudoun would advise it. This his lordship did not chuse to do, though I once thought I had nearly prevail'd with him to do it; but finally he rather chose to urge the compliance of the Assembly; and he entreated me to use my endeavours with them for that purpose, declaring that he would spare none of the king's troops for the defense of our frontiers, and that, if we did not continue to provide for that defense ourselves, they must remain expos'd to the enemy.

I acquainted the House with what had pass'd, and, presenting them with a set of resolutions I had drawn up, declaring our rights, and that we did not relinquish our claim to those rights, but only suspended the exercise of them on this occasion thro' *force,* against which we protested, they at length agreed to drop that bill, and frame another conformable to the proprietary instructions. This of course the governor pass'd, and I was then at liberty to proceed on my voyage. But, in the meantime, the paquet had sailed with my sea-stores, which was some loss to me, and my only recompense was his lordship's thanks for my service, all the credit of obtaining the accommodation falling to his share.

He set out for New York before me; and, as the time for dispatching the paquet-boats was at his disposition, and there were two then remaining there, one of which, he said, was to sail very soon, I requested to know the precise time, that I might not miss her by any delay of mine. His answer was, "I have given out that she is to sail on Saturday next; but I may let you know, *entre nous,* that if you are there by Monday morning, you will be in time, but do not delay longer." By some accidental hinderance at a ferry, it was Monday noon before I arrived, and I was much afraid she might have sailed, as the wind was fair; but I was soon made easy by the information that she was still in the harbor, and would not move till the next day. One would imagine that I was now on the very point of departing for Europe. I thought so; but I was not then so well acquainted with his lordship's character, of which *indecision* was one of the strongest features. I shall give some instances. It was about the beginning of April that I came to New York, and I think it was near the end of June before we sail'd. There were then two of the paquet-boats, which had been long in port, but were detained for the general's letters, which were always to be ready to-morrow. Another paquet arriv'd; she too was detain'd; and, before we sail'd, a fourth was expected. Ours was the first to be dispatch'd, as having been there longest. Passengers were engag'd in all, and some extremely impatient to be gone, and the merchants uneasy about their letters, and the orders they had given for insurance (it being war time) for fall goods! but their anxiety avail'd nothing; his lordship's letters were not ready; and yet whoever waited on him found him always at his desk, pen in hand, and concluded he must needs write abundantly.

Going myself one morning to pay my respects, I found in his antechamber one Innis, a messenger of Philadelphia, who had come from thence express with a paquet from Governor Denny for the General. He delivered to me some letters from my friends there, which occasion'd my inquiring when he was to return, and where he lodg'd, that I might send some letters by him. He told me he was order'd to call to-morrow at nine for the general's answer to the governor, and should set off immediately. I put my letters into his hands the same day. A fortnight after I met him again in the same place. "So, you are soon return'd, Innis?" *"Return'd! no, I am not gone yet."* "How so?" "I have called here by order every morning these two weeks past for his lordship's letter, and it is not yet ready." "Is it possible, when he is so great a writer? for I see him constantly at his escritoire." "Yes," says Innis, "but he is like St. George on the signs, *always on horseback, and never rides on."* This observation of the messenger was, it seems, well founded; for, when in England, I understood that Mr. Pitt gave it as one reason for removing this general, and sending Generals Amherst and Wolfe, *that the minister never heard from him, and could not know what he was doing.*

This daily expectation of sailing, and all the three paquets going down to Sandy Hook, to join the fleet there, the passengers thought it best to be on board, lest by a sudden order the ships should sail, and they be left behind. There, if I remember right, we were about six weeks, consuming our sea-stores, and oblig'd to procure more. At length the fleet sail'd, the General and all his army on board, bound to Louisburg, with intent to besiege and take that fortress; all the paquet-boats in company ordered to attend the General's ship, ready to receive his dispatches when they should be ready. We were out five days before we got a letter with leave to part, and then our ship quitted the fleet and steered for England. The other two paquets he still detained, carried them with him to Halifax, where he stayed some time to exercise the men in sham attacks upon sham forts, then alter'd his mind as to besieging Louisburg, and return'd to New York, with all his troops, together with the two paquets above mentioned, and all their passengers! During his absence the French and savages had taken Fort George, on the frontier of that province, and the savages had massacred many of the garrison after capitulation.

I saw afterwards in London Captain Bonnell, who commanded one of those paquets. He told me that, when he had been detain'd a month, he acquainted his lordship that his ship was grown foul, to a degree that must necessarily hinder her fast sailing, a point of consequence for a paquet-boat, and requested an allowance of time to heave her down and clean her bottom. He was asked how long time that would require. He answer'd, three days. The general replied, "If you can do it in one day, I give leave; otherwise not; for you must certainly sail the day after to-morrow." So he never obtain'd leave, though detained afterwards from day to day during full three months.

I saw also in London one of Bonnell's passengers, who was so enrag'd against his lordship for deceiving and detaining him so long at New York, and then carrying him to Halifax and back again, that he swore he would sue for damages. Whether he did or not, I never heard; but, as he represented the injury to his affairs, it was very considerable.

On the whole, I wonder'd much how such a man came to be intrusted with so important a business as the conduct of a great army; but, having since seen more of the great world, and the means of obtaining, and motives for giving places, my wonder is diminished. General Shirley, on whom the command of the army devolved upon the death of Braddock, would, in my opinion, if continued in place, have made a much better campaign than that of Loudoun in 1757, which was frivolous, expensive, and disgraceful to our nation beyond conception; for, tho' Shirley was not a bred soldier, he was sensible and sagacious in himself, and attentive to good advice from others, capable of forming judicious plans, and quick and active in carrying them into execution. Loudoun, instead of defending the colonies with his great army, left them totally expos'd while he paraded idly at Halifax, by which means Fort George was lost, besides, he derang'd all our mercantile operations, and distress'd our trade, by a long embargo on the exportation of provisions, on pretence of keeping supplies from being obtain'd by the enemy, but in reality for beating down their price in favor of the contractors, in whose profits, it was said, perhaps from suspicion only, he had a share. And, when at length the embargo was taken off, by neglecting to send notice of it to Charlestown, the Carolina fleet was detain'd near three months longer, whereby their bottoms were so much damaged by the worm that a great part of them foundered in their passage home.

Shirley was, I believe, sincerely glad of being relieved from so burdensome a charge as the conduct of an army must be to a man unacquainted with military business. I was at the entertainment given by the city of New York to Lord Loudoun, on his taking upon him the command. Shirley, tho' thereby superseded, was present also. There was a great company of officers, citizens, and strangers, and, some chairs having been borrowed in the neighborhood, there was one among them very low, which fell to the lot of Mr. Shirley. Perceiving it as I sat by him, I said, "They have given you, sir, too low a seat." "No matter," says he, "Mr. Franklin. I find *a low seat* the easiest."

While I was, as afore mention'd, detain'd at New York, I receiv'd all the accounts of the provisions, etc., that I had furnish'd to Braddock, some of which accounts could not sooner be obtain'd from the different persons I had employ'd to assist in the business. I presented them to Lord Loudoun, desiring to be paid the ballance. He caus'd them to be regularly examined by the proper officer, who, after comparing every article with its voucher, certified them to be right; and the balance due for which his lordship promis'd to give me an order on the paymaster. This was, however, put off from time to time; and, tho' I call'd often for it by appointment, I did not get it. At length, just before my departure, he told me he had, on better consideration, concluded not to mix his accounts with those of his predecessors. "And you," says he, "when in England, have only to exhibit your accounts at the treasury, and you will be paid immediately."

I mention'd, but without effect, the great and unexpected expense I had been put to by being detain'd so long at New York, as a reason for my desiring to be presently paid; and on my observing that it was not right I should be put to any further trouble or delay in obtaining the money I had advanc'd, as I charged no commission for my service, "O, sir," says he, "you must not think of persuading us that you are no gainer; we understand better those affairs, and know that every one concerned in supplying the army finds means, in the doing it, to fill his own pockets." I assur'd him that was not my case, and that I had not pocketed a farthing; but he appear'd clearly not to believe me; and, indeed, I have since learnt that immense fortunes are often made in such employments. As to my ballance, I am not paid it to this day, of which more hereafter.

Our captain of the paquet had boasted much, before we sailed, of the swiftness of his ship; unfortunately, when we came to sea, she proved the dullest of ninety-six sail, to his no small mortification. After many conjectures respecting the cause, when we were near another ship almost as dull as ours, which, however, gain'd upon us, the captain ordered all hands to come aft, and stand as near the ensign staff as possible. We were, passengers included, about forty persons. While we stood there, the ship mended her pace, and soon left her neighbour far behind, which prov'd clearly what our captain suspected, that she was loaded too much by the head. The casks of water, it seems, had been all plac'd forward; these he therefore order'd to be mov'd further aft, on which the ship recover'd her character, and proved the sailer in the fleet.

The captain said she had once gone at the rate of thirteen knots, which is accounted thirteen miles per hour. We had on board, as a passenger, Captain Kennedy, of the Navy, who contended that it was impossible, and that no ship ever sailed so fast, and that there must have been some error in the division of the log-line, or some mistake in heaving the log. A wager ensu'd between the two captains, to be decided when there should be sufficient wind. Kennedy thereupon examin'd rigorously the log-line, and, being satisfi'd with that, he determin'd to throw the log himself. Accordingly some days after, when the wind blew very fair and fresh, and the captain of the paquet, Lutwidge, said he believ'd she then went at the rate of thirteen knots, Kennedy made the experiment, and own'd his wager lost.

The above fact I give for the sake of the following observation. It has been remark'd, as an imperfection in the art of ship-building, that it can never be known, till she is tried, whether a new ship will or will not be a good sailer; for that the model of a good-sailing ship has been exactly follow'd in a new one, which has prov'd, on the contrary, remarkably dull. I apprehend that this may partly be occasion'd by the different opinions of seamen respecting the modes of lading, rigging, and sailing of a ship; each has his system; and the same vessel, laden by the judgment and orders of one captain, shall sail better or worse than when by the orders of another. Besides, it scarce ever happens that a ship is form'd, fitted for the sea, and sail'd by the same person. One man builds the hull, another

rigs her, a third lades and sails her. No one of these has the advantage of knowing all the ideas and experience of the others, and,
therefore, can not draw just conclusions from a combination of
the whole.

Even in the simple operation of sailing when at sea, I have often
observ'd different judgments in the officers who commanded the
successive watches, the wind being the same. One would have the
sails trimm'd sharper or flatter than another, so that they seem'd
to have no certain rule to govern by. Yet I think a set of experiments
might be instituted, first, to determine the most proper form of the
hull for swift sailing; next, the best dimensions and properest place
for the masts: then the form and quantity of sails, and their position,
as the wind may be; and, lastly, the disposition of the lading. This
is an age of experiments, and I think a set accurately made and
combin'd would be of great use. I am persuaded, therefore, that ere
long some ingenious philosopher will undertake it, to whom I wish
success.

We were several times chas'd in our passage, but outsail'd every
thing, and in thirty days had soundings. We had a good observation, and the captain judg'd himself so near our port, Falmouth, that,
if we made a good run in the night, we might be off the mouth of
that harbor in the morning, and by running in the night might
escape the notice of the enemy's privateers, who often crus'd near the
entrance of the channel. Accordingly, all the sail was set that we
could possibly make, and the wind being very fresh and fair, we
went right before it, and made great way. The captain, after his
observation, shap'd his course, as he thought, so as to pass wide of
the Scilly Isles; but it seems there is sometimes a strong indraught
setting up St. George's Channel, which deceives seamen and caused
the loss of Sir Cloudesley Shovel's squadron. This indraught was
probably the cause of what happened to us.

We had a watchman plac'd in the bow, to whom they often called,
"*Look well out before there,*" and he as often answered, "*Ay ay;*"
but perhaps had his eyes shut, and was half asleep at the time, they
sometimes answering, as is said, mechanically; for he did not see
a light just before us, which had been hid by the studdingsails from
the man at the helm, and from the rest of the watch, but by an

accidental yaw of the ship was discover'd, and occasion'd a great alarm, we being very near it, the light appearing to me as big as a cart-wheel. It was midnight, and our captain fast asleep; but Captain Kennedy, jumping upon deck, and seeing the danger, ordered the ship to wear round, all sails standing; an operation dangerous to the masts, but it carried us clear, and we escaped shipwreck, for we were running right upon the rocks on which the light-house was erected. This deliverance impressed me strongly with the utility of light-houses, and made me resolve to encourage the building more of them in America, if I should live to return there.

In the morning it was found by the soundings, etc., that we were near our port, but a thick fog hid the land from our sight. About nine o'clock the fog began to rise, and seem'd to be lifted up from the water like the curtain at a play-house, discovering underneath, the town of Falmouth, the vessels in its harbor, and the fields that surrounded it. This was a most pleasing spectacle to those who had been so long without any other prospects than the uniform view of a vacant ocean, and it gave us the more pleasure as we were now free from the anxieties which the state of war occasion'd.

I set out immediately, with my son, for London, and we only stopt a little by the way to view Stonehenge on Salisbury Plain, and Lord Pembroke's house and gardens, with his very curious antiquities at Wilton. We arrived in London the 27th of July, 1757.[17]

[17] Here terminates the Autobiography, as published by Wm. Temple Franklin and his successors. What follows was written in the last year of Dr. Franklin's life, and was first printed (in English) in Mr. Bigelow's edition of 1868.—ED.

AS SOON as I was settled in a lodging Mr. Charles had provided for me, I went to visit Dr. Fothergill, to whom I was strongly recommended, and whose counsel respecting my proceedings I was advis'd to obtain. He was against an immediate complaint to government, and thought the proprietaries should first be personally appli'd to, who might possibly be induc'd by the interposition and persuasion of some private friends, to accommodate matters amicably. I then waited on my old friend and correspondent, Mr. Peter Collinson, who told me that John Hanbury, the great Virginia merchant, had requested to be informed when I should arrive, that he might carry me to Lord Granville's, who was then President of the Council and wished to see me as soon as possible. I agreed to go with him the next morning. Accordingly Mr. Hanbury called for me and took me in his carriage to that nobleman's, who receiv'd me with great civility; and after some questions respecting the present state of affairs in America and discourse thereupon, he said to me: "You Americans have wrong ideas of the nature of your constitution; you contend that the king's instructions to his governors are not laws, and think yourselves at liberty to regard or disregard them at your own discretion. But those instructions are not like the pocket instructions given to a minister going abroad, for regulating his conduct in some trifling point of ceremony. They are first drawn up by judges learned in the laws; they are then considered, debated, and perhaps amended in Council, after which they are signed by the king. They are then, so far as they relate to you, the *law of the land,* for the king is the LEGISLATOR OF THE COLONIES." I told his lordship this was new doctrine to me. I had always understood from our charters that our laws were to be made by our Assemblies, to be presented indeed to the king for his royal assent, but that being once given the king could not repeal or alter them. And as the Assemblies could not make permanent laws without his assent, so neither could he make a law for them without theirs. He assur'd me I was totally mistaken. I did not think so, however, and his lordship's conversation having a little alarm'd me as to what might be the sentiments of the court concerning us, I wrote it down as soon as I return'd to my lodgings. I recollected that about 20 years before, a clause in a bill brought into Parliament by the ministry had propos'd to make the king's instructions laws in the colonies, but the clause was thrown out by the Commons, for which we adored them as our friends and friends of liberty, till by their conduct towards us in 1765 it seem'd that they had refus'd that point of sovereignty to the king only that they might reserve it for themselves.

After some days, Dr. Fothergill having spoken to the proprietaries, they agreed to a meeting with me at Mr. T. Penn's house in Spring Garden. The conversation at first consisted of mutual declarations of disposition to reasonable accommodations, but I suppose each party had its own ideas of what should be meant by *reasonable*. We then went into consideration of our several points of complaint, which I enumerated. The proprietaries justify'd their conduct as well as they could, and I the Assembly's. We now appeared very wide, and so far from each other in our opinions as to discourage all hope of agreement. However, it was concluded that I should give them the heads of our complaints in writing, and they promis'd then to consider them. I did so soon after, but they put the paper into the hands of their solicitor, Ferdinand John Paris, who managed for them all their law business in their great suit with the neighbouring proprietary of Maryland, Lord Baltimore, which had subsisted 70 years, and wrote for them all their papers and messages in their dispute with the Assembly. He was a proud, angry man, and as I had occasionally in the answers of the Assembly treated his papers with some severity, they being really weak in point of argument and haughty in expression, he had conceived a mortal enmity to me, which discovering itself whenever we met, I declin'd the proprietary's proposal that he and I should discuss the heads of complaint between our two selves, and refus'd treating with any one but them. They then by his advice put the paper into the hands of the Attorney and Solicitor-General for their opinion and counsel upon it, where it lay unanswered a year wanting eight days, during which time I made frequent demands of an answer from the proprietaries, but without obtaining any other than that they had not yet received the opinion of the Attorney and Solicitor-General. What it was when they did receive it I never learnt, for they did not communicate it to me, but sent a long message to the Assembly drawn and signed by Paris, reciting my paper, complaining of its want of formality, as a rudeness on my part, and giving a flimsy justification of their conduct, adding that they should be willing to accommodate matters if the Assembly would send out *some person of candour* to treat with them for that purpose, intimating thereby that I was not such.

The want of formality or rudeness was, probably, my not having address'd the paper to them with their assum'd titles of True and Absolute Proprietaries of the Province of Pennsylvania, which I omitted as not thinking it necessary in a paper, the intention of which was only to reduce to a certainty by writing, what in conversation I had delivered *viva voce*.

But during this delay, the Assembly having prevailed with Gov'r Denny to pass an act taxing the proprietary estate in common with the estates of the people, which was the grand point in dispute, they omitted answering the message.

When this act however came over, the proprietaries, counselled by Paris, determined to oppose its receiving the royal assent. Accordingly they petition'd the king in Council, and a hearing was appointed in which two lawyers were employ'd by them against the act, and two by me in support of it. They alledg'd that the act was intended to load the proprietary estate in order to spare those of the people, and that if it were suffer'd to continue in force, and the proprietaries who were in odium with the people, left to their mercy in proportioning the taxes, they would inevitably be ruined. We reply'd that the act had no such intention, and would have no such effect. That the assessors were honest and discreet men under an oath to assess fairly and equitably, and that any advantage each of them might expect in lessening his own tax by augmenting that of the proprietaries was too trifling to induce them to perjure themselves. This is the purport of what I remember as urged by both sides, except that we insisted strongly on the mischievous consequences that must attend a repeal, for that the money, £100,000, being printed and given to the king's use, expended in his service, and now spread among the people, the repeal would strike it dead in their hands to the ruin of many, and the total discouragement of future grants, and the selfishness of the proprietors in soliciting such a general catastrophe, merely from a groundless fear of their estate being taxed too highly, was insisted on in the strongest terms. On this, Lord Mansfield, one of the counsel rose, and beckoning me took me into the clerk's chamber, while the lawyers were pleading, and asked me if I was really of opinion that no injury would be done the proprietary estate in the execution of the act. I said certainly. "Then," says he, "you can have little objection to enter into an engagement to assure that point." I answer'd, "None at all." He then call'd in Paris, and after some discourse, his lordship's proposition was accepted on both sides; a paper to the purpose was drawn up by the Clerk of the Council, which I sign'd with Mr. Charles, who was also an Agent of the Province for their ordinary affairs, when Lord Mansfield returned to the Council Chamber, where finally the law was allowed to pass. Some changes were however recommended and we also engaged they should be made by a subsequent law, but the Assembly did not think them necessary; for one year's tax having been levied by the act before the order of Council arrived, they appointed a committee to examine the proceedings of the assessors, and on this committee they put several particular friends of the proprietaries. After a full enquiry, they unanimously sign'd a report that they found the tax had been assess'd with perfect equity.

The Assembly looked into my entering into the first part of the engagement, as an essential service to the Province, since it secured the credit of the paper money then spread over all the country. They gave me their thanks in form when I return'd. But the proprietaries were enraged at Governor Denny for having pass'd the act, and turn'd him out with threats of suing him for breach of instructions which he had given bond to observe. He, however, having done it at the instance of the General, and for His Majesty's service, and having some powerful interest at court, despis'd the threats and they were never put in execution. . . . [*Unfinished.*]

CHIEF EVENTS IN FRANKLIN'S LIFE

[Ending, as it does, with the year 1757, the autobiography leaves important facts unrecorded. It has seemed advisable, therefore, to detail the chief events in Franklin's life, from the beginning, in the following list:

1706 He is born, in Boston, and baptized in the Old South Church.

1714 At the age of eight, enters the Grammar School.

1716 Becomes his father's assistant in the tallow-chandlery business.

1718 Apprenticed to his brother James, printer.

1721 Writes ballads and peddles them, in printed form, in the streets; contributes, anonymously, to the "New England Courant," and temporarily edits that paper; becomes a free-thinker, and a vegetarian.

1723 Breaks his indenture and removes to Philadelphia; obtains employment in Keimer's printing-office; abandons vegetarianism.

1724 Is persuaded by Governor Keith to establish himself independently, and goes to London to buy type; works at his trade there, and publishes "Dissertation on Liberty and Necessity, Pleasure and Pain."

1726 Returns to Philadelphia; after serving as clerk in a dry-goods store, becomes manager of Keimer's printing-house.

1727 Founds the Junto, or "Leathern Apron" Club.

1728 With Hugh Meredith, opens a printing-office.

1729 Becomes proprietor and editor of the "Pennsylvania Gazette"; prints, anonymously, "Nature and Necessity of a Paper Currency"; opens a stationer's shop.

1730 Marries Deborah Read.

1731 Founds the Philadelphia Library.

1732 Publishes the first number of "Poor Richard's Almanac" under the pseudonym of "Richard Saunders." The Almanac, which continued for twenty-five years to contain his witty, worldly-wise sayings, played a very large part in bringing together and molding the American character which was at that time made up of so many diverse and scattered types.

1733 Begins to study French, Italian, Spanish, and Latin.

1736 Chosen clerk of the General Assembly; forms the Union Fire Company of Philadelphia.

1737 Elected to the Assembly; appointed Deputy Postmaster-General; plans a city police.

1742 Invents the open, or "Franklin," stove.

1743 Proposes a plan for an Academy, which is adopted 1749 and develops into the University of Pennsylvania.

1744 Establishes the American Philosophical Society.

1746 Publishes a pamphlet, "Plain Truth," on the necessity for disciplined defense, and forms a military company; begins electrical experiments.

1748 Sells out his printing business; is appointed on the Commission of the Peace, chosen to the Common Council, and to the Assembly.

1749 Appointed a Commissioner to trade with the Indians.

1751 Aids in founding a hospital.

1752 Experiments with a kite and discovers that lightning is an electrical discharge.

1753 Awarded the Copley medal for this discovery, and elected a member of the Royal Society; receives the degree of M.A. from Yale and Harvard. Appointed joint Postmaster-General.

1754 Appointed one of the Commissioners from Pennsylvania to the Colonial Congress at Albany; proposes a plan for the union of the colonies.

1755 Pledges his personal property in order that supplies may be raised for Braddock's army; obtains a grant from the Assembly in aid of the Crown Point expedition; carries through a bill establishing a voluntary militia; is appointed Colonel, and takes the field.

1757 Introduces a bill in the Assembly for paving the streets of Philadelphia; publishes his famous "Way to Wealth"; goes to England to plead the cause of the Assembly against the Proprietaries; remains as agent for Pennsylvania; enjoys the friendship of the scientific and literary men of the kingdom.

[HERE THE AUTOBIOGRAPHY BREAKS OFF]

1760 Secures from the Privy Council, by a compromise, a decision obliging the Proprietary estates to contribute to the public revenue.

1762 Receives the degree of D. C. L. from Oxford; returns to America.

1763 Makes a five months' tour of the northern colonies for the purpose of inspecting the post-offices.

1764 Defeated by the Penn faction for reelection to the Assembly; sent to England as agent for Pennsylvania.

1765 Endeavors to prevent the passage of the Stamp Act.

1766 Examined before the House of Commons relative to the passage of the Stamp Act; appointed agent of Massachusetts, New Jersey, and Georgia; visits Göttingen University.

1767 Travels in France and is presented at court.

1769 Procures a telescope for Harvard College.

1772 Elected Associé Etranger of the French Academy.

1774 Dismissed from the office of Postmaster-General; influences Thomas Paine to emigrate to America.

1775 Returns to America; chosen a delegate to the Second Continental Congress; placed on the committee of secret correspondence; appointed one of the commissioners to secure the cooperation of Canada.

1776 Placed on the committee to draft a Declaration of Independence; chosen president of the Constitutional Committee of Pennsylvania; sent to France as agent of the colonies.

1778 Concludes treaties of defensive alliance, and of amity and commerce; is received at court.

1779 Appointed Minister Plenipotentiary to France.

1780 Appoints Paul Jones commander of the "Alliance."

1782 Signs the preliminary articles of peace.

1783 Signs the definite treaty of peace.

1785 Returns to America; is chosen President of Pennsylvania; reelected 1786.

1787 Reelected President; sent as delegate to the convention for framing a Federal Constitution.

1788 Retires from public life.

1790 April 17, dies. His grave is in the churchyard at Fifth and Arch streets, Philadelphia.   EDITOR.]

THE JOURNAL OF
JOHN WOOLMAN

INTRODUCTORY NOTE

JOHN WOOLMAN was born at Northampton, N. J., in 1720, and died at York, England, in 1772. He was the child of Quaker parents, and from his youth was a zealous member of the Society of Friends. His "Journal," published posthumously in 1774, sufficiently describes his way of life and the spirit in which he did his work; but his extreme humility prevents him from making clear the importance of the part he played in the movement against slaveholding among the Quakers.

During the earlier years of their settlement in America, the Friends took part in the traffic in slaves with apparently as little hesitation as their fellow colonists; but in 1671 George Fox, visiting the Barbados, was struck by the inconsistency of slaveholding with the religious principles of his Society. His protests, along with those of others, led to the growth of an agitation which spread from section to section. In 1742, Woolman, then a young clerk in the employment of a storekeeper in New Jersey, was asked to make out a bill of sale for a negro woman; and the scruples which then occurred to him were the beginning of a life-long activity against the traffic. Shortly afterward he began his laborious foot-journeys, pleading everywhere with his co-religionists, and inspiring others to take up the crusade. The result of the agitation was that the various Yearly Meetings one by one decided that emancipation was a religious duty; and within twenty years after Woolman's death the practise of slavery had ceased in the Society of Friends. But his influence did not stop there, for no small part of the enthusiasm of the general emancipation movement is traceable to his labors.

His own words in this "Journal," of an extraordinary simplicity and charm, are the best expression of a personality which in its ardor, purity of motive, breadth of sympathy, and clear spiritual insight, gives Woolman a place among the uncanonized saints of America.

THE JOURNAL OF JOHN WOOLMAN

(1720–1772)

CHAPTER I

1720–1742

His Birth and Parentage—Some Account of the Operations of Divine Grace on his Mind in his Youth—His first Appearance in the Ministry—And his Considerations, while Young, on the Keeping of Slaves.

I HAVE often felt a motion of love to leave some hints in writing of my experience of the goodness of God, and now, in the thirty-sixth year of my age, I begin this work.

I was born in Northampton, in Burlington County, West Jersey, in the year 1720. Before I was seven years old I began to be acquainted with the operations of Divine love. Through the care of my parents, I was taught to read nearly as soon as I was capable of it; and as I went from school one day, I remember that while my companions were playing by the way, I went forward out of sight, and, sitting down, I read the twenty-second chapter of Revelation: "He showed me a pure river of water of life, clear as crystal, proceeding out of the throne of God and of the Lamb, &c." In reading it, my mind was drawn to seek after that pure habitation which I then believed God had prepared for his servants. The place where I sat, and the sweetness that attended my mind, remain fresh in my memory. This, and the like gracious visitations, had such an effect upon me that when boys used ill language it troubled me; and, through the continued mercies of God, I was preserved from that evil.

The pious instructions of my parents were often fresh in my mind, when I happened to be among wicked children, and were of use to me. Having a large family of children, they used frequently, on first-days, after meeting, to set us one after another to read the Holy Scriptures, or some religious books, the rest sitting by without much conversation; I have since often thought it was a good practice. From what I had read and heard, I believed there had been, in past ages, people who walked in uprightness before God in a degree exceeding any that I knew or heard of now living: and the apprehension of there being less steadiness and firmness amongst people in the present age often troubled me while I was a child.

I may here mention a remarkable circumstance that occurred in my childhood. On going to a neighbor's house, I saw on the way a robin sitting on her nest, and as I came near she went off; but having young ones, she flew about, and with many cries expressed her concern for them. I stood and threw stones at her, and one striking her she fell down dead. At first I was pleased with the exploit, but after a few minutes was seized with horror, at having, in a sportive way, killed an innocent creature while she was careful for her young. I beheld her lying dead, and thought those young ones, for which she was so careful, must now perish for want of their dam to nourish them. After some painful considerations on the subject, I climbed up the tree, took all the young birds, and killed them, supposing that better than to leave them to pine away and die miserably. In this case I believed that Scripture proverb was fulfilled, "The tender mercies of the wicked are cruel." I then went on my errand, and for some hours could think of little else but the cruelties I had committed, and was much troubled. Thus He whose tender mercies are over all his works hath placed a principle in the human mind, which incites to exercise goodness towards every living creature; and this being singly attended to, people become tender-hearted and sympathizing; but when frequently and totally rejected, the mind becomes shut up in a contrary disposition.

About the twelfth year of my age, my father being abroad, my mother reproved me for some misconduct, to which I made an undutiful reply. The next first-day, as I was with my father returning from meeting, he told me that he understood I had behaved amiss to my mother, and advised me to be more careful in future. I knew myself blamable, and in shame and confusion remained silent. Being thus awakened to a sense of my wickedness, I felt remorse in my mind, and on getting home I retired and prayed to the Lord to forgive me, and I do not remember that I ever afterwards spoke unhandsomely to either of my parents, however foolish in some other things.

Having attained the age of sixteen years, I began to love wanton company and though I was preserved from profane language or scandalous conduct, yet I perceived a plant in me which produced much wild grapes; my merciful Father did not, however, forsake me utterly, but at times, through his grace, I was brought seriously to consider my ways; and the sight of my backslidings affected me with sorrow, yet for want of rightly attending to the reproofs of instruction, vanity was added to vanity, and repentance to repentance. Upon the whole, my mind became more and more alienated from the truth, and I hastened toward destruction. While I meditate on the gulf towards which I travelled, and reflect on my youthful disobedience, for these things I weep, mine eye runneth down with water.

Advancing in age, the number of my acquaintance increased, and thereby my way grew more difficult. Though I had found comfort in reading the Holy Scriptures and thinking on heavenly things, I was now estranged therefrom. I knew I was going from the flock of Christ and had no resolution to return, hence serious reflections were uneasy to me, and youthful vanities and diversions were my greatest pleasure. In this road I found many like myself, and we associated in that which is adverse to true friendship.

In this swift race it pleased God to visit me with sickness, so that I doubted of recovery; then did darkness, horror, and amazement with full force seize me, even when my pain and distress of body were very great. I thought it would have been better for me never to have had being, than to see the day which I now saw. I was filled with confusion, and in great affliction, both of mind and body, I lay and bewailed myself. I had not confidence to lift up my cries to God, whom I had thus offended; but in a deep sense of my great folly I was humbled before him. At length that word which is as a fire and a hammer broke and dissolved my rebellious heart; my cries were put up in contrition; and in the multitude of his mercies

I found inward relief, and a close engagement that if he was pleased to restore my health I might walk humbly before him.

After my recovery this exercise remained with me a considerable time, but by degrees giving way to youthful vanities, and associating with wanton young people, I lost ground. The Lord had been very gracious, and spoke peace to me in the time of my distress, and I now most ungratefully turned again to folly; at times I felt sharp reproof, but I did not get low enough to cry for help. I was not so hardy as to commit things scandalous, but to exceed in vanity and to promote mirth was my chief study. Still I retained a love and esteem for pious people, and their company brought an awe upon me. My dear parents several times admonished me in the fear of the Lord, and their admonition entered into my heart and had a good effect for a season; but not getting deep enough to pray rightly, the tempter, when he came, found entrance. Once having spent a part of the day in wantonness, when I went to bed at night there lay in a window near my bed a Bible, which I opened, and first cast my eye on the text, "We lie down in our shame, and our confusion covereth us." This I knew to be my case, and meeting with so unexpected a reproof I was somewhat affected with it, and went to bed under remorse of conscience, which I soon cast off again.

Thus time passed on; my heart was replenished with mirth and wantonness, while pleasing scenes of vanity were presented to my imagination, till I attained the age of eighteen years, near which time I felt the judgments of God in my soul, like a consuming fire, and looking over my past life the prospect was moving. I was often sad, and longed to be delivered from those vanities; then again my heart was strongly inclined to them, and there was in me a sore conflict. At times I turned to folly, and then again sorrow and confusion took hold of me. In a while I resolved totally to leave off some of my vanities, but there was a secret reserve in my heart of the more refined part of them, and I was not low enough to find true peace. Thus for some months I had great troubles; my will was unsubjected, which rendered my labors fruitless. At length, through the merciful continuance of heavenly visitations, I was made to bow down in spirit before the Lord. One evening I had spent some time in reading a pious author, and walking out alone

I humbly prayed to the Lord for his help, that I might be delivered from all those vanities which so ensnared me. Thus being brought low, he helped me, and as I learned to bear the cross I felt refreshment to come from his presence, but not keeping in that strength which gave victory I lost ground again, the sense of which greatly affected me. I sought deserts and lonely places, and there with tears did confess my sins to God and humbly craved his help. And I may say with reverence, he was near to me in my troubles, and in those times of humiliation opened my ear to discipline. I was now led to look seriously at the means by which I was drawn from the pure truth, and learned that if I would live such a life as the faithful servants of God lived, I must not go into company as heretofore in my own will, but all the cravings of sense must be governed by a Divine principle. In times of sorrow and abasement these instructions were sealed upon me, and I felt the power of Christ prevail over selfish desires, so that I was preserved in a good degree of steadiness, and being young, and believing at that time that a single life was best for me, I was strengthened to keep from such company as had often been a snare to me.

I kept steadily to meetings, spent first-day afternoons chiefly in reading the Scriptures and other good books, and was early convinced in my mind that true religion consisted in an inward life, wherein the heart does love and reverence God the Creator, and learns to exercise true justice and goodness, not only toward all men, but also toward the brute creatures; that, as the mind was moved by an inward principle to love God as an invisible, incomprehensible Being, so, by the same principle, it was moved to love him in all his manifestations in the visible world; that, as by his breath the flame of life was kindled in all animal sensible creatures, to say we love God as unseen, and at the same time exercise cruelty toward the least creature moving by his life, or by life derived from him, was a contradiction in itself. I found no narrowness respecting sects and opinions, but believed that sincere, upright-hearted people, in every society, who truly love God, were accepted of him.

As I lived under the cross, and simply followed the opening of truth, my mind, from day to day, was more enlightened, my former acquaintance were left to judge of me as they would, for I found it safest for me to live in private, and keep these things sealed up in my own breast. While I silently ponder on that change wrought in me, I find no language equal to convey to another a clear idea of it. I looked upon the works of God in this visible creation, and an awfulness covered me. My heart was tender and often contrite, and universal love to my fellow-creatures increased in me. This will be understood by such as have trodden in the same path. Some glances of real beauty may be seen in their faces who dwell in true meekness. There is a harmony in the sound of that voice to which Divine love gives utterance, and some appearance of right order in their temper and conduct whose passions are regulated; yet these do not fully show forth that inward life to those who have not felt it; this white stone and new name is only known rightly by such as receive it.

Now, though I had been thus strengthened to bear the cross, I still found myself in great danger, having many weaknesses attending me, and strong temptations to wrestle with; in the feeling whereof I frequently withdrew into private places, and often with tears besought the Lord to help me, and his gracious ear was open to my cry.

All this time I lived with my parents, and wrought on the plantation; and having had schooling pretty well for a planter, I used to improve myself in winter evenings, and other leisure times. Being now in the twenty-first year of my age, with my father's consent I engaged with a man, in much business as a shop-keeper and baker, to tend shop and keep books. At home I had lived retired; and now having a prospect of being much in the way of company, I felt frequent and fervent cries in my heart to God, the Father of Mercies, that he would preserve me from all taint and corruption; that, in this more public employment, I might serve him, my gracious Redeemer, in that humility and self-denial which I had in a small degree exercised in a more private life.

The man who employed me furnished a shop in Mount Holly, about five miles from my father's house, and six from his own, and there I lived alone and tended his shop. Shortly after my settlement here I was visited by several young people, my former acquaintance, who supposed that vanities would be as agreeable to me now as ever. At these times I cried to the Lord in secret for wisdom and strength; for I felt myself encompassed with difficulties, and had fresh occasion to bewail the follies of times past, in contracting a familiarity with libertine people; and as I had now left my father's house outwardly, I found my Heavenly Father to be merciful to me beyond what I can express.

By day I was much amongst people, and had many trials to go through; but in the evenings I was mostly alone, and I may with thankfulness acknowledge, that in those times the spirit of supplication was often poured upon me; under which I was frequently exercised, and felt my strength renewed.

After a while, my former acquaintance gave over expecting me as one of their company, and I began to be known to some whose conversation was helpful to me. And now, as I had experienced the love of God, through Jesus Christ, to redeem me from many pollutions, and to be a succor to me through a sea of conflicts, with which no person was fully acquainted, and as my heart was often enlarged in this heavenly principle, I felt a tender compassion for the youth who remained entangled in snares like those which had entangled me. This love and tenderness increased, and my mind was strongly engaged for the good of my fellow-creatures. I went to meetings in an awful frame of mind, and endeavored to be inwardly acquainted with the language of the true Shepherd. One day, being under a strong exercise of spirit, I stood up and said some words in a meeting; but not keeping close to the Divine opening, I said more than was required of me. Being soon sensible of my error, I was afflicted in mind some weeks, without any light or comfort, even to that degree that I could not take satisfaction in anything. I remembered God, and was troubled, and in the depth of my distress he had pity upon me, and sent the Comforter. I then felt forgiveness for my offence; my mind became calm and quiet, and I was truly thankful to my gracious Redeemer for his mercies. About six weeks after this, feeling the spring of Divine love opened, and a concern to speak, I said a few words in a meeting, in which I found peace. Being thus humbled and disciplined under the cross, my understanding became more strengthened to distinguish the pure spirit which inwardly moves upon the heart, and which taught me to wait in silence sometimes many weeks together, until I felt that rise which prepares the creature to stand like a trumpet, through which the Lord speaks to his flock.

From an inward purifying, and steadfast abiding under it springs a lively operative desire for the good of others. All the faithful are not called to the public ministry; but whoever are, are called to minister of that which they have tasted and handled spiritually. The outward modes of worship are various; but whenever any are true ministers of Jesus Christ, it is from the operation of his Spirit upon their hearts, first purifying them, and thus giving them a just sense of the conditions of others. This truth was early fixed in my mind, and I was taught to watch the pure opening, and to take heed lest, while I was standing to speak, my own will should get uppermost, and cause me to utter words from worldly wisdom, and depart from the channel of the true gospel ministry.

In the management of my outward affairs, I may say with thankfulness, I found truth to be my support; and I was respected in my master's family, who came to live in Mount Holly within two years after my going there.

In a few months after I came here, my master bought several Scotchmen servants, from on board a vessel, and brought them to Mount Holly to sell, one of whom was taken sick and died. In the latter part of his sickness, being delirious, he used to curse and swear most sorrowfully; and the next night after his burial I was left to sleep alone in the chamber where he died. I perceived in me a timorousness; I knew, however, I had not injured the man, but assisted in taking care of him according to my capacity. I was not free to ask any one on that occasion to sleep with me. Nature was feeble; but every trial was a fresh incitement to give myself up wholly to the service of God, for I found no helper like him in times of trouble.

About the twenty-third year of my age, I had many fresh and heavenly openings, in respect to the care and providence of the Almighty over his creatures in general, and over man as the most noble amongst those which are visible. And being clearly convinced in my judgment that to place my whole trust in God was best for me, I felt renewed engagements that in all things I might act on an inward principle of virtue, and pursue worldly business no further than as truth opened my way.

About the time called Christmas I observed many people, both in town and from the country, resorting to public-houses, and spending their time in drinking and vain sports, tending to corrupt one another; on which account I was much troubled. At one house in particular there was much disorder; and I believed it was a duty incumbent on me to speak to the master of that house. I considered I was young, and that several elderly friends in town had opportunity to see these things; but though I would gladly have been excused, yet I could not feel my mind clear.

The exercise was heavy; and as I was reading what the Almighty said to Ezekiel, respecting his duty as a watchman, the matter was set home more clearly. With prayers and tears I besought the Lord for his assistance, and He, in loving-kindness, gave me a resigned heart. At a suitable opportunity I went to the public-house; and seeing the man amongst much company, I called him aside, and in the fear and dread of the Almighty expressed to him what rested on my mind. He took it kindly, and afterwards showed more regard to me than before. In a few years afterwards he died, middle-aged; and I often thought that had I neglected my duty in that case it would have given me great trouble; and I was humbly thankful to my gracious Father, who had supported me herein.

My employer, having a negro woman,[1] sold her, and desired me to write a bill of sale, the man being waiting who bought her. The thing was sudden; and though I felt uneasy at the thoughts of writing an instrument of slavery for one of my fellow-creatures, yet I remembered that I was hired by the year, that it was my master who directed me to do it, and that it was an elderly man, a member of our Society, who bought her; so through weakness I gave way, and wrote it; but at the executing of it I was so afflicted in my mind, that I said before my master and the Friend that I believed slave-keeping to be a practice inconsistent with the Christian religion. This, in some degree, abated my uneasiness; yet as often as I

---

[1] The number of slaves in New Jersey at this time must have been considerable, for even as late as 1800 there were over 12,000 of them. The newly imported Africans were deposited at Perth Amboy. In 1734 there were enough of them to make a formidable though unsuccessful insurrection.

reflected seriously upon it I thought I should have been clearer if I had desired to be excused from it, as a thing against my conscience; for such it was. Some time after this a young man of our Society spoke to me to write a conveyance of a slave to him, he having lately taken a negro into his house. I told him I was not easy to write it; for, though many of our meeting and in other places kept slaves, I still believed the practice was not right, and desired to be excused from the writing. I spoke to him in goodwill; and he told me that keeping slaves was not altogether agreeable to his mind; but that the slave being a gift made to his wife he had accepted her.

CHAPTER II

1743-1748

His first Journey, on a Religious Visit, in East Jersey—Thoughts on Merchandising, and Learning a Trade—Second Journey into Pennsylvania, Maryland, Virginia, and North Carolina—Third Journey through part of West and East Jersey—Fourth Journey through New York and Long Island, to New England—And his fifth Journey to the Eastern Shore of Maryland, and the Lower Counties on Delaware.

MY esteemed friend Abraham Farrington being about to make a visit to Friends on the eastern side of this province, and having no companion, he proposed to me to go with him; and after a conference with some elderly Friends I agreed to go. We set out on the 5th of ninth month, 1743; had an evening meeting at a tavern in Brunswick, a town in which none of our Society dwelt; the room was full, and the people quiet. Thence to Amboy, and had an evening meeting in the court-house, to which came many people, amongst whom were several members of Assembly, they being in town on the public affairs of the province. In both these meetings my ancient companion was engaged to preach largely in the love of the gospel. Thence we went to Woodbridge, Rahway, and Plainfield, and had six or seven meetings in places where Friends' meetings are not usually held, chiefly attended by Presbyterians, and my beloved companion was frequently strengthened to publish the word of life amongst them. As for me, I was often silent through the meetings, and when I spake it was with much care, that I might speak only what truth opened. My mind was often tender, and I learned some profitable lessons. We were out about two weeks.

Near this time, being on some outward business in which several families were concerned, and which was attended with difficulties, some things relating thereto not being clearly stated, nor rightly understood by all, there arose some heat in the minds of the parties, and one valuable friend got off his watch. I had a great regard for him, and felt a strong inclination, after matters were settled, to speak to him concerning his conduct in that case; but being a youth, and he far advanced in age and experience, my way appeared difficult; after some days' deliberation, and inward seeking to the Lord for assistance, I was made subject, so that I expressed what lay upon me in a way which became my youth and his years; and though it was a hard task to me it was well taken, and I believe was useful to us both.

Having now been several years with my employer, and he doing less in merchandise than heretofore, I was thoughtful about some other way of business, perceiving merchandise to be attended with much cumber in the way of trading in these parts.

My mind, through the power of truth, was in a good degree weaned from the desire of outward greatness, and I was learning to be content with real conveniences, that were not costly, so that a way of life free from much entanglement appeared best for me, though the income might be small. I had several offers of business that appeared profitable, but I did not see my way clear to accept of them, believing they would be attended with more outward care and cumber than was required of me to engage in. I saw that an humble man, with the blessing of the Lord, might live on a little, and that where the heart was set on greatness, success in business did not satisfy the craving; but that commonly with an increase of wealth the desire of wealth increased. There was a care on my mind so to pass my time that nothing might hinder me from the most steady attention to the voice of the true Shepherd.

My employer, though now a retailer of goods, was by trade a tailor, and kept a servant-man at that business; and I began to think about learning the trade, expecting that if I should settle I might by this trade and a little retailing of goods get a living in a plain way, without the load of great business. I mentioned it to my employer, and we soon agreed on terms, and when I had leisure from the affairs of merchandise I worked with his man. I believed the hand of Providence pointed out this business for me, and I was taught to be content with it, though I felt at times a disposition that would have sought for something greater; but through the revelation of Jesus Christ I had seen the happiness of humility, and there was an earnest desire in me to enter deeply into it; at times this desire arose to a degree of fervent supplication, wherein my soul was so environed with heavenly light and consolation that things were made easy to me which had been otherwise.

After some time my employer's wife died; she was a virtuous woman, and generally beloved of her neighbors. Soon after this he left shop-keeping, and we parted. I then wrought at my trade as a tailor; carefully attended meetings for worship and discipline; and found an enlargement of gospel love in my mind, and therein a concern to visit Friends in some of the back settlements of Pennsylvania and Virginia. Being thoughtful about a companion, I expressed it to my beloved friend, Isaac Andrews, who told me that he had drawings to the same places, and also to go through Maryland, Virginia, and Carolina. After a considerable time, and several conferences with him, I felt easy to accompany him throughout, if way opened for it. I opened the case in our Monthly Meeting, and, Friends expressing their unity therewith, we obtained certificates to travel as companions,—he from Haddonfield, and I from Burlington.

We left our province on the 12th of third month, 1746, and had several meetings in the upper part of Chester County, and near Lancaster; in some of which the love of Christ prevailed, uniting us together in his service. We then crossed the river Susquehanna, and had several meetings in a new settlement, called the Red Lands. It is the poorer sort of people that commonly begin to improve remote deserts; with a small stock they have houses to build, lands to clear and fence, corn to raise, clothes to provide, and children to educate, so that Friends who visit such may well sympathize with them in their hardships in the wilderness; and though the best entertainment that they can give may seem coarse to some who are used to cities or old settled places, it becomes the disciples of Christ to be therewith content. Our hearts were sometimes enlarged in the love of our Heavenly Father amongst these people, and the sweet influence of his Spirit supported us through some difficulties: to him be the praise.

We passed on to Manoquacy, Fairfax, Hopewell, and Shanando,

and had meetings, some of which were comfortable and edifying. From Shanando, we set off in the afternoon for the settlements of Friends in Virginia; the first night we, with our guide, lodged in the woods, our horses feeding near us; but he being poorly provided with a horse, and we young, and having good horses, were free the next day to part with him. In two days after we reached our friend John Cheagle's, in Virginia. We took the meetings in our way through Virginia; were in some degree baptized into a feeling sense of the conditions of the people, and our exercise in general was more painful in these old settlements than it had been amongst the back inhabitants; yet through the goodness of our Heavenly Father the well of living waters was at times opened to our encouragement, and the refreshment of the sincere-hearted. We went on to Perquimans, in North Carolina; had several large meetings, and found some openness in those parts, and a hopeful appearance amongst the young people. Afterwards we turned again to Virginia, and attended most of the meetings which we had not been at before, laboring amongst Friends in the love of Jesus Christ, as ability was given; thence went to the mountains, up James River to a new settlement, and had several meetings amongst the people, some of whom had lately joined in membership with our Society. In our journeying to and fro, we found some honest-hearted Friends, who appeared to be concerned for the cause of truth among a backsliding people.

From Virginia we crossed over the river Potomac, at Hoe's Ferry, and made a general visit to the meetings of Friends on the western shore of Maryland, and were at their Quarterly Meeting. We had some hard labor amongst them, endeavoring to discharge our duty honestly as way opened, in the love of truth. Thence, taking sundry meetings in our way, we passed towards home, which, through the favor of Divine Providence, we reached the 16th of sixth month, 1746; and I may say, that through the assistance of the Holy Spirit, which mortifies selfish desires, my companion and I travelled in harmony, and parted in the nearness of true brotherly love.

Two things were remarkable to me in this journey: first, in regard to my entertainment. When I ate, drank, and lodged free-cost with people who lived in ease on the hard labor of their slaves I felt uneasy; and as my mind was inward to the Lord, I found this uneasiness return upon me, at times, through the whole visit. Where the masters bore a good share of the burden, and lived frugally, so that their servants were well provided for, and their labor moderate, I felt more easy; but where they lived in a costly way, and laid heavy burdens on their slaves, my exercise was often great, and I frequently had conversation with them in private concerning it. Secondly, this trade of importing slaves from their native country being much encouraged amongst them, and the white people and their children so generally living without much labor, was frequently the subject of my serious thoughts. I saw in these southern provinces so many vices and corruptions, increased by this trade and this way of life, that it appeared to me as a dark gloominess hanging over the land; and though now many willingly run into it, yet in future the consequence will be grievous to posterity. I express it as it hath appeared to me, not once, nor twice, but as a matter fixed on my mind.

Soon after my return home I felt an increasing concern for Friends on our seacoast; and on the 8th of eighth month, 1746, I left home with the unity of Friends, and in company with my beloved friend and neighbor Peter Andrews, brother to my companion before mentioned, and visited them in their meetings generally about Salem, Cape May, Great and Little Egg Harbor; we had meetings also at Barnagat, Manahockin, and Mane Squan, and so to the Yearly Meeting at Shrewsbury. Through the goodness of the Lord way was opened, and the strength of Divine love was sometimes felt in our assemblies, to the comfort and help of those who were rightly concerned before him. We were out twenty-two days, and rode, by computation, three hundred and forty miles. At Shrewsbury Yearly Meeting we met with our dear friends Michael Lightfoot and Abraham Farrington, who had good service there.

The winter following died my eldest sister Elizabeth Woolman, of the small-pox, aged thirty-one years.

Of late I found drawings in my mind to visit Friends in New England, and having an opportunity of joining in company with my beloved friend Peter Andrews, we obtained certificates from our Monthly Meeting, and set forward on the 16th of third month, 1747. We reached the Yearly Meeting at Long Island, at which were our friends, Samuel Nottingham from England, John Griffith, Jane

Hoskins, and Elizabeth Hudson from Pennsylvania, and Jacob Andrews from Chesterfield, several of whom were favored in their public exercise; and, through the goodness of the Lord, we had some edifying meetings. After this my companion and I visited Friends on Long Island; and through the mercies of God we were helped in the work.

Besides going to the settled meetings of Friends, we were at a general meeting at Setawket, chiefly made up of other societies; we had also a meeting at Oyster Bay in a dwelling-house, at which were many people. At the former there was not much said by way of testimony, but it was, I believe, a good meeting; at the latter, through the springing up of living waters, it was a day to be thankfully remembered. Having visited the island, we went over to the main, taking meetings in our way, to Oblong, Nine-partners, and New Milford. In these back settlements we met with several people who, through the immediate workings of the Spirit of Christ on their minds, were drawn from the vanities of the world to an inward acquaintance with him. They were educated in the way of the Presbyterians. A considerable number of the youth, members of that society, used often to spend their time together in merriment, but some of the principal young men of the company, being visited by the powerful workings of the Spirit of Christ, and thereby led humbly to take up his cross, could no longer join in those vanities. As these stood steadfast to that inward convincement, they were made a blessing to some of their former companions; so that through the power of truth several were brought into a close exercise concerning the eternal well-being of their souls. These young people continued for a time to frequent their public worship; and, besides that, had meetings of their own, which meetings were awhile allowed by their preacher, who sometimes met with them; but in time their judgment in matters of religion disagreeing with some of the articles of the Presbyterians their meetings were disapproved by that society; and such of them as stood firm to their duty, as it was inwardly manifested, had many difficulties to go through. In a while their meetings were dropped; some of them returned to the Presbyterians, and others joined to our religious society.

I had conversation with some of the latter to my help and edification, and believe several of them are acquainted with the nature of that worship which is performed in spirit and in truth. Amos Powel, a friend from Long Island, accompanied me through Connecticut, which is chiefly inhabited by Presbyterians, who were generally civil to us. After three days' riding, we came amongst Friends in the colony of Rhode Island, and visited them in and about Newport, Dartmouth, and generally in those parts; we then went to Boston, and proceeded eastward as far as Dover. Not far from thence we met our friend Thomas Gawthrop, from England, who was then on a visit to these provinces. From Newport we sailed to Nantucket; were there nearly a week; and from thence came over to Dartmouth. Having finished our visit in these parts, we crossed the Sound from New London to Long Island, and taking some meetings on the island proceeded towards home, which we reached the 13th of seventh month, 1747, having rode about fifteen hundred miles, and sailed about one hundred and fifty.

In this journey, I may say in general, we were sometimes in much weakness, and labored under discouragements, and at other times, through the renewed manifestations of Divine love, we had seasons of refreshment wherein the power of truth prevailed. We were taught by renewed experience to labor for an inward stillness; at no time to seek for words, but to live in the spirit of truth, and utter that to the people which truth opened in us. My beloved companion and I belonged both to one meeting, came forth in the ministry near the same time, and were inwardly united in the work. He was about thirteen years older than I, bore the heaviest burden, and was an instrument of the greatest use.

Finding a concern to visit Friends in the lower counties of Delaware, and on the eastern shore of Maryland, and having an opportunity to join with my well-beloved ancient friend, John Sykes, we obtained certificates, and set off the 7th of eighth month, 1748, were at the meetings of Friends in the lower counties, attended the Yearly Meeting at Little Creek, and made a visit to most of the meetings on the eastern shore, and so home by the way of Nottingham. We were abroad about six weeks, and rode, by computation, about five hundred and fifty miles.

Our exercise at times was heavy, but through the goodness of the

Lord we were often refreshed, and I may say by experience "he is a stronghold in the day of trouble." Though our Society in these parts appeared to me to be in a declining condition, yet I believe the Lord hath a people amongst them who labor to serve him uprightly, but they have many difficulties to encounter.

CHAPTER III

1749–1756

His Marriage—The Death of his Father—His Journeys into the upper part of New Jersey, and afterwards into Pennsylvania—Considerations on keeping Slaves, and Visits to the Families of Friends at several times and places—An Epistle from the General Meeting—His journey to Long Island—Considerations on Trading and on the Use of Spirituous Liquors and Costly Apparel—Letter to a Friend.

ABOUT this time, believing it good for me to settle, and thinking seriously about a companion, my heart was turned to the Lord with desires that he would give me wisdom to proceed therein agreeably to his will, and he was pleased to give me a well-inclined damsel, Sarah Ellis, to whom I was married the 18th of eighth month, 1749.

In the fall of the year 1750 died my father, Samuel Woolman, of a fever, aged about sixty years. In his lifetime he manifested much care for us his children, that in our youth we might learn to fear the Lord; and often endeavored to imprint in our minds the true principles of virtue, and particularly to cherish in us a spirit of tenderness, not only towards poor people, but also towards all creatures of which we had the command.

After my return from Carolina in 1746, I made some observations on keeping slaves, which some time before his decease I showed to him; he perused the manuscript, proposed a few alterations, and appeared well satisfied that I found a concern on that account. In his last sickness, as I was watching with him one night, he being so far spent that there was no expectation of his recovery, though he had the perfect use of his understanding, he asked me concerning the manuscript, and whether I expected soon to proceed to take the advice of friends in publishing it? After some further conversation thereon, he said, "I have all along been deeply affected with the oppression of the poor negroes; and now, at last, my concern for them is as great as ever."

By his direction I had written his will in a time of health, and that night he desired me to read it to him, which I did; and he said it was agreeable to his mind. He then made mention of his end, which he believed was near; and signified that though he was sensible of many imperfections in the course of his life, yet his experience of the power of truth, and of the love and goodness of God from time to time, even till now, was such that he had no doubt that on leaving this life he should enter into one more happy.

The next day his sister Elizabeth came to see him, and told him of the decease of their sister Anne, who died a few days before; he then said, "I reckon Sister Anne was free to leave this world?" Elizabeth said she was. He then said, "I also am free to leave it"; and being in great weakness of body said, "I hope I shall shortly go to rest." He continued in a weighty frame of mind, and was sensible till near the last.

Second of ninth month, 1751.—Feeling drawings in my mind to visit Friends at the Great Meadows, in the upper part of West Jersey, with the unity of our Monthly Meeting, I went there, and had some searching laborious exercise amongst Friends in those parts, and found inward peace therein.

Ninth month, 1753.—In company with my well-esteemed friend, John Sykes, and with the unity of Friends, I travelled about two weeks, visiting Friends in Buck's County. We labored in the love of the gospel, according to the measure received; and through the mercies of Him who is strength to the poor who trust in him, we found satisfaction in our visit. In the next winter, way opening to visit Friends' families within the compass of our Monthly Meeting, partly by the labors of two Friends from Pennsylvania, I joined in some part of the work, having had a desire some time that it might go forward amongst us.

About this time, a person at some distance lying sick, his brother came to me to write his will. I knew he had slaves, and, asking his brother, was told he intended to leave them as slaves to his children. As writing is a profitable employ, and as offending sober people was disagreeable to my inclination, I was straitened in my mind; but as I looked to the Lord, he inclined my heart to his testimony. I told the man that I believed the practice of continuing slavery to this people was not right, and that I had a scruple in my mind against doing writings of that kind; that though many in our Society kept them as slaves, still I was not easy to be concerned in it, and desired to be excused from going to write the will. I spake to him in the fear of the Lord, and he made no reply to what I said, but went away; he also had some concerns in the practice, and I thought he was displeased with me. In this case I had fresh confirmation that acting contrary to present outward interest, from a motive of Divine love and in regard to truth and righteousness, and thereby incurring the resentments of people, opens the way to a treasure better than silver, and to a friendship exceeding the friendship of men.

The manuscript before mentioned having laid by me several years, the publication of it rested weightily upon me, and this year I offered it to the revisal of my friends, who, having examined and made some small alterations in it, directed a number of copies thereof to be published and dispersed amongst members of our Society.[2]

In the year 1754 I found my mind drawn to join in a visit to Friends' families belonging to Chesterfield Monthly Meeting, and having the approbation of our own, I went to their Monthly meeting in order to confer with Friends, and see if way opened for it. I had conference with some of their members, the proposal having been opened before in their meeting, and one Friend agreed to join with me as a companion for a beginning; but when meeting was ended, I felt great distress of mind, and doubted what way to take, or whether to go home and wait for greater clearness. I kept my distress secret, and going with a friend to his house, my desires were to the great Shepherd for his heavenly instruction. In the morning I felt easy to proceed on the visit, though very low in my mind. As mine eye was turned to the Lord, waiting in families in deep reverence before him, he was pleased graciously to afford help, so that we had many comfortable opportunities, and it appeared as a fresh visitation to some young people. I spent several weeks this winter in the service, part of which time was employed near home. And again in the following winter I was several weeks in the same service; some part of the time at Shrewsbury, in company with my beloved friend, John Sykes; and I have cause humbly to acknowl-

2 This pamphlet was published by Benjamin Franklin, 1754.

edge that through the goodness of the Lord our hearts were at times enlarged in his love, and strength was given to go through the trials which, in the course of our visit, attended us.

From a disagreement between the powers of England and France, it was now a time of trouble on this continent, and an epistle to Friends went forth from our general spring meeting, which I thought good to give a place in this Journal.

An Epistle from our general Spring Meeting of ministers and elders for Pennsylvania and New Jersey, held at Philadelphia, from the 29th of the third month to the 1st of the fourth month, inclusive, 1755.

To Friends on the Continent of America:—

Dear Friends,—In an humble sense of Divine goodness, and the gracious continuation of God's love to his people, we tenderly salute you, and are at this time therein engaged in mind, that all of us who profess the truth, as held forth and published by our worthy predecessors in this latter age of the world, may keep near to that Life which is the light of men, and be strengthened to hold fast the profession of our faith without wavering, that our trust may not be in man, but in the Lord alone, who ruleth in the army of heaven and in the kingdoms of men, before whom the earth is "as the dust of the balance, and her inhabitants as grasshoppers." (Isa. xl. 22.)

Being convinced that the gracious design of the Almighty in sending his Son into the world was to repair the breach made by disobedience, to finish sin and transgression, that his kingdom might come, and his will be done on earth as it is in heaven, we have found it to be our duty to cease from those national contests which are productive of misery and bloodshed, and submit our cause to him, the Most High, whose tender love to his children exceeds the most warm affections of natural parents, and who hath promised to his seed throughout the earth, as to one individual, "I will never leave thee, nor forsake thee." (Heb. xiii. 5.) And we, through the gracious dealings of the Lord our God, have had experience of that work which is carried on, not by earthly might, "nor by power, but by my Spirit, saith the Lord of Hosts." (Zech. iv. 6.) By which operation that spiritual kingdom is set up, which is to subdue and break in pieces all kingdoms that oppose it, and shall stand forever.

In a deep sense thereof, and of the safety, stability, and peace that are in it, we are desirous that all who profess the truth may be inwardly acquainted with it, and thereby be qualified to conduct ourselves in all parts of our life as becomes our peaceable profession; and we trust as there is a faithful continuance to depend wholly upon the almighty arm, from one generation to another, the peaceable kingdom will gradually be extended "from sea to sea, and from the river to the ends of the earth" (Zech. ix. 10), to the completion of those prophecies already begun, that "nation shall not lift up a sword against nation, nor learn war any more." (Isa. ii. 4. Micah iv. 3.)

And, dearly beloved friends, seeing that we have these promises, and believe that God is beginning to fulfil them, let us constantly endeavor to have our minds sufficiently disentangled from the surfeiting cares of this life, and redeemed from the love of the world, that no earthly possessions nor enjoyments may bias our judgments, or turn us from that resignation and entire trust in God to which his blessing is most surely annexed; then may we say, "Our Redeemer is mighty, he will plead our cause for us." (Jer. l. 34.) And if, for the further promoting of his most gracious purposes in the earth, he should give us to taste of that bitter cup of which his faithful ones have often partaken, O that we might be rightly prepared to receive it!

And now, dear friends, with respect to the commotions and stirrings of the powers of the earth at this time near us, we are desirous that none of us may be moved thereat, but repose ourselves in the munition of that rock which all these shakings shall not move, even in the knowledge and feeling of the eternal power of God, keeping us subjectly given up to his heavenly will, and feeling it daily to mortify that which remains in any of us which is of this world; for the worldly part in any is the changeable part, and that is up and down, full and empty, joyful and sorrowful, as things go well or ill in this world. For as the truth is but one, and many are made partakers of its spirit, so the world is but one, and many are made partakers of the spirit of it; and so many as do partake of it, so many will be straitened and perplexed with it. But they who are single to the truth, waiting daily to feel the life and virtue of it in their hearts, shall rejoice in the midst of adversity, and have to experience with the prophet, that, "although the fig-tree shall not blossom, neither shall fruit be in the vines; the labor of the olive shall fail, and the fields shall yield no meat; the flock shall be cut off from the fold, and there shall be no herd in the stalls; yet will they rejoice in the Lord, and joy in the God of their salvation." (Hab. iii. 17, 18.)

If, contrary to this, we profess the truth, and, not living under the power and influence of it, are producing fruits disagreeable to the purity thereof, and trust to the strength of man to support ourselves, our confidence therein will be vain. For he who removed the hedge from his vineyard, and gave it to be trodden under foot by reason of the wild grapes it produced (Isa. v. 6), remains unchangeable; and if, for the chastisement of wickedness and the further promoting of his own glory, he doth arise, even to shake terribly the earth, who then may oppose him, and prosper?

We remain, in the love of the gospel, your friends and brethren.

(Signed by fourteen Friends.)

Scrupling to do writings relative to keeping slaves has been a means of sundry small trials to me, in which I have so evidently felt my own will set aside that I think it good to mention a few of them. Tradesmen and retailers of goods, who depend on their business for a living, are naturally inclined to keep the good-will of their customers; nor is it a pleasant thing for young men to be under any necessity to question the judgment or honesty of elderly men, and more especially of such as have a fair reputation. Deep-rooted customs, though wrong, are not easily altered; but it is the duty of all to be firm in that which they certainly know is right for them. A charitable, benevolent man, well acquainted with a negro, may, I believe, under some circumstances, keep him in his family as a servant, on no other motives than the negro's good; but man, as man, knows not what shall be after him, nor hath he any assurance that his children will attain to that perfection in wisdom and goodness necessary rightly to exercise such power; hence it is clear to me, that I ought not to be the scribe where wills are drawn in which some children are made ales masters over others during life.

About this time an ancient man of good esteem in the neighborhood came to my house to get his will written. He had young negroes, and I asked him privately how he purposed to dispose of them. He told me; I then said, "I cannot write thy will without breaking my own peace," and respectfully gave him my reasons for it. He signified that he had a choice that I should have written it, but as I could not, consistently with my conscience, he did not desire it, and so he got it written by some other person. A few years after, there being great alterations in his family, he came again to get me to write his will. His negroes were yet young, and his son, to whom he intended to give them, was, since he first spoke to me, from a libertine become a sober young man, and he supposed that I would have been free on that account to write it. We had much friendly talk on the subject, and then deferred it. A few days after he came again and directed their freedom, and I then wrote his will.

Near the time that the last-mentiond Friend first spoke to me, a neighbor received a bad bruise in his body and sent for me to bleed him, which having done, he desired me to write his will. I took notes, and amongst other things he told me to which of his children he gave his young negro. I considered the pain and distress he was in, and knew not how it would end, so I wrote his will, save only that part concerning his slave, and carrying it to his bedside read it to him. I then told him in a friendly way that I could not write any instruments by which my fellow-creatures were made slaves, without bringing trouble on my own mind. I let him know that I charged nothing for what I had done, and desired to be excused from doing the other part in the way he proposed. We then had a serious conference on the subject; at length, he agreeing to set her free, I finished his will.

Having found drawings in my mind to visit Friends on Long Island, after obtaining a certificate from our Monthly Meeting, I set off 12th of fifth month, 1756. When I reached the island, I lodged the first night at the house of my dear friend, Richard Hallett. The next day being the first of the week, I was at the meeting in New Town, in which we experienced the renewed manifestations of the love of Jesus Christ to the comfort of the honest-hearted. I went that night to Flushing, and the next day I and my beloved friend, Matthew Franklin, crossed the ferry at White Stone; were at three meetings on the main, and then returned to the island, where I spent the remainder of the week in visiting meetings. The Lord, I believe, hath a people in those parts who are honestly inclined to serve him; but many I fear, are too much clogged with the things of this life, and do not come forward bearing the cross in such faithfulness as he calls for.

My mind was deeply engaged in this visit, both in public and private, and at several places where I was, on observing that they had slaves, I found myself under a necessity, in a friendly way, to labor with them on that subject; expressing, as way opened, the inconsistency of that practice with the purity of the Christian religion, and the ill effects of it manifested amongst us.

The latter end of the week their Yearly Meeting began; at which were our friends, John Scarborough, Jane Hoskins, and Susannah Brown, from Pennsylvania. The public meetings were large, and measurably favored with Divine goodness. The exercise of my mind at this meeting was chiefly on account of those who were considered as the foremost rank in the Society; and in a meeting of ministers and elders way opened for me to express in some measure what lay upon me; and when Friends were met for transacting the affairs of the church, having sat awhile silent, I felt a weight on my mind, and stood up; and through the gracious regard of our Heavenly Father, strength was given fully to clear myself of a burden which for some days had been increasing upon me.

Through the humbling dispensations of Divine Providence, men are sometimes fitted for his service. The messages of the prophet Jeremiah were so disagreeable to the people, and so adverse to the spirit they lived in, that he became the object of their reproach, and in the weakness of nature he thought of desisting from his prophetic office; but saith he, "His word was in my heart as a burning fire shut up in my bones; and I was weary with forbearing, and could not stay." I saw at this time that if I was honest in declaring that which truth opened in me, I could not please all men; and I labored to be content in the way of my duty, however disagreeable to my own inclination. After this I went homeward, taking Woodbridge and Plainfield in my way, in both which meetings the pure influence of Divine love was manifested, in an humbling sense whereof I went home. I had been out about twenty-four days, and rode about three hundred and sixteen miles.

While I was out on this journey my heart was much affected with a sense of the state of the churches in our southern provinces; and believing the Lord was calling me to some further labor amongst them, I was bowed in reverence before him, with fervent desires that I might find strength to resign myself to his heavenly will.

Until this year, 1756, I continued to retail goods, besides following my trade as a tailor; about which time I grew uneasy on account of my business growing too cumbersome. I had begun with selling trimmings for garments, and from thence proceeded to sell cloths and linens; and at length, having got a considerable shop of goods, my trade increased every year, and the way to large business appeared open, but I felt a stop in my mind.

Through the mercies of the Almighty, I had, in a good degree, learned to be content with a plain way of living. I had but a small family; and, on serious consideration, believed truth did not require me to engage much in cumbering affairs. It had been my general practice to buy and sell things really useful. Things that served chiefly to please the vain mind in people, I was not easy to trade in; seldom did it; and whenever I did I found it weaken me as a Christian.

The increase of business became my burden; for though my natural inclination was toward merchandise, yet I believed truth required me to live more free from outward cumbers; and there was now a strife in my mind between the two. In this exercise my prayers were put up to the Lord, who graciously heard me, and gave me a heart resigned to his holy will. Then I lessened my outward business, and, as I had opportunity, told my customers of my intentions, that they might consider what shop to turn to; and in a while I wholly laid down merchandise, and followed my trade as a tailor by myself, having no apprentice. I also had a nursery of apple-trees, in which I employed some of my time in hoeing, grafting, trimming, and inoculating.[2] In merchandise it is the custom where I lived to sell chiefly on credit, and poor people often get in debt; when payment is expected, not having wherewith to pay, their creditors often sue for it at law. Having frequently observed occurrences of this kind, I found it good for me to advise poor people to take such goods as were most useful, and not costly.

In the time of trading I had an opportunity of seeing that the too liberal use of spirituous liquors and the custom of wearing too costly apparel led some people into great inconveniences; and that these two things appear to be often connected with each other. By not attending to that use of things which is consistent with universal righteousness, there is an increase of labor which extends beyond what our Heavenly Father intends for us. And by great labor, and often of much sweating, there is even among such as are not drunkards a craving of liquors to revive the spirits; that partly by the luxurious drinking of some, and partly by the drinking of others (led to it through immoderate labor), very great quantities of rum are every year expended in our colonies; the greater part of which we should have no need of, did we steadily attend to pure wisdom.

When men take pleasure in feeling their minds elevated with strong drink, and so indulge their appetite as to disorder their understandings, neglect their duty as members of a family or civil society, and cast off all regard to religion, their case is much to be pitied. And where those whose lives are for the most part regular, and whose examples have a strong influence on the minds of others, adhere to some customs which powerfully draw to the use of more strong

[2] He seems to have regarded agriculture as the business most conducive to moral and physical health. He thought "if the leadings of the Spirit were more attended to, more people would be engaged in the sweet employment of husbandry, where labor is agreeable and healthful." He does not condemn the honest acquisition of wealth in other business free from oppression; even "merchandising," he thought, *might* be carried on innocently and in pure reason. Christ does not forbid the laying up of a needful support for family and friends; the command is, "Lay not up for YOURSELVES treasures on earth." From his little farm on the Rancocas he looked out with a mingled feeling of wonder and sorrow upon the hurry and unrest of the world; and especially was he pained to see luxury and extravagance overgrowing the early plainness and simplicity of his own religious society. He regarded the merely rich man with unfeigned pity. With nothing of his scorn, he had all of Thoreau's commiseration, for people who went about bowed down with the weight of broad acres and great houses on their backs.—*Note in edition published by Messrs. Houghton, Mifflin & Co.*

liquor than pure wisdom allows, it hinders the spreading of the spirit of meekness, and strengthens the hands of the more excessive drinkers. This is a case to be lamented.

Every degree of luxury hath some connection with evil; and if those who profess to be disciples of Christ, and are looked upon as leaders of the people, have that mind in them which was also in Christ, and so stand separate from every wrong way, it is a means of help to the weaker. As I have sometimes been much spent in the heat and have taken spirits to revive me, I have found by experience, that in such circumstances the mind is not so calm, nor so fitly disposed for Divine meditation, as when all such extremes are avoided. I have felt an increasing care to attend to that Holy Spirit which sets right bounds to our desires, and leads those who faithfully follow it to apply all the gifts of Divine Providence to the purposes for which they were intended. Did those who have the care of great estates attend with singleness of heart to this heavenly Instructor, which so opens and enlarges the mind as to cause men to love their neighbors as themselves, they would have wisdom given them to manage their concerns, without employing some people in providing luxuries of life, or others in laboring too hard; but for want of steadily regarding this principle of Divine love, a selfish spirit takes place in the minds of people, which is attended with darkness and manifold confusions in the world.

Though trading in things useful is an honest employ, yet through the great number of superfluities which are bought and sold, and through the corruption of the times, they who apply to merchandise for a living have great need to be well experienced in that precept which the Prophet Jeremiah laid down for his scribe: "Seekest thou great things for thyself? seek them not."

In the winter this year I was engaged with friends in visiting families, and through the goodness of the Lord we oftentimes experienced his heart-tendering presence amongst us.

A Copy of a Letter written to a Friend

"In this, thy late affliction, I have found a deep fellow-feeling with thee, and have had a secret hope throughout that it might please the Father of Mercies to raise thee up and sanctify thy troubles to thee;

that thou being more fully acquainted with that way which the world esteems foolish, mayst feel the clothing of Divine fortitude, and be strengthened to resist that spirit which leads from the simplicity of the everlasting truth.

"We may see ourselves crippled and halting, and from a strong bias to things pleasant and easy find an impossibility to advance forward; but things impossible with men are possible with God; and our wills being made subject to his, all temptations are surmountable.

"This work of subjecting the will is compared to the mineral in the furnace, which, through fervent heat, is reduced from its first principle: 'He refines them as silver is refined; he shall sit as a refiner and purifier of silver.' By these comparisons we are instructed in the necessity of the melting operation of the hand of God upon us, to prepare our hearts truly to adore him, and manifest that adoration by inwardly turning away from that spirit, in all its workings, which is not of him. To forward this work the all-wise God is sometimes pleased, through outward distress, to bring us near the gates of death; that life being painful and afflicting, and the prospect of eternity opened before us, all earthly bonds may be loosened, and the mind prepared for that deep and sacred instruction which otherwise would not be received. If kind parents love their children and delight in their happiness, then he who is perfect goodness in sending abroad mortal contagions doth assuredly direct their use. Are the righteous removed by it? their change is happy. Are the wicked taken away in their wickedness? the Almighty is clear. Do we pass through with anguish and great bitterness, and yet recover? He intends that we should be purged from dross, and our ear opened to discipline.

"And now, as thou art again restored, after thy sore affliction and doubts of recovery, forget not Him who hath helped thee, but in humble gratitude hold fast his instructions, and thereby shun those by-paths which lead from the firm foundation. I am sensible of that variety of company to which one in thy business must be exposed; I have painfully felt the force of conversation proceeding from men deeply rooted in an earthly mind, and can sympathize with others in such conflicts, because much weakness still attends me.

"I find that to be a fool as to worldly wisdom, and to commit my cause to God, not fearing to offend men, who take offence at the simplicity of truth, is the only way to remain unmoved at the sentiments of others.

"The fear of man brings a snare. By halting in our duty, and giving back in the time of trial, our hands grow weaker, our spirits get mingled with the people, our ears grow dull as to hearing the language of the true Shepherd, so that when we look at the way of the righteous, it seems as though it was not for us to follow them.

"A love clothes my mind while I write, which is superior to all expression; and I find my heart open to encourage to a holy emulation, to advance forward in Christian firmness. Deep humility is a strong bulwark, and as we enter into it we find safety and true exaltation. The foolishness of God is wiser than man, and the weakness of God is stronger than man. Being unclothed of our own wisdom, and knowing the abasement of the creature, we find that power to arise which gives health and vigor to us."

CHAPTER IV

1757, 1758

Visit to the Families of Friends at Burlington—Journey to Pennsylvania, Maryland, Virginia, and North Carolina—Considerations on the State of Friends there, and the Exercise he was under in Travelling among those so generally concerned in keeping Slaves, with some Observations on this Subject—Epistle to Friends at New Garden and Crane Creek—Thoughts on the Neglect of a Religious Care in the Education of the Negroes.

THIRTEENTH fifth month, 1757.—Being in good health, and abroad with Friends visiting families, I lodged at a Friend's house in Burlington. Going to bed about the time usual with me, I awoke in the night, and my meditations, as I lay, were on the goodness and mercy of the Lord, in a sense whereof my heart was contrited. After this I went to sleep again; in a short time I awoke; it was yet dark, and no appearance of day or moonshine, and as I opened mine eyes I saw a light in my chamber, at the apparent distance of five feet, about nine inches in diameter, of a clear, easy brightness, and near its centre the most radiant. As I lay still looking upon it without any surprise, words were spoken to my inward ear, which filled my whole inward man. They were not the effect of thought, nor any conclusion in relation to the appearance, but as the language of the Holy One spoken in my mind. The words were, CERTAIN EVIDENCE OF DIVINE TRUTH. They were again repeated exactly in the same manner, and then the light disappeared.

Feeling the exercise in relation to a visit to the Southern Provinces to increase upon me, I acquainted our Monthly Meeting therewith, and obtained their certificate. Expecting to go alone, one of my brothers who lived in Philadelphia, having some business in North Carolina, proposed going with me part of the way; but as he had a view of some outward affairs, to accept of him as a companion was some difficulty with me, whereupon I had conversation with him at sundry times. At length feeling easy in my mind, I had conversation with several elderly Friends of Philadelphia on the subject, and he obtaining a certificate suitable to the occasion, we set off in the fifth month, 1757. Coming to Nottingham week-day meeting, we lodged at John Churchman's, where I met with our friend, Benjamin Buffington, from New England, who was returning from a visit to the Southern Provinces. Thence we crossed the river Susquehanna, and lodged at William Cox's in Maryland.

Soon after I entered this province a deep and painful exercise came upon me, which I often had some feeling of, since my mind was drawn toward these parts, and with which I had acquainted my brother before we agreed to join as companions. As the people in this and the Southern Provinces live much on the labor of slaves, many of whom are used hardly, my concern was that I might attend with singleness of heart to the voice of the true Shepherd and be so supported as to remain unmoved at the faces of men.

As it is common for Friends on such a visit to have entertainment free of cost, a difficulty arose in my mind with respect to saving my money by kindness received from what appeared to me to be the gain of oppression. Receiving a gift, considered as a gift, brings the receiver under obligations to the benefactor, and has a natural tendency to draw the obliged into a party with the giver. To prevent difficulties of this kind, and to preserve the minds of judges from any bias, was that Divine prohibition: "Thou shalt not receive any gift; for a gift bindeth the wise, and perverteth the words of the righteous." (Exod. xxiii. 8.) As the disciples were sent forth without any provision for their journey, and our Lord said the workman is worthy of his meat, their labor in the gospel was considered as a reward for their entertainment, and therefore not received as a gift; yet, in regard to my present journey, I could not see my way clear in that respect. The difference appeared thus: the entertainment the disciples met with was from them whose hearts God had opened to receive them, from a love to them and the truth they published; but we, considered as members of the same religious society, look upon it as a piece of civility to receive each other in such visits; and such receptions, at times, is partly in regard to reputation, and not from an inward unity of heart and spirit. Conduct is more convincing than language, and where people, by their actions, manifest that the slave-trade is not so disagreeable to their principles but that it may be encouraged, there is not a sound uniting with some Friends who visit them.

The prospect of so weighty a work, and of being so distinguished from many whom I esteemed before myself, brought me very low, and such were the conflicts of my soul that I had a near sympathy with the Prophet, in the time of his weakness, when he said: "If thou deal thus with me, kill me, I pray thee, if I have found favor in thy sight." (Num. xi. 15.) But I soon saw that this proceeded from the want of a full resignation to the Divine will. Many were the afflictions which attended me, and in great abasement, with many tears, my cries were to the Almighty for his gracious and fatherly assistance, and after a time of deep trial I was favored to understand the state mentioned by the Psalmist more clearly than ever I had done before; to wit: "My soul is even as a weaned child." (Psalm cxxxi. 2.) Being thus helped to sink down into resignation, I felt a deliverance from that tempest in which I had been sorely exercised, and in calmness of mind went forward, trusting that the Lord Jesus Christ, as I faithfully attended to him, would be a counsellor to me in all difficulties, and that by His strength I should be enabled even to leave money with the members of society where I had entertainment, when I found that omitting it would obstruct that work to which I believed He had called me. As I copy this after my return, I may here add, that oftentimes I did so under a sense of duty. The way in which I did it was thus: when I expected soon to leave a Friend's house where I had entertainment, if I believed that I should not keep clear from the gain of oppression without leaving money, I spoke to one of the heads of the family privately, and desired them to accept of those pieces of silver, and give them to such of their negroes as they believed would make the best use of them; and at other times I gave them to the negroes myself, as the way looked clearest to me. Before I came out, I had provided a large number of small pieces for this purpose and thus offering them to some who appeared to be wealthy people was a trial both to me and them. But the fear of the Lord so covered me at times that my way was made easier than I expected; and few, if any, manifested any resentment at the offer, and most of them, after some conversation, accepted of them.

Ninth of fifth month.—A Friend at whose house we breakfasted setting us a little on our way, I had conversation with him, in the fear of the Lord, concerning his slaves, in which my heart was tender; I used much plainness of speech with him, and he appeared to take it kindly. We pursued our journey without appointing meetings, being pressed in my mind to be at the Yearly Meeting in Virginia. In my travelling on the road, I often felt a cry rise from the centre of my mind, thus: "O Lord, I am a stranger on the earth, hide not thy face from me." On the 11th, we crossed the rivers Patowmack and Rapahannock, and lodged at Port Royal. On the way we had the company of a colonel of the militia, who appeared to be a thoughtful man. I took occasion to remark on the difference in general betwixt a people used to labor moderately for their living, training up their children in frugality and business, and those who live on the labor of slaves; the former, in my view, being the most happy life. He concurred in the remark, and mentioned the trouble arising from the untoward, slothful disposition of the negroes, adding that one of our laborers would do as much in a day as two of their slaves. I replied, that free men, whose minds were properly on their business, found a satisfaction in improving, cultivating, and providing for their families; but negroes, laboring to support others who claim them as their property, and expecting nothing but slavery during life, had not the like inducement to be industrious.

After some further conversation I said, that men having power too often misapplied it; that though we made slaves of the negroes, and the Turks made slaves of the Christians, I believed that liberty was the natural right of all men equally. This he did not deny, but said the lives of the negroes were so wretched in their own country that many of them lived better here than there. I replied, "There is great odds in regard to us on what principle we act"; and so the conversation on that subject ended. I may here add that another person, some time afterwards, mentioned the wretchedness of the negroes, occasioned by their intestine wars, as an argument in favor of our fetching them away for slaves. To which I replied, if compassion for the Africans, on account of their domestic troubles, was the real motive of our purchasing them, that spirit of tenderness being attended to, would incite us to use them kindly that, as strangers brought out of affliction, their lives might be happy among us. And as they are human creatures, whose souls are as precious as ours, and who may receive the same help and comfort from the Holy Scriptures as we do, we could not omit suitable endeavors to instruct them therein; but that while we manifest by our conduct that our views in purchasing them are to advance ourselves, and while our buying captives taken in war animates those parties to push on the war, and increase desolation amongst them, to say they live unhappily in Africa is far from being an argument in our favor. I further said, the present circumstances of these provinces to me appear difficult; the slaves look like a burdensome stone to such as burden themselves with them; and that if the white people retain a resolution to prefer their outward prospects of gain to all other considerations, and do not act conscientiously toward them as fellow-creatures, I believe that burden will grow heavier and heavier, until times change in a way disagreeable to us. The person appeared very serious, and owned that in considering their condition and the manner of their treatment in these provinces he had sometimes thought it might be just in the Almighty so to order it.

Having travelled through Maryland, we came amongst Friends at Cedar Creek in Virginia, on the 12th; and the next day rode, in company with several of them, a day's journey to Camp Creek. As I was riding along in the morning, my mind was deeply affected in a sense I had of the need of Divine aid to support me in the various difficulties which attended me, and in uncommon distress of mind I cried in secret to the Most High, "O Lord be merciful, I beseech thee, to thy poor afflicted creature!" After some time, I felt inward relief, and, soon after, a Friend in company began to talk in support of the slave-trade, and said the negroes were understood to be the offspring of Cain, their blackness being the mark which God set upon him after he murdered Abel his brother; that it was the design of Providence they should be slaves, as a condition proper to the race of so wicked a man as Cain was. Then another spake in support of what had been said. To all which I replied in substance as follows: that

Noah and his family were all who survived the flood, according to Scripture; and as Noah was of Seth's race, the family of Cain was wholly destroyed. One of them said that after the flood Ham went to the land of Nod and took a wife; that Nod was a land far distant, inhabited by Cain's race, and that the flood did not reach it; and as Ham was sentenced to be a servant of servants to his brethren, these two families, being thus joined, were undoubtedly fit only for slaves. I replied, the flood was a judgment upon the world for their abominations, and it was granted that Cain's stock was the most wicked, and therefore unreasonable to suppose that they were spared. As to Ham's going to the land of Nod for a wife, no time being fixed, Nod might be inhabited by some of Noah's family before Ham married a second time; moreover the text saith "That all flesh died that moved upon the earth." (Gen. vii. 21.) I further reminded them how the prophets repeatedly declare "that the son shall not suffer for the iniquity of the father, but every one be answerable for his own sins." I was troubled to perceive the darkness of their imaginations, and in some pressure of spirit said, "The love of ease and gain are the motives in general of keeping slaves, and men are wont to take hold of weak arguments to support a cause which is unreasonable. I have no interest on either side, save only the interest which I desire to have in the truth. I believe liberty is their right, and as I see they are not only deprived of it, but treated in other respects with inhumanity in many places, I believe He who is a refuge for the oppressed will, in his own time, plead their cause, and happy will it be for such as walk in uprightness before him." And thus our conversation ended.

Fourteenth of fifth month.—I was this day at Camp Creek Monthly Meeting, and then rode to the mountains up James River, and had a meeting at a Friend's house, in both which I felt sorrow of heart, and my tears were poured out before the Lord, who was pleased to afford a degree of strength by which way was opened to clear my mind amongst Friends in those places. From thence I went to Fork Creek, and so to Cedar Creek again, at which place I now had a meeting. Here I found a tender seed, and as I was preserved in the ministry to keep low with the truth, the same truth in their hearts answered it, that it was a time of mutual refreshment from the presence of the Lord. I lodged at James Standley's, father of William Standley, one of the young men who suffered imprisonment at Winchester last summer on account of their testimony against fighting, and I had some satisfactory conversation with him concerning it. Hence I went to the Swamp Meeting, and to Wayanoke Meeting, and then crossed James River, and lodged near Burleigh. From the time of my entering Maryland I have been much under sorrow, which of late so increased upon me that my mind was almost overwhelmed, and I may say with the Psalmist, "In my distress I called upon the Lord, and cried to my God," who, in infinite goodness, looked upon my affliction, and in my private retirement sent the Comforter for my relief, for which I humbly bless His holy name.

The sense I had of the state of the churches brought a weight of distress upon me. The gold to me appeared dim, and the fine gold changed, and though this is the case too generally, yet the sense of it in these parts hath in a particular manner borne heavy upon me. It appeared to me that through the prevailing of the spirit of this world the minds of many were brought to an inward desolation, and instead of the spirit of meekness, gentleness, and heavenly wisdom, which are the necessary companions of the true sheep of Christ, a spirit of fierceness and the love of dominion too generally prevailed. From small beginnings in error great buildings by degrees are raised, and from one age to another are more and more strengthened by the general concurrence of the people; and as men obtain reputation by their profession of the truth, their virtues are mentioned as arguments in favor of general error; and those of less note, to justify themselves, say, such and such good men did the like. By what other steps could the people of Judah arise to that height in wickedness as to give just ground for the Prophet Isaiah to declare, in the name of the Lord, "that none calleth for justice, nor any pleadeth for truth" (Isa. lix. 4), or for the Almighty to call upon the great city of Jerusalem just before the Babylonish captivity, "If ye can find a man, if there be any who executeth judgment, that seeketh the truth, and I will pardon it"? (Jer. v. 1.)

The prospect of a way being open to the same degeneracy, in some parts of this newly settled land of America, in respect to our conduct towards the negroes, hath deeply bowed my mind in this journey, and though briefly to relate how these people are treated is no agree-able work yet, after often reading over the notes I made as I trav-elled, I find my mind engaged to preserve them. Many of the white people in those provinces take little or no care of negro marriages; and when negroes marry after their own way, some make so little account of those marriages that with views of outward interest they often part men from their wives by selling them far asunder, which is common when estates are sold by executors at vendue. Many whose labor is heavy being followed at their business in the field by a man with a whip, hired for that purpose, have in common little else allowed but one peck of Indian corn and some salt, for one week, with a few potatoes; the potatoes they commonly raise by their labor on the first day of the week. The correction ensuing on their disobe-dience to overseers, or slothfulness in business, is often very severe, and sometimes desperate.

Men and women have many times scarcely clothes sufficient to hide their nakedness, and boys and girls ten and twelve years old are often quite naked amongst their master's children. Some of our Society, and some of the society called Newlights, use some endeav-ors to instruct those they have in reading; but in common this is not only neglected, but disapproved. These are the people by whose labor the other inhabitants are in a great measure supported, and many of them in the luxuries of life. These are the people who have made no agreement to serve us, and who have not forfeited their liberty that we know of. These are the souls for whom Christ died, and for our conduct towards them we must answer before Him who is no respecter of persons. They who know the only true God, and Jesus Christ whom he hath sent, and are thus acquainted with the merciful, benevolent, gospel spirit, will therein perceive that the in-dignation of God is kindled against oppression and cruelty, and in beholding the great distress of so numerous a people will find cause for mourning.

From my lodgings I went to Burleigh Meeting, where I felt my mind drawn in a quiet, resigned state. After a long silence I felt an engagement to stand up, and through the powerful operation of Divine love we were favored with an edifying meeting. The next meeting we had was at Black-Water, and from thence went to the

Yearly Meeting at the Western Branch. When business began, some queries were introduced by some of their members for consideration, and, if approved, they were to be answered hereafter by their respective Monthly Meetings. They were the Pennsylvania queries, which had been examined by a committee of Virginia Yearly Meeting appointed the last year, who made some alterations in them, one of which alterations was made in favor of a custom which troubled me. The query was, "Are there any concerned in the importation of negroes, or in buying them after imported?" which was thus altered, "Are there any concerned in the importation of negroes, or buying them to trade in?" As one query admitted with unanimity was, "Are any concerned in buying or vending goods unlawfully imported, or prize goods?" I found my mind engaged to say that as we profess the truth, and were there assembled to support the testimony of it, it was necessary for us to dwell deep and act in that wisdom which is pure, or otherwise we could not prosper. I then mentioned their alteration, and referring to the last-mentioned query, added, that as purchasing any merchandise taken by the sword was always allowed to be inconsistent with our principles, so negroes being captives of war, or taken by stealth, it was inconsistent with our testimony to buy them; and their being our fellow-creatures, and sold as slaves, added greatly to the iniquity. Friends appeared attentive to what was said; some expressed a care and concern about their negroes; none made any objection, by way of reply to what I said, but the query was admitted as they had altered it.

As some of their members have heretofore traded in negroes, as in other merchandise, this query being admitted will be one step further than they have hitherto gone, and I did not see it my duty to press for an alteration, but felt easy to leave it all to Him who alone is able to turn the hearts of the mighty, and make way for the spreading of truth on the earth, by means agreeable to his infinite wisdom. In regard to those they already had, I felt my mind engaged to labor with them, and said that as we believe the Scriptures were given forth by holy men, as they were moved by the Holy Ghost, and many of us know by experience that they are often helpful and comfortable, and believe ourselves bound in duty to teach our children to read them; I believed that if we were divested of all selfish views, the same good spirit that gave them forth would engage us to teach the negroes to read, that they might have the benefit of them. Some present manifested a concern to take more care in the education of their negroes.

Twenty-ninth fifth month.—At the house where I lodged was a meeting of ministers and elders. I found an engagement to speak freely and plainly to them concerning their slaves; mentioning how they as the first rank in the society, whose conduct in that case was much noticed by others, were under the stronger obligations to look carefully to themselves. Expressing how needful it was for them in that situation to be thoroughly divested of all selfish views; that, living in the pure truth, and acting conscientiously towards those people in their education and otherwise, they might be instrumental in helping forward a work so exceedingly necessary, and so much neglected amongst them. At the twelfth hour the meeting of worship began, which was a solid meeting.

The next day, about the tenth hour, Friends met to finish their business, and then the meeting for worship ensued, which to me was a laborious time; but through the goodness of the Lord, truth, I believed, gained some ground, and it was a strengthening opportunity to the honest-hearted.

About this time I wrote an epistle to Friends in the back settlements of North Carolina, as follows:—

To Friends at their Monthly Meeting at New Garden and Cane Creek, in North Carolina:—

Dear Friends,—It having pleased the Lord to draw me forth on a visit to some parts of Virginia and Carolina, you have often been in my mind; and though my way is not clear to come in person to visit you, yet I feel it in my heart to communicate a few things, as they arise in the love of truth. First, my dear friends, dwell in humility; and take heed that no views of outward gain get too deep hold of you, that so your eyes being single to the Lord, you may be preserved in the way of safety. Where people let loose their minds after the love of outward things, and are more engaged in pursuing the profits and seeking the friendships of this world than to be inwardly acquainted with the way of true peace, they walk in a vain shadow, while the true comfort of life is wanting. Their examples are often hurtful to others; and their treasures thus collected do many times prove dangerous snares to their children.

But where people are sincerely devoted to follow Christ, and dwell under the influence of his Holy Spirit, their stability and firmness, through a Divine blessing, is at times like dew on the tender plants round about them, and the weightiness of their spirits secretly works on the minds of others. In this condition, through the spreading influence of Divine love, they feel a care over the flock, and way is opened for maintaining good order in the Society. And though we may meet with opposition from another spirit, yet, as there is a dwelling in meekness, feeling our spirits subject, and moving only in the gentle, peaceable wisdom, the inward reward of quietness will be greater than all our difficulties. Where the pure life is kept to, and meetings of discipline are held in the authority of it, we find by experience that they are comfortable, and tend to the health of the body.

While I write, the youth come fresh in my way. Dear young people, choose God for your portion; love his truth, and be not ashamed of it; choose for your company such as serve him in uprightness; and shun as most dangerous the conversation of those whose lives are of an ill savor; for by frequenting such company some hopeful young people have come to great loss, and been drawn from less evils to greater, to their utter ruin. In the bloom of youth no ornament is so lovely as that of virtue, nor any enjoyments equal to those which we partake of in fully resigning ourselves to the Divine will. These enjoyments add sweetness to all other comforts, and give true satisfaction in company and conversation, where people are mutually acquainted with it; and as your minds are thus seasoned with the truth, you will find strength to abide steadfast to the testimony of it, and be prepared for services in the church.

And now, dear friends and brethren, as you are improving a wilderness, and may be numbered amongst the first planters in one part of a province, I beseech you, in the love of Jesus Christ, wisely to consider the force of your examples, and think how much your successors may be thereby affected. It is a help in a country, yea, and a great favor and blessing, when customs first settled are agreeable to sound wisdom; but when they are otherwise the effect of them is grievous; and children feel themselves encompassed with difficulties prepared for them by their predecessors.

As moderate care and exercise, under the direction of true wisdom, are useful both to mind and body, so by these means in general the real wants of life are easily supplied, our gracious Father having so proportioned one to the other that keeping in the medium we may pass on quietly. Where slaves are purchased to do our labor numerous difficulties attend it. To rational creatures bondage is uneasy, and frequently occasions sourness and discontent in them; which affects the family and such as claim the mastery over them. Thus people and their children are many times encompassed with vexations, which arise from their applying to wrong methods to get a living.

I have been informed that there is a large number of Friends in your parts who have no slaves; and in tender and most affectionate love I beseech you to keep clear from purchasing any. Look, my dear friends, to Divine Providence, and follow in simplicity that exercise of body, that plainness and frugality, which true wisdom leads to; so may you be preserved from those dangers which attend such as are aiming at outward ease and greatness.

Treasures, though small, attained on a true principle of virtue, are sweet; and while we walk in the light of the Lord there is true comfort and satisfaction in the possession; neither the murmurs of an oppressed people, nor a throbbing, uneasy conscience, nor anxious thoughts about the events of things, hinder the enjoyment of them.

When we look towards the end of life, and think on the division of our substance among our successors, if we know that it was collected in the fear of the Lord, in honesty, in equity, and in uprightness of heart before him, we may consider it as his gift to us, and with a single eye to his blessing, bestow it on those we leave behind us. Such is the happiness of the plain ways of true virtue. "The work of righteousness shall be peace; and the effect of righteousness, quietness and assurance forever." (Isa. xxxii. 17.)

Dwell here, my dear friends; and then in remote and solitary deserts you may find true peace and satisfaction. If the Lord be our

God, in truth and reality, there is safety for us: for he is a stronghold in the day of trouble, and knoweth them that trust in him.

ISLE OF WIGHT COUNTY, in Virginia,
20th of the 5th month, 1757.

From the Yearly Meeting in Virginia I went to Carolina, and on the first of sixth month was at Wells Monthly Meeting, where the spring of the gospel ministry was opened, and the love of Jesus Christ experienced among us; to his name be the praise.

Here my brother joined with some Friends from New Garden who were going homeward; and I went next to Simons Creek Monthly Meeting, where I was silent during the meeting for worship. When business came on, my mind was exercised concerning the poor slaves, but I did not feel my way clear to speak. In this condition I was bowed in spirit before the Lord, and with tears and inward supplication besought him so to open my understanding that I might know his will concerning me; and, at length, my mind was settled in silence. Near the end of their business a member of their meeting expressed a concern that had some time lain upon him, on account of Friends so much neglecting their duty in the education of their slaves, and proposed having meetings sometimes appointed for them on a weekday, to be attended only by some Friends to be named in their Monthly Meetings. Many present appeared to unite with the proposal. One said he had often wondered that they, being our fellow-creatures, and capable of religious understanding, had been so exceedingly neglected; another expressed the like concern, and appeared zealous that in future it might be more closely considered. At length a minute was made, and the further consideration of it referred to their next Monthly Meeting. The Friend who made this proposal hath negroes; he told me that he was at New Garden, about two hundred and fifty miles from home, and came back alone; that in this solitary journey this exercise, in regard to the education of their negroes, was from time to time renewed in his mind. A Friend of some note in Virginia, who hath slaves, told me that he being far from home on a lonesome journey had many serious thoughts about them; and his mind was so impressed therewith that he believed he saw a time coming when Divine Providence would alter the circumstance of these people, respecting their condition as slaves.

From hence I went to a meeting at Newbegun Creek, and sat a considerable time in much weakness; then I felt truth open the way to speak a little in much plainness and simplicity, till at length, through the increase of Divine love amongst us, we had a seasoning opportunity. This was also the case at the head of Little River, where we had a crowded meeting on a first-day. I went thence to the Old Neck, where I was led into a careful searching out of the secret workings of the mystery of iniquity, which, under a cover of religion exalts itself against that pure spirit which leads in the way of meekness and self-denial. Pineywoods was the last meeting I was at in Carolina; it was large, and my heart being deeply engaged, I was drawn forth into a fervent labor amongst them.

When I was at Newbegun Creek a Friend was there who labored for his living, having no negroes, and who had been a minister many years. He came to me the next day, and as we rode together, he signified that he wanted to talk with me concerning a difficulty he had been under, which he related nearly as follows: That as moneys had of late years been raised by a tax to carry on the wars, he had a scruple in his mind in regard to paying it, and chose rather to suffer restraint of his goods; but as he was the only person who refused it in those parts, and knew not that any one else was in the like circumstances, he signified that it had been a heavy trial to him, especially as some of his brethren had been uneasy with his conduct in that case. He added, that from a sympathy he felt with me yesterday in meeting, he found freedom thus to open the matter in the way of querying concerning Friends in our parts; I told him the state of Friends amongst us as well as I was able, and also that I had for some time been under the like scruple. I believed him to be one who was concerned to walk uprightly before the Lord, and esteemed it my duty to preserve this note concerning him, Samuel Newby.

From hence I went back into Virginia, and had a meeting near James Cowpland's; it was a time of inward suffering, but through the goodness of the Lord I was made content; at another meeting, through the renewings of pure love, we had a very comfortable season.

Travelling up and down of late, I have had renewed evidences that to be faithful to the Lord, and content with his will concerning me, is a most necessary and useful lesson for me to be learning; looking less at the effects of my labor than at the pure motion and reality of the concern, as it arises from heavenly love. In the Lord Jehovah is everlasting strength; and as the mind, by humble resignation, is united to Him, and we utter words from an inward knowledge that they arise from the heavenly spring, though our way may be difficult, and it may require close attention to keep in it, and though the matter in which we may be led may tend to our own abasement; yet, if we continue in patience and meekness, heavenly peace will be the reward of our labors.

I attended Curles Meeting, which, though small, was reviving to the honest-hearted. Afterwards I went to Black Creek and Caroline Meetings, from whence, accompanied by William Standley before mentioned, I rode to Goose Creek, being much through the woods, and about one hundred miles. We lodged the first night at a public-house; the second in the woods; and the next day we reached a Friend's house at Goose Creek. In the woods we were under some disadvantage, having no fire-works nor bells for our horses, but we stopped a little before night and let them feed on the wild grass, which was plentiful, in the mean time cutting with our knives a store against night. We then secured our horses, and gathering some bushes under an oak we lay down; but the mosquitoes being numerous and the ground damp I slept but little. Thus lying in the wilderness, and looking at the stars, I was led to contemplate on the condition of our first parents when they were sent forth from the garden; how the Almighty, though they had been disobedient, continued to be a father to them, and showed them what tended to their felicity as intelligent creatures, and was acceptable to him. To provide things relative to our outward living, in the way of true wisdom, is good, and the gift of improving in things useful is a good gift, and comes from the Father of Lights. Many have had this gift; and from age to age there have been improvements of this kind made in the world. But some, not keeping to the pure gift, have in the creaturely cunning and self-exaltation sought out many inventions. As the first motive to these inventions of men, as distinct from that uprightness in which man was created, was evil, so the effects have been and are evil. It is, therefore, as necessary for us at this day constantly to attend on the heavenly gift, to be qualified to use rightly the good things in this life, amidst great improvements, as it was for our first parents when they were without any improvements, without any friend or father but God only.

I was at a meeting at Goose Creek, and next at a Monthly Meeting at Fairfax, where, through the gracious dealing of the Almighty with us, his power prevailed over many hearts. From thence I went to Monoquacy and Pipe Creek in Maryland; at both places I had cause humbly to adore Him who had supported me through many exercises, and by whose help I was enabled to reach the true witness in the hearts of others. There were some hopeful young people in those parts. I had meetings afterwards at John Everit's, in Monalen, and at Huntingdon, and I was made humbly thankful to the Lord, who opened my heart amongst the people in these new settlements, so that it was a time of encouragement to the honest-minded.

At Monalen a Friend gave me some account of a religious society among the Dutch called Mennonists, and amongst other things related a passage in substance as follows: One of the Mennonists having acquaintance with a man of another society at a considerable distance, and being with his wagon on business near the house of his said acquaintance, and night coming on, he had thoughts of putting up with him, but passing by his fields, and observing the distressed appearance of his slaves, he kindled a fire in the woods hard by, and lay there that night. His said acquaintance hearing where he lodged, and afterward meeting the Mennonist, told him of it, adding he should have been heartily welcome at his house, and from their acquaintance in former time wondered at his conduct in that case. The Mennonist replied, "Ever since I lodged by thy field I have wanted an opportunity to speak with thee. I had intended to come to thy house for entertainment, but seeing thy slaves at their work, and observing the manner of their dress, I had no liking to come to partake with thee." He then admonished him to use them with more humanity, and added, "As I lay by the fire that night, I thought that as I was a man of substance thou wouldst have received me freely; but if I had been as poor as one of thy slaves, and had no power to help myself, I should have received from thy hand no kinder usage than they."

In this journey I was out about two months, and travelled about eleven hundred and fifty miles. I returned home under an humbling sense of the gracious dealings of the Lord with me, in preserving me through many trials and afflictions.

CHAPTER V

1757, 1758

Considerations on the Payment of a Tax laid for Carrying on the War against the Indians—Meetings of the Committee of the Yearly Meeting at Philadelphia—Some Notes on Thomas à Kempis and John Huss—The present Circumstances of Friends in Pennsylvania and New Jersey very Different from those of our Predecessors—The Drafting of the Militia in New Jersey to serve in the Army, with some Observations on the State of the Members of our Society at that time—Visit to Friends in Pennsylvania, accompanied by Benjamin Jones—Proceedings at the Monthly, Quarterly, and Yearly Meetings in Philadelphia, respecting those who keep Slaves.

A FEW years past, money being made current in our province for carrying on wars, and to be called in again by taxes laid on the inhabitants, my mind was often affected with the thoughts of paying such taxes; and I believe it right for me to preserve a memorandum concerning it. I was told that Friends in England frequently paid taxes, when the money was applied to such purposes. I had conversation with several noted Friends on the subject, who all favored the payment of such taxes; some of them I preferred before myself, and this made me easier for a time; yet there was in the depth of my mind a scruple which I never could get over; and at certain times I was greatly distressed on that account.

I believed that there were some upright-hearted men who paid such taxes, yet could not see that their example was a sufficient reason for me to do so, while I believe that the spirit of truth required of me, as an individual, to suffer patiently the distress of goods, rather than pay actively.

To refuse the active payment of a tax which our Society generally paid was exceedingly disagreeable; but to do a thing contrary to my conscience appeared yet more dreadful. When this exercise came upon me, I knew of none under the like difficulty; and in my dis-

217

tress I besought the Lord to enable me to give up all that so I might follow him wheresoever he was pleased to lead me. Under this exercise I went to our Yearly Meeting at Philadelphia in the year 1755; at which a committee was appointed of some from each Quarterly Meeting, to correspond with the meeting for sufferers in London; and another to visit our Monthly and Quarterly Meetings. After their appointment, before the last adjournment of the meeting, it was agreed that these two committees should meet together in Friends' school-house in the city, to consider some things in which the cause of truth was concerned. They accordingly had a weighty conference in the fear of the Lord; at which time I perceived there were many Friends under a scruple like that before mentioned.[1]

As scrupling to pay a tax on account of the application hath seldom been heard of heretofore, even amongst men of integrity, who have steadily borne their testimony against outward wars in their time, I may therefore note some things which have occurred to my mind, as I have been inwardly exercised on that account. From the steady opposition which faithful Friends in early times made to wrong things then approved, they were hated and persecuted by men living in the spirit of this world, and suffering with firmness, they were made a blessing to the church, and the work prospered. It equally concerns men in every age to take heed to their own spirits; and in comparing their situation with ours, to me it appears that there was less danger of their being infected with the spirit of this world, in paying such taxes, than is the case with us now. They had little or no share in civil government, and many of them declared that they were, through the power of God, separated from the spirit in which wars were, and being afflicted by the rulers on account of their testimony, there was less likelihood of their uniting in spirit with them in things inconsistent with the purity of truth. We, from the first settlement of this land, have known little or no troubles of that sort. The profession of our predecessors was for a time accounted reproachful, but at length their uprightness being understood by the rulers, and their innocent sufferings moving them, our way of worship was tolerated, and many of our members in these

[1] Christians refused to pay taxes to support heathen temples. See Cave's Primitive Christianity, Part III., p. 327.

colonies became active in civil government. Being thus tried with favor and prosperity, this world appeared inviting; our minds have been turned to the improvement of our country, to merchandise and the sciences, amongst which are many things useful, if followed in pure wisdom; but in our present condition I believe it will not be denied that a carnal mind is gaining upon us. Some of our members, who are officers in civil government, are in one case or other, called upon in their respective stations to assist in things relative to the wars; but being in doubt whether to act or to crave to be excused from their office, if they see their brethren united in the payment of a tax to carry on the said wars, may think their case not much different, and so might quench the tender movings of the Holy Spirit in their minds. Thus, by small degrees, we might approach so near to fighting that the distinction would be little else than the name of a peaceable people.

It requires great self-denial and resignation of ourselves to God, to attain that state wherein we can freely cease from fighting when wrongfully invaded, if, by our fighting, there were a probability of overcoming the invaders. Whoever rightly attains to it does in some degree feel that spirit in which our Redeemer gave his life for us; and through Divine goodness many of our predecessors, and many now living, have learned this blessed lesson; but many others, having their religion chiefly by education, and not being enough acquainted with that cross which crucifies to the world, do manifest a temper distinguishable from that of an entire trust in God. In calmly considering these things, it hath not appeared strange to me that an exercise hath now fallen upon some, which, with respect to the outward means, is different from what was known to many of those who went before us.

Some time after the Yearly Meeting, the said committees met at Philadelphia, and, by adjournments, continued sitting several days. The calamities of war were now increasing; the frontier inhabitants of Pennsylvania were frequently surprised; some were slain, and many taken captive by the Indians; and while these committees sat, the corpse of one so slain was brought in a wagon, and taken through the streets of the city in his bloody garments, to alarm the people and rouse them to war.

Friends thus met were not all of one mind in relation to the tax, which, to those who scrupled it, made the way more difficult. To refuse an active payment at such a time might be construed into an act of disloyalty, and appeared likely to displease the rulers, not only here but in England; still there was a scruple so fixed on the minds of many Friends that nothing moved it. It was a conference the most weighty that ever I was at, and the hearts of many were bowed in reverence before the Most High. Some Friends of the said committees who appeared easy to pay the tax, after several adjournments, withdrew; others of them continued till the last. At length an epistle of tender love and caution to Friends in Pennsylvania was drawn up, and being read several times and corrected, was signed by such as were free to sign it, and afterward sent to the Monthly and Quarterly Meetings.

Ninth of eight month, 1757.—Orders came at night to the military officers in our county (Burlington), directing them to draft the militia, and prepare a number of men to go off as soldiers, to the relief of the English at Fort William Henry, in New York government; a few days after which, there was a general review of the militia at Mount Holly, and a number of men were chosen and sent off under some officers. Shortly after, there came orders to draft three times as many, who were to hold themselves in readiness to march when fresh orders came. On the 17th there was a meeting of the military officers at Mount Holly, who agreed on draft; orders were sent to the men so chosen to meet their respective captains at set times and places, those in our township to meet at Mount Holly, amongst whom were a considerable number of our Society. My mind being affected herewith, I had fresh opportunity to see and consider the advantage of living in the real substance of religion, where practice doth harmonize with principle. Amongst the officers are men of understanding, who have some regard to sincerity where they see it; and when such in the execution of their office have men to deal with whom they believe to be upright-hearted, it is a painful task to put them to trouble on account of scruples of conscience, and they will be likely to avoid it as much as easily may be. But where men profess to be so meek and heavenly-minded, and to have their trust so firmly settled in God that they cannot join in wars, and yet by their spirit and conduct in common life manifest a contrary disposition, their difficulties are great at such a time.

When officers who are anxiously endeavoring to get troops to answer the demands of their superiors see men who are insincere pretend scruple of conscience in hopes of being excused from a dangerous employment, it is likely they will be roughly handled. In this time of commotion some of our young men left these parts and tarried abroad till it was over; some came, and proposed to go as soldiers; others appeared to have a real tender scruple in their minds against joining in wars, and were much humbled under the apprehension of a trial so near. I had conversation with several of them to my satisfaction. When the captain came to town, some of the last-mentioned went and told him in substance as follows: That they could not bear arms for conscience' sake; nor could they hire any to go in their places, being resigned as to the event. At length the captain acquainted them all that they might return home for the present, but he required them to provide themselves as soldiers, and be in readiness to march when called upon. This was such a time as I had not seen before; and yet I may say, with thankfulness to the Lord, that I believed the trial was intended for our good; and I was favored with resignation to him. The French army having taken the fort they were besieging, destroyed it and went away; the company of men who were first drafted, after some days' march, had orders to return home, and those on the second draft were no more called upon on that occasion.

Fourth of fourth month, 1758.—Orders came to some officers in Mount Holly to prepare quarters for a short time for about one hundred soldiers. An officer and two other men, all inhabitants of our town came to my house. The officer told me that he came to desire me to provide lodging and entertainment for two soldiers, and that six shillings a week per man would be allowed as pay for it. The case being new and unexpected I made no answer suddenly, but sat a time silent, my mind being inward. I was fully convinced that the proceedings in wars are inconsistent with the purity of the Christian religion; and to be hired to entertain men, who were then under pay as soldiers, was a difficulty with me. I expected they had legal authority for what they did; and after a short time I said to the officer, if the men are sent here for entertainment I believe I shall not refuse to admit them into my house, but the nature of the case is such that I expect I cannot keep them on hire; one of the men intimated that he thought I might do it consistently with my religious principles. To which I made no reply, believing silence at that time best for me. Though they spake of two, there came only one, who tarried at my house about two weeks, and behaved himself civilly. When the officer came to pay me, I told him I could not take pay, having admitted him into my house in a passive obedience to authority. I was on horseback when he spake to me, and as I turned from him, he said he was obliged to me; to which I said nothing; but, thinking on the expression, I grew uneasy; and afterwards, being near where he lived, I went and told him on what grounds I refused taking pay for keeping the soldier.

I have been informed that Thomas à Kempis lived and died in the profession of the Roman Catholic religion; and, in reading his writings, I have believed him to be a man of a true Christian spirit, as fully so as many who died martyrs because they could not join with some superstitions in that church. All true Christians are of the same spirit, but their gifts are diverse, Jesus Christ appointing to each one his peculiar office, agreeably to his infinite wisdom.

John Huss contended against the errors which had crept into the church, in opposition to the Council of Constance, which the historian reports to have consisted of some thousand persons. He modestly vindicated the cause which he believed was right; and though his language and conduct towards his judges appear to have been respectful, yet he never could be moved from the principles settled in his mind. To use his own words: "This I most humbly require and desire of you all, even for his sake who is the God of us all, that I be not compelled to the thing which my conscience doth repugn or strive against." And again, in his answer to the Emperor: "I refuse nothing, most noble Emperor, whatsoever the council shall decree or determine upon me, only this one thing I except, that I do not offend God and my conscience."[2] At length, rather than act contrary to that which he believed the Lord required of him, he chose to suffer death by fire. Thomas à Kempis, without disputing against the

[2] Fox's Acts and Monuments, p. 233.

articles then generally agreed to, appears to have labored, by a pious example as well as by preaching and writing, to promote virtue and the inward spiritual religion; and I believe they were both sincere-hearted followers of Christ. True charity is an excellent virtue; and sincerely to labor for their good, whose belief in all points doth not agree with ours, is a happy state.

Near the beginning of the year 1758, I went one evening, in company with a friend, to visit a sick person; and before our return we were told of a woman living near, who had for several days been disconsolate, occasioned by a dream, wherein death, and the judgments of the Almighty after death, were represented to her mind in a moving manner. Her sadness on that account being worn off, the friend with whom I was in company went to see her, and had some religious conversation with her and her husband. With this visit they were somewhat affected, and the man, with many tears, expressed his satisfaction. In a short time after the poor man, being on the river in a storm of wind, was with one more drowned.

Eighth month, 1758.—Having had drawings in my mind to be at the Quarterly Meeting in Chester County, and at some meetings in the county of Philadelphia, I went first to said Quarterly Meeting, which was large. Several weighty matters came under consideration and debate, and the Lord was pleased to qualify some of his servants with strength and firmness to bear the burden of the day. Though I said but little, my mind was deeply exercised; and, under a sense of God's love, in the anointing and fitting of some young men for his work, I was comforted, and my heart was tendered before him. From hence I went to the Youth's Meeting at Darby, where my beloved friend and brother Benjamin Jones met me by appointment before I left home, to join in the visit. We were at Radnor, Merion, Richland, North Wales, Plymouth, and Abington meetings, and had cause to bow in reverence before the Lord, our gracious God, by whose help way was opened for us from day to day. I was out about two weeks, and rode about two hundred miles.

The Monthly Meeting of Philadephia having been under a concern on account of some Friends who this summer (1758) had bought negro slaves, proposed to their Quarterly Meeting to have the minute reconsidered in the Yearly Meeting, which was made last on that subject, and the said Quarterly Meeting appointed a committee to consider it, and to report to their next. This committee having met once and adjourned, and I, going to Philadelphia to meet a committee of the Yearly Meeting, was in town the evening on which the Quarterly Meeting's committee met the second time, and finding an inclination to sit with them, I, with some others, was admitted, and Friends had a weighty conference on the subject. Soon after their next Quarterly meeting I heard that the case was coming to our Yearly Meeting. This brought a weighty exercise upon me, and under a sense of my own infirmities, and the great danger I felt of turning aside from perfect purity, my mind was often drawn to retire alone, and put up my prayers to the Lord that he would be graciously pleased to strengthen me; that setting aside all views of self-interest and the friendship of this world, I might stand fully resigned to his holy will.

In this Yearly Meeting several weighty matters were considered, and toward the last that in relation to dealing with persons who purchase slaves. During the several sittings of the said meeting, my mind was frequently covered with inward prayer, and I could say with David, "that tears were my meat day and night." The case of slave-keeping lay heavy upon me, nor did I find any engagement to speak directly to any other matter before the meeting. Now when this case was opened several faithful Friends spake weightily thereto, with which I was comforted; and feeling a concern to cast in my mite, I said in substance as follows:—

"In the difficulties attending us in this life nothing is more precious than the mind of truth inwardly manifested; and it is my earnest desire that in this weighty matter we may be so truly humbled as to be favored with a clear understanding of the mind of truth, and follow it; this would be of more advantage to the Society than any medium not in the clearness of Divine wisdom. The case is difficult to some who have slaves, but if such set aside all self-interest, and come to be weaned from the desire of getting estates, or even from holding them together, when truth requires the contrary, I believe way will so open that they will know how to steer through those difficulties."

Many Friends appeared to be deeply bowed under the weight of the work, and manifested much firmness in their love to the cause of truth and universal righteousness on the earth. And though none did openly justify the practice of slave-keeping in general, yet some appeared concerned lest the meeting should go into such measures as might give uneasiness to many brethren, alleging that if Friends patiently continued under the exercise the Lord in his time might open a way for the deliverance of these people. Finding an engagement to speak, I said, "My mind is often led to consider the purity of the Divine Being, and the justice of his judgments; and herein my soul is covered with awfulness. I cannot omit to hint of some cases where people have not been treated with the purity of justice, and the event hath been lamentable. Many slaves on this continent are oppressed, and their cries have reached the ears of the Most High. Such are the purity and certainty of his judgments, that he cannot be partial in our favor. In infinite love and goodness he hath opened our understanding from one time to another concerning our duty towards this people, and it is not a time for delay. Should we now be sensible of what he requires of us, and through a respect to the private interest of some persons, or through a regard to some friendships which do not stand on an immutable foundation, neglect to do our duty in firmness and constancy, still waiting for some extraordinary means to bring about their deliverance, God may by terrible things in righteousness answer us in this matter."

Many faithful brethren labored with great firmness, and the love of truth in a good degree prevailed. Several who had negroes expressed their desire that a rule might be made to deal with such Friends as offenders who bought slaves in future. To this it was answered that the root of this evil would never be effectually struck at until a thorough search was made in the circumstances of such Friends as kept negroes, with respect to the righteousness of their motives in keeping them, that impartial justice might be administered throughout. Several Friends expressed their desire that a visit might be made to such Friends as kept slaves, and many others said that they believed liberty was the negro's right; to which, at length, no opposition was publicly made. A minute was made more full on that subject than any heretofore; and the names of several Friends entered who were free to join in a visit to such as kept slaves.

CHAPTER VI

1758, 1759

Visit to the Quarterly Meetings in Chester County—Joins Daniel Stanton and John Scarborough in a Visit to such as kept Slaves there—Some Observations on the Conduct which those should maintain who speak in Meetings for Discipline—More Visits to such as kept Slaves, and to Friends near Salem—Account of the Yearly Meeting in the Year 1759, and of the increasing Concern in Divers Provinces to Labor against Buying and Keeping Slaves—The Yearly Meeting Epistle—Thoughts on the Small-pox spreading, and on Inoculation.

ELEVENTH of eleventh month, 1758.—This day I set out for Concord; the Quarterly Meeting heretofore held there was now, by reason of a great increase of members, divided into two by the agreement of Friends at our last Yearly Meeting. Here I met with our beloved friends Samuel Spavold and Mary Kirby from England, and with Joseph White from Buck's County; the latter had taken leave of his family in order to go on a religious visit to Friends in England, and, through Divine goodness, we were favored with a strengthening opportunity together.

After this meeting I joined with my friends, Daniel Stanton and John Scarborough, in visiting Friends who had slaves. At night we had a family meeting at William Trimble's, many young people being there; and it was a precious, reviving opportunity. Next morning we had a comfortable sitting with a sick neighbor, and thence to the burial of the corpse of a Friend at Uwchland Meeting, at which were many people, and it was a time of Divine favor, after which we visited some who had slaves. In the evening we had a family meeting at a Friend's house, where the channel of the gospel love was opened, and my mind was comforted after a hard day's labor. The next day we were at Goshen Monthly Meeting, and on the 18th attended the Quarterly Meeting at London Grove, it being first held at that place. Here we met again with all the before-mentioned Friends, and had some edifying meetings. Near the conclusion of the meeting for business, Friends were incited to constancy in supporting the testimony of truth, and reminded of the necessity which the disciples of Christ are under to attend principally to his business as he is pleased to open it to us, and to be particularly careful to have our minds redeemed from the love of wealth, and our outward affairs in as little room as may be, that no temporal concerns may entangle our affections or hinder us from diligently following the dictates of truth in laboring to promote the pure spirit of meekness and heavenly-mindedness amongst the children of men in these days of calamity and distress, wherein God is visiting our land with his just judgments.

Each of these Quarterly Meetings was large and sat near eight hours. I had occasion to consider that it is a weighty thing to speak much in large meetings for business, for except our minds are rightly prepared, and we clearly understand the case we speak to, instead of forwarding, we hinder business, and make more labor for those on whom the burden of the work is laid. If selfish views or a partial spirit have any room in our minds, we are unfit for the Lord's work; if we have a clear prospect of the business, and proper weight on our minds to speak, we should avoid useless apologies and repetitions. Where people are gathered from far, and adjourning a meeting of business is attended with great difficulty, it behoves all to be cautious how they detain a meeting, especially when they have sat six or seven hours, and have a great distance to ride home. After this meeting I rode home.

In the beginning of the twelfth month I joined, in company with my friends John Sykes and Daniel Stanton, in visiting such as had slaves. Some whose hearts were rightly exercised about them appeared to be glad of our visit, but in some places our way was more difficult. I often saw the necessity of keeping down to that root from whence our concern proceeded, and have cause, in reverent thankfulness, humbly to bow down before the Lord, who was near to me, and preserved my mind in calmness under some sharp conflicts, and begat a spirit of sympathy and tenderness in me towards some who were grievously entangled by the spirit of this world.

First month, 1759.—Having found my mind drawn to visit some of the more active members in our Society at Philadelphia, who had slaves, I met my friend John Churchman there by agreement, and we continued about a week in the city. We visited some that were sick, and some widows and their families, and the other part of our time was mostly employed in visiting such as had slaves. It was a time of deep exercise, but looking often to the Lord for his assistance, he in unspeakable kindness favored us with the influence of that spirit which crucifies to the greatness and splendor of this world, and enabling us to go through some heavy labors, in which we found peace.

Twenty-fourth of third month, 1759.—After attending our general Spring Meeting at Philadelphia I again joined with John Churchman on a visit to some who had slaves in Philadelphia, and with thankfulness to our Heavenly Father I may say that Divine love and a true sympathizing tenderness of heart prevailed at times in this service.

Having at times perceived a shyness in some Friends of considerable note towards me, I found an engagement in gospel love to pay a visit to one of them; and as I dwelt under the exercise, I felt a resignedness in my mind to go and tell him privately that I had a desire to have an opportunity with him alone; to this proposal he readily agreed, and then, in the fear of the Lord, things relating to that shyness were searched to the bottom, and we had a large conference, which, I believe was of use to both of us, and I am thankful that way was opened for it.

Fourteenth of sixth month.—Having felt drawings in my mind to visit Friends about Salem, and having the approbation of our Monthly Meeting, I attended their Quarterly Meeting, and was out seven days, and attended seven meetings; in some of them I was chiefly silent; in others, through the baptizing power of truth, my heart was enlarged in heavenly love, and I found a near fellowship with the brethren and sisters, in the manifold trials attending their Christian progress through this world.

Seventh month.—I have found an increasing concern on my mind to visit some active members in our Society who have slaves, and having no opportunity of the company of such as were named in the minutes of the Yearly Meeting, I went alone to their houses, and, in the fear of the Lord, acquainted them with the exercise I was under; and, thus, sometimes by a few words, I found myself discharged from a heavy burden. After this, our friend John Churchman coming into our province with a view to be at some meetings, and to join again in the visit to those who had slaves, I bore him company in the said visit to some active members, and found inward satisfaction.

At our Yearly Meeting this year, we had some weighty seasons, in which the power of truth was largely extended, to the strengthening of the honest-minded. As the epistles which were to be sent to the Yearly Meetings on this continent were read, I observed that in most of them, both this year and the last, it was recommended to Friends to labor against buying and keeping slaves, and in some of them the subject was closely treated upon. As this practice hath long been a heavy exercise to me, and I have often waded through mortifying labors on that account, and at times in some meetings have been almost alone therein, I was humbly bowed in thankfulness in observing the increasing concern in our religious society, and seeing how the Lord was raising up and qualifying servants for his work, not only in this respect, but for promoting the cause of truth in general.

This meeting continued near a week. For several days, in the fore part of it, my mind was drawn into a deep inward stillness, and being at times covered with the spirit of supplication, my heart was secretly poured out before the Lord. Near the conclusion of the meeting for business, way opened in the pure flowings of Divine love for me to express what lay upon me, which, as it then arose in my mind, was first to show how deep answers to deep in the hearts of the sincere and upright; though, in their different growths, they may not all have attained to the same clearness in some points relating to our testimony. And I was then led to mention the integrity and constancy of many martyrs who gave their lives for the testimony of Jesus, and yet, in some points, they held doctrines distinguishable from some which we hold, that, in all ages, where people were faithful to the light and understanding which the Most High afforded them, they found acceptance with Him, and though there may be different ways of thinking amongst us in some particulars, yet, if we mutually keep to that spirit and power which crucifies to the world, which teaches us to be content with things really needful, and to avoid all superfluities, and give up our hearts to fear and serve the Lord, true unity may still be preserved amongst us; that if those who were at times under sufferings on account of some scruples of conscience kept low and humble, and in their conduct in life manifested a spirit of true charity, it would be more likely to reach the witness in others, and be of more service in the church, than if their sufferings were attended with a contrary spirit and conduct. In this exercise I was drawn into a sympathizing tenderness with the sheep of Christ, however distinguished one from another in this world, and the like disposition appeared to spread over others in the meeting. Great is the goodness of the Lord towards his poor creatures.

An epistle went forth from this Yearly Meeting which I think good to give a place in this Journal. It is as follows.

From the Yearly Meeting held at Philadelphia, for Pennsylvania and New Jersey, from the twenty-second day of the ninth month to the twenty-eighth of the same, inclusive, 1759.

To the Quarterly and Monthly Meetings of Friends belonging to the said Yearly Meeting:—

Dearly beloved Friends and Brethren,—In an awful sense of the wisdom and goodness of the Lord our God, whose tender mercies have been continued to us in this land, we affectionately salute you, with sincere and fervent desires that we may reverently regard the dispensations of his providence, and improve under them.

The empires and kingdoms of the earth are subject to his almighty power. He is the God of the spirits of all flesh, and deals with his people agreeable to that wisdom, the depth whereof is to us unsearchable. We in these provinces may say, He hath, as a gracious and tender parent, dealt bountifully with us, even from the days of our fathers. It was he who strengthened them to labor through the difficulties attending the improvement of a wilderness, and made way for them in the hearts of the natives, so that by them they were comforted in times of want and distress. It was by the gracious influences of his Holy Spirit that they were disposed to work righteousness, and walk uprightly towards each other, and towards the natives; in life and conversation to manifest the excellency of the principles and doctrines of the Christian religion whereby they retain their esteem and friendship. Whilst they were laboring for the necessaries of life, many of them were fervently engaged to promote piety and virtue in the earth, and to educate their children in the fear of the Lord.

If we carefully consider the peaceable measures pursued in the first settlement of land, and that freedom from the desolations of wars which for a long time we enjoyed, we shall find ourselves under strong obligations to the Almighty, who, when the earth is so generally polluted with wickedness, gives us a being in a part so signally favored with tranquillity and plenty, and in which the glad tidings of the gospel of Christ are so freely published that we may justly say with the Psalmist, "What shall we render unto the Lord for all his benefits?"

Our own real good, and the good of our posterity, in some measure depends on the part we act, and it nearly concerns us to try our foundations impartially. Such are the different rewards of the just and unjust in a future state, that to attend diligently to the dictates of the spirit of Christ, to devote ourselves to his service, and to engage fervently in his cause, during our short stay in this world, is a choice well becoming a free, intelligent creature. We shall thus clearly see and consider that the dealings of God with mankind, in a national capacity, as recorded in Holy Writ, do sufficiently evidence the truth of that saying, "It is righteousness which exalteth a nation"; and though he doth not at all times suddenly execute his judgments on a sinful people in this life, yet we see in many instances that when "men follow lying vanities they forsake their own mercies"; and as a proud, selfish spirit prevails and spreads among a people, so partial judgment, oppression, discord, envy, and confusions increase, and provinces and kingdoms are made to drink the cup of adversity as a reward of their own doings. Thus the inspired prophet, reasoning with the degenerated Jews, saith, "Thine own wickedness shall correct thee, and thy backsliding shall reprove thee; know, therefore, that it is an evil thing and bitter that thou hast forsaken the Lord thy God, and that my fear is not in thee, saith the Lord God of Hosts." (Jeremiah ii. 19.)

The God of our fathers, who hath bestowed on us many benefits, furnished a table for us in the wilderness, and made the deserts and solitary places to rejoice. He doth now mercifully call upon us to serve him more faithfully. We may truly say with the Prophet, "It is his voice which crieth to the city, and men of wisdom see his name. They regard the rod, and Him who hath appointed it." People who look chiefly at things outward too little consider the original cause of the present troubles; but they who fear the Lord and think often upon his name, see and feel that a wrong spirit is spreading amongst the inhabitants of our country; that the hearts of many are waxed fat, and their ears dull of hearing; that the Most High, in his visitations to us, instead of calling, lifteth up his voice and crieth: he crieth to our country, and his voice waxeth louder and louder. In former wars between the English and other nations, since the settlement of our provinces, the calamities attending them have fallen chiefly on other places, but now of late they have reached to our borders; many of our fellow-subjects have suffered on and near our frontiers, some have been slain in battle, some killed in their houses, and some in their fields, some wounded and left in great misery, and others separated from their wives and little children, who have been carried captives among the Indians. We have seen men and women who have been witnesses of these scenes of sorrow, and, being reduced to want, have come to our houses asking relief. It is not long since that many young men in one of these provinces were drafted, in order to be taken as soldiers; some were at that time in great distress, and had occasion to consider that their lives had been too little conformable to the purity and spirituality of that religion which we profess, and found themselves too little acquainted with that inward humility, in which true fortitude to endure hardness for the truth's sake is experienced. Many parents were concerned for their children, and in that time of trial were led to consider that their care to get outward treasure for them had been greater than their care for their settlement in that religion which crucifieth to the world, and enableth to bear testimony to the peaceable government of the Messiah. These troubles are removed, and for a time we are released from them.

Let us not forget that "The Most High hath his way in the deep, in clouds, and in thick darkness"; that it is his voice which crieth to the city and to the country, and O! that these loud and awakening cries may have a proper effect upon us, that heavier chastisement may not become necessary! For though things, as to the outward, may for a short time afford a pleasing prospect, yet, while a selfish spirit, that is not subject to the cross of Christ, continueth to spread and prevail, there can be no long continuance in outward peace and tranquillity. If we desire an inheritance incorruptible, and to be at rest in that state of peace and happiness which ever continues; if we desire in this life to dwell under the favor and protection of that Almighty Being whose habitation is in holiness, whose ways are all equal, and whose anger is now kindled because of our backslidings, —let us then awfully regard these beginnings of his sore judgments, and with abasement and humiliation turn to him whom we have offended.

Contending with one equal in strength is an uneasy exercise; but if the Lord is become our enemy, if we persist in contending with him who is omnipotent, our overthrow will be unavoidable.

Do we feel an affectionate regard to posterity? and are we employed to promote their happiness? Do our minds, in things outward, look beyond our own dissolution? and are we contriving for the prosperity of our children after us? Let us then, like wise builders, lay the foundation deep, and by our constant uniform regard to an inward piety and virtue let them see that we really value it. Let us labor in the fear of the Lord, that their innocent minds, while young and tender, may be preserved from corruptions; that as they advance in age they may rightly understand their true interest, may consider the uncertainty of temporal things, and, above all, have their hope and confidence firmly settled in the blessing of that Almighty Being who inhabits eternity and preserves and supports the world.

In all our cares about worldly treasures, let us steadily bear in mind that riches possessed by children who do not truly serve God are likely to prove snares that may more grievously entangle them in that spirit of selfishness and exaltation which stands in opposition to real peace and happiness, and renders those who submit to the influence of it enemies to the cross of Christ.

To keep a watchful eye towards real objects of charity, to visit the poor in their lonesome dwelling-places, to comfort those who, through the dispensations of Divine Providence, are in strait and painful circumstances in this life, and steadily to endeavor to honor God with our substance, from a real sense of the love of Christ influencing our minds, is more likely to bring a blessing to our children, and will afford more satisfaction to a Christian favored with plenty, than an earnest desire to collect much wealth to leave behind us; for, "here we have no continuing city"; may we therefore diligently "seek one that is to come, whose builder and maker is God."

"Finally, brethren, whatsoever things are true, whatsoever things are just, whatsoever things are pure, whatsoever things are lovely, whatsoever things are of good report, if there be any virtue, if there be any praise, think on these things, and do them, and the God of peace shall be with you."

(Signed by appointment, and on behalf of said meeting.)

Twenty-eighth eleventh month.—This day I attended the Quarterly Meeting in Bucks County. In the meeting of ministers and elders my heart was enlarged in the love of Jesus Christ, and the favor of the Most High was extended to us in that and the ensuing meeting.

I had conversation at my lodging with my beloved friend Samuel Eastburn, who expressed a concern to join in a visit to some Friends in that county who had negroes, and as I had felt a drawing in my mind to the said work, I came home and put things in order. On 11th of twelfth month I went over the river, and on the next day was at Buckingham Meeting, where, through the descendings of heavenly dew, my mind was comforted and drawn into a near unity with the flock of Jesus Christ.

Entering upon this business appeared weighty, and before I left home my mind was often sad, under which exercise I felt at times the Holy Spirit which helps our infirmities, and through which my prayers were at times put up to God in private that he would be pleased to purge me from all selfishness, that I might be strengthened to discharge my duty faithfully, how hard soever to the natural part. We proceeded on the visit in a weighty frame of spirit, and went to the houses of the most active members who had negroes throughout the county. Through the goodness of the Lord my mind was preserved in resignation in times of trial, and though the work was hard to nature, yet through the strength of that love which is stronger than death, tenderness of heart was often felt amongst us in our visits, and we parted from several families with greater satisfaction than we expected.

We visited Joseph White's family, he being in England; we had also a family-sitting at the house of an elder who bore us company, and were at Makefield on a first day: at all which times my heart was truly thankful to the Lord who was graciously pleased to renew his loving-kindness to us, his poor servants, uniting us together in his work.

In the winter of this year, the small-pox being in our town, and many being inoculated, of whom a few died, some things were opened in my mind, which I wrote as follows:—

The more fully our lives are conformable to the will of God, the better it is for us; I have looked on the small-pox as a messenger from the Almighty, to be an assistant in the cause of virtue, and to incite us to consider whether we employ our time only in such things as are consistent with perfect wisdom and goodness. Building houses suitable to dwell in, for ourselves and our creatures; preparing clothing suitable for the climate and season, and food convenient, are all duties incumbent on us. And under these general heads are many branches of business in which we may venture health and life, as necessity may require.

This disease being in a house, and my business calling me to go near it, incites me to consider whether this is a real indispensable duty; whether it is not in conformity to some custom which would be better laid aside, or, whether it does not proceed from too eager a pursuit after some outward treasure. If the business before me springs not from a clear understanding and a regard to that use of things which perfect wisdom approves, to be brought to a sense of it and stopped in my pursuit is a kindness, for when I proceed to business without some evidence of duty, I have found by experience that it tends to weakness.

If I am so situated that there appears no probability of missing the infection, it tends to make me think whether my manner of life in things outward has nothing in it which may unfit my body to receive this messenger in a way the most favorable to me. Do I use food and drink in no other sort and in no other degree than was designed by Him who gave these creatures for our sustenance? Do I never abuse my body by inordinate labor, striving to accomplish some end which I have unwisely proposed? Do I use action enough in some useful employ, or do I sit too much idle while some persons who labor to support me have too great a share of it? If in any of these things I am deficient, to be incited to consider it is a favor to me. Employment is necessary in social life, and this infection, which often proves mortal, incites me to think whether these social acts of mine are real duties. If I go on a visit to the widows and fatherless, do I go purely on a principle of charity, free from any selfish views? If I go to a religious meeting it puts me on thinking whether I go in sincerity and in a clear sense of duty, or whether it is not partly in conformity to custom, or partly from a sensible delight which my animal spirits feel in the company of other people, and whether to support my reputation as a religious man has no share in it.

Do affairs relating to civil society call me near this infection? If I go, it is at the hazard of my health and life, and it becomes me to think seriously whether love to truth and righteousness is the motive of my attending; whether the manner of proceeding is altogether equitable, or whether aught of narrowness, party interest, respect to outward dignities, names, or distinctions among men, do not stain the beauty of those assemblies, and render it doubtful; in point of duty, whether a disciple of Christ ought to attend as a member united to the body or not. Whenever there are blemishes which for a series of time remain such, that which is a means of stirring us up to look attentively on these blemishes, and to labor according to our capacities, to have health and soundness restored in our country, we may justly account a kindness from our gracious Father, who appointed that means.

The care of a wise and good man for his only son is inferior to the regard of the great Parent of the universe for his creatures. He hath the command of all the powers and operations in nature, and "doth not afflict willingly, nor grieve the children of men." Chastisement is intended for instruction, and instruction being received by gentle chastisement, greater calamities are prevented. By an earthquake hundreds of houses are sometimes shaken down in a few minutes, multitudes of people perish suddenly, and many more, being crushed and bruised in the ruins of the buildings, pine away and die in great misery.

By the breaking in of enraged merciless armies, flourishing countries have been laid waste, great numbers of people have perished in a short time, and many more have been pressed with poverty and grief. By the pestilence, people have died so fast in a city, that, through fear, grief, and confusion, those in health have found great difficulty in burying the dead, even without coffins. By famine, great numbers of people in some places have been brought to the utmost distress, and have pined away from want of the necessaries of life. Thus, when the kind invitations and gentle chastisements of a gracious God have not been attended to, his sore judgments have at times been poured out upon people.

While some rules approved in civil society and conformable to human policy, so called, are distinguishable from the purity of truth and righteousness,—while many professing the truth are declining from that ardent love and heavenly-mindedness which was amongst the primitive followers of Jesus Christ, it is time for us to attend diligently to the intent of every chastisement, and to consider the most deep and inward design of them.

The Most High doth not often speak with an outward voice to our outward ears, but if we humbly meditate on his perfections, consider that he is perfect wisdom and goodness, and that to afflict his creatures to no purpose would be utterly averse to his nature, we shall hear and understand his language both in his gentle and more heavy chastisements, and shall take heed that we do not, in the wisdom of this world, endeavor to escape his hand by means too powerful for us.

Had he endowed men with understanding to prevent this disease (the small-pox) by means which had never proved hurtful nor mortal, such a discovery might be considered as the period of chastisement by this distemper, where that knowledge extended. But as life and health are his gifts, and are not to be disposed of in our own wills, to take upon us by inoculation when in health a disorder of which some die, requires great clearness of knowledge that it is our duty to do so.

CHAPTER VII

1760

FOURTH month, 1760.—Having for some time past felt a sympathy in my mind with Friends eastward, I opened my concern in our Monthly Meeting, and, obtaining a certificate, set forward on the 17th of this month, in company with my beloved friend Samuel Eastburn. We had meetings at Woodbridge, Rahway, and Plainfield, and were at their Monthly Meeting of ministers and elders in Rahway. We labored under some discouragement, but through the invisible power of truth our visit was made reviving to the lowly-minded, with whom I felt a near unity of spirit, being much reduced in my mind. We passed on and visited most of the meetings on Long Island. It was my concern from day to day to say neither more nor less than what the spirit of truth opened in me, being jealous over myself lest I should say anything to make my testimony look agreeable to that mind in people which is not in pure obedience to the cross of Christ.

The spring of the ministry was often low, and through the subjecting power of truth we were kept low with it; from place to place they whose hearts were truly concerned for the cause of Christ appeared to be comforted in our labors, and though it was in general a time of abasement of the creature, yet through his goodness who is a helper of the poor we had some truly edifying seasons both in meetings and in families where we tarried; sometimes we found strength to labor earnestly with the unfaithful, especially with those whose station in families or in the Society was such that their example had a powerful tendency to open the way for others to go aside from the purity and soundness of the blessed truth.

At Jericho, on Long Island, I wrote home as follows:—

24th of the fourth month, 1760.

DEARLY BELOVED WIFE!

We are favored with health; have been at sundry meetings in East Jersey and on this island. My mind hath been much in an inward, watchful frame since I left thee, greatly desiring that our proceedings may be singly in the will of our Heavenly Father.

As the present appearance of things is not joyous, I have been much shut up from outward cheerfulness, remembering that promise, "Then shalt thou delight thyself in the Lord"; as this from day to day has been revived in my memory, I have considered that his internal presence in our minds is a delight of all others the most pure, and that the honest-hearted not only delight in this, but in the effect of it upon them. He regards the helpless and distressed, and reveals his love to his children under affliction, who delight in beholding his benevolence, and in feeling Divine charity moving in them. Of this I may speak a little, for though since I left you I have often an engaging love and affection towards thee and my daughter, and friends about home, and going out at this time, when sickness is so great amongst you, is a trial upon me; yet I often remember there are many widows and fatherless, many who have poor tutors, many who have evil examples before them, and many whose minds are in captivity; for whose sake my heart is at times moved with compassion, so that I feel my mind resigned to leave you for a season, to exercise that gift which the Lord hath bestowed on me, which though small compared with some, yet in this I rejoice, that I feel love unfeigned towards my fellow-creatures. I recommend you to the Almighty, who I trust, cares for you, and under a sense of his heavenly love remain,

Thy loving husband,

J. W.

We crossed from the east end of Long Island to New London, about thirty miles, in a large open boat; while we were out, the wind rising high, the waves several times beat over us, so that to me it appeared dangerous, but my mind was at that time turned to Him who made and governs the deep, and my life was resigned to him; as he was mercifully pleased to preserve us I had fresh occasion to

consider every day as a day lent to me, and felt a renewed engagement to devote my time, and all I had, to him who gave it.

We had five meetings in Narraganset, and went thence to Newport on Rhode Island. Our gracious Father preserved us in an
humble dependence on him through deep exercises that were mortifying to the creaturely will. In several families in the country where
we lodged, I felt an engagement on my mind to have a conference
with them in private, concerning their slaves; and through Divine
aid I was favored to give up thereto. Though in this concern I
differ from many whose service in travelling is, I believe, greater
than mine, yet I do not think hardly of them for omitting it; I do
not repine at having so unpleasant a task assigned me, but look
with awfulness to him who appoints to his servants their respective
employments, and is good to all who serve him sincerely.

We got to Newport in the evening, and on the next day visited
two sick persons, with whom we had comfortable sittings, and in
the afternoon attended the burial of a Friend. The next day we were
at meetings at Newport, in the forenoon and afternoon; the spring
of the ministry was opened, and strength was given to declare the
Word of Life to the people.

The day following we went on our journey, but the great number
of slaves in these parts, and the continuance of that trade from
thence to Guinea, made a deep impression on me, and my cries
were often put up to my Heavenly Father in secret, that he would
enable me to discharge my duty faithfully in such way as he might
be pleased to point out to me.

We took Swansea, Freetown, and Taunton in our way to Boston,
where also we had a meeting; our exercise was deep, and the love
of truth prevailed, for which I bless the Lord. We went eastward
about eighty miles beyond Boston, taking meetings, and were in a
good degree preserved in an humble dependence on that arm which
drew us out; and though we had some hard labor with the disobedient, by laying things home and close to such as were stout
against the truth, yet through the goodness of God we had at times
to partake of heavenly comfort with those who were meek, and
were often favored to part with Friends in the nearness of true
gospel fellowship. We returned to Boston and had another com-

fortable opportunity with Friends there, and thence rode back a
day's journey eastward of Boston. Our guide being a heavy man,
and the weather hot, my companion and I expressed our freedom to
go on without him, to which he consented, and we respectfully
took our leave of him; this we did as believing the journey would
have been hard to him and his horse.

In visiting the meetings in those parts we were measurably baptized into a feeling of the state of the Society, and in bowedness of
spirit went to the Yearly Meeting at Newport, where we met with
John Storer from England, Elizabeth Shipley, Ann Gaunt, Hannah
Foster, and Mercy Redman, from our parts, all ministers of the
gospel, of whose company I was glad. Understanding that a large
number of slaves had been imported from Africa into that town
and were then on sale by a member of our Society, my appetite
failed, and I grew outwardly weak, and had a feeling of the condition of Habakkuk, as thus expressed, "When I heard, my belly
trembled, my lips quivered, I trembled in myself, that I might rest
in the day of trouble." I had many cogitations, and was sorely distressed. I was desirous that Friends might petition the Legislature
to use their endeavors to discourage the future importation of slaves,
for I saw that this trade was a great evil, and tended to multiply
troubles, and to bring distresses on the people for whose welfare
my heart was deeply concerned. But I perceived several difficulties
in regard to petitioning, and such was the exercise of my mind that
I thought of endeavoring to get an opportunity to speak a few words
in the House of Assembly, then sitting in town.

This exercise came upon me in the afternoon on the second day
of the Yearly Meeting, and on going to bed I got no sleep till my
mind was wholly resigned thereto. In the morning I inquired of a
Friend how long the Assembly was likely to continue sitting, who
told me it was expected to be prorogued that day or the next. As
I was desirous to attend the business of the meeting, and perceived
the Assembly was likely to separate before the business was over,
after considerable exercise, humbly seeking to the Lord for instruction, my mind settled to attend on the business of the meeting; on
the last day of which I had prepared a short essay of a petition to
be presented to the Legislature, if way opened. And being informed

that there were some appointed by that Yearly Meeting to speak with those in authority on cases relating to the Society, I opened my mind to several of them, and showed them the essay I had made, and afterwards I opened the case in the meeting for business, in substance as follows:—

"I have been under a concern for some time on account of the great number of slaves which are imported into this colony. I am aware that it is a tender point to speak to, but apprehend I am not clear in the sight of Heaven without doing so. I have prepared an essay of a petition to be presented to the Legislature, if way open; and what I have to propose to this meeting is that some Friends may be named to withdraw and look over it, and report whether they believe it suitable to be read in the meeting. If they should think well of reading it, it will remain for the meeting to consider whether to take any further notice of it, as a meeting, or not." After a short conference some Friends went out, and, looking over it, expressed their willingness to have it read, which being done, many expressed their unity with the proposal, and some signified that to have the subjects of the petition enlarged upon, and signed out of meeting by such as were free, would be more suitable than to do it there. Though I expected at first that if it was done it would be in that way, yet such was the exercise of my mind that to move it in the hearing of Friends when assembled appeared to me as a duty, for my heart yearned towards the inhabitants of these parts, believing that by this trade there had been an increase of inquietude amongst them, and way had been made for the spreading of a spirit opposite to that meekness and humility which is a sure resting-place for the soul; and that the continuance of this trade would not only render their healing more difficult, but would increase their malady.

Having proceeded thus far, I felt easy to leave the essay amongst Friends, for them to proceed in it as they believed best. And now an exercise revived in my mind in relation to lotteries, which were common in those parts. I had mentioned the subject in a former sitting of this meeting, when arguments were used in favor of Friends being held excused who were only concerned in such lotteries as were agreeable to law. And now, on moving it again, it was opposed as before; but the hearts of some solid Friends appeared to be united to discourage the practice amongst their members, and the matter was zealously handled by some on both sides. In this debate it appeared very clear to me that the spirit of lotteries was a spirit of selfishness, which tended to confuse and darken the understanding, and that pleading for it in our meetings, which were set apart for the Lord's work, was not right. In the heat of zeal, I made reply to what an ancient Friend said, and when I sat down I saw that my words were not enough seasoned with charity. After this I spoke no more on the subject. At length a minute was made, a copy of which was to be sent to their several Quarterly Meetings, inciting Friends to labor to discourage the practice amongst all professing with us.

Some time after this minute was made I remained uneasy with the manner of my speaking to the ancient Friend, and could not see my way clear to conceal my uneasiness, though I was concerned that I might say nothing to weaken the cause in which I had labored. After some close exercise and hearty repentence for not having attended closely to the safe guide, I stood up, and, reciting the passage, acquainted Friends that though I durst not go from what I had said as to the matter, yet I was uneasy with the manner of my speaking, believing milder language would have been better. As this was uttered in some degree of creaturely abasement after a warm debate, it appeared to have a good savor amongst us.

The Yearly Meeting being now over, there yet remained on my mind a secret though heavy exercise, in regard to some leading active members about Newport, who were in the practice of keeping slaves. This I mentioned to two ancient Friends who came out of the country, and proposed to them, if way opened, to have some conversation with those members. One of them and I, having consulted one of the most noted elders who had slaves, he, in a respectful manner, encouraged me to proceed to clear myself of what lay upon me. Near the beginning of the Yearly Meeting, I had had a private conference with this said elder and his wife, concerning their slaves, so that the way seemed clear to me to advise with him about the manner of proceeding. I told him I was free to have a conference with them all together in a private house; or if he thought they would take it unkind to be asked to come together, and to be spoken with in the hearing of one another, I was free to spend some time amongst them, and to visit them all in their own houses. He expressed his liking to the first proposal, not doubting their willingness to come together; and, as I proposed a visit to only ministers, elders, and overseers, he named some others whom he desired might also be present. A careful messenger being wanted to acquaint them in a proper manner, he offered to go to all their houses, to open the matter to them,—and did so. About the eighth hour the next morning we met in the meeting-house chamber, the last-mentioned country Friend, my companion, and John Storer being with us. After a short time of retirement, I acquainted them with the steps I had taken in procuring that meeting, and opened the concern I was under, and we then proceeded to a free conference upon the subject. My exercise was heavy, and I was deeply bowed in spirit before the Lord, who was pleased to favor with the seasoning virtue of truth, which wrought a tenderness amongst us; and the subject was mutually handled in a calm and peaceable spirit. At length, feeling my mind released from the burden which I had been under, I took my leave of them in a good degree of satisfaction; and by the tenderness they manifested in regard to the practice, and the concern several of them expressed in relation to the manner of disposing of their negroes after their decease, I believed that a good exercise was spreading amongst them; and I am humbly thankful to God, who supported my mind and preserved me in a good degree of resignation through these trials.

Thou who sometimes travellest in the work of the ministry, and art made very welcome by thy friends, seest many tokens of their satisfaction in having thee for their guest. It is good for thee to dwell deep, that thou mayest feel and understand the spirits of people. If we believe truth points towards a conference on some subjects in a private way, it is needful for us to take heed that their kindness, their freedom, and affability do not hinder us from the Lord's work. I have experienced that, in the midst of kindness and smooth conduct, to speak close and home to them who entertain us, on points that relate to outward interest, is hard labor. Sometimes, when I have felt truth lead towards it, I have found myself disqualified by a superficial friendship; and as the sense thereof hath abased me, and my cries have been to the Lord, so I have been humbled and made content to appear weak, or as a fool for his sake; and thus a door hath been opened to enter upon it. To attempt to do the Lord's work in our own way, and to speak of that which is the burden of the Word, in a way easy to the natural part, doth not reach the bottom of the disorder. To see the failings of our friends, and think hard of them, without opening that which we ought to open, and still carry a face of friendship, tends to undermine the foundation of true unity. The office of a minister of Christ is weighty. And they who now go forth as watchmen have need to be steadily on their guard against the snares of prosperity and an outside friendship.

After the Yearly Meeting we were at meetings at Newtown, Cushnet, Long Plain, Rochester, and Dartmouth. From thence we sailed for Nantucket, in company with Ann Gaunt, Mercy Redman, and several other Friends. The wind being slack we only reached Tarpawling Cove the first day; where, going on shore, we found room in a public-house, and beds for a few of us,—the rest slept on the floor. We went on board again about break of day, and though the wind was small, we were favored to come within about four miles of Nantucket; and then about ten of us got into our boat and rowed to the harbor before dark; a large boat went off and brought in the rest of the passengers about midnight. The next day but one was their Yearly Meeting, which held four days, the last of which was their Monthly Meeting for business. We had a laborious time amongst them; our minds were closely exercised, and I believe it was a time of great searching of heart. The longer I was on the Island the more I became sensible that there was a considerable number of valuable Friends there, though an evil spirit, tending to strife, had been at work amongst them. I was cautious of making any visits except as my mind was particularly drawn to them; and in that way we had some sittings in Friends' houses, where the heavenly wing was at times spread over us, to our mutual comfort. My beloved companion had very acceptable service on this island.

When meeting was over we all agreed to sail the next day if the weather was suitable and we were well; and being called up the latter part of the night, about fifty of us went on board a vessel;

but, the wind changing, the seamen thought best to stay in the harbor till it altered, so we returned on shore. Feeling clear as to any further visits, I spent my time in my chamber, chiefly alone; and after some hours, my heart being filled with the spirit of supplication, my prayers and tears were poured out before my Heavenly Father for his help and instruction in the manifold difficulties which attended me in life. While I was waiting upon the Lord, there came a messenger from the women Friends who lodged at another house, desiring to confer with us about appointing a meeting, which to me appeared weighty, as we had been at so many before; but after a short conference, and advising with some elderly Friends, a meeting was appointed, in which the Friend who first moved it, and who had been much shut up before, was largely opened in the love of the gospel. The next morning about break of day going again on board the vessel, we reached Falmouth on the Main before night, where our horses being brought, we proceeded towards Sandwich Quarterly Meeting.

Being two days in going to Nantucket, and having been there once before, I observed many shoals in their bay, which make sailing more dangerous, especially in stormy nights; also, that a great shoal, which encloses their harbor, prevents the entrance of sloops except when the tide is up. Waiting without for the rising of the tide is sometimes hazardous in storms, and by waiting within they sometimes miss a fair wind. I took notice that there was on that small island a great number of inhabitants, and the soil not very fertile, the timber being so gone that for vessels, fences, and firewood, they depend chiefly on buying from the Main, for the cost whereof, with most of their other expenses, they depend principally upon the whale fishery. I considered that as towns grew larger, and lands near navigable waters were more cleared, it would require more labor to get timber and wood. I understood that the whales, being much hunted and sometimes wounded and not killed, grow more shy and difficult to come at. I considered that the formation of the earth, the seas, the islands, bays, and rivers, the motions of the winds, and great waters, which cause bars and shoals in particular places, were all the works of Him who is perfect wisdom and goodness; and as people attend to his heavenly instruction, and put their trust in him, he provides for them in all parts where he gives them a being; and as in this visit to these people I felt a strong desire for their firm establishment on the sure foundation, besides what was said more publicly, I was concerned to speak with the women Friends in their Monthly Meeting of business, many being present, and in the fresh spring of pure love to open before them the advantage, both inwardly and outwardly, of attending singly to the pure guidance of the Holy Spirit, and therein to educate their children in true humility and the disuse of all superfluities. I reminded them of the difficulties their husbands and sons were frequently exposed to at sea, and that the more plain and simple their way of living was the less need there would be of running great hazards to support them. I also encouraged the young women to continue their neat, decent way of attending themselves on the affairs of the house; showing, as the way opened, that where people were truly humble, used themselves to business, and were content with a plain way of life, they had ever had more true peace and calmness of mind than they who, aspiring to greatness and outward show, have grasped hard for an income to support themselves therein. And as I observed they had so few or no slaves, I had to encourage them to be content without them, making mention of the numerous troubles and vexations which frequently attended the minds of the people who depend on slaves to do their labor.

We attended the Quarterly Meeting at Sandwich, in company with Ann Gaunt and Mercy Redman, which was preceded by a Monthly Meeting, and in the whole held three days. We were in various ways exercised amongst them, in gospel love, according to the several gifts bestowed on us, and were at times overshadowed with the virtue of truth, to the comfort of the sincere and stirring up of the negligent. Here we parted with Ann and Mercy, and went to Rhode Island, taking one meeting in our way, which was a satisfactory time. Reaching Newport the evening before their Quarterly Meeting, we attended it, and after that had a meeting with our young people, separated from those of other societies. We went through much labor in this town; and now, in taking leave of it, though I felt close inward exercise to the last, I found inward peace, and was in some degree comforted in a belief that a good number remain in that place who retain a sense of truth, and that there are some young people attentive to the voice of the Heavenly Shepherd. The last meeting, in which Friends from the several parts of the quarter came together, was a select meeting, and through the renewed manifestation of the Father's love the hearts of the sincere were united together.

The poverty of spirit and inward weakness, with which I was much tried the fore part of this journey, has of late appeared to me a dispensation of kindness. Appointing meetings never appeared more weighty to me, and I was led into a deep search, whether in all things my mind was resigned to the will of God; often querying with myself what should be the cause of such inward poverty, and greatly desiring that no secret reserve in my heart might hinder my access to the Divine fountain. In these humbling times I was made watchful, and excited to attend to the secret movings of the heavenly principle in my mind, which prepared the way to some duties that in more easy and prosperous times as to the outward, I believe I should have been in danger of omitting.

From Newport we went to Greenwich, Shanticut, and Warwick, and were helped to labor amongst Friends in the love of our gracious Redeemer. Afterwards, accompanied by our friend John Casey from Newport, we rode through Connecticut to Oblong, visited the meetings in those parts, and thence proceeded to the Quarterly Meeting at Ryewoods. Through the gracious extendings of Divine help, we had some seasoning opportunities in those places. We also visited Friends at New York and Flushing, and thence to Rahway. Here our roads parting, I took leave of my beloved companion and true yokemate Samuel Eastburn, and reached home the 10th of eighth month, where I found my family well. For the favors and protection of the Lord, both inward and outward, extended to me in this journey, my heart is humbled in grateful acknowledgments, and I find renewed desires to dwell and walk in resignedness before him.

CHAPTER VIII

1761, 1762

Visits Pennsylvania, Shrewsbury, and Squan—Publishes the Second Part of his Considerations on keeping Negroes—The Grounds of his appearing in some Respects singular in his Dress—Visit to the Families of Friends of Ancocas and Mount Holly Meetings—Visits to the Indians at Wehaloosing on the River Susquehanna.

HAVING felt my mind drawn towards a visit to a few meetings in Pennsylvania, I was very desirous to be rightly instructed as to the time of setting off. On the 10th of the fifth month, 1761, being the first day of the week, I went to Haddonfield Meeting, concluding to seek for heavenly instruction, and come home, or go on as I might then believe best for me, and there through the springing up of pure love I felt encouragement, and so crossed the river. In this visit I was at two quarterly and three monthly meetings, and in the love of truth I felt my way open to labor with some noted Friends who kept negroes. As I was favored to keep to the root, and endeavor to discharge what I believed was required of me, I found inward peace therein, from time to time, and thankfulness of heart to the Lord, who was graciously pleased to be a guide to me.

Eighth month, 1761.—Having felt drawings in my mind to visit Friends in and about Shrewsbury, I went there, and was at their Monthly Meeting, and their first-day meeting; I had also a meeting at Squan, and another at Squanquam, and, as way opened, had conversation with some noted Friends concerning their slaves. I returned home in a thankful sense of the goodness of the Lord.

From the concern I felt growing in me for some years, I wrote part the second of a work entitled "Considerations on keeping Negroes," which was printed this year, 1762. When the overseers of the press had done with it, they offered to get a number printed, to be paid for out of the Yearly Meeting's stock, to be given away;

but I being most easy to publish it at my own expense, and offering my reasons, they appeared satisfied.

This stock is the contribution of the members of our religious society in general, among whom are some who keep negroes, and, being inclined to continue them in slavery, are not likely to be satisfied with such books being spread among a people, especially at their own expense, many of whose slaves are taught to read, and such, receiving them as a gift, often conceal them. But as they who make a purchase generally buy that which they have a mind for, I believed it best to sell them, expecting by that means they would more generally be read with attention. Advertisements were signed by order of the overseers of the press, and directed to be read in the Monthly Meetings of business within our own Yearly Meeting, informing where the books were, and that the price was no more than the cost of printing and binding them. Many were taken off in our parts; some I sent to Virginia, some to New York, some to my acquaintance at Newport, and some I kept, intending to give part of them away, where there appeared a prospect of service.

In my youth I was used to hard labor, and though I was middling healthy, yet my nature was not fitted to endure so much as many others. Being often weary, I was prepared to sympathize with those whose circumstances in life, as free men, required constant labor to answer the demands of their creditors, as well as with others under oppression. In the uneasiness of body which I have many times felt by too much labor, not as a forced but a voluntary oppression, I have often been excited to think on the original cause of that oppression which is imposed on many in the world. The latter part of the time wherein I labored on our plantation, my heart, through the fresh visitations of heavenly love, being often tender, and my leisure time being frequently spent in reading the life and doctrines of our blessed Redeemer, the account of the sufferings of martyrs, and the history of the first rise of our Society, a belief was gradually settled in my mind, that if such as had great estates generally lived in that humility and plainness which belong to a Christian life, and laid much easier rents and interests on their lands and moneys, and thus led the way to a right use of things, so great a number of people might be employed in things useful, that labor both for men and other creatures would need to be no more than an agreeable employ, and divers branches of business, which serve chiefly to please the natural inclinations of our minds, and which at present seem necessary to circulate that wealth which some gather, might, in this way of pure wisdom, be discontinued. As I have thus considered these things, a query at times hath arisen: Do I, in all my proceedings, keep to that use of things which is agreeable to universal righteousness? And then there hath some degree of sadness at times come over me, because I accustomed myself to some things which have occasioned more labor than I believe Divine wisdom intended for us.

From my early acquaintance with truth I have often felt an inward distress, occasioned by the striving of a spirit in me against the operation of the heavenly principle; and in this state I have been affected with a sense of my own wretchedness, and in a mourning condition have felt earnest longings for that Divine help which brings the soul into true liberty. Sometimes, on retiring into private places, the spirit of supplication hath been given me, and under a heavenly covering I have asked my gracious Father to give me a heart in all things resigned to the direction of his wisdom; in uttering language like this, the thought of my wearing hats and garments dyed with a dye hurtful to them, has made lasting impression on me.

In visiting people of note in the Society who had slaves, and laboring with them in brotherly love on that account, I have seen, and the sight has affected me, that a conformity to some customs distinguishable from pure wisdom has entangled many, and that the desire of gain to support these customs has greatly opposed the work of truth. Sometimes when the prospect of the work before me has been such that in bowedness of spirit I have been drawn into retired places, and have besought the Lord with tears that he would take me wholly under his direction, and show me the way in which I ought to walk, it hath revived with strength of conviction that if I would be his faithful servant I must in all things attend to his wisdom, and be teachable, and so cease from all customs contrary thereto, however used among religious people.

As he is the perfection of power, of wisdom, and of goodness, so I believe he hath provided that so much labor shall be necessary for men's support in this world as would, being rightly divided, be a suitable employment of their time; and that we cannot go into superfluities, or grasp after wealth in a way contrary to his wisdom, without having connection with some degree of oppression, and with that spirit which leads to self-exaltation and strife, and which frequently brings calamities on countries by parties contending about their claims.

Being thus fully convinced, and feeling an increasing desire to live in the spirit of peace, I have often been sorrowfully affected with thinking on the unquiet spirit in which wars are generally carried on, and with the miseries of many of my fellow-creatures engaged therein; some suddenly destroyed: some wounded, and after much pain remaining cripples; some deprived of all their outward substance and reduced to want; and some carried into captivity. Thinking often on these things, the use of hats and garments dyed with a dye hurtful to them, and wearing more clothes in summer than are useful, grew more uneasy to me, believing them to be customs which have not their foundation in pure wisdom. The apprehension of being singular from my beloved friends was a strait upon me, and thus I continued in the use of some things contrary to my judgment.

On the 31st of fifth month, 1761, I was taken ill of a fever, and after it had continued near a week I was in great distress of body. One day there was a cry raised in me that I might understand the cause of my affliction, and improve under it, and my conformity to some customs which I believed were not right was brought to my remembrance. In the continuance of this exercise I felt all the powers in me yield themselves up into the hands of Him who gave me being, and was made thankful that he had taken hold of me by his chastisements. Feeling the necessity of further purifying, there was now no desire in me for health until the design of my correction was answered. Thus I lay in abasement and brokenness of spirit, and as I felt a sinking down into a calm resignation, so I felt, as in an instant, an inward healing in my nature, and from that time forward I grew better.

Though my mind was thus settled in relation to hurtful dyes, I felt easy to wear my garments heretofore made, and continued to do so about nine months. Then I thought of getting a hat the natural color of the fur, but the apprehension of being looked upon as one affecting singularity felt uneasy to me. Here I had occasion to consider that things, though small in themselves, being clearly enjoined by Divine authority, become great things to us; and I trusted that the Lord would support me in the trials that might attend singularity, so long as singularity was only for his sake. On this account I was under close exercise of mind in the time of our General Spring Meeting, 1762, greatly desiring to be rightly directed; when, being deeply bowed in spirit before the Lord, I was made willing to submit to what I apprehended was required of me, and when I returned home got a hat of the natural color of the fur.

In attending meetings this singularity was a trial to me, and more especially at this time, as white hats were used by some who were fond of following the changeable modes of dress, and as some Friends who knew not from what motives I wore it grew shy of me, I felt my way for a time shut up in the exercise of the ministry. In this condition, my mind being turned toward my Heavenly Father with fervent cries that I might be preserved to walk before him in the meekness of wisdom, my heart was often tender in meetings, and I felt an inward consolation which to me was very precious under these difficulties.

I had several dyed garments fit for use which I believed it best to wear till I had occasion for new ones. Some Friends were apprehensive that my wearing such a hat savored of an affected singularity; those who spoke with me in a friendly way I generally informed, in a few words, that I believed my wearing it was not in my own will. I had at times been sensible that a superficial friendship had been dangerous to me; and many Friends being now uneasy with me, I had an inclination to acquaint some with the manner of my being led into these things; yet upon a deeper thought I was for a time most easy to omit it, believing the present dispensation was profitable, and trusting that if I kept my place the Lord in his own time would open the hearts of Friends towards me. I have since had cause to admire his goodness and loving-kindness in leading about and instructing me, and in opening and enlarging my heart in some of our meetings.

In the eleventh month this year, feeling an engagement of mind to visit some families in Mansfield, I joined my beloved friend Benjamin Jones, and we spent a few days together in that service. In the second month, 1763, I joined, in company with Elizabeth Smith and Mary Noble, in a visit to the families of Friends at Ancocas. In both these visits, through the baptizing power of truth, the sincere laborers were often comforted, and the hearts of Friends opened to receive us. In the fourth month following, I accompanied some Friends in a visit to the families of Friends in Mount Holly; during this visit my mind was often drawn into an inward awfulness, wherein strong desires were raised for the everlasting welfare of my fellow-creatures, and through the kindness of our Heavenly Father our hearts were at times enlarged, and Friends were invited, in the flowings of Divine love, to attend to that which would settle them on the sure foundation.

Having for many years felt love in my heart towards the natives of this land who dwell far back in the wilderness, whose ancestors were formerly the owners and possessors of the land where we dwell, and who for a small consideration assigned their inheritance to us, and being at Philadelphia in the 8th month, 1761, on a visit to some Friends who had slaves, I fell in company with some of those natives who lived on the east branch of the river Susquehanna, at an Indian town called Wehaloosing, two hundred miles from Philadelphia. In conversation with them by an interpreter, as also by observations on their countenances and conduct, I believed some of them were measurably acquainted with that Divine power which subjects the rough and froward will of the creature. At times I felt inward drawings towards a visit to that place, which I mentioned to none except my dear wife until it came to some ripeness. In the winter of 1762 I laid my prospects before my friends at our Monthly and Quarterly, and afterwards at our General Spring Meeting; and having the unity of Friends, and being thoughtful about an Indian pilot, there came a man and three women from a little beyond that town to Philadelphia on business. Being informed thereof by letter, I met them in town in the 5th month, 1763; and after some conversation, finding they were sober people, I, with the concurrence of Friends in that place, agreed to join them as companions in their return, and we appointed to meet at Samuel Foulk's, at Richland, in Bucks County, on the 7th of sixth month. Now, as this visit felt weighty, and was performed at a time when travelling appeared perilous, so the dispensations of Divine Providence in preparing my mind for it have been memorable, and I believe it good for me to give some account thereof.

After I had given up to go, the thoughts of the journey were often attended with unusual sadness; at which times my heart was frequently turned to the Lord with inward breathings for his heavenly support, that I might not fail to follow him wheresoever he might lead me. Being at our youth's meeting at Chesterfield, about a week before the time I expected to set off, I was there led to speak on that prayer of our Redeemer to the Father: "I pray not that thou shouldest take them out of the world, but that thou shouldest keep them from the evil." And in attending to the pure openings of truth, I had to mention what he elsewhere said to his Father: "I know that thou hearest me at all times"; so, as some of his followers kept their places, and as his prayer was granted, it followed necessarily that they were kept from evil; and as some of those met with great hardships and afflictions in this world, and at last suffered death by cruel men, so it appears that whatsoever befalls men while they live in pure obedience to God certainly works for their good, and may not be considered an evil as it relates to them. As I spake on this subject my heart was much tendered, and great awfulness came over me. On the first day of the week, being at our own afternoon meeting, and my heart being enlarged in love, I was led to speak on the care and protection of the Lord over his people, and to make mention of that passage where a band of Syrians, who were endeavoring to take captive the prophet, were disappointed; and how the Psalmist said, "The angel of the Lord encampeth round about them that fear him." Thus, in true love and tenderness, I parted from Friends, expecting the next morning to proceed on my journey. Being weary I went early to bed. After I had been asleep a short time I was awoke by a man calling at my door, and inviting me to meet some Friends at a public-house in our town, who came from Philadelphia so late that Friends were generally gone to bed. These Friends informed me that an express had arrived the last morning from Pittsburg, and brought news that the Indians had taken a fort from the English westward, and had slain and scalped some English people near the said Pittsburg, and in divers places. Some elderly Friends in Philadelphia, knowing the time of my intending to set off, had conferred together, and thought good to inform me of these things before I left home, that I might consider them and proceed as I believed best. Going to bed again, I told not my wife till morning. My heart was turned to the Lord for his heavenly instruction; and it was an humbling time to me. When I told my dear wife, she appeared to be deeply concerned about it; but in a few hours' time my mind became settled in a belief that it was my duty to proceed on my journey, and she bore it with a good degree of resignation. In this conflict of spirit there were great searchings of heart and strong cries to the Lord, that no motion might in the least degree be attended to but that of the pure spirit of truth.

The subjects before mentioned, on which I had so lately spoken in public, were now fresh before me, and I was brought inwardly to commit myself to the Lord, to be disposed of as he saw best. I took leave of my family and neighbors in much bowedness of spirit, and went to our Monthly Meeting at Burlington. After taking leave of Friends there, I crossed the river, accompanied by my friends Israel and John Pemberton; and parting the next morning with Israel, John bore me company to Samuel Foulk's, where I met the before-mentioned Indians; and we were glad to see each other. Here my friend Benjamin Parvin met me, and proposed joining me as a companion,—we had before exchanged some letters on the subject,—and now I had a sharp trial on his account; for, as the journey appeared perilous, I thought if he went chiefly to bear me company, and we should be taken captive, my having been the means of drawing him into these difficulties would add to my own afflictions; so I told him my mind freely, and let him know that I was resigned to go alone; but after all, if he really believed it to be his duty to go on, I believed his company would be very comfortable to me. It was, indeed, a time of deep exercise, and Benjamin appeared to be so fastened to the visit that he could not be easy to leave me; so we went on, accompanied by our friends John Pemberton and William Lightfoot of Pikeland. We lodged at Bethlehem, and there parting with John, William and we went forward on the 9th of the sixth month, and got lodging on the floor of a house, about five miles from Fort Allen. Here we parted with William, and at this place we met with an Indian trader lately come from Wyoming. In conversation with him, I perceived that many white people often sell rum to the Indians, which I believe is a great evil. In the first place, they are thereby deprived of the use of reason, and their spirits being violently agitated, quarrels often arise which end in mischief, and the bitterness and resentment occasioned hereby are frequently of long continuance. Again, their skins and furs, gotten through much fatigue and hard travels in hunting, with which they intended to buy clothing, they often sell at a low rate for more rum, when they become intoxicated; and afterward, when they suffer for want of the necessaries of life, are angry with those who, for the sake of gain, took advantage of their weakness. Their chiefs have often complained of this in their treaties with the English. Where cunning people pass counterfeits and impose on others that which is good for nothing, it is considered as wickedness; but for the sake of gain to sell that which we know does people harm, and which often works their ruin, manifests a hardened and corrupt heart, and is an evil which demands the care of all true lovers of virtue to suppress. While my mind this evening was thus employed, I also remembered that the people on the frontiers, among whom this evil is too common, are often poor; and that they venture to the outside of a colony in order to live more independently of the wealthy, who often set high rents on their land. I was renewedly confirmed in a belief, that if all our inhabitants lived according to sound wisdom, laboring to promote universal love and righteousness, and ceased from every inordinate desire after wealth, and from all customs which are tinctured with luxury, the way would be easy for our inhabitants, though they might be much more numerous than at present, to live comfortably on honest employments, without the temptation they are so often under of being drawn into schemes to make settlements on lands which have not been purchased of the Indians, or of applying to that wicked practice of selling rum to them.

Tenth of sixth month.—We set out early this morning and crossed the western branch of Delaware, called the Great Lehie, near Fort Allen. The water being high, we went over in a canoe. Here we met an Indian, had friendly conversation with him, and gave him some biscuit; and he, having killed a deer, gave some of it to the Indians with us. After travelling some miles, we met several Indian men and women with a cow and horse, and some household goods, who were lately come from their dwelling at Wyoming, and were going to settle at another place. We made them some small presents, and, as some of them understood English, I told them my motive for coming into their country, with which they appeared satisfied. One of our guides talking awhile with an ancient woman concerning us, the poor old woman came to my companion and me and took her leave of us with an appearance of sincere affection. We pitched our tent near the banks of the same river, having labored hard in crossing some of those mountains called the Blue Ridge. The roughness of the stones and the cavities between them, with the steepness of the hills, made it appear dangerous. But we were preserved in safety, through the kindness of Him whose works in these mountainous deserts appeared awful, and towards whom my heart was turned during this day's travel.

Near our tent, on the sides of large trees peeled for that purpose, were various representations of men going to and returning from the wars, and of some being killed in battle. This was a path heretofore used by warriors, and as I walked about viewing those Indian histories, which were painted mostly in red or black, and thinking on the innumerable afflictions which the proud, fierce spirit produceth in the world, also on the toils and fatigues of warriors in travelling over mountains and deserts; on their miseries and distresses when far from home and wounded by their enemies; of their bruises and great weariness in chasing one another over the rocks and mountains; of the restless, unquiet state of mind of those who live in this spirit, and of the hatred which mutually grows up in the minds of their children,—the desire to cherish the spirit of love and peace among these people arose very fresh in me.

This was the first night that we lodged in the woods, and being wet with travelling in the rain, as were also our blankets, the ground, our tent, and the bushes under which we purposed to lay, all looked discouraging; but I believed that it was the Lord who had thus far brought me forward, and that he would dispose of me as he saw good, and so I felt easy. We kindled a fire, with our tent open to it, then laid some bushes next the ground, and put our blankets upon them for our bed, and, lying down, got some sleep. In the morning, feeling a little unwell, I went into the river; the water was cold, but soon after I felt fresh and well. About eight o'clock we set forward and crossed a high mountain supposed to be upward of four miles over, the north side being the steepest. About noon we were overtaken by one of the Moravian brethren going to Wehaloosing, and an Indian man with him who could talk English; and we being together while our horses ate grass had some friendly conversation; but they, travelling faster than we, soon left us. This Moravian, I understood, has this spring spent some time at Wehaloosing, and was invited by some of the Indians to come again.

Twelfth of sixth month being the first of the week and a rainy day, we continued in our tent, and I was led to think on the nature of the exercise which hath attended me. Love was the first motion, and thence a concern arose to spend some time with the Indians, that I might feel and understand their life and the spirit they live in, if haply I might receive some instruction from them, or they might be in any degree helped forward by my following the leadings of truth among them; and as it pleased the Lord to make way for my going at a time when the troubles of war were increasing, and when, by reason of much wet weather, travelling was more difficult than usual at that season, I looked upon it as a more favorable opportunity to season my mind, and to bring me into a nearer sympathy with them. As mine eye was to the great Father of Mercies, humbly desiring to learn his will concerning me, I was made quiet and content.

Our guide's horse strayed, though hoppled, in the night, and after searching some time for him his footsteps were discovered in the path going back, whereupon my kind companion went off in the rain, and after about seven hours returned with him. Here we lodged again, tying up our horses before we went to bed, and loosing them to feed about break of day.

Thirteenth of sixth month.—The sun appearing, we set forward, and as I rode over the barren hills my meditations were on the alterations in the circumstances of the natives of this land since the coming in of the English. The lands near the sea are conveniently situated for fishing; the lands near the rivers, where the tides flow, and some above, are in many places fertile, and not mountainous, while the changing of the tides makes passing up and down easy with any kind of traffic. The natives have in some places, for trifling considerations, sold their inheritance so favorably situated, and in other places have been driven back by superior force; their way of clothing themselves is also altered from what it was, and they being far removed from us have to pass over mountains, swamps, and barren deserts, so that travelling is very troublesome in bringing their skins and furs to trade with us. By the extension of English settlements, and partly by the increase of English hunters, the wild beasts on which the natives chiefly depend for subsistence are not so plentiful as they were, and people too often, for the sake of gain, induce them to waste their skins and furs in purchasing a liquor which tends to the ruin of them and their families.

My own will and desires were now very much broken, and my heart was with much earnestness turned to the Lord, to whom alone I looked for help in the dangers before me. I had a prospect of the English along the coast for upwards of nine hundred miles, where I travelled, and their favorable situation and the difficulties attending the natives as well as the negroes in many places were open before me. A weighty and heavenly care came over my mind, and love filled my heart towards all mankind, in which I felt a strong engagement that we might be obedient to the Lord while in tender mercy he is yet calling to us, and that we might so attend to pure universal righteousness as to give no just cause of offence to the gentiles, who do not profess Christianity, whether they be the blacks from Africa, or the native inhabitants of this continent. Here I was led into a close and laborious inquiry whether I, as an individual, kept clear from all things which tended to stir up or were connected with wars, either in this land or in Africa; my heart was

deeply concerned that in future I might in all things keep steadily
to the pure truth, and live and walk in the plainness and simplicity
of a sincere follower of Christ. In this lonely journey I did greatly
bewail the spreading of a wrong spirit, believing that the prosperous, convenient situation of the English would require a constant
attention in us to Divine love and wisdom, in order to their being
guided and supported in a way answerable to the will of that good,
gracious, and Almighty Being, who hath an equal regard to all
mankind. And here luxury and covetousness, with the numerous
oppressions and other evils attending them, appeared very afflicting
to me, and I felt in that which is immutable that the seeds of great
calamity and desolation are sown and growing fast on this continent.
Nor have I words sufficient to set forth the longing I then felt, that
we who are placed along the coast, and have tasted the love and
goodness of God, might arise in the strength thereof, and like faithful messengers labor to check the growth of these seeds, that they
may not ripen to the ruin of our posterity.

On reaching the Indian settlement at Wyoming, we were told
that an Indian runner had been at that place a day or two before us,
and brought news of the Indians having taken an English fort
westward, and destroyed the people, and that they were endeavoring
to take another; also that another Indian runner came there about
the middle of the previous night from a town about ten miles from
Wehaloosing, and brought the news that some Indian warriors
from distant parts came to that town with two English scalps, and
told the people that it was war with the English.

Our guides took us to the house of a very ancient man. Soon
after we had put in our baggage there came a man from another
Indian house some distance off. Perceiving there was a man near
the door I went out; the man had a tomahawk wrapped under his
match-coat out of sight. As I approached him he took it in his hand;
I went forward, and, speaking to him in a friendly way, perceived
he understood some English. My companion joining me, we had
some talk with him concerning the nature of our visit in these parts;
he then went into the house with us, and, talking with our guides,
soon appeared friendly, sat down and smoked his pipe. Though
taking his hatchet in his hand at the instant I drew near to him had

a disagreeable appearance, I believe he had no other intent than to be in readiness in case any violence were offered to him.

On hearing the news brought by these Indian runners, and being told by the Indians where we lodged, that the Indians about Wyoming expected in a few days to move to some larger towns, I thought, to all outward appearance, it would be dangerous travelling at this time. After a hard day's journey I was brought into a painful exercise at night, in which I had to trace back and view the steps I had taken from my first moving in the visit; and though I had to bewail some weakness which at times had attended me, yet I could not find that I had ever given way to wilful disobedience. Believing I had, under a sense of duty, come thus far, I was now earnest in spirit, beseeching the Lord to show me what I ought to do. In this great distress I grew jealous of myself, lest the desire of reputation as a man firmly settled to persevere through dangers, or the fear of disgrace from my returning without performing the visit, might have some place in me. Full of these thoughts, I lay great part of the night, while my beloved companion slept by me, till the Lord, my gracious Father, who saw the conflicts of my soul, was pleased to give quietness. Then I was again strengthened to commit my life, and all things relating thereto, into his heavenly hands, and got a little sleep towards day.

Fourteenth of sixth month.—We sought out and visited all the Indians hereabouts that we could meet with, in number about twenty. They were chiefly in one place, about a mile from where we lodged. I expressed to them the care I had on my mind for their good, and told them that true love had made me willing thus to leave my family to come and see the Indians and speak with them in their houses. Some of them appeared kind and friendly. After taking leave of them, we went up the river Susquehanna about three miles, to the house of an Indian called Jacob January. He had killed his hog, and the women were making store of bread and preparing to move up the river. Here our pilots had left their canoe when they came down in the spring, and lying dry it had become leaky. This detained us some hours, so that we had a good deal of friendly conversation with the family; and, eating dinner with them, we made them some small presents. Then putting our baggage into the canoe, some of them pushed slowly up the stream, and the rest of us rode our horses. We swam them over a creek called Lahawahamunk, and pitched our tent above it in the evening. In a sense of God's goodness in helping me in my distress, sustaining me under trials, and inclining my heart to trust in him, I lay down in an humble, bowed frame of mind, and had a comfortable night's lodging.

Fifteenth of sixth month.—We proceeded forward till the afternoon, when, a storm appearing, we met our canoe at an appointed place and stayed all night, the rain continuing so heavy that it beat through our tent and wet both us and our baggage. The next day we found abundance of trees blown down by the storm yesterday, and had occasion reverently to consider the kind dealings of the Lord who provided a safe place for us in a valley while this storm continued. We were much hindered by the trees which had fallen across our path, and in some swamps our way was so stopped that we got through with extreme difficulty. I had this day often to consider myself as a sojourner in this world. A belief in the all-sufficiency of God to support his people in their pilgrimage felt comfortable to me, and I was industriously employed to get to a state of perfect resignation.

We seldom saw our canoe but at appointed places, by reason of the path going off from the river. This afternoon Job Chilaway, an Indian from Wehaloosing, who talks good English and is acquainted with several people in and about Philadelphia, met our people on the river. Understanding where we expected to lodge, he pushed back about six miles, and came to us after night; and in a while our own canoe arrived, it being hard work pushing up the stream. Job told us that an Indian came in haste to their town yesterday and told them that three warriors from a distance lodged in a town above Wehaloosing a few nights past, and that these three men were going against the English at Juniata. Job was going down the river to the province-store at Shamokin. Though I was so far favored with health as to continue travelling, yet, through the various difficulties in our journey, and the different way of living from which I had been used to, I grew sick. The news of these warriors being on their march so near us, and not knowing whether we might not fall in with them, was a fresh trial of my faith; and though, through the strength of Divine love, I had several times been enabled to commit myself to the Divine disposal, I still found the want of a renewal of my strength, that I might be able to persevere therein; and my cries for help were put up to the Lord, who, in great mercy, gave me a resigned heart, in which I found quietness.

Parting from Job Chilaway on the 17th, we went on and reached Wehaloosing about the middle of the afternoon. The first Indian that we saw was a woman of a modest countenance, with a Bible, who spake first to our guide, and then with an harmonious voice expressed her gladness at seeing us, having before heard of our coming. By the direction of our guide we sat down on a log while he went to the town to tell the people we were come. My companion and I, sitting thus together in a deep inward stillness, the poor woman came and sat near us; and, great awfulness coming over us, we rejoiced in a sense of God's love manifested to our poor souls. After a while we heard a conch-shell blow several times, and then came John Curtis and another Indian man, who kindly invited us into a house near the town, where we found about sixty people sitting in silence. After sitting with them a short time I stood up, and in some tenderness of spirit acquainted them, in a few short sentences, with the nature of my visit, and that a concern for their good had made me willing to come thus far to see them; which some of them understanding interpreted to the others, and there appeared gladness among them. I then showed them my certificate, which was explained to them; and the Moravian who overtook us on the way, being now here, bade me welcome. But the Indians knowing that this Moravian and I were of different religious societies, and as some of their people had encouraged him to come and stay awhile with them, they were, I believe, concerned that there might be no jarring or discord in their meetings; and having, I suppose, conferred together, they acquainted me that the people, at my request, would at any time come together and hold meetings. They also told me that they expected the Moravian would speak in their settled meetings, which are commonly held in the morning and near evening. So finding liberty in my heart to speak to the

Moravian, I told him of the care I felt on my mind for the good of these people, and my belief that no ill effects would follow if I sometimes spake in their meetings when love engaged me thereto, without calling them together at times when they did not meet of course. He expressed his good-will towards my speaking at any time all that I found in my heart to say.

On the evening of the 18th I was at their meeting, where pure gospel love was felt, to the tendering of some of our hearts. The interpreters endeavored to acquaint the people with what I said, in short sentences, but found some difficulty, as none of them were quite perfect in the English and Delaware tongues, so they helped one another, and we labored along, Divine love attending. Afterwards, feeling my mind covered with the spirit of prayer, I told the interpreters that I found it in my heart to pray to God, and believed, if I prayed aright, he would hear me; and I expressed my willingness for them to omit interpreting; so our meeting ended with a degree of Divine love. Before the people went out, I observed Papunehang (the man who had been zealous in laboring for a reformation in that town, being then very tender) speaking to one of the interpreters, and I was afterwards told that he said in substance as follows: "I love to feel where words come from."

Nineteenth of sixth month and first of the week.—This morning the Indian who came with the Moravian, being also a member of that society, prayed in the meeting, and then the Moravian spake a short time to the people. In the afternoon, my heart being filled with a heavenly care for their good, I spake to them awhile by interpreters; but none of them being perfect in the work, and I feeling the current of love run strong, told the interpreters that I believed some of the people would understand me, and so I proceeded without them; and I believe the Holy Ghost wrought on some hearts to edification where all the words were not understood. I looked upon it as a time of Divine favor, and my heart was tendered and truly thankful before the Lord. After I sat down, one of the interpreters seemed spirited to give the Indians the substance of what I said.

Before our first meeting this morning, I was led to meditate on the manifold difficulties of these Indians who, by the permission of the Six Nations, dwell in these parts. A near sympathy with them was raised in me, and, my heart being enlarged in the love of Christ, I thought that the affectionate care of a good man for his only brother in affliction does not exceed what I then felt for that people. I came to this place through much trouble; and though through the mercies of God I believed that if I died in the journey it would be well with me, yet the thoughts of falling into the hands of Indian warriors were, in times of weakness, afflicting to me; and being of a tender constitution of body, the thoughts of captivity among them were also grievous; supposing that as they were strong and hardy they might demand service of me beyond what I could well bear. But the Lord alone was my keeper, and I believed that if I went into captivity it would be for some good end. Thus, from time to time, my mind was centred in resignation, in which I always found quietness. And this day, though I had the same dangerous wilderness between me and home, I was inwardly joyful that the Lord had strengthened me to come on this visit, and had manifested a fatherly care over me in my poor lowly condition, when, in mine own eyes, I appeared inferior to many among the Indians.

When the last-mentioned meeting was ended, it being night, Papunehang went to bed; and hearing him speak with an harmonious voice, I suppose for a minute or two, I asked the interpreter, who told me that he was expressing his thankfulness to God for the favors he had received that day, and prayed that he would continue to favor him with the same, which he had experienced in that meeting. Though Papunehang had before agreed to receive the Moravian and join with them, he still appeared kind and loving to us.

I was at two meetings on the 20th, and silent in them. The following morning, in meeting, my heart was enlarged in pure love among them, and in short plain sentences I expressed several things that rested upon me, which one of the interpreters gave the people pretty readily. The meeting ended in supplication, and I had cause humbly to acknowledge the loving-kindness of the Lord towards us; and then I believed that a door remained open for the faithful disciples of Jesus Christ to labor among these people. And now, feeling my mind at liberty to return, I took my leave of them in general at the conclusion of what I said in meeting, and we then prepared to go homeward. But some of their most active men told us that when we were ready to move the people would choose to come and shake hands with us. Those who usually came to meeting did so; and from a secret draught in my mind I went among some who did not usually go to meeting, and took my leave of them also. The Moravian and his Indian interpreter appeared respectful to us at parting. This town, Wehaloosing, stands on the bank of the Susquehanna, and consists, I believe, of about forty houses, mostly compact together, some about thirty feet long and eighteen wide,—some bigger, some less. They are built mostly of split plank, one end being set in the ground, and the other pinned to a plate on which rafters are laid, and then covered with bark. I understand a great flood last winter overflowed the greater part of the ground where the town stands, and some were now about moving their houses to higher ground.

We expected only two Indians to be of our company, but when we were ready to go we found many of them were going to Bethlehem with skins and furs, and chose to go in company with us. So they loaded two canoes in which they desired us to go, telling us that the waters were so raised with the rains that the horses should be taken by such as were better acquainted with the fording-places. We, therefore, with several Indians, went in the canoes, and others went on horses, there being seven besides ours. We met with the horsemen once on the way by appointment, and at night we lodged a little below a branch called Tankhannah, and some of the young men, going out a little before dusk with their guns, brought in a deer.

Through diligence we reached Wyoming before night, the 22d, and understood that the Indians were mostly gone from this place. We went up a small creek into the woods with our canoes, and, pitching our tent, carried out our baggage, and before dark our horses came to us. Next morning, the horses being loaded and our baggage prepared, we set forward, being in all fourteen, and with diligent travelling were favored to get near half-way to Fort Allen. The land on this road from Wyoming to our frontier being mostly poor, and good grass being scarce, the Indians chose a piece of low ground to lodge on, as the best for grazing. I had sweat much in travelling, and, being weary, slept soundly. In the night I perceived that I had taken cold, of which I was favored soon to get better.

Twenty-fourth of sixth month.—This day we passed Fort Allen and lodged near it in the woods. We forded the westerly branch of the Delaware three times, which was a shorter way than going over the top of the Blue Mountains called the Second Ridge. In the second time of fording where the river cuts through the mountain, the waters being rapid and pretty deep, my companion's mare, being a tall, tractable animal, was sundry times driven back through the river, being laden with the burdens of some small horses which were thought unable to come through with their loads. The troubles westward, and the difficulty for Indians to pass through our frontier, was, I apprehend, one reason why so many came, expecting that our being in company would prevent the outside inhabitants being surprised. We reached Bethlehem on the 25th, taking care to keep foremost, and to acquaint people on and near the road who these Indians were. This we found very needful, for the frontier inhabitants were often alarmed at the report of the English being killed by Indians westward. Among our company were some whom I did not remember to have seen at meeting, and some of these at first were very reserved; but we being several days together, and behaving in a friendly manner towards them, and making them suitable return for the services they did us, they became more free and sociable.

Twenty-sixth of sixth month.—Having carefully endeavored to settle all affairs with the Indians relative to our journey, we took leave of them, and I thought they generally parted from us affectionately. We went forward to Richland and had a very comfortable meeting among our friends, it being the first day of the week. Here I parted with my kind friend and companion Benjamin Parvin, and, accompanied by my friend Samuel Foulk, we rode to John Cadwallader's, from whence I reached home the next day, and found my family tolerably well. They and my friends appeared glad to see me return from a journey which they apprehended would be dangerous; but my mind, while I was out, had been so employed in striving for perfect resignation, and had so often been confirmed in a belief, that, whatever the Lord might be pleased to allot for me, it would work for good, that I was careful lest I should admit any degree of selfishness in being glad overmuch, and labored to improve by those trials in such a manner as my gracious Father and Protector designed. Between the English settlements and Wehaloosing we had only a narrow path, which in many places is much grown up with bushes, and interrupted by abundance of trees lying across it. These, together with the mountain swamps and rough stones, make it a difficult road to travel, and the more so because rattlesnakes abound here, of which we killed four. People who have never been in such places have but an imperfect idea of them; and I was not only taught patience, but also made thankful to God, who thus led about and instructed me, that I might have a quick and lively feeling of the afflictions of my fellow-creatures, whose situation in life is difficult.

CHAPTER IX

1763–1769

Religious Conversation with a Company met to see the Tricks of a Juggler—Account of John Smith's Advice and of the Proceedings of a Committee at the Yearly Meeting in 1764—Contemplations on the Nature of True Wisdom—Visit to the Families of Friends at Mount Holly, Mansfield, and Burlington, and to the Meetings on the Sea-Coast from Cape May towards Squan—Some Account of Joseph Nichols and his Followers—On the different State of the First Settlers in Pennsylvania who depended on their own Labor, compared with those of the Southern Provinces who kept Negroes—Visit to the Northern Parts of New Jersey and the Western Parts of Maryland and Pennsylvania; also to the Families of Friends at Mount Holly and several Parts of Maryland—Further Considerations on keeping Slaves, and his Concern for having been a Party to the Sale of One—Thoughts on Friends exercising Offices in Civil Government.

THE latter part of the summer, 1763, there came a man to Mount Holly who had previously published a printed advertisement that at a certain public-house he would show many wonderful operations, which were therein enumerated. At the appointed time he did, by sleight of hand, perform sundry things which appeared strange to the spectators. Understanding that the show was to be repeated the next night, and that the people were to meet about sunset, I felt an exercise on that account. So I went to the public-house in the evening, and told the man of the house that I had an inclination to spend a part of the evening there; with which he signified that he was content. Then, sitting down by the door, I spoke to the people in the fear of the Lord, as they came together, concerning this show, and labored to convince them that their thus assembling to see these sleight-of-hand tricks, and bestowing their money to support men who, in that capacity, were of no use to the world, was contrary to the nature of the Christian religion. One of the company endeavored to show by arguments the reasonableness of their proceedings herein; but after considering some texts of Scripture and calmly debating the matter he gave up the point. After spending about an hour among them, and feeling my mind easy, I departed.

Twenty-fifth* of ninth month, 1764.—At our Yearly Meeting at Philadelphia this day, John Smith, of Marlborough, aged upwards of eighty years, a faithful minister, though not eloquent, stood up in our meeting of ministers and elders, and, appearing to be under a great exercise of spirit, informed Friends in substance as follows: "That he had been a member of our Society upwards of sixty years, and he well remembered, that, in those early times, Friends were a plain, lowly-minded people, and that there was much tenderness and contrition in their meetings. That, at twenty years from that time, the Society increasing in wealth and in some degree conforming to the fashions of the world, true humility was less apparent, and their meetings in general were not so lively and edifying. That at the end of forty years many of them were grown very rich, and many of the Society made a specious appearance in the world; that wearing fine costly garments, and using silver and other watches, became customary with them, their sons, and their daughters. These marks of outward wealth and greatness appeared on some in our meetings of ministers and elders; and, as such things became more prevalent, so the powerful overshadowings of the Holy Ghost were less manifest in the Society. That there had been a continued increase of such ways of life, even until the present time; and that the weakness which hath now overspread the Society and the barrenness manifest among us is matter of much sorrow." He then mentioned the uncertainty of his attending these meetings in future, expecting his dissolution was near; and, having tenderly expressed his concern for us, signified that he had seen in the true light that the Lord would bring back his people from these things, into which they were thus degenerated, but that his faithful servants must go through great and heavy exercises.

Twentieth† of ninth month.—The committee appointed by the Yearly Meeting to visit the Quarterly and Monthly Meetings gave

*[Twentieth?—Ed.]   †[Twenty-fifth?—Ed.]

an account in writing of their proceedings in that service. They signified that in the course of the visit they had been apprehensive that some persons holding offices in government inconsistent with our principles, and others who kept slaves, remaining active members in our meetings for discipline, had been one means of weakness prevailing in some places. After this report was read, an exercise revived in my mind which had attended me for several years, and inward cries to the Lord were raised in me that the fear of man might not prevent me from doing what he required of me, and, standing up, I spoke in substance as follows: "I have felt a tenderness in my mind towards persons in two circumstances mentioned in that report; namely, towards such active members as keep slaves and such as hold offices in civil government; and I have desired that Friends, in all their conduct, may be kindly affectioned one towards another. Many Friends who keep slaves are under some exercise on that account; and at times think about trying them with freedom, but find many things in their way. The way of living and the annual expenses of some of them are such that it seems impracticable for them to set their slaves free without changing their own way of life. It has been my lot to be often abroad; and I have observed in some places, at Quarterly and Yearly Meetings, and at some houses where travelling Friends and their horses are often entertained, that the yearly expense of individuals therein is very considerable. And Friends in some places crowding much on persons in these circumstances for entertainment hath rested as a burden on my mind for some years past. I now express it in the fear of the Lord, greatly desiring that Friends here present may duly consider it."

In the fall of this year, having hired a man to work, I perceived in conversation with him that he had been a soldier in the late war on this continent; and he informed me in the evening, in a narrative of his captivity among the Indians, that he saw two of his fellow-captives tortured to death in a very cruel manner. This relation affected me with sadness, under which I went to bed; and the next morning, soon after I awoke, a fresh and living sense of Divine love overspread my mind, in which I had a renewed prospect of the nature of that wisdom from above which leads to a right use of all gifts, both spiritual and temporal, and gives content therein. Under a feeling thereof, I wrote as follows:—

"Hath He who gave me a being attended with many wants unknown to brute creatures given me a capacity superior to theirs, and shown me that a moderate application to business is suitable to my present condition; and that this, attended with his blessing, may supply all my outward wants while they remain within the bounds he hath fixed, and while no imaginary wants proceeding from an evil spirit have any place in me? Attend then, O my soul! to this pure wisdom as thy sure conductor through the manifold dangers of this world.

"Doth pride lead to vanity? Doth vanity form imaginary wants? Do these wants prompt men to exert their power in requiring more from others than they would be willing to perform themselves, were the same required of them? Do these proceedings beget hard thoughts? Do hard thoughts, when ripe, become malice? Does malice, when ripe, become revengeful, and in the end inflict terrible pains on our fellow-creatures and spread desolations in the world?

"Do mankind, walking in uprightness, delight in each other's happiness? And do those who are capable of this attainment, by giving way to an evil spirit, employ their skill and strength to afflict and destroy one another? Remember then, O my soul! the quietude of those in whom Christ governs, and in all thy proceedings feel after it.

"Doth he condescend to bless thee with his presence? To move and influence thee to action? To dwell and to walk in thee? Remember then thy station as being sacred to God. Accept of the strength freely offered to thee, and take heed that no weakness in conforming to unwise, expensive, and hard-hearted customs, gendering to discord and strife, be given way to. Doth he claim my body as his temple, and graciously require that I may be sacred to him? O that I may prize this favor, and that my whole life may be conformable to this character! Remember, O my soul! that the Prince of Peace is thy Lord; that he communicates his unmixed wisdom to his family, that they, living in perfect simplicity, may give no just cause of offence to any creature, but that they may walk as He walked!"

Having felt an openness in my heart towards visiting families in our own meeting, and especially in the town of Mount Holly, the place of my abode, I mentioned it at our Monthly Meeting in the fore part of the winter of 1764, which being agreed to, and several Friends of our meeting being united in the exercise, we proceeded therein; and through Divine favor we were helped in the work, so that it appeared to me as a fresh reviving of godly care among Friends. The latter part of the same winter I joined my friend William Jones in a visit to Friends' families in Mansfield, in which labor I had cause to admire the goodness of the Lord toward us.

My mind being drawn towards Friends along the seacoast from Cape May to near Squan, and also to visit some people in those parts, among whom there is no settled worship, I joined with my beloved friend Benjamin Jones in a visit to them, having Friends' unity therein. We set off the 24th of tenth month, 1765, and had a prosperous and very satisfactory journey, feeling at times, through the goodness of the Heavenly Shepherd, the gospel to flow freely towards a poor people scattered in these places. Soon after our return I joined my friends John Sleeper and Elizabeth Smith in a visit to Friends' families at Burlington, there being at this time about fifty families of our Society in that city; and we had cause humbly to adore our Heavenly Father, who baptized us into a feeling of the state of the people, and strengthened us to labor in true gospel love among them.

Having had a concern at times for several years to pay a religious visit to Friends on the Eastern Shore of Maryland, and to travel on foot among them, that by so travelling I might have a more lively feeling of the condition of the oppressed slaves, set an example of lowliness before the eyes of their masters, and be more out of the way of temptation to unprofitable converse; and the time drawing near in which I believed it my duty to lay my concern before our Monthly Meeting, I perceived, in conversation with my beloved friend John Sleeper, that he also was under a similar concern to travel on foot in the form of a servant among them, as he expressed it. This he told me before he knew aught of my exercise. Being thus drawn the same way, we laid our exercise and the nature of it before Friends; and, obtaining certificates, we set off the 6th of fifth month, 1766, and were at meetings with Friends at Wilmington, Duck

Creek, Little Creek, and Motherkill. My heart was often tendered under the Divine influence, and enlarged in love towards the people among whom we travelled.

From Motherkill we crossed the country about thirty-five miles to Tuckahoe, in Maryland, and had a meeting there, and also at Marshy Creek. At the last three meetings there were a considerable number of the followers of one Joseph Nichols, a preacher, who, I understand, is not in outward fellowship with any religious society, but professeth nearly the same principles as those of our Society, and often travels up and down, appointing meetings which many people attend. I heard of some who had been irreligious people that were now his followers, and were become sober, well-behaved men and women. Some irregularities, I hear, have been among the people at several of his meetings; but from what I have perceived I believe the man and some of his followers are honestly disposed, but that skilful fathers are wanting among them.

We then went to Choptank and Third Haven, and thence to Queen Anne's. The weather for some days past having been hot and dry, and we having travelled pretty steadily and having hard labor in meetings, I grew weakly, at which I was for a time discouraged; but looking over our journey and considering how the Lord had supported our minds and bodies, so that we had gone forward much faster than I expected before we came out, I saw that I had been in danger of too strongly desiring to get quickly through the journey, and that the bodily weakness now attending me was a kindness; and then, in contrition of spirit, I became very thankful to my gracious Father for this manifestation of his love, and in humble submission to his will my trust in him was renewed.

In this part of our journey I had many thoughts on the different circumstances of Friends who inhabit Pennsylvania and Jersey from those who dwell in Maryland, Virginia, and Carolina. Pennsylvania and New Jersey were settled by Friends who were convinced of our principles in England in times of suffering; these, coming over, bought lands of the natives, and applied to husbandry in a peaceable way, and many of their children were taught to labor for their living. Few of these, I believe, settled in any of the southern provinces; but by the faithful labors of travelling Friends in early times there was considerable convincement among the inhabitants of these parts. I also remembered having read of the warlike disposition of many of the first settlers in those provinces, and of their numerous engagements with the natives in which much blood was shed even in the infancy of the colonies. Some of the people inhabiting those places, being grounded in customs contrary to the pure truth, were affected with the powerful preaching of the Word of Life and joined in fellowship with our Society, and in so doing they had a great work to go through. In the history of the reformation from Popery it is observable that the progress was gradual from age to age. The uprightness of the first reformers in attending to the light and understanding given to them opened the way for sincere-hearted people to proceed further afterwards; and thus each one truly fearing God and laboring in the works of righteousness appointed for him in his day findeth acceptance with Him. Through the darkness of the times and the corruption of manners and customs, some upright men may have had little more for their day's work than to attend to the righteous principle in their minds as it related to their own conduct in life without pointing out to others the whole extent of that into which the same principle would lead succeeding ages. Thus, for instance, among an imperious, warlike people, supported by oppressed slaves, some of these masters, I suppose, are awakened to feel and to see their error, and through sincere repentance cease from oppression and become like fathers to their servants, showing by their example a pattern of humility in living, and moderation in governing, for the instruction and admonition of their oppressing neighbors; these, without carrying the reformation further, have, I believe, found acceptance with the Lord. Such was the beginning; and those who succeeded them, and who faithfully attended to the nature and spirit of the reformation, have seen the necessity of proceeding forward, and have not only to instruct others by their own example in governing well, but have also to use means to prevent their successors from having so much power to oppress others.

Here I was renewedly confirmed in my mind that the Lord (whose tender mercies are over all his works, and whose ear is open to the cries and groans of the oppressed) is graciously moving in the hearts of people to draw them off from the desire of wealth and to bring them into such an humble, lowly way of living that they may see their way clearly to repair to the standard of true righteousness, and may not only break the yoke of oppression, but may know him to be their strength and support in times of outward affliction.

We crossed Chester River, had a meeting there, and also at Cecil and Sassafras. My bodily weakness, joined with a heavy exercise of mind, was to me an humbling dispensation, and I had a very lively feeling of the state of the oppressed; yet I often thought that what I suffered was little compared with the sufferings of the blessed Jesus and many of his faithful followers; and I may say with thankfulness that I was made content. From Sassafras we went pretty directly home, where we found our families well. For several weeks after our return I had often to look over our journey; and though to me it appeared as a small service, and that some faithful messengers will yet have more bitter cups to drink in those southern provinces for Christ's sake than we have had, yet I found peace in that I had been helped to walk in sincerity according to the understanding and strength given to me.

Thirteenth of eleventh month.—With the unity of Friends at our monthly meeting, and in company with my beloved friend Benjamin Jones, I set out on a visit to Friends in the upper part of this province, having had drawings of love in my heart that way for a considerable time. We travelled as far as Hardwick, and I had inward peace in my labors of love among them. Through the humbling dispensations of Divine Providence my mind hath been further brought into a feeling of the difficulties of Friends and their servants southwestward; and being often engaged in spirit on their account I believed it my duty to walk into some parts of the western shore of Maryland on a religious visit. Having obtained a certificate from Friends of our Monthly Meeting, I took leave of my family under the heart-tendering operation of truth, and on the 20th of fourth month, 1767, rode to the ferry opposite to Philadelphia, and thence walked to William Horne's, at Derby, the same evening. Next day I pursued my journey alone and reached Concord Week-Day Meeting.

Discouragements and a weight of distress had at times attended me in this lonesome walk, but through these afflictions I was mercifully preserved. Sitting down with Friends, my mind was turned towards the Lord to wait for his holy leadings; and in infinite love he was pleased to soften my heart into humble contrition, and renewedly to strengthen me to go forward, so that to me it was a time of heavenly refreshment in a silent meeting. The next day I came to New Garden Week-Day Meeting, in which I sat in bowedness of spirit, and being baptized into a feeling of the state of some present, the Lord gave us a heart-tendering season; to his name be the praise. Passing on, I was at Nottingham Monthly Meeting, and at a meeting at Little Britain on first-day; in the afternoon several Friends came to the house where I lodged and we had a little afternoon meeting, and through the humbling power of truth I had to admire the loving-kindness of the Lord manifested to us.

Twenty-sixth of fourth month.—I crossed the Susquehanna, and coming among people in outward ease and greatness, supported chiefly on the labor of slaves, my heart was much affected, and in awful retiredness my mind was gathered inward to the Lord, humbly desiring that in true resignation I might receive instruction from him respecting my duty among this people. Though travelling on foot was wearisome to my body, yet it was agreeable to the state of my mind. Being weakly, I was covered with sorrow and heaviness on account of the prevailing spirit of this world by which customs grievous and oppressive are introduced on the one hand, and pride and wantonness on the other.

In this lonely walk and state of abasement and humiliation, the condition of the church in these parts was opened before me, and I may truly say with the Prophet, "I was bowed down at the hearing of it; I was dismayed at the seeing of it." Under this exercise I attended the Quarterly Meeting at Gunpowder, and in bowedness of spirit I had to express with much plainness my feelings respecting Friends living in fulness on the labors of the poor oppressed negroes; and that promise of the Most High was now revived, "I will gather all nations and tongues, and they shall come and see my glory." Here the sufferings of Christ and his tasting death for every man, and the travels, sufferings, and martyrdom of the Apostles and primitive Christians in laboring for the conversion of the Gentiles, were livingly revived in me, and according to the measure of strength afforded I labored in some tenderness of spirit, being deeply affected among them. The difference between the present treatment which these gentiles, the negroes, receive at our hands, and the labors of the primitive Christians for the conversion of the Gentiles, were pressed home, and the power of truth came over us, under a feeling of which my mind was united to a tender-hearted people in these parts. The meeting concluded in a sense of God's goodness towards his humble, dependent children.

The next day was a general meeting for worship, much crowded, in which I was deeply engaged in inward cries to the Lord for help, that I might stand wholly resigned, and move only as he might be pleased to lead me. I was mercifully helped to labor honestly and fervently among them, in which I found inward peace, and the sincere were comforted. From this place I turned towards Pipe Creek and the Red Lands, and had several meetings among Friends in those parts. My heart was often tenderly affected under a sense of the Lord's goodness in sanctifying my troubles and exercises, turning them to my comfort, and I believe to the benefit of many others, for I may say with thankfulness that in this visit it appeared like a tendering visitation in most places.

I passed on to the Western Quarterly Meeting in Pennsylvania. During the several days of this meeting I was mercifully preserved in an inward feeling after the mind of truth, and my public labors tended to my humiliation, with which I was content. After the Quarterly Meeting for worship ended, I felt drawings to go to the women's meeting for business, which was very full; here the humility of Jesus Christ as a pattern for us to walk by was livingly opened before me, and in treating on it my heart was enlarged, and it was a baptizing time. I was afterwards at meetings at Concord, Middletown, Providence, and Haddonfield, whence I returned home and found my family well. A sense of the Lord's merciful preservation in this my journey excites reverent thankfulness to him.

Second of ninth month, 1767.—With the unity of Friends, I set off on a visit to Friends in the upper part of Berks and Philadelphia counties; was at eleven meetings in about two weeks, and have renewed cause to bow in reverence before the Lord, who, by the powerful extendings of his humbling goodness, opened my way among Friends, and I trust made the meetings profitable to us. The following winter I joined some Friends in a family visit to some part of our meeting, in which exercise the pure influence of Divine love made our visits reviving.

Fifth of fifth month, 1768.—I left home under the humbling hand of the Lord, with a certificate to visit some meetings in Maryland, and to proceed without a horse seemed clearest to me. I was at the Quarterly Meetings at Philadelphia and Concord, whence I proceeded to Chester River, and, crossing the bay, was at the Yearly Meeting at West River; I then returned to Chester River, and, taking a few meetings in my way, proceeded home. It was a journey of much inward waiting, and as my eye was to the Lord, way was several times opened to my humbling admiration when things appeared very difficult. On my return I felt a very comfortable relief of mind, having through Divine help labored in much plainness, both with Friends selected and in the more public meetings, so that I trust the pure witness in many minds was reached.

Eleventh of sixth month, 1769.—There have been sundry cases of late years within the limits of our Monthly Meeting, respecting the exercising of pure righteousness towards the negroes, in which I have lived under a labor of heart that equity might be steadily preserved. On this account I have had some close exercises among Friends, in which, I may thankfully say, I find peace. And as my meditations have been on universal love, my own conduct in time past became of late very grievous to me. As persons setting negroes free in our province are bound by law to maintain them in case they have need of relief, some in the time of my youth who scrupled to keep slaves for term of life were wont to detain their young negroes in their service without wages till they were thirty years of age. With this custom I so far agreed that being joined with another Friend in executing the will of a deceased Friend, I once sold a negro lad till he might attain the age of thirty years, and applied the money to the use of the estate.

With abasement of heart I may now say that sometimes as I have sat in a meeting with my heart exercised towards that awful Being who respecteth not persons nor colors, and have thought upon this lad, I have felt that all was not clear in my mind respecting him; and as I have attended to this exercise and fervently sought the Lord it hath appeared to me that I should make some restitution; but in what way I saw not till lately, when being under some concern that I might be resigned to go on a visit to some part of the West Indies, and under close engagement of spirit seeking to the Lord for counsel herein, the aforesaid transaction came heavily upon me, and my mind for a time was covered with darkness and sorrow. Under this sore affliction my heart was softened to receive instruction, and I now first perceived that as I had been one of the two executors who had sold this lad for nine years longer than is common for our own children to serve, so I should now offer part of my substance to redeem the last half of the nine years; but as the time was not yet come, I executed a bond, binding myself and my executors to pay to the man to whom he was sold what to candid men might appear equitable for the last four and a half years of his time, in case the said youth should be living, and in a condition likely to provide comfortably for himself.

Ninth of tenth month.—My heart hath often been deeply afflicted under a feeling that the standard of pure righteousness is not lifted up to the people by us, as a society, in that clearness which it might have been, had we been as faithful as we ought to be to the teachings of Christ. And as my mind hath been inward to the Lord, the purity of Christ's government hath been made clear to my understanding, and I have believed, in the opening of universal love, that where a people who are convinced of the truth of the inward teachings of Christ are active in putting laws in execution which are not consistent with pure wisdom, it hath a necessary tendency to bring dimness over their minds. My heart having been thus exercised for several years with a tender sympathy towards my fellow-members, I have within a few months past expressed my concern on this subject in several meetings for discipline.

CHAPTER X

1769, 1770

Bodily Indisposition—Exercise of his Mind for the Good of the People in the West Indies—Communicates to Friends his Concern to visit some of those Islands—Preparations to embark—Considerations on the Trade to the West Indies—Release from his Concern and return Home—Religious Engagements—Sickness, and Exercise of his Mind therein.

TWELFTH of third month, 1769.—Having for some years past dieted myself on account of illness and weakness of body, and not having ability to travel by land as heretofore, I was at times favored to look with awfulness towards the Lord, before whom are all my ways, who alone hath the power of life and death, and to feel thankfulness raised in me for this fatherly chastisement, believing that if I was truly humbled under it all would work for good. While under this bodily weakness, my mind was at times exercised for my fellow-creatures in the West Indies, and I grew jealous over myself lest the disagreeableness of the prospect should hinder me from obediently attending thereto; for, though I knew not that the Lord required me to go there, yet I believed that resignation was now called for in that respect. Feeling a danger of not being wholly devoted to him, I was frequently engaged to watch unto prayer that I might be preserved; and upwards of a year having passed, as I one day walked in a solitary wood, my mind being covered with awfulness, cries were raised in me to my merciful Father, that he would graciously keep me in faithfulness; and it then settled on my mind, as a duty, to open my condition to Friends at our Monthly Meeting, which I did soon after, as follows:—

"An exercise hath attended me for some time past, and of late hath been more weighty upon me, which is, that I believe it is required of me to be resigned to go on a visit to some parts of the West Indies." In the Quarterly and General Spring Meetings I found no clearness to express anything further than that I believed resignation herein was required of me. Having obtained certificates from all the said meetings, I felt like a sojourner at my outward habitation, and kept free from worldly encumbrances, and I was often bowed in spirit before the Lord, with inward breathings to him that I might be rightly directed. I may here note that the circumstance before related of my having, when young, joined with another executor in selling a negro lad till he might attain the age of thirty years, was now the cause of much sorrow to me; and, after having settled matters relating to this youth, I provided a sea-store and bed, and things for the voyage. Hearing of a vessel likely to sail from Philadelphia for Barbadoes, I spake with one of the owners at Burlington, and soon after went to Philadelphia on purpose to speak to him again. He told me there was a Friend in town who was part owner of the said vessel. I felt no inclination to speak with the latter, but returned home. Awhile after I took leave of my family, and, going to Philadelphia, had some weighty conversation with the first-mentioned owner, and showed him a writing, as follows:—

"On the 25th of eleventh month, 1769, as an exercise with respect to a visit to Barbadoes hath been weighty on my mind, I may express some of the trials which have attended me, under which I have at times rejoiced that I have felt my own self-will subjected.

"Some years ago I retailed rum, sugar, and molasses, the fruits of the labor of slaves, but had not then much concern about them save only that the rum might be used in moderation; nor was this concern so weightily attended to as I now believe it ought to have been. Having of late years been further informed respecting the oppressions too generally exercised in these islands, and thinking often on the dangers there are in connections of interest and fellowship with the works of darkness (Eph. v. 11), I have felt an increasing concern to be wholly given up to the leadings of the Holy Spirit, and it hath seemed right that my small gain from this branch of trade should be applied in promoting righteousness on the earth. This was the first motion towards a visit to Barbadoes. I believed also that part of my outward substance should be applied in paying my passage, if I went, and providing things in a lowly way for my subsistence; but when the time drew near in which I believed it required of me to be in readiness, a difficulty arose which hath been a continual trial for some months past, under which I have, with abasement of mind from day to day, sought the Lord for instruction, having often had a feeling of the condition of one formerly, who bewailed himself because the Lord hid his face from him. During these exercises my heart hath often been contrite, and I have had a tender feeling of the temptations of my fellow-creatures, laboring under expensive customs not agreeable to the simplicity that 'there is in Christ' (2 Cor. ii. 3), and sometimes in the renewings of gospel love I have been helped to minister to others.

"That which hath so closely engaged my mind, in seeking to the Lord for instruction, is, whether, after the full information I have had of the oppression which the slaves lie under who raise the West India produce, which I have gained by reading a caution and warning to Great Britain and her colonies, written by Anthony Benezet, it is right for me to take passage in a vessel employed in the West India trade.

"To trade freely with oppressors without laboring to dissuade them from such unkind treatment, and to seek for gain by such traffic, tends, I believe, to make them more easy respecting their conduct than they would be if the cause of universal righteousness was humbly and firmly attended to by those in general with whom they have commerce; and that complaint of the Lord by his prophet, "They have strengthened the hands of the wicked," hath very often revived in my mind. I may here add some circumstances which occurred to me before I had any prospect of a visit there. David longed for some water in a well beyond an army of Philistines who were at war with Israel, and some of his men, to please him, ventured their lives in passing through this army, and brought that water.

"It doth not appear that the Israelites were then scarce of water, but rather that David gave way to delicacy of taste; and having reflected on the danger to which these men had been exposed, he considered this water as their blood, and his heart smote him that he could not drink it, but he poured it out to the Lord. The oppression of the slaves which I have seen in several journeys southward on this continent, and the report of their treatment in the West Indies, have deeply affected me, and a care to live in the spirit of peace and minister no just cause of offence to my fellow-creatures having from time to time livingly revived in my mind, I have for some years past declined to gratify my palate with those sugars.

"I do not censure my brethren in these things, but I believe the Father of Mercies, to whom all mankind by creation are equally related, hath heard the groans of this oppressed people and that he is preparing some to have a tender feeling of their condition. Trading in or the frequent use of any produce known to be raised by the labor of those who are under such lamentable oppression hath appeared to be a subject which may hereafter require the more serious consideration of the humble followers of Christ, the Prince of Peace.

"After long and mournful exercise I am now free to mention how things have opened in my mind, with desires that if it may please the Lord further to open his will to any of his children in this matter they may faithfully follow him in such further manifestation.

"The number of those who decline the use of West India produce, on account of the hard usage of the slaves who raise it, appears small, even among people truly pious; and the labors in Christian love on that subject of those who do are not very extensive. Were the trade from this continent to the West Indies to be stopped at once, I believe many there would suffer for want of bread. Did we on this continent and the inhabitants of the West Indies generally dwell in pure righteousness, I believe a small trade between us might be right. Under these considerations, when the thoughts of wholly declining the use of trading-vessels and of trying to hire a vessel to go under ballast have arisen in my mind, I have believed that the labors in gospel love hitherto bestowed in the cause of universal righteousness have not reached that height. If the trade to the West Indies were no more than was consistent with pure wisdom, I believe the passage-money would for good reasons be higher than it is now; and therefore, under deep exercise of mind, I have believed that I should not take advantage of this great trade and small passage-money, but, as a testimony in favor of less trading, should pay more than is common for others to pay if I go at this time."

The first-mentioned owner, having read the paper, went with me to the other owner, who also read over the paper, and we had some solid conversation, under which I felt myself bowed in reverence before the Most High. At length one of them asked me if I would go and see the vessel. But not having clearness in my mind to go, I went to my lodging and retired in private under great exercise of mind; and my tears were poured out before the Lord with inward cries that he would graciously help me under these trials. I believe my mind was resigned, but I did not feel clearness to proceed; and my own weakness and the necessity of Divine instruction were impressed upon me.

I was for a time as one who knew not what to do and was tossed as in a tempest; under which affliction the doctrine of Christ, "Take no thought for the morrow," arose livingly before me, and I was favored to get into a good degree of stillness. Having been near two days in town, I believed my obedience to my Heavenly Father consisted in returning homeward; I therefore went over among Friends on the Jersey shore and tarried till the morning on which the vessel was appointed to sail. As I lay in bed the latter part of that night my mind was comforted, and I felt what I esteemed a fresh confirmation that it was the Lord's will that I should pass through some further exercises near home; so I went thither, and still felt like a sojourner with my family. In the fresh spring of pure love I had some labors in a private way among Friends on a subject relating to truth's testimony, under which I had frequently been exercised in heart for some years. I remember, as I walked on the road under this exercise, that passage in Ezekiel came fresh upon me, "Whithersoever their faces were turned thither they went." And I was graciously helped to discharge my duty in the fear and dread of the Almighty.

In the course of a few weeks it pleased the Lord to visit me with a pleurisy; and after I had lain a few days and felt the disorder very grievous, I was thoughtful how it might end. I had of late, through various exercises, been much weaned from the pleasant things of this life; and I now thought if it were the Lord's will to put an end to my labors and graciously to receive me into the arms of his mercy, death would be acceptable to me; but if it were his will further to refine me under affliction, and to make me in any degree useful in his church, I desired not to die. I may with thankfulness say that in this case I felt resignedness wrought in me and had no inclination to send for a doctor, believing, if it were the Lord's will through outward means to raise me up, some sympathizing Friends would be sent to minister to me; which accordingly was the case. But though I was carefully attended, yet the disorder was at times so heavy that I had no expectation of recovery. One night in particular my bodily distress was great; my feet grew cold, and the cold increased up my legs towards my body; at that time I had no inclination to ask my nurse to apply anything warm to my feet, expecting my end was near. After I had lain near ten hours in this condition, I closed my eyes, thinking whether I might now be delivered out of the body; but in these awful moments my mind was livingly opened to behold the church; and strong engagements were begotten in me for the everlasting well-being of my fellow-creatures. I felt in the spring of pure love that I might remain some time longer in the body, to fill up according to my measure that which remains of the afflictions of Christ, and to labor for the good of the church; after which I requested my nurse to apply warmth to my feet, and I revived. The next night, feeling a weighty exercise of spirit and having a solid friend sitting up with me, I requested him to write what I said, which he did as follows:—

"Fourth day of the first month, 1770, about five in the morning.—I have seen in the Light of the Lord that the day is approaching when the man that is most wise in human policy shall be the greatest fool; and the arm that is mighty to support injustice shall be broken to pieces; the enemies of righteousness shall make a terrible rattle, and shall mightily torment one another; for He that is omnipotent is rising up to judgment, and will plead the cause of the oppressed; and He commanded me to open the vision."

Near a week after this, feeling my mind livingly opened, I sent for a neighbor, who, at my request, wrote as follows:—

"The place of prayer is a precious habitation; for I now saw that the prayers of the saints were precious incense; and a trumpet was given to me that I might sound forth this language; that the children might hear it and be invited together to this precious habitation, where the prayers of the saints, as sweet incense, arise before the throne of God and the Lamb. I saw this habitation to be safe,—to be inwardly quiet when there were great stirrings and commotions in the world.

"Prayer, at this day, in pure resignation, is a precious place: the trumpet is sounded; the call goes forth to the church that she gather to the place of pure inward prayer: and her habitation is safe."

CHAPTER XI

1772

Embarks at Chester, with Samuel Emlen, in a Ship bound for London—
Exercise of Mind respecting the Hardships of the Sailors—Consid-
erations on the Dangers of training Youth to a Seafaring Life—
Thoughts during a Storm at Sea—Arrival in London.

HAVING been some time under a religious concern to prepare
for crossing the seas, in order to visit Friends in the northern parts of England, and more particularly in Yorkshire,
after consideration I thought it expedient to inform Friends of it at
our Monthly Meeting at Burlington, who, having unity with me
therein, gave me a certificate. I afterwards communicated the same
to our Quarterly Meeting, and they likewise certified their concurrence. Some time after, at the General Spring Meeting of ministers
and elders, I thought it my duty to acquaint them with the religious
exercise which attended my mind; and they likewise signified their
unity therewith by a certificate, dated the 24th of third month, 1772,
directed to Friends in Great Britain.

In the fourth month following I thought the time was come for
me to make some inquiry for a suitable conveyance; and as my concern was principally towards the northern parts of England, it seemed
most proper to go in a vessel bound to Liverpool or Whitehaven.
While I was at Philadelphia deliberating on this subject I was informed that my beloved friend Samuel Emlen, junior, intended to
go to London, and had taken a passage for himself in the cabin of
the ship called the Mary and Elizabeth, of which James Sparks was
master, and John Head, of the city of Philadelphia, one of the owners; and feeling a draught in my mind towards the steerage of the
same ship, I went first and opened to Samuel the feeling I had concerning it.

My beloved friend wept when I spake to him, and appeared glad
that I had thoughts of going in the vessel with him, though my pros-

pect was toward the steerage: and he offering to go with me, we went on board, first into the cabin,—a commodious room,—and then into the steerage, where we sat down on a chest, the sailors being busy about us. The owner of the ship also came and sat down with us. My mind was turned towards Christ, the Heavenly Counsellor, and feeling at this time my own will subjected, my heart was contrite before him. A motion was made by the owner to go and sit in the cabin, as a place more retired; but I felt easy to leave the ship, and making no agreement as to a passage in her, told the owner if I took a passage in the ship I believed it would be in the steerage; but did not say much as to my exercise in that case.

After I went to my lodgings, and the case was a little known in town, a Friend laid before me the great inconvenience attending a passage in the steerage, which for a time appeared very discouraging to me.

I soon after went to bed, and my mind was under a deep exercise before the Lord, whose helping hand was manifested to me as I slept that night, and his love strengthened my heart. In the morning I went with two Friends on board the vessel again, and after a short time spent therein, I went with Samuel Emlen to the house of the owner, to whom, in the hearing of Samuel only, I opened my exercise in relation to a scruple I felt with regard to a passage in the cabin, in substance as follows:—

"That on the outside of that part of the ship where the cabin was I observed sundry sorts of carved work and imagery; that in the cabin I observed some superfluity of workmanship of several sorts; and that according to the ways of men's reckoning, the sum of money to be paid for a passage in that apartment has some relation to the expense of furnishing it to please the minds of such as give way to a conformity to this world; and that in this, as in other cases, the moneys received from the passengers are calculated to defray the cost of these superfluities, as well as the other expenses of their passage. I therefore felt a scruple with regard to paying my money to be applied to such purposes."

As my mind was now opened, I told the owner that I had, at several times, in my travels, seen great oppressions on this continent, at which my heart had been much affected and brought into a feeling of the state of the sufferers; and having many times been engaged in the fear and love of God to labor with those under whom the oppressed have been borne down and afflicted, I have often perceived that with a view to get riches and to provide estates for children, that they may live conformably to the customs and honors of this world, many are entangled in the spirit of oppression, and the exercise of my soul had been such that I could not find peace in joining in anything which I saw was against that wisdom which is pure.

After this I agreed for a passage in the steerage; and hearing that Joseph White had desired to see me, I went to his house, and the next day home, where I tarried two nights. Early the next morning I parted with my family under a sense of the humbling hand of God upon me, and, going to Philadelphia, had an opportunity with several of my beloved friends, who appeared to be concerned for me on account of the unpleasant situation of that part of the vessel in which I was likely to lodge. In these opportunities my mind, through the mercies of the Lord, was kept low in an inward waiting for his help; and Friends having expressed their desire that I might have a more convenient place than the steerage, did not urge it, but appeared disposed to leave me to the Lord.

Having stayed two nights at Philadelphia, I went the next day to Derby Monthly Meeting, where through the strength of Divine love my heart was enlarged towards the youth there present, under which I was helped to labor in some tenderness of spirit. I lodged at William Horn's and afterwards went to Chester, where I met with Samuel Emlen, and we went on board 1st of fifth month, 1772. As I sat alone on the deck I felt a satisfactory evidence that my proceedings were not in my own will, but under the power of the cross of Christ.

Seventh of fifth month.—We have had rough weather mostly since I came on board, and the passengers, James Reynolds, John Till Adams, Sarah Logan and her hired maid, and John Bispham, all seasick at times; from which sickness, through the tender mercies of my Heavenly Father, I have been preserved, my afflictions now being of another kind. There appeared an openness in the minds of the master of the ship and in the cabin passengers towards me. We are often together on the deck, and sometimes in the cabin. My mind, through the merciful help of the Lord, hath been preserved in a good degree watchful and quiet, for which I have great cause to be thankful.

As my lodging in the steerage, now near a week, hath afforded me sundry opportunities of seeing, hearing, and feeling with respect to the life and spirit of many poor sailors, an exercise of soul hath attended me in regard to placing our children and youth where they may be likely to be exampled and instructed in the pure fear of the Lord.

Being much among the seamen I have, from a motion of love, taken sundry opportunities with one of them at a time, and have in free conversation labored to turn their minds toward the fear of the Lord. This day we had a meeting in the cabin, where my heart was contrite under a feeling of Divine love.

I believe a communication with different parts of the world by sea is at times consistent with the will of our Heavenly Father, and to educate some youth in the practice of sailing, I believe may be right; but how lamentable is the present corruption of the world! How impure are the channels through which trade is conducted! How great is the danger to which poor lads are exposed when placed on shipboard to learn the art of sailing! Five lads training up for the seas were on board this ship. Two of them were brought up in our Society, and the other, by name James Naylor, is a member, to whose father James Naylor, mentioned in Sewel's history, appears to have been uncle. I often feel a tenderness of heart towards these poor lads, and at times look at them as though they were my children according to the flesh.

O that all may take heed and beware of covetousness! O that all may learn of Christ, who was meek and lowly of heart. Then in faithfully following him he will teach us to be content with food and raiment without respect to the customs or honors of this world. Men thus redeemed will feel a tender concern for their fellow-creatures, and a desire that those in the lowest stations may be assisted and encouraged, and where owners of ships attain to the perfect law of liberty and are doers of the Word, these will be blessed in their deeds.

A ship at sea commonly sails all night, and the seamen take their watches four hours at a time. Rising to work in the night, it is not commonly pleasant in any case, but in dark rainy nights it is very disagreeable, even though each man were furnished with all conveniences. If, after having been on deck several hours in the night, they come down into the steerage soaking wet, and are so closely stowed that proper convenience for change of garments is not easily come at, but for want of proper room their wet garments are thrown in heaps, and sometimes, through much crowding, are trodden under foot in going to their lodgings and getting out of them, and it is difficult at times for each to find his own. Here are trials for the poor sailors.

Now, as I have been with them in my lodge, my heart hath often yearned for them, and tender desires have been raised in me that all owners and masters of vessels may dwell in the love of God and therein act uprightly, and by seeking less for gain and looking carefully to their ways they may earnestly labor to remove all cause of provocation from the poor seamen, so that they may neither fret nor use excess of strong drink; for, indeed, the poor creatures, in the wet and cold, seem to apply at times to strong drink to supply the want of other convenience. Great reformation is wanting in the world, and the necessity of it among those who do business on great waters hath at this time been abundantly opened before me.

Eighth of fifth month.—This morning the clouds gathered, the wind blew strong from the southeast, and before noon so increased that sailing appeared dangerous. The seamen then bound up some of their sails and took down others, and the storm increasing they put the dead-lights, so called, into the cabin windows and lighted a lamp as at night. The wind now blew vehemently, and the sea wrought to that degree that an awful seriousness prevailed in the cabin, in which I spent, I believe, about seventeen hours, for the cabin passengers had given me frequent invitations, and I thought the poor wet toiling seamen had need of all the room in the crowded steerage. They now ceased from sailing and put the vessel in the posture called lying to.

My mind during this tempest, through the gracious assistance of the Lord, was preserved in a good degree of resignation; and at times I expressed a few words in his love to my shipmates in regard to the all-sufficiency of Him who formed the great deep, and whose care is so extensive that a sparrow falls not without his notice; and thus in a tender frame of mind I spoke to them of the necessity of our yielding in true obedience to the instructions of our Heavenly Father, who sometimes through adversities intendeth our refinement.

About eleven at night I went out on the deck. The sea wrought exceedingly, and the high, foaming waves round about had in some sort the appearance of fire, but did not give much if any light. The sailor at the helm said he lately saw a corposant at the head of the mast. I observed that the master of the ship ordered the carpenter to keep on the deck; and, though he said little, I apprehended his care was that the carpenter with his axe might be in readiness in case of any emergency. Soon after this the vehemency of the wind abated, and before morning they again put the ship under sail.

Tenth of fifth month.—It being the first day of the week and fine weather, we had a meeting in the cabin, at which most of the seamen were present; this meeting was to me a strengthening time. 13th.— As I continue to lodge in the steerage I feel an openness this morning to express something further of the state of my mind in respect to poor lads bound apprentice to learn the art of sailing. As I believe sailing is of use in the world, a labor of soul attends me that the pure counsel of truth may be humbly waited for in this case by all concerned in the business of the seas. A pious father whose mind is exercised for the everlasting welfare of his child may not with a peaceable mind place him out to an employment among a people whose common course of life is manifestly corrupt and profane. Great is the present defect among seafaring men in regard to virtue and piety; and, by reason of an abundant traffic and many ships being used for war, so many people are employed on the sea that the subject of placing lads to this employment appears very weighty.

When I remember the saying of the Most High through his prophet, "This people have I formed for myself; they shall show forth my praise," and think of placing children among such to learn the practice of sailing, the consistency of it with a pious education seems to me like that mentioned by the prophet, "There is no answer from God."

Profane examples are very corrupting and very forcible. And as my mind day after day and night after night hath been affected with a sympathizing tenderness towards poor children who are put to the employment of sailors, I have sometimes had weighty conversation with the sailors in the steerage, who were mostly respectful to me and became more so the longer I was with them. They mostly appeared to take kindly what I said to them; but their minds were so deeply impressed with the almost universal depravity among sailors that the poor creatures in their answers to me have revived in my remembrance that of the degenerate Jews a little before the captivity, as repeated by Jeremiah the prophet, "There is no hope."

Now under this exercise a sense of the desire of outward gain prevailing among us felt grievous; and a strong call to the professed followers of Christ was raised in me that all may take heed lest, through loving this present world, they be found in a continued neglect of duty with respect to a faithful labor for reformation.

To silence every motion proceeding from the love of money and humbly to wait upon God to know his will concerning us have appeared necessary. He alone is able to strengthen us to dig deep, to remove all which lies between us and the safe foundation, and so to direct us in our outward employments that pure universal love may shine forth in our proceedings. Desires arising from the spirit of truth are pure desires; and when a mind divinely opened towards a young generation is made sensible of corrupting examples powerfully working and extensively spreading among them, how moving is the prospect! In a world of dangers and difficulties, like a desolate, thorny wilderness, how precious, how comfortable, how safe, are the leadings of Christ the good Shepherd, who said, "I know my sheep, and am known of mine!"

Sixteenth of sixth* month.—Wind for several days past often high, what the sailors call squally, with a rough sea and frequent rains. This last night has been a very trying one to the poor seamen, the water the most part of the night running over the main-deck, and sometimes breaking waves came on the quarter-deck. The latter part of the night, as I lay in bed, my mind was humbled under the power of Divine love; and resignedness to the great Creator of the earth and the seas was renewedly wrought in me, and his fatherly care over his children felt precious to my soul. I was now desirous to embrace every opportunity of being inwardly acquainted with the

*[Fifth?—Ed.]

hardships and difficulties of my fellow-creatures, and to labor in his love for the spreading of pure righteousness on the earth. Opportunities were frequent of hearing conversation among the sailors respecting the voyages to Africa and the manner of bringing the deeply oppressed slaves into our islands. They are frequently brought on board the vessels in chains and fetters, with hearts loaded with grief under the apprehension of miserable slavery; so that my mind was frequently engaged to meditate on these things.

Seventeenth of fifth month and first of the week.—We had a meeting in the cabin, to which the seamen generally came. My spirit was contrite before the Lord, whose love at this time affected my heart. In the afternoon I felt a tender sympathy of soul with my poor wife and family left behind, in which state my heart was enlarged in desires that they may walk in that humble obedience wherein the everlasting Father may be their guide and support through all their difficulties in this world; and a sense of that gracious assistance, through which my mind hath been strengthened to take up the cross and leave them to travel in the love of truth, hath begotten thankfulness in my heart to our great Helper.

Twenty-fourth of fifth month.—A clear, pleasant morning. As I sat on deck I felt a reviving in my nature, which had been weakened through much rainy weather and high winds and being shut up in a close, unhealthy air. Several nights of late I have felt my breathing difficult; and a little after the rising of the second watch, which is about midnight, I have got up and stood near an hour with my face near the hatchway, to get the fresh air at the small vacancy under the hatch door, which is commonly shut down, partly to keep out rain and sometimes to keep the breaking waves from dashing into the steerage. I may with thankfulness to the Father of Mercies acknowledge that in my present weak state my mind hath been supported to bear this affliction with patience; and I have looked at the present dispensation as a kindness from the great Father of mankind, who, in this my floating pilgrimage, is in some degree bringing me to feel what many thousands of my fellow-creatures often suffer in a greater degree.

My appetite failing, the trial hath been the heavier; and I have felt tender breathings in my soul after God, the fountain of comfort, whose inward help hath supplied at times the want of outward convenience; and strong desires have attended me that his family, who are acquainted with the movings of his Holy Spirit, may be so redeemed from the love of money and from that spirit in which men seek honor one of another, that in all business, by sea or land, they may constantly keep in view the coming of his kingdom on earth as it is in Heaven, and, by faithfully following this safe guide, may show forth examples tending to lead out of that under which the creation groans. This day we had a meeting in the cabin, in which I was favored in some degree to experience the fulfilling of that saying of the prophet, "The Lord hath been a strength to the poor, a strength to the needy in their distress"; for which my heart is bowed in thankfulness before him.

Twenty-eighth of fifth month.—Wet weather of late and small winds, inclining to calms. Our seamen cast a lead, I suppose about one hundred fathoms, but found no bottom. Foggy weather this morning. Through the kindness of the great Preserver of men my mind remains quiet; and a degree of exercise from day to day attends me, that the pure peaceable government of Christ may spread and prevail among mankind.

The leading of a young generation in that pure way in which the wisdom of this world hath no place, where parents and tutors, humbly waiting for the heavenly Counsellor, may example them in the truth as it is in Jesus, hath for several days been the exercise of my mind. O, how safe, how quiet, is that state where the soul stands in pure obedience to the voice of Christ and a watchful care is maintained not to follow the voice of the stranger! Here Christ is felt to be our Shepherd, and under his leading people are brought to a stability; and where he doth not lead forward, we are bound in the bonds of pure love to stand still and wait upon him.

In the love of money and in the wisdom of this world, business is proposed, then the urgency of affairs push forward, and the mind cannot in this state discern the good and perfect will of God concerning us. The love of God is manifested in graciously calling us to come out of that which stands in confusion; but if we bow not in the name of Jesus, if we give not up those prospects of gain which in the wisdom of this world are open before us, but say in our hearts,

"I must needs go on; and in going on I hope to keep as near the purity of truth as the business before me will admit of," the mind remains entangled and the shining of the light of life into the soul is obstructed.

Surely the Lord calls to mourning and deep humiliation that in his fear we may be instructed and led safely through the great difficulties and perplexities in this present age. In an entire subjection of our wills the Lord graciously opens a way for his people, where all their wants are bounded by his wisdom; and here we experience the substance of what Moses the prophet figured out in the water of separation as a purification from sin.

Esau is mentioned as a child red all over like a hairy garment. In Esau is represented the natural will of man. In preparing the water of separation a red heifer without blemish, on which there had been no yoke, was to be slain and her blood sprinkled by the priest seven times towards the tabernacle of the congregation; then her skin, her flesh, and all pertaining to her, was to be burnt without the camp, and of her ashes the water was prepared. Thus, the crucifying of the old man, or natural will, is represented; and hence comes a separation from that carnal mind which is death. "He who toucheth the dead body of a man and purifieth not himself with the water of separation, defileth the tabernacle of the Lord; he is unclean." (Num. xix. 13.)

If any through the love of gain engage in business wherein they dwell as among the tombs and touch the bodies of those who are dead should through the infinite love of God feel the power of the cross of Christ to crucify them to the world, and therein learn humbly to follow the divine Leader, here is the judgment of this world, here the prince of this world is cast out. The water of separation is felt; and though we have been among the slain, and through the desire of gain have touched the dead body of a man, yet in the purifying love of Christ we are washed in the water of separation; we are brought off from that business, from that gain and from that fellowship which is not agreeable to his holy will. I have felt a renewed confirmation in the time of this voyage, that the Lord, in his infinite love, is calling to his visited children, so to give up all outward possessions and means of getting treasures, that his Holy Spirit may have free course in their hearts and direct them in all their proceedings. To feel the substance pointed at in this figure man must know death as to his own will.

"No man can see God and live." This was spoken by the Almighty to Moses the prophet and opened by our blessed Redeemer. As death comes on our own wills, and a new life is formed in us, the heart is purified and prepared to understand clearly, "Blessed are the pure in heart, for they shall see God." In purity of heart the mind is divinely opened to behold the nature of universal righteousness, or the righteousness of the kingdom of God. "No man hath seen the Father save he that is of God, he hath seen the Father."

The natural mind is active about the things of this life, and in this natural activity business is proposed and a will is formed in us to go forward in it. And so long as this natural will remains unsubjected, so long there remains an obstruction to the clearness of Divine light operating in us; but when we love God with all our heart and with all our strength, in this love we love our neighbor as ourselves; and a tenderness of heart is felt towards all people for whom Christ died, even those who, as to outward circumstances, may be to us as the Jews were to the Samaritans. "Who is my neighbor?" See this question answered by our Saviour, Luke x. 30. In this love we can say that Jesus is the Lord; and in this reformation in our souls, manifested in a full reformation of our lives, wherein all things are new, and all things are of God (2 Cor. v. 18), the desire of gain is subjected.

When employment is honestly followed in the light of truth, and people become diligent in business, "fervent in spirit, serving the Lord" (Rom. xii. 11), the meaning of the name is opened to us: "This is the name by which he shall be called, THE LORD OUR RIGHTEOUSNESS." (Jer. xxiii. 6.) O, how precious is this name! it is like ointment poured out. The chaste virgins are in love with the Redeemer; and for promoting his peaceable kingdom in the world are content to endure hardness like good soldiers; and are so separated in spirit from the desire of riches, that in their employments they become extensively careful to give no offence, either to Jew or Heathen, or to the church of Christ.

Thirty-first of fifth month and first of the week.—We had a meeting in the cabin, with nearly all the ship's company, the whole being near thirty. In this meeting the Lord in mercy favored us with the extending of his love.

Second of sixth month.—Last evening the seamen found bottom at about seventy fathoms. This morning, a fair wind and pleasant. I sat on deck; my heart was overcome with the love of Christ, and melted into contrition before him. In this state the prospect of that work to which I found my mind drawn when in my native land being, in some degree, opened before me, I felt like a little child; and my cries were put up to my Heavenly Father for preservation, that in an humble dependence on him my soul might be strengthened in his love and kept inwardly waiting for his counsel. This afternoon we saw that part of England called the Lizard.

Some fowls yet remained of those the passengers took for their sea-store. I believe about fourteen perished in the storms at sea, by the waves breaking over the quarter-deck, and a considerable number with sickness at different times. I observed the cocks crew as we came down the Delaware, and while we were near the land, but afterwards I think I did not hear one of them crow till we came near the English coast, when they again crowed a few times. In observing their dull appearance at sea, and the pining sickness of some of them, I often remembered the Fountain of goodness, who gave being to all creatures, and whose love extends to caring for the sparrows. I believe where the love of God is verily perfected, and the true spirit of government watchfully attended to, a tenderness towards all creatures made subject to us will be experienced, and a care felt in us that we do not lessen that sweetness of life in the animal creation which the great Creator intends for them under our government.

Fourth of sixth month.—Wet weather, high winds, and so dark that we could see but a little way. I perceived our seamen were apprehensive of the danger of missing the channel, which I understood was narrow. In a while it grew lighter, and they saw the land and knew where we were. Thus the Father of Mercies was pleased to try us with the sight of dangers, and then graciously, from time to time, deliver us from them; thus sparing our lives, that in humility and reverence we might walk before him and put our trust in him.

About noon a pilot came off from Dover, where my beloved friend Samuel Emlen went on shore and thence to London, about seventy-two miles by land; but I felt easy in staying in the ship.

Seventh of sixth month and first of the week.—A clear morning; we lay at anchor for the tide, and had a parting meeting with the ship's company, in which my heart was enlarged in a fervent concern for them, that they may come to experience salvation through Christ. Had a head-wind up the Thames; lay sometimes at anchor; saw many ships passing, and some at anchor near; and I had large opportunity of feeling the spirit in which the poor bewildered sailors too generally live. That lamentable degeneracy which so much prevails in the people employed on the seas so affected my heart that I cannot easily convey the feeling I had to another.

The present state of the seafaring life in general appears so opposite to that of a pious education, so full of corruption and extreme alienation from God, so full of the most dangerous examples to young people that in looking towards a young generation I feel a care for them, that they may have an education different from the present one of lads at sea, and that all of us who are acquainted with the pure gospel spirit may lay this case to heart, may remember the lamentable corruptions which attend the conveyance of merchandise across the seas, and so abide in the love of Christ that, being delivered from the entangling expenses of a curious, delicate, and luxurious life, we may learn contentment with a little, and promote the seafaring life no further than that spirit which leads into all truth attends us in our proceedings.

CHAPTER XII

1772

Attends the Yearly Meeting in London—Then proceeds towards Yorkshire—Visits Quarterly and other Meetings in the Counties of Hertford, Warwick, Oxford, Nottingham, York, and Westmoreland—
Returns to Yorkshire—Instructive Observations and Letters—Hears
of the Decease of William Hunt—Some Account of him—The
Author's Last Illness and Death at York.

ON the 8th of sixth month, 1772, we landed at London, and
I went straightway to the Yearly Meeting of ministers
and elders, which had been gathered, I suppose, about
half an hour.[1]

In this meeting my mind was humbly contrite. In the afternoon
the meeting for business was opened, which by adjournments held
near a week. In these meetings I often felt a living concern for the
establishment of Friends in the pure life of truth. My heart was en-

[1] There is a story told of his first appearance in England which I have from my
friend, William J. Allinson, editor of the Friends' Review, and which he assures
me is well authenticated. The vessel reached London on the morning of the fifth
day of the week, and John Woolman, knowing that the meeting was then in session,
lost no time in reaching it. Coming in late and unannounced, his peculiar dress
and manner excited attention and apprehension that he was an itinerant enthusiast.
He presented his certificate from Friends in America, but the dissatisfaction still
remained, and some one remarked that perhaps the stranger Friend might feel that
his dedication of himself to this apprehended service was accepted, without further
labor, and that he might now feel free to return to his home. John Woolman sat
silent for a space, seeking the unerring counsel of Divine Wisdom. He was pro-
foundly affected by the unfavorable reception he met with, and his tears flowed
freely. In the love of Christ and his fellow-men he had, at a painful sacrifice, taken
his life in his hands, and left behind the peace and endearments of home. That
love still flowed out toward the people of England; must it henceforth be pent up
in his own heart? He rose at last, and stated that he could not feel himself released
from his prospect of labor in England. Yet he could not travel in the ministry without the unity of Friends; and while that was withheld he could not feel easy to be
of any cost to them. He could not go back as had been suggested; but he was
acquainted with a mechanical trade, and while the impediment to his services
continued he hoped Friends would be kindly willing to employ him in such business as he was capable of, that he might not be chargeable to any.

A deep silence prevailed over the assembly, many of whom were touched by the
wise simplicity of the stranger's words and manner. After a season of waiting,
John Woolman felt that words were given him to utter as a minister of Christ.

larged in the meetings of ministers, that for business, and in several meetings for public worship, and I felt my mind united in true love to the faithful laborers now gathered at this Yearly Meeting. On the 15th I went to a Quarterly Meeting at Hertford.

First of seventh month.—I have been at Quarterly Meetings at Sherrington, Northampton, Banbury, and Shipton, and have had sundry meetings between. My mind hath been bowed under a sense of Divine goodness manifested among us; my heart hath been often enlarged in true love, both among ministers and elders and in public meetings, and through the Lord's goodness I believe it hath been a fresh visitation to many, in particular to the youth.

Seventeenth.—I was this day at Birmingham; I have been at meetings at Coventry, Warwick, in Oxfordshire, and sundry other places, and have felt the humbling hand of the Lord upon me; but through his tender mercies I find peace in the labors I have gone through.

Twenty-sixth.—I have continued travelling northward, visiting meetings. Was this day at Nottingham; the forenoon meeting was especially, through Divine love, a heart-tendering season. Next day I had a meeting in a Friend's family, which, through the strengthening arm of the Lord, was a time to be thankfully remembered.

Second of eighth month and first of the week.—I was this day at Sheffield, a large inland town. I was at sundry meetings last week, and feel inward thankfulness for that Divine support which hath been graciously extended to me. On the 9th I was at Rushworth. I have lately passed through some painful labor, but have been comforted under a sense of that Divine visitation which I feel extended towards many young people.

The spirit of his Master bore witness to them in the hearts of his hearers. When he closed, the Friend who had advised against his further service rose up and humbly confessed his error, and avowed his full unity with the stranger. All doubt was removed; there was a general expression of unity and sympathy, and John Woolman, owned by his brethren, passed on to his work.

There is no portrait of John Woolman; and had photography been known in his day it is not at all probable that the sun-artist would have been permitted to delineate his features. That, while eschewing all superfluity and expensive luxury, he was scrupulously neat in his dress and person may be inferred from his general character and from the fact that one of his serious objections to dyed clothing was that it served to conceal uncleanness, and was, therefore, detrimental to real purity. It is, however, quite probable that his outer man, on the occasion referred to, was suggestive of a hasty toilet in the crowded steerage.—*Note from the edition published by Messrs. Houghton, Mifflin & Co.*

Sixteenth of eighth month and the first of the week, I was at Settle. It hath of late been a time of inward poverty, under which my mind hath been preserved in a watchful, tender state, feeling for the mind of the Holy Leader, and I find peace in the labors I have passed through.

On inquiry in many places I find the price of rye about five shillings; wheat, eight shillings per bushel; oatmeal, twelve shillings for a hundred and twenty pounds; mutton from threepence to fivepence per pound; bacon from sevenpence to ninepence; cheese from fourpence to sixpence; butter from eightpence to tenpence; house-rent for a poor man from twenty-five shillings to forty shillings per year, to be paid weekly; wood for fire very scarce and dear; coal in some places two shillings and sixpence per hundredweight; but near the pits not a quarter so much. O, may the wealthy consider the poor!

The wages of laboring men in several counties toward London at tenpence per day in common business, the employer finds small beer and the laborer finds his own food; but in harvest and hay time wages are about one shilling per day, and the laborer hath all his diet. In some parts of the north of England poor laboring men have their food where they work, and appear in common to do rather better than nearer London. Industrious women who spin in the factories get some fourpence, some fivepence, and so on to six, seven, eight, nine, or ten pence per day, and find their own house-room and diet. Great numbers of poor people live chiefly on bread and water in the southern parts of England, as well as in the northern parts; and there are many poor children not even taught to read. May those who have abundance lay these things to heart!

Stage-coaches frequently go upwards of one hundred miles in twenty-four hours; and I have heard Friends say in several places that it is common for horses to be killed with hard driving, and that many others are driven till they grow blind. Post-boys pursue their business, each one to his stage, all night through the winter. Some boys who ride long stages suffer greatly in winter nights, and at several places I have heard of their being frozen to death. So great is the hurry in the spirit of this world, that in aiming to do business quickly and to gain wealth the creation at this day doth loudly groan.

As my journey hath been without a horse, I have had several of-fers of being assisted on my way in these stage-coaches, but have not been in them; nor have I had freedom to send letters by these posts in the present way of riding, the stages being so fixed, and one boy dependent on another as to time, and going at great speed, that in long cold winter nights the poor boys suffer much. I heard in Amer-ica of the way of these posts, and cautioned Friends in the General Meeting of ministers and elders at Philadelphia, and in the Yearly Meeting of ministers and elders in London, not to send letters to me on any common occasion by post. And though on this account I may be likely not to hear so often from my family left behind, yet for righteousness' sake I am, through Divine favor, made content.

I have felt great distress of mind since I came on this island, on account of the members of our Society being mixed with the world in various sorts of traffic, carried on in impure channels. Great is the trade to Africa for slaves; and for the loading of these ships a great number of people are employed in their factories, among whom are many of our Society. Friends in early times refused on a religious principle to make or trade in superfluities, of which we have many testimonies on record; but for want of faithfulness, some, whose examples were of note in our Society, gave way, from which others took more liberty. Members of our Society worked in superfluities, and bought and sold them, and thus dimness of sight came over many; at length Friends got into the use of some superfluities in dress and in the furniture of their houses, which hath spread from less to more, till superfluity of some kinds is common among us.

In this declining state many look at the example of others and too much neglect the pure feeling of truth. Of late years a deep exercise hath attended my mind, that Friends may dig deep, may carefully cast forth the loose matter and get down to the rock, the sure founda-tion, and there hearken to that Divine voice which gives a clear and certain sound; and I have felt in that which doth not receive, that if Friends who have known the truth keep in that tenderness of heart where all views of outward gain are given up, and their trust is only in the Lord, he will graciously lead some to be patterns of deep self-denial in things relating to trade and handicraft labor; and others who have plenty of the treasures of this world will be examples of a plain frugal life, and pay wages to such as they may hire more liberally than is now customary in some places.

Twenty-third of eighth month.—I was this day at Preston Patrick, and had a comfortable meeting. I have several times been entertained at the houses of Friends, who had sundry things about them that had the appearance of outward greatness, and as I have kept inward, way hath opened for conversation with such in private, in which Divine goodness hath favored us together with heart-tendering times.

Twenty-sixth of eighth month.—Being now at George Crosfield's, in the county of Westmoreland, I feel a concern to commit to writing the following uncommon circumstance.

In a time of sickness, a little more than two years and a half ago, I was brought so near the gates of death that I forgot my name. Being then desirous to know who I was, I saw a mass of matter of a dull gloomy color between the south and the east, and was informed that this mass was human beings in as great misery as they could be, and live, and that I was mixed with them, and that henceforth I might not consider myself as a distinct or separate being. In this state I remained several hours. I then heard a soft melodious voice, more pure and harmonious than any I had heard with my ears before; I believed it was the voice of an angel who spake to the other angels; the words were, "John Woolman is dead." I soon remembered that I was once John Woolman, and being assured that I was alive in the body, I greatly wondered what that heavenly voice could mean. I believed beyond doubting that it was the voice of an holy angel, but as yet it was a mystery to me.

I was then carried in spirit to the mines where poor oppressed people were digging rich treasures for those called Christians, and heard them blaspheme the name of Christ, at which I was grieved, for his name to me was precious. I was then informed that these heathens were told that those who oppressed them were the followers of Christ, and they said among themselves, "If Christ directed them to use us in this sort, then Christ is a cruel tyrant."

All this time the song of the angel remained a mystery; and in the morning, my dear wife and some others coming to my bedside, I asked them if they knew who I was, and they telling me I was John Woolman, thought I was lightheaded, for I told them not what the angel said, nor was I disposed to talk much to any one, but was very desirous to get so deep that I might understand this mystery.

My tongue was often so dry that I could not speak till I had moved it about and gathered some moisture, and as I lay still for a time I at length felt a Divine power prepare my mouth that I could speak, and I then said, "I am crucified with Christ, nevertheless I live; yet not I, but Christ liveth in me. And the life which I now live in the flesh I live by the faith of the Son of God, who loved me and gave himself for me." Then the mystery was opened and I perceived there was joy in heaven over a sinner who had repented, and that the language "John Woolman is dead," meant no more than the death of my own will.

My natural understanding now returned as before, and I saw that people setting off their tables with silver vessels at entertainments was often stained with worldly glory, and that in the present state of things I should take heed how I fed myself out of such vessels. Going to our Monthly Meeting soon after my recovery, I dined at a Friend's house where drink was brought in silver vessels, and not in any other. Wanting something to drink, I told him my case with weeping, and he ordered some drink for me in another vessel. I afterwards went through the same exercise in several Friends' houses in America, as well as in England, and I have cause to acknowledge with humble reverence the loving-kindness of my Heavenly Father, who hath preserved me in such a tender frame of mind, that none, I believe, have ever been offended at what I have said on that subject.

After this sickness I spake not in public meetings for worship for nearly one year, but my mind was very often in company with the oppressed slaves as I sat in meetings; and though under his dispensation I was shut up from speaking, yet the spring of the gospel ministry was many times livingly opened in me, and the Divine gift operated by abundance of weeping, in feeling the oppression of this people. It being so long since I passed through this dispensation, and the matter remaining fresh and lively in my mind, I believe it safest for me to commit it to writing.

Thirtieth of eighth month.—This morning I wrote a letter in substance as follows:—

BELOVED FRIEND,—My mind is often affected as I pass along under a sense of the state of many poor people who sit under that sort of ministry which requires much outward labor to support it; and the loving-kindness of our Heavenly Father in opening a pure gospel ministry in this nation hath often raised thankfulness in my heart to him. I often remember the conflicts of the faithful under persecution, and now look at the free exercise of the pure gift uninterrupted by outward laws, as a trust committed to us, which requires our deepest gratitude and most careful attention. I feel a tender concern that the work of reformation so prosperously carried on in this land within a few ages past may go forward and spread among the nations, and may not go backward through dust gathering on our garments, who have been called to a work so great and so precious.

Last evening during thy absence I had a little opportunity with some of thy family, in which I rejoiced, and feeling a sweetness on my mind towards thee, I now endeavor to open a little of the feeling I had there.

I have heard that you in these parts have at certain seasons Meetings of Conference in relation to Friends living up to our principles, in which several meetings unite in one. With this I feel unity, having in some measure felt truth lead that way among Friends in America, and I have found, my dear friend, that in these labors all superfluities in our own living are against us. I feel that pure love towards thee in which there is freedom.

I look at that precious gift bestowed on thee with awfulness before Him who gave it, and feel a desire that we may be so separated to the gospel of Christ, that those things which proceed from the spirit of this world may have no place among us.   Thy friend,

JOHN WOOLMAN.

I rested a few days in body and mind with our friend, Jane Crosfield, who was once in America. On the sixth day of the week I was at Kendal, in Westmoreland, and at Greyrig Meeting the 30th day of the month, and first of the week. I have known poverty of late, and have been graciously supported to keep in the patience, and am thankful under a sense of the goodness of the Lord towards those who are of a contrite spirit.

Sixth of ninth month and first of the week.—I was this day at Counterside, a large meeting-house, and very full. Through the opening of pure love, it was a strengthening time to me, and I believe to many more.

Thirteenth of ninth month.—This day I was at Leyburn, a small meeting; but, the towns-people coming in, the house was crowded. It was a time of heavy labor, and I believe was a profitable meeting. At this place I heard that my kinsman, William Hunt, from North Carolina, who was on a religious visit to Friends in England, departed this life on the 9th of this month, of the small-pox, at Newcastle. He appeared in the ministry when a youth, and his labors therein were of good savor. He travelled much in that work in America. I once heard him say in public testimony, that his concern in that visit was to be devoted to the service of Christ so fully that he might not spend one minute in pleasing himself, which words, joined with his example, was a means of stirring up the pure mind in me.

Having of late often travelled in wet weather through narrow streets in towns and villages, where dirtiness under foot and the scent arising from that filth which more or less infects the air of all thickly settled towns were disagreeable; and, being but weakly, I have felt distress both in body and mind with that which is impure. In these journeys I have been where much cloth hath been dyed, and have, at sundry times, walked over ground where much of their dye-stuffs has drained away. This hath produced a longing in my mind that people might come into cleanness of spirit, cleanness of person, and cleanness about their houses and garments.

Some of the great carry delicacy to a great height themselves, and yet real cleanliness is not generally promoted. Dyes being invented partly to please the eye and partly to hide dirt, I have felt in this weak state, when travelling in dirtiness, and affected with unwholesome scents, a strong desire that the nature of dyeing cloth to hide dirt may be more fully considered.

Washing our garments to keep them sweet is cleanly, but it is the opposite to real cleanliness to hide dirt in them. Through giving way to hiding dirt in our garments a spirit which would conceal that which is disagreeable is strengthened. Real cleanliness becometh a holy people; but hiding that which is not clean by coloring our garments seems contrary to the sweetness of sincerity. Through some sorts of dyes cloth is rendered less useful. And if the value of dyestuffs, and expense of dyeing, and the damage done to cloth, were all added together, and that cost applied to keeping all sweet and clean, how much more would real cleanliness prevail.

On this visit to England I have felt some instructions sealed on my mind, which I am concerned to leave in writing for the use of such as are called to the station of a minister of Christ.

Christ being the Prince of Peace, and we being no more than ministers, it is necessary for us not only to feel a concern in our first going forth, but to experience the renewing thereof in the appointment of meetings. I felt a concern in America to prepare for this voyage, and being through the mercy of God brought safe hither, my heart was like a vessel that wanted vent. For several weeks after my arrival, when my mouth was opened in meetings, it was like the raising of a gate in a water-course when a weight of water lay upon it. In these labors there was a fresh visitation to many, especially to the youth; but sometimes I felt poor and empty, and yet there appeared a necessity to appoint meetings. In this I was exercised to abide in the pure life of truth, and in all my labors to watch diligently against the motions of self in my own mind.

I have frequently found a necessity to stand up when the spring of the ministry was low, and to speak from the necessity in that which subjecteth the will of the creature; and herein I was united with the suffering seed, and found inward sweetness in these mortifying labors. As I have been preserved in a watchful attention to the divine Leader, under these dispensations enlargement at times hath followed, and the power of truth hath risen higher in some meetings than I ever knew it before through me. Thus I have been more and more instructed as to the necessity of depending, not upon a concern which I felt in America to come on a visit to England, but upon the daily instructions of Christ, the Prince of Peace.

Of late I have sometimes felt a stop in the appointment of meetings, not wholly, but in part: and I do not feel liberty to appoint them so quickly, one after another, as I have done heretofore. The work of the ministry being a work of Divine love, I feel that the openings thereof are to be waited for in all our appointments. O, how deep is Divine wisdom! Christ puts forth his ministers and goeth before them; and O, how great is the danger of departing from the pure feeling of that which leadeth safely! Christ knoweth the state of the people, and in the pure feeling of the gospel ministry their states are opened to his servants. Christ knoweth when the fruit-bearing branches themselves have need of purging. O that these lessons may be remembered by me! and that all who appoint meetings may proceed in the pure feeling of duty!

I have sometimes felt a necessity to stand up, but that spirit which is of the world hath so much prevailed in many, and the pure life of truth hath been so pressed down, that I have gone forward, not as one travelling in a road cast up and well prepared, but as a man walking through a miry place in which are stones here and there safe to step on, but so situated that one step being taken, time is necessary to see where to step next. Now I find that in a state of pure obedience the mind learns contentment in appearing weak and foolish to that wisdom which is of the world; and in these lowly labors, they who stand in a low place and are rightly exercised under the cross will find nourishment. The gift is pure; and while the eye is single in attending thereto the understanding is preserved clear; self is kept out. We rejoice in filling up that which remains of the afflictions of Christ for his body's sake, which is the church.

The natural man loveth eloquence, and many love to hear eloquent orations, and if there be not a careful attention to the gift, men who have once labored in the pure gospel ministry, growing weary of suffering, and ashamed of appearing weak, may kindle a fire, compass themselves about with sparks, and walk in the light, not of Christ, who is under suffering, but of that fire which they in departing from the gift have kindled, in order that those hearers who have left the meek, suffering state for worldly wisdom may be warmed with this fire and speak highly of their labors. That which is of God gathers to God, and that which is of the world is owned by the world.

In this journey a labor hath attended my mind, that the ministers among us may be preserved in the meek, feeling life of truth, where we may have no desire but to follow Christ and to be with him, that when he is under suffering, we may suffer with him, and never desire to rise up in dominion, but as he, by the virtue of his own spirit, may raise us.

THE DEATH OF JOHN WOOLMAN

JOHN WOOLMAN died at York, England, October 7, 1772. His last days are memorialized in the following extract from "The testimony of Friends in Yorkshire at their Quarterly Meeting, held at York the 24th and 25th of the third month, 1773, concerning John Woolman, of Mount Holly, in the Province of New Jersey, North America, who departed this life at the house of our Friend Thomas Priestman, in the suburbs of this city, the 7th of the tenth month, 1772, and was interred in the burial-ground of Friends the 9th of the same, aged about fifty-two years:

"This our valuable friend having been under a religious engagement for some time to visit Friends in this nation, and more especially us in the northern parts, undertook the same in full concurrence and near sympathy with his friends and brethren at home, as appeared by certificates from the Monthly and Quarterly Meetings to which he belonged, and from the Spring Meeting of ministers and elders held at Philadelphia for Pennsylvania and New Jersey.

"He arrived in the city of London the beginning of the last Yearly Meeting, and, after attending that meeting, traveled northward, visiting the Quarterly Meetings of Hertfordshire, Buckinghamshire, Northamptonshire, Oxfordshire, and Worcestershire, and divers particular meetings in his way.

"He visited many meetings on the west side of this country, also some in Lancashire and Westmoreland, from whence he came to our Quarterly Meeting in the last ninth month, and though much out of health, yet was enabled to attend all the sittings of that meeting except the last.

"His disorder, which proved the small-pox, increased speedily upon him, and was very afflicting, under which he was supported in much meekness, patience, and Christian fortitude. To those who attended him in his illness, his mind appeared to be centred in Divine love, under the precious influence whereof we believe he finished his course, and entered into the mansions of everlasting rest.

"In the early part of his illness he requested a Friend to write, and he broke forth thus:

" 'O Lord my God! the amazing horrors of darkness were gathered around me and covered me all over, and I saw no way to go forth; I felt the misery of my fellow-creatures separated from the Divine harmony, and it was heavier than I could bear, and I was crushed down under it; I lifted up my hand and stretched out my arm, but there was none to help me; I looked round about and was amazed. In the depth of misery, O Lord! I remembered that thou art omnipotent, that I had called thee Father, and I felt that I loved thee, and I was made quiet in thy will, and I waited for deliverance from thee; thou hadst pity upon me when no man could help me; I saw that meekness under suffering was showed to us in the most affecting example of thy Son, and thou taught me to follow him, and I said, Thy will, O Father, be done.'

"Many more of his weighty expressions might have been inserted here, but it was deemed unnecessary, they being already published in print."

SOME FRUITS OF SOLITUDE

BY
WILLIAM PENN

INTRODUCTORY NOTE

WILLIAM PENN, the founder of Pennsylvania, was the son of Sir William Penn, a distinguished English Admiral. He was born in 1644. His boyhood was marked by a combination of pietism with a strong interest in athletics, and he was expelled from Oxford for nonconformity. After leaving the University he traveled on the Continent, served in the navy, and studied law. In 1667 he became a Quaker, and in the next year he was committed to the Tower for an attack on the orthodoxy of the day. During his imprisonment he wrote his well-known treatise on self-sacrifice, "No Cross, No Crown"; and after his release he suffered from time to time renewed imprisonments, till he finally turned his attention to America as a possible refuge for the persecuted Friends. In 1682 he obtained a charter creating him proprietor and governor of East New Jersey and Pennsylvania, and, after drawing up a constitution for the colony on the basis of religious toleration, he sailed for his new province. After two years, during which the population of the colony grew rapidly through emigration from Germany, Holland, and Scandinavia, as well as Great Britain, he returned to England, where his consultations with James II, whom he believed to be sincere in his professions of toleration, led to much misunderstanding of his motives and character. At the Revolution of 1688 he was treated as a Jacobite, but finally obtained the good-will of William III, and resumed his preaching and writing. In 1699 he again came to America, this time with the intention of remaining; but two years later he went home to oppose the proposal to convert his province into a crown colony. Queen Anne received him favorably, and he remained in England till his death in 1718.

Penn's voluminous writings are largely controversial, and often concerned with issues no longer vital. But his interpretation and defense of Quaker doctrine remain important; and the "Fruits of Solitude," here printed, is a mine of pithy comment upon human life, which combines with the acute common sense of Franklin the spiritual elevation of Woolman.

CONTENTS

PART I

THE PREFACE

READER,—This Enchiridion, I present thee with, is the Fruit of Solitude: A School few care to learn in, tho' None instructs us better. Some Parts of it are the Result of serious Reflection: Others the Flashings of Lucid Intervals: Writ for private Satisfaction, and now publish'd for an Help to Human Conduct.

The Author blesseth God for his Retirement, and kisses that Gentle Hand which led him into it: For though it should prove Barren to the World, it can never do so to him.

He has now had some Time he could call his own; a Property he was never so much Master of before: In which he has taken a View of himself and the World; and observed wherein he hath hit and mist the Mark; What might have been done, what mended, and what avoided in his Human Conduct: Together with the Omissions and Excesses of others, as well Societies and Governments, as private Families, and Persons. And he verily thinks, were he to live over his Life again, he could not only, with God's Grace, serve Him, but his Neighbor and himself, better than he hath done, and have Seven Years of his Time to spare. And yet perhaps he hath not been the Worst or the Idlest Man in the World; nor is he the Oldest. And this is the rather said, that it might quicken, Thee, Reader, to lose none of the Time that is yet thine.

There is nothing of which we are apt to be so lavish as of Time, and about which we ought to be more solicitous; since without it we can do nothing in this World. Time is what we want most, but what, alas! we use worst; and for which God will certainly most strictly reckon with us, when Time shall be no more.

It is of that Moment to us in Reference to both Worlds, that I can hardly wish any Man better, than that he would seriously consider what he does with his Time: How and to What Ends he Employs it; and what Returns he makes to God, his Neighbor and Himself for it. Will he ne'er have a Leidger for this? This, the greatest Wisdom and Work of Life.

To come but once into the World, and Trifle away our true Enjoyment of it, and of our selves in it, is lamentable indeed. This one Reflection would yield a thinking Person great Instruction. And since nothing below Man·can so Think; Man, in being Thoughtless, must needs fall below himself. And that, to be sure, such do, as are unconcern'd in the Use of their most Precious Time.

This is but too evident, if we will allow our selves to consider, that there's hardly any Thing we take by the Right End, or improve to its just Advantage.

We understand little of the Works of God, either in Nature or Grace. We pursue False Knowledge, and Mistake Education extreamly. We are violent in our Affections, Confused and Immethodical in our whole Life; making That a Burthen, which was given for a Blessing; and so of little Comfort to our selves or others; Misapprehending the true Notion of Happiness, and so missing of the Right Use of Life, and Way of happy Living.

And till we are perswaded to stop, and step a little aside, out of the noisy Crowd and Incumbering Hurry of the World, and Calmly take a Prospect of Things, it will be impossible we should be able to make a right Judgment of our Selves or know our own Misery. But after we have made the just Reckonings which Retirement will help us to, we shall begin to think the World in great measure Mad, and that we have been in a sort of Bedlam all this while.

Reader, whether Young or Old, think it not too soon or too late to turn over the Leaves of thy past Life: And be sure to fold down where any Passage of it may affect thee; And bestow thy Remainder of Time, to correct those Faults in thy future Conduct; Be it in Relation to this or the next life. What thou wouldst do, if what thou hast done were to do again, be sure to do as long as thou livest, upon the like Occasions.

Our Resolutions seem to be Vigorous, as often as we reflect upon our past Errors; But, Alas! they are apt to flat again upon fresh Temptations to the same Things.

The Author does not pretend to deliver thee an Exact Piece; his Business not being Ostentation, but Charity. 'T is Miscellaneous in the Matter of it, and by no means Artificial in the Composure. But it contains Hints, that it may serve thee for Texts to Preach to thy Self upon, and which comprehend Much of the Course of Human Life: Since whether thou art Parent or Child, Prince or Subject, Master or Servant, Single or Married, Publick or Private, Mean or Honorable, Rich or Poor, Prosperous or Improsperous, in Peace or Controversy, in Business or Solitude; Whatever be thy Inclination or Aversion, Practice or Duty, thou wilt find something not unsuitably said for thy Direction and Advantage. Accept and Improve what deserves thy Notice; The rest excuse, and place to account of good Will to Thee and the whole Creation of God.

SOME FRUITS OF SOLITUDE
IN REFLECTIONS AND MAXIMS

PART I

IGNORANCE

IT IS admirable to consider how many Millions of People come into, and go out of the World, Ignorant of themselves, and of the World they have lived in.

2. If one went to see Windsor-Castle, or Hampton-Court, it would be strange not to observe and remember the Situation, the Building, the Gardens, Fountains, &c. that make up the Beauty and Pleasure of such a Seat? And yet few People know themselves; No, not their own Bodies, the Houses of their Minds, the most curious Structure of the World; a living walking Tabernacle: Nor the World of which it was made, and out of which it is fed; which would be so much our Benefit, as well as our Pleasure, to know. We cannot doubt of this when we are told that the Invisible Things of God are brought to light by the Things that are seen; and consequently we read our Duty in them as often as we look upon them, to him that is the Great and Wise Author of them, if we look as we should do.

3. The World is certainly a great and stately Volume of natural Things; and may be not improperly styled the Hieroglyphicks of a better: But, alas! how very few Leaves of it do we seriously turn over! This ought to be the Subject of the Education of our Youth, who, at Twenty, when they should be fit for Business, know little or nothing of it.

EDUCATION

4. We are in Pain to make them Scholars, but not Men! To talk, rather than to know, which is true Canting.

5. The first Thing obvious to Children is what is sensible; and that we make no Part of their rudiments.

6. We press their Memory too soon, and puzzle, strain, and load them with Words and Rules; to know Grammer and Rhetorick, and a strange Tongue or two, that it is ten to one may never be useful to them; Leaving their natural Genius to Mechanical and Physical, or natural Knowledge uncultivated and neglected; which would be of exceeding Use and Pleasure to them through the whole Course of their Life.

7. To be sure, Languages are not to be despised or neglected. But Things are still to be preferred.

8. Children had rather be making of Tools and Instruments of Play; Shaping, Drawing, Framing, and Building, &c. than getting some Rules of Propriety of Speech by Heart: And those also would follow with more Judgment, and less Trouble and Time.

9. It were Happy if we studied Nature more in natural Things; and acted according to Nature; whose rules are few, plain and most reasonable.

10. Let us begin where she begins, go her Pace, and close always where she ends, and we cannot miss of being good Naturalists.

11. The Creation would not be longer a Riddle to us: The Heavens, Earth, and Waters, with their respective, various and numerous Inhabitants: Their Productions, Natures, Seasons, Sympathies and Antipathies; their Use, Benefit and Pleasure, would be better understood by us: And an eternal Wisdom, Power, Majesty, and Goodness, very conspicuous to us, thro' those sensible and passing Forms: The World wearing the Mark of its Maker, whose Stamp is everywhere visible, and the Characters very legible to the Children of Wisdom.

12. And it would go a great way to caution and direct People in their Use of the World, that they were better studied and known in the Creation of it.

13. For how could Man find the Confidence to abuse it, while they should see the Great Creator stare them in the Face, in all and every part thereof?

14. Their Ignorance makes them insensible, and that Insensibility hardy in misusing this noble Creation, that has the Stamp

and Voice of a Deity every where, and in every Thing to the Observing.

15. It is pity therefore that Books have not been composed for Youth, by some curious and careful Naturalists, and also Mechanicks, in the Latin Tongue, to be used in Schools, that they might learn Things with Words: Things obvious and familiar to them, and which would make the Tongue easier to be obtained by them.

16. Many able Gardiners and Husbandmen are yet Ignorant of the Reason of their Calling; as most Artificers are of the Reason of their own Rules that govern their excellent Workmanship. But a Naturalist and Mechanick of this sort is Master of the Reason of both, and might be of the Practice too, if his Industry kept pace with his Speculation; which were very commendable; and without which he cannot be said to be a complete Naturalist or Mechanick.

17. Finally, if Man be the Index or Epitomy of the World, as Philosophers tell us, we have only to read our selves well to be learned in it. But because there is nothing we less regard than the Characters of the Power that made us, which are so clearly written upon us and the World he has given us, and can best tell us what we are and should be, we are even Strangers to our own Genius: The Glass in which we should see that true instructing and agreeable Variety, which is to be observed in Nature, to the Admiration of that Wisdom and Adoration of that Power which made us all.

PRIDE

18. And yet we are very apt to be full of our selves, instead of Him that made what we so much value; and, but for whom we can have no Reason to value our selves. For we have nothing that we can call our own; no, not our selves: For we are all but Tenants, and at Will too, of the great Lord of our selves, and the rest of this great Farm, the World that we live upon.

19. But methinks we cannot answer it to our Selves as well as our Maker, that we should live and die ignorant of our Selves, and thereby of Him and the Obligations we are under to Him for our Selves.

20. If the worth of a Gift sets the Obligation, and directs the

return of the Party that receives it; he that is ignorant of it, will be at a loss to value it and the Giver, for it.

21. Here is Man in his Ignorance of himself. He knows not how to estimate his Creator, because he knows not how to value his Creation. If we consider his Make, and lovely Compositure; the several Stories of his lovely Structure. His divers Members, their Order, Function and Dependency: The Instruments of Food, the Vessels of Digestion, the several Transmutations it passes. And how Nourishment is carried and diffused throughout the whole Body, by most innate and imperceptible Passages. How the Animal Spirit is thereby refreshed, and with an unspeakable Dexterity and Motion sets all Parts at work to feed themselves. And last of all, how the Rational Soul is seated in the Animal, as its proper House, as is the Animal in the Body: I say if this rare Fabrick alone were but considered by us, with all the rest by which it is fed and comforted, surely Man would have a more reverent Sense of the Power, Wisdom and Goodness of God, and of that Duty he owes to Him for it. But if he would be acquainted with his own Soul, its noble Faculties, its Union with the Body, its Nature and End, and the Providences by which the whole Frame of Humanity is preserved, he would Admire and Adore his Good and Great God. But Man is become a strange Contradiction to himself; but it is of himself; Not being by Constitution, but Corruption, such.

22. He would have others obey him, even his own kind; but he will not obey God, that is so much above him, and who made him.

23. He will lose none of his Authority; no, not bate an Ace of it: He is humorous[1] to his Wife, he beats his Children, is angry with his Servants, strict with his Neighbors, revenges all Affronts to Extremity; but, alas, forgets all the while that he is the Man; and is more in Arrear to God, that is so very patient with him, than they are to him with whom he is so strict and impatient.

24. He is curious to wash, dress, and perfume his Body, but careless of his Soul. The one shall have many Hours, the other not so many Minutes. This shall have three or four new Suits in a Year, but that must wear its old Cloaths still.

25. If he be to receive or see a great Man, how nice and anxious

[1] Capricious.

is he that all things be in order? And with what Respect and
Address does he approach and make his Court? But to God, how
dry and formal and constrained in his Devotion?

26. In his Prayers he says, Thy Will be done: But means his own:
At least acts so.

27. It is too frequent to begin with God and end with the World.
But He is the good Man's Beginning and End; his Alpha and
Omega.

LUXURY

28. Such is now become our Delicacy, that we will not eat ordinary
Meat, nor drink small, pall'd[2] Liquor; we must have the best, and
the best cook'd for our Bodies, while our Souls feed on empty or
corrupted Things.

29. In short, Man is spending all upon a bare House, and hath little
or no Furniture within to recommend it; which is preferring the
Cabinet before the Jewel, a Lease of seven Years before an inheritance. So absurd a thing is Man, after all his proud Pretences to
Wit and Understanding.

INCONSIDERATION

30. The want of due Consideration is the Cause of all the Unhappiness Man brings upon himself. For his second Thoughts rarely
agree with his first, which pass not without a considerable Retrench-
ment or Correction. And yet that sensible Warning is, too frequently, not Precaution enough for his future Conduct.

31. Well may we say our Infelicity is of our selves; since there is
nothing we do that we should not do, but we know it, and yet do it.

DISAPPOINTMENT AND RESIGNATION

32. For Disappointments, that come not by our own Folly, they
are the Tryals or Corrections of Heaven: And it is our own Fault,
if they prove not our Advantage.

33. To repine at them does not mend the Matter: It is only to
grumble at our Creator. But to see the Hand of God in them,

[2] Stale.

with an humble submission to his Will, is the Way to turn our Water into Wine, and engage the greatest Love and Mercy on our side.

34. We must needs disorder our selves, if we only look at our Losses. But if we consider how little we deserve what is left, our Passion will cool, and our Murmurs will turn into Thankfulness.

35. If our Hairs fall not to the Ground, less do we or our Substance without God's Providence.

36. Nor can we fall below the Arms of God, how low soever it be we fall.

37. For though our Saviour's Passion is over, his Compassion is not. That never fails his humble, sincere Disciples: In him, they find more than all that they lose in the World.

MURMURING

38. Is it reasonable to take it ill, that any Body desires of us that which is their own? All we have is the Almighty's: And shall not God have his own when he calls for it?

39. Discontentedness is not only in such a Case Ingratitude, but Injustice. For we are both unthankful for the time we had it, and not honest enough to restore it, if we could keep it.

40. But it is hard for us to look on things in such a Glass, and at such a Distance from this low World; and yet it is our Duty, and would be our Wisdom and our Glory to do so.

CENSORIOUSNESS

41. We are apt to be very pert at censuring others, where we will not endure advice our selves. And nothing shews our Weakness more than to be so sharp-sighted at spying other Men's Faults; and so purblind about our own.

42. When the Actions of a Neighbor are upon the Stage, we can have all our Wits about us, are so quick and critical we can split an Hair, and find out ever Failure and Infirmity: But are without feeling, or have but very little Sense of our own.

43. Much of this comes from Ill Nature, as well as from an inordinate Value of our selves: For we love Rambling better than

home, and blaming the unhappy, rather than covering and relieving them.

44. In such Occasions some shew their Malice, and are witty upon Misfortunes; others their Justice, they can reflect a pace: But few or none their Charity; especially if it be about Money Matters.

45. You shall see an old Miser come forth with a set Gravity, and so much Severity against the distressed, to excuse his Purse, that he will, e'er he has done, put it out of all Question, That Riches is Righteousness with him. This, says he, is the Fruit of your Prodigality (as if, poor Man, Covetousness were no Fault) Or, of your Projects, or grasping after a great Trade: While he himself would have done the same thing, but that he had not the Courage to venture so much ready Money out of his own trusty Hands, though it had been to have brought him back the Indies in return. But the Proverb is just, Vice should not correct Sin.

46. They have a Right to censure, that have a Heart to help: The rest is Cruelty, not Justice.

BOUNDS OF CHARITY

47. Lend not beyond thy Ability, nor refuse to lend out of thy Ability; especially when it will help others more than it can hurt thee.

48. If thy Debtor be honest and capable, thou hast thy Mony again, if not with Encrease, with Praise: If he prove insolvent, don't ruin him to get that, which it will not ruin thee to lose: For thou art but a Steward, and another is thy Owner, Master and Judge.

49. The more merciful Acts thou dost, the more Mercy thou wilt receive; and if with a charitable Imployment of thy Temporal Riches, thou gainest eternal Treasure, thy Purchase is infinite: Thou wilt have found the Art of Multiplying[3] indeed.

FRUGALITY OR BOUNTY

50. Frugality is good if Liberality be join'd with it. The first is leaving off superfluous Expences; the last bestowing them to the Benefit of others that need. The first without the last begins Covetousness; the last without the first begins Prodigality: Both together

[3] The term used by the alchemists for increasing the precious metals.

make an excellent Temper. Happy the Place where ever that is found.

51. Were it universal, we should be Cur'd of two Extreams, Want and Excess: and the one would supply the other, and so bring both nearer to a Mean; the just Degree of earthly Happiness.

52. It is a Reproach to Religion and Government to suffer so much Poverty and Excess.

53. Were the Superfluities of a Nation valued, and made a perpetual Tax or Benevolence, there would be more Almshouses than Poor; Schools than Scholars; and enough to spare for Government besides.

54. Hospitality is good, if the poorer sort are the subjects of our Bounty; else too near a Superfluity.

DISCIPLINE

55. If thou wouldst be happy and easie in thy Family, above all things observe Discipline.

56. Every one in it should know their Duty; and there should be a Time and Place for every thing; and whatever else is done or omitted, be sure to begin and end with God.

INDUSTRY

57. Love Labor: For if thou dost not want it for Food, thou mayest for Physick. It is wholesom for thy Body, and good for thy Mind. It prevents the Fruits of Idleness, which many times comes of nothing to do, and leads too many to do what is worse than nothing.

58. A Garden, an Elaboratory, a Work-house, Improvements and Breeding, are pleasant and Profitable Diversions to the Idle and Ingenious: For here they miss Ill Company, and converse with Nature and Art; whose Variety are equally grateful and instructing; and preserve a good Constitution of Body and Mind.

TEMPERANCE

59. To this a spare Diet contributes much. Eat therefore to live, and do not live to eat. That's like a Man, but this below a Beast.

60. Have wholesome, but not costly Food, and be rather cleanly than dainty in ordering it.

61. The Receipts of Cookery are swell'd to a Volume, but a good Stomach excels them all; to which nothing contributes more than Industry and Temperance.

62. It is a cruel Folly to offer up to Ostentation so many Lives of Creatures, as make up the State of our Treats; as it is a prodigal one to spend more in Sawce than in Meat.

63. The Proverb says, That enough is as good as a Feast: But it is certainly better, if Superfluity be a Fault, which never fails to be at Festivals.

64. If thou rise with an Appetite, thou art sure never to sit down without one.

65. Rarely drink but when thou art dry; nor then, between Meals, if it can be avoided.

66. The smaller[4] the Drink, the clearer the Head, and the cooler the Blood; which are great Benefits in Temper and Business.

67. Strong Liquors are good at some Times, and in small Proportions; being better for Physick than Food, for Cordials than common Use.

68. The most common things are the most useful; which shews both the Wisdom and Goodness of the great Lord of the Family of the World.

69. What therefore he has made rare, don't thou use too commonly: Lest thou shouldest invert the Use and Order of things, become Wanton and Voluptuous; and thy Blessings prove a Curse.

70. Let nothing be lost, said our Saviour. But that is lost that is misused.

71. Neither urge another to that thou wouldst be unwilling to do thy self, nor do thy self what looks to thee unseemly, and intemperate in another.

72. All Excess is ill: But Drunkenness is of the worst Sort. It spoils Health, dismounts the Mind, and unmans Men: It reveals Secrets, is Quarrelsome, Lascivious, Impudent, Dangerous and Mad. In fine, he that is drunk is not a Man: Because he is so long void of Reason, that distinguishes a Man from a Beast.

[4] Weaker.

APPAREL

73. Excess in Apparel is another costly Folly. The very Trimming of the vain World would cloath all the naked one.

74. Chuse thy Cloaths by thine own Eyes, not another's. The more plain and simple they are, the better. Neither unshapely, nor fantastical; and for Use and Decency, and not for Pride.

75. If thou art clean and warm, it is sufficient; for more doth but rob the Poor, and please the Wanton.

76. It is said of the true Church, the King's Daughter is all glorious within. Let our Care therefore be of our Minds more than of our Bodies, if we would be of her Communion.

77. We are told with Truth, that Meekness and Modesty are the Rich and Charming Attire of the Soul: And the plainer the Dress, the more Distinctly, and with greater Lustre, their Beauty shines.

78. It is great Pity such Beauties are so rare, and those of Jezebel's Forehead are so common: Whose Dresses are Incentives to Lust; but Bars instead of Motives, to Love or Vertue.

RIGHT MARRIAGE

79. Never Marry but for Love; but see that thou lov'st what is lovely.

80. If Love be not thy chiefest Motive, thou wilt soon grow weary of a Married State, and stray from thy Promise, to search out thy Pleasures in forbidden Places.

81. Let not Enjoyment lessen, but augment Affection; it being the basest of Passions to like when we have not, what we slight when we possess.

82. It is the difference betwixt Lust and Love, that this is fixt, that volatile. Love grows, Lust wastes by Enjoyment: And the Reason is, that one springs from an Union of Souls, and the other from an Union of Sense.

83. They have Divers Originals, and so are of different Families: That inward and deep, this superficial; this transient, and that parmanent.

84. They that Marry for Money cannot have the true Satisfaction of Marriage; the requisite Means being wanting.

85. Men are generally more careful of the Breed of their Horses and Dogs than of their Children.

86. Those must be of the best Sort, for Shape, Strength, Courage and good Conditions: But as for these, their own Posterity, Money shall answer all Things. With such, it makes the Crooked Streight, sets Squint-Eyes Right, cures Madness, covers Folly, changes ill Conditions, mends the Skin, gives a sweet Breath, repairs Honors, makes Young, works Wonders.

87. O how sordid is Man grown! Man, the noblest Creature in the World, as a God on Earth, and the Image of him that made it; thus to mistake Earth for Heaven, and worship Gold for God!

AVARICE

88. Covetousness is the greatest of Monsters, as well as the Root of all Evil. I have once seen the Man that dyed to save Charges. What! Give Ten Shillings to a Doctor, and have an Apothecary's Bill besides, that may come to I know not what! No, not he: Valuing Life less than Twenty Shillings. But indeed such a Man could not well set too low a Price upon himself; who, though he liv'd up to the Chin in Bags, had rather die than find in his Heart to open one of them, to help to save his Life.

89. Such a Man is *felo de se*,[5] and deserves not Christian Burial.

90. He is a common Nusance, a Weyer[6] cross the Stream, that stops the Current: An Obstruction, to be remov'd by a Purge of the Law. The only Gratification he gives his Neighbors, is to let them see that he himself is as little the better for what he has, as they are. For he always looks like Lent; a Sort of Lay Minim.[7] In some Sense he may be compar'd to Pharoah's lean Kine, for all that he has does him no good. He commonly wears his Cloaths till they leave him, or that no Body else can wear them. He affects to be thought poor, to escape Robbery and Taxes: And by looking as if he wanted an Alms, excusing himself from giving any. He ever goes late to Markets, to cover buying the worst: But does it because that is cheapest. He lives of the Offal. His Life were an insupportable Punishment to any Temper but his own: And no

---

[5] A suicide.   [6] Dam.   [7] One of an order of monks pledged to the observance of perpetual Lent.

greater Torment to him on Earth, than to live as other Men do. But the Misery of his Pleasure is, that he is never satisfied with getting, and always in Fear of losing what he cannot use.

91. How vilely has he lost himself, that becomes a Slave to his Servant, and exalts him to the Dignity of his Maker! Gold is the God, the Wife, the Friend of the Money-Monger of the World.

92. But in Marriage do thou be wise; prefer the Person before Money; Vertue before Beauty, the Mind before the Body: Then thou hast a Wife, a Friend, a Companion, a Second Self; one that bears an equal Share with thee in all thy Toyls and Troubles.

93. Chuse one that Measures her satisfaction, Safety and Danger, by thine; and of whom thou art sure, as of thy secretest Thoughts: A Friend as well as a Wife, which indeed a Wife implies: For she is but half a Wife that is not, or is not capable of being such a Friend.

94. Sexes make no Difference; since in Souls there is none: And they are the Subjects of Friendship.

95. He that minds a Body and not a Soul, has not the better Part of that Relation; and will consequently want the Noblest Comfort of a Married Life.

96. The Satisfaction of our Senses is low, short, and transient: But the Mind gives a more raised and extended Pleasure, and is capable of an Happiness founded upon Reason; not bounded and limited by the Circumstances that Bodies are confin'd to.

97. Here it is we ought to search out our Pleasure, where the Field is large and full of Variety, and of an induring Nature: Sickness, Poverty, or Disgrace, being not able to shake it, because it is not under the moving Influences of Worldly Contingencies.

98. The Satisfaction of those that do so is in well-doing, and in the Assurance they have of a future Reward: That they are best loved of those they love most, and that they enjoy and value the Liberty of their Minds above that of their Bodies; having the whole Creation for their Prospect, the most Noble and Wonderful Works and Providences of God, the Histories of the Antients, and in them the Actions and Examples of the Vertuous; and lastly, themselves, their Affairs and Family, to exercise their Minds and Friendship upon.

99. Nothing can be more entire and without Reserve; nothing more zealous, affectionate and sincere; nothing more contented and constant than such a Couple; nor no greater temporal Felicity than to be one of them.

100. Between a Man and his Wife nothing ought to rule but Love. Authority is for Children and Servants; yet not without Sweetness.

101. As Love ought to bring them together, so it is the best Way to keep them well together.

102. Wherefore use her not as a Servant, whom thou would'st, perhaps, have serv'd Seven Years to have obtained.

103. An Husband and Wife that love and value one another, shew their Children and Servants, That they should do so too. Others visibly lose their Authority in their Families by their Contempt of one another; and teach their Children to be unnatural by their own Example.

104. It is a general Fault, not to be more careful to preserve Nature in Children; who, at least in the second Descent, hardly have the Feeling of their Relation; which must be an unpleasant Reflection to affectionate Parents.

105. Frequent Visits, Presents, intimate Correspondence and Inter-marriages within allowed Bounds, are Means of keeping up the Concern and Affection that Nature requires from Relations.

FRIENDSHIP

106. Friendship is the next Pleasure we may hope for: And where we find it not at home, or have no home to find it in, we may seek it abroad. It is an Union of Spirits, a Marriage of Hearts, and the Bond thereof Vertue.

107. There can be no Friendship where there is no Freedom. Friendship loves a free Air, and will not be penned up in streight and narrow Enclosures. It will speak freely, and act so too; and take nothing ill where no ill is meant; nay, where it is, 'twill easily forgive, and forget too, upon small Acknowledgments.

108. Friends are true Twins in Soul; they Sympathize in every thing, and have the Love and Aversion.

109. One is not happy without the other, nor can either of them

be miserable alone. As if they could change Bodies, they take their turns in Pain as well as in Pleasure; relieving one another in their most adverse Conditions.

110. What one enjoys, the other cannot Want. Like the Primitive Christians, they have all things in common, and no Property but in one another.

QUALITIES OF A FRIEND

111. A true Friend unbosoms freely, advises justly, assists readily, adventures boldly, takes all patiently, defends courageously, and continues a Friend unchangeably.

112. These being the Qualities of a Friend, we are to find them before we chuse one.

113. The Covetous, the Angry, the Proud, the Jealous, the Talkative, cannot but make ill Friends, as well as the False.

114. In short, chuse a Friend as thou dost a Wife, till Death seperate you.

115. Yet be not a Friend beyond the Altar: but let Virtue bound thy Friendship: Else it is not Friendship, but an Evil Confederacy.

116. If my Brother or Kinsman will be my Friend, I ought to prefer him before a Stranger, or I shew little Duty or Nature to my Parents.

117. And as we ought to prefer our Kindred in Point of Affection, so too in Point of Charity, if equally needing and deserving.

CAUTION AND CONDUCT

118. Be not easily acquainted, lest finding Reason to cool, thou makest an Enemy instead of a good Neighbor.

119. Be Reserved, but not Sour; Grave, but not Formal; Bold, but not Rash; Humble, but not Servile; Patient, not Insensible; Constant, not Obstinate; Chearful, not Light; Rather Sweet than Familiar; Familiar, than Intimate; and Intimate with very few, and upon very good Grounds.

120. Return the Civilities thou receivest, and be grateful for Favors.

REPARATION

121. If thou hast done an Injury to another, rather own it than defend it. One way thou gainest Forgiveness, the other, thou doubl'st the Wrong and Reckoning.

122. Some oppose Honor to Submission: But it can be no Honor to maintain, what it is dishonorable to do.

123. To confess a Fault, that is none, out of Fear, is indeed mean: But not to be afraid of standing in one, is Brutish.

124. We should make more Haste to Right our Neighbor, than we do to wrong him, and instead of being Vindicative, we should leave him to be Judge of his own Satisfaction.

125. True Honor will pay treble Damages, rather than justifie one wrong with another.

126. In such Controversies, it is but too common for some to say, Both are to blame, to excuse their own Unconcernedness, which is a base Neutrality. Others will cry, They are both alike; thereby involving the Injured with the Guilty, to mince the Matter for the Faulty, or cover their own Injustice to the wronged Party.

127. Fear and Gain are great Perverters of Mankind, and where either prevail, the Judgment is violated.

RULES OF CONVERSATION

128. Avoid Company where it is not profitable or necessary; and in those Occasions speak little, and last.

129. Silence is Wisdom, where Speaking is Folly; and always safe.

130. Some are so Foolish as to interrupt and anticipate those that speak, instead of hearing and thinking before they answer; which is uncivil as well as silly.

131. If thou thinkest twice, before thou speakest once, thou wilt speak twice the better for it.

132. Better say nothing than not to the Purpose. And to speak pertinently, consider both what is fit, and when it is fit to speak.

133. In all Debates, let Truth be thy Aim, not Victory, or an unjust Interest: And endeavor to gain, rather than to expose thy Antagonist.

134. Give no Advantage in Argument, nor lose any that is offered. This is a Benefit which arises from Temper.

135. Don't use thy self to dispute against thine own Judgment, to shew Wit, lest it prepare thee to be too indifferent about what is Right: Nor against another Man, to vex him, or for mere Trial

of Skill; since to inform, or to be informed, ought to be the End of all Conferences.

136. Men are too apt to be concerned for their Credit, more than for the Cause.

ELOQUENCE

137. There is a Truth and Beauty in Rhetorick; but it oftener serves ill Turns than good ones.

138. Elegancy is a good Meen and Address given to Matter, be it by proper or figurative Speech: Where the Words are apt, and allusions very natural, Certainly it has a moving Grace: But it is too artificial for Simplicity, and oftentimes for Truth. The Danger is, lest it delude the Weak, who in such Cases may mistake the Handmaid for the Mistress, if not Error for Truth.

139. 'T is certain Truth is least indebted to it, because she has least need of it, and least uses it.

140. But it is a reprovable Delicacy in them, that despise Truth in plain Cloths.

141. Such Luxuriants have but false Appetites; like those Gluttons, that by Sawces force them, where they have no Stomach, and Sacrifice to their Pallate, not their Health: Which cannot be without great Vanity, nor That without some Sin.

TEMPER

142. Nothing does Reason more Right, than the Coolness of those that offer it: For Truth often suffers more by the Heat of its Defenders, than from the Arguments of its Opposers.

143. Zeal ever follows an Appearance of Truth, and the Assured are too apt to be warm; but 't is their weak side in Argument; Zeal being better shewn against Sin, than Persons or their Mistakes.

TRUTH

144. Where thou art Obliged to speak, be sure speak the Truth: For Equivocation is half way to Lying, as Lying, the whole way to Hell.

JUSTICE

145. Believe nothing against another but upon good Authority: Nor report what may hurt another, unless it be a greater hurt to others to conceal it.

SECRECY

146. It is wise not to seek a Secret, and honest not to reveal one.

147. Only trust thy self, and another shall not betray thee.

148. Openness has the Mischief, though not the Malice of Treachery.

COMPLACENCY

149. Never assent merely to please others. For that is, besides Flattery, oftentimes Untruth; and discovers a Mind liable to be servile and base: Nor contradict to vex others, for that shows an ill Temper, and provokes, but profits no Body.

SHIFTS

150. Do not accuse others to excuse thy self; for that is neither Generous nor Just. But let Sincerity and Ingenuity be thy Refuge, rather than Craft and Falsehood: for Cunning borders very near upon Knavery.

151. Wisdom never uses nor wants it. Cunning to Wise, is as an Ape to a Man.

INTEREST

152. Interest has the Security, tho' not the Virtue of a Principle. As the World goes 't is the surer side; For Men daily leave both Relations and Religion to follow it.

153. 'T is an odd Sight, but very evident, That Families and Nations, of cross Religions and Humors unite against those of their own, where they find an Interest to do it.

154. We are tied down by our Senses to this World; and where that is in Question, it can be none with Worldly Men, whether they should not forsake all other Considerations for it.

INQUIRY

155. Have a care of Vulgar Errors. Dislike, as well as Allow Reasonably.

156. Inquiry is Human; Blind Obedience Brutal. Truth never loses by the one, but often suffers by the other.

157. The usefulest Truths are plainest: And while we keep to them, our Differences cannot rise high.

158. There may be a Wantonness in Search, as well as a Stupidity in Trusting. It is great Wisdom equally to avoid the Extreams.

RIGHT-TIMING

159. Do nothing improperly. Some are Witty, Kind, Cold, Angry, Easie, Stiff, Jealous, Careless, Cautious, Confident, Close, Open, but all in the wrong Place.

160. It is all mistaking where the Matter is of Importance.

161. It is not enough that a thing be Right, if it be not fit to be done. If not Imprudent, tho' Just, it is not advisable. He that loses by getting, had better lose than get.

KNOWLEDGE

162. Knowledge is the Treasure, but Judgment the Treasurer of a Wise Man.

163. He that has more Knowledge than Judgment, is made for another Man's use more than his own.

164. It cannot be a good Constitution, where the Appetite is great and the Digestion is weak.

165. There are some Men like Dictionaries; to be lookt into upon occasions, but have no Connection, and are little entertaining.

166. Less Knowledge than Judgment will always have the advantage upon the Injudicious knowing Man.

167. A Wise Man makes what he learns his own, 'tother shows he's but a Copy, or a Collection at most.

WIT

168. Wit is an happy and striking way of expressing a Thought.

169. 'Tis not often tho' it be lively and mantling, that it carries a great Body with it.

170. Wit therefore is fitter for Diversion than Business, being more grateful to Fancy than Judgment.

171. Less Judgment than Wit, is more Sale than Ballast.

172. Yet it must be confessed, that Wit gives an Edge to Sense, and recommends it extreamly.

173. Where Judgment has Wit to express it, there's the best Orator.

OBEDIENCE TO PARENTS

174. If thou wouldest be obeyed, being a Father; being a Son, be Obedient.

175. He that begets thee, owes thee; and has a natural Right over thee.

176. Next to God, thy Parents; next them, the Magistrate.

177. Remember that thou are not more indebted to thy Parents for thy Nature, than for thy Love and Care.

178. Rebellion therefore in Children, was made Death by God's Law, and the next Sin to Idolatry, in the People; which is renouncing of God, the Parent of all.

179. Obedience to Parents is not only our Duty, but our Interest. If we received our Life from them, We prolong it by obeying them: For Obedience is the first Commandment with Promise.

180. The Obligation is as indissolvable as the Relation.

181. If we must not disobey God to obey them; at least we must let them see, that there is nothing else in our refusal. For some unjust Commands cannot excuse the general Neglect of our Duty. They will be our Parents and we must be their Children still: And if we cannot act for them against God, neither can we act against them for ourselves or anything else.

BEARING

182. A Man in Business must put up many Affronts, if he loves his own Quiet.

183. We must not pretend to see all that we see, if we would be easie.

184. It were endless to dispute upon everything that is disput.. able.

185. A vindictive Temper is not only uneasie to others, but to them that have it.

PROMISING

186. Rarely Promise: But, if Lawful, constantly perform.

187. Hasty Resolutions are of the Nature of Vows; and to be equally avoided.

188. I will never do this, says one, yet does it: I am resolved to do this, says another; but flags upon second Thoughts: Or does it, tho' awkwardly, for his Word's sake: As if it were worse to break his Word, than to do amiss in keeping it.

189. Wear none of thine own Chains; but keep free, whilst thou art free.

190. It is an Effect of Passion that Wisdom corrects, to lay thy self under Resolutions that cannot be well made, and must be worse performed.

FIDELITY

191. Avoid all thou canst to be Entrusted: But do thy utmost to discharge the Trust thou undertakest: For Carelessness is Injurious, if not Unjust.

192. The Glory of a Servant is Fidelity; which cannot be without Diligence, as well as Truth.

193. Fidelity has Enfranchised Slaves, and Adopted Servants to be Sons.

194. Reward a good Servant well: And rather quit than Disquiet thy self with an ill one.

MASTER

195. Mix Kindness with Authority; and rule more by Discretion than Rigor.

196. If thy Servant be faulty, strive rather to convince him of his Error, than discover thy Passion: And when he is sensible, forgive him.

197. Remember he is thy Fellow-Creature, and that God's Good-

ness, not thy Merit, has made the Difference betwixt Thee and Him.

198. Let not thy Children Domineer over thy Servants: Nor suffer them to slight thy Children.

199. Suppress Tales in the general: But where a Matter requires notice, encourage the Complaint, and right the Aggrieved.

200. If a Child, he ought to Entreat, and not to Command; and if a Servant, to comply where he does not obey.

201. Tho' there should be but one Master and Mistress in a Family, yet Servants should know that Children have the Reversion.

SERVANT

202. Indulge not unseemly Things in thy Master's Children, nor refuse them what is fitting: For one is the highest Unfaithfulness, and the other, Indiscretion as well as Disrespect.

203. Do thine own Work honestly and chearfully: And when that is done, help thy Fellow; that so another time he may help thee.

204. If thou wilt be a Good Servant, thou must be True; and thou canst not be True if thou Defraud'st thy Master.

205. A Master may be Defrauded many ways by a servant: As in Time, Care, Pains, Money, Trust.

206. But, a True Servant is the Contrary: He's Diligent, Careful, Trusty. He Tells no Tales, Reveals no Secrets, Refuses no Pains: Not to be Tempted by Gain, nor aw'd by Fear, to Unfaithfulness.

207. Such a Servant, serves God in serving his Master; and has double Wages for his Work, to wit, Here and Hereafter.

JEALOUSY

208. Be not fancifully Jealous: For that is Foolish; as, to be reasonably so, is Wise.

209. He that superfines up another Man's Actions, cozens himself, as well as injures them.

210. To be very subtil and scrupulous in Business, is as hurtful, as being over-confident and secure.

211. In difficult Cases, such a Temper is Timorous; and in dispatch Irresolute.

212. Experience is a safe Guide: And a Practical Head, is a great Happiness in Business.

POSTERITY

213. We are too careless of Posterity; not considering that as they are, so the next Generation will be.

214. If we would amend the World, we should mend Our selves; and teach our Children to be, not what we are, but what they should be.

215. We are too apt to awaken and turn up their Passions by the Examples of our own; and to teach them to be pleased, not with what is best, but with what pleases best.

216. It is our Duty, and ought to be our Care, to ward against that Passion in them, which is more especially our Own Weakness and Affliction: For we are in great measure accountable for them, as well as for our selves.

217. We are in this also true Turners of the World upside down; For Money is first, and Virtue last, and least in our care.

218. It is not How we leave our Children, but What we leave them.

219. To be sure Virtue is but a Supplement, and not a Principal in their Portion and Character: And therefore we see so little Wisdom or Goodness among the Rich, in proportion to their Wealth.

A COUNTRY LIFE

220. The Country Life is to be preferr'd; for there we see the Works of God; but in Cities little else but the Works of Men: And the one makes a better Subject for our Contemplation than the other.

221. As Puppets are to Men, and Babies[8] to Children, so is Man's Workmanship to God's: We are the Picture, he the Reality.

222. God's Works declare his Power, Wisdom and Goodness; but Man's Works, for the most part, his Pride, Folly and Excess. The one is for use, the other, chiefly, for Ostentation and Lust.

223. The Country is both the Philosopher's Garden and his Library, in which he Reads and Contemplates the Power, Wisdom and Goodness of God.

[8] Dolls.

224. It is his Food as well as Study; and gives him Life, as well as Learning.

225. A Sweet and Natural Retreat from Noise and Talk, and allows opportunity for Reflection, and gives the best Subjects for it.

226. In short, 't is an Original, and the Knowledge and Improvement of it, Man's oldest Business and Trade, and the best he can be of.

ART AND PROJECT

227. Art, is Good, where it is beneficial. Socrates wisely bounded his Knowledge and Instruction by Practice.

228. Have a care therefore of Projects: And yet despise nothing rashly, or in the Lump.

229. Ingenuity, as well as Religion, sometimes suffers between two Thieves; Pretenders and Despisers.

230. Though injudicious and dishonest Projectors often discredit Art, yet the most useful and extraordinary Inventions have not, at first, escap'd the Scorn of Ignorance; as their Authors, rarely, have cracking of their Heads, or breaking their backs.

231. Undertake no Experiment, in Speculation, that appears not true in Art; nor then, at thine own Cost, if costly or hazardous in making.

232. As many Hands make light Work, so several Purses make cheap Experiments.

INDUSTRY

233. Industry, is certainly very commendable, and supplies the want of Parts.

234. Patience and Diligence, like Faith, remove Mountains.

235. Never give out while there is Hope; but hope not beyond Reason, for that shews more Desire than Judgment.

236. It is a profitable Wisdom to know when we have done enough: Much Time and Pains are spared, in not flattering our selves against Probabilities.

TEMPORAL HAPPINESS

237. Do Good with what thou hast, or it will do thee no good.

238. Seek not to be Rich, but Happy. The one lies in Bags, the other in Content: which Wealth can never give.

239. We are apt to call things by wrong Names. We will have Prosperity to be Happiness, and Adversity to be Misery; though that is the School of Wisdom, and oftentimes the way to Eternal Happiness.

240. If thou wouldest be Happy, bring thy Mind to thy Condition, and have an Indifferency for more than what is sufficient.

241. Have but little to do, and do it thy self: And do to others as thou wouldest have them do to thee: So, thou canst not fail of Temporal Felicity.

242. The generality are the worse for their Plenty: The Voluptuous consumes it, the Miser hides it: 'T is the good Man that uses it, and to good Purposes. But such are hardly found among the Prosperous.

243. Be rather Bountiful, than Expensive.

244. Neither make nor go to Feasts, but let the laborious Poor bless thee at Home in their Solitary Cottages.

245. Never voluntarily want what thou hast in Possession; nor so spend it as to involve thyself in want unavoidable.

246. Be not tempted to presume by Success: For many that have got largely, have lost all, by coveting to get more.

247. To hazard much to get much, has more of Avarice than Wisdom.

248. It is great Prudence both to Bound and Use Prosperity.

249. Too few know when they have Enough; and fewer know how to employ it.

250. It is equally adviseable not to part lightly with what is hardly gotten, and not to shut up closely what flows in freely.

251. Act not the Shark upon thy Neighbors; nor take Advantage of the Ignorance, Prodigality or Necessity of any one: For that is next door to Fraud, and, at best, makes but an Unblest Gain.

252. It is oftentimes the Judgment of God upon Greedy Rich Men, that he suffers them to push on their Desires of Wealth to the Excess of over-reaching, grinding or oppression, which poisons all the rest they have gotten: So that it commonly runs away as fast, and by as bad ways as it was heap'd up together.

RESPECT

253. Never esteem any Man, or thy self, the more for Money; nor think the meaner of thy self or another for want of it: Vertue being the just Reason of respecting, and the want of it, of slighting any one.

254. A Man like a Watch, is to be valued for his Goings.

255. He that prefers him upon other accounts, bows to an Idol.

256. Unless Virtue guide us, our Choice must be wrong.

257. An able bad Man, is an ill Instrument, and to be shunned as the Plague.

258. Be not deceived with the first appearances of things, but give thy self Time to be in the right.

259. Show, is not Substance: Realities Govern Wise Men.

260. Have a Care therefore where there is more Sail than Ballast.

HAZARD

261. In all Business it is best to put nothing to hazard: But where it is unavoidable, be not rash, but firm and resign'd.

262. We should not be troubled for what we cannot help: But if it was our Fault, let it be so no more. Amendment is Repentance, if not Reparation.

263. As a Desperate Game needs an able Gamester, so Consideration often would prevent, what the best skill in the World Cannot Recover.

264. Where the Probability of Advantage exceeds not that of Loss, Wisdom never Adventures.

265. To Shoot well Flying is well; but to Chose it, has more of Vanity than Judgment.

266. To be Dextrous in Danger is a Virtue; but to Court Danger to show it, is Weakness.

DETRACTION

267. Have a care of that base Evil Detraction. It is the Fruit of Envy, as that is of Pride; the immediate Offspring of the Devil: Who, of an Angel, a Lucifer, a Son of the Morning, made himself

a Serpent, a Devil, a Beelzebub, and all that is obnoxious to the Eternal Goodness.

268. Vertue is not secure against Envy. Men will Lessen what they won't Imitate.

269. Dislike what deserves it, but never Hate: For that is of the Nature of Malice; which is almost ever to Persons, not Things, and is one of the blackest Qualities Sin begets in the Soul.

MODERATION

270. It were an happy Day if Men could bound and qualifie their Resentments with Charity to the Offender: For then our Anger would be without Sin, and better convict and edifie the Guilty; which alone can make it lawful.

271. Not to be provok'd is best: But if mov'd, never correct till the Fume is spent; For every Stroke our Fury strikes, is sure to hit our selves at last.

272. If we did but observe the Allowances our Reason makes upon Reflection, when our Passion is over, we could not want a Rule how to behave our selves again in the like Occasions.

273. We are more prone to Complain than Redress, and to Censure than Excuse.

274. It is next to unpardonable, that we can so often Blame what we will not once mend. It shews, we know, but will not do our Master's Will.

275. They that censure, should Practice: Or else let them have the first stone, and the last too.

TRICK

276. Nothing needs a Trick but a Trick; Sincerity loathes one.

277. We must take care to do Right Things Rightly: For a just Sentence may be unjustly executed.

278. Circumstances give great Light to true Judgment, if well weigh'd.

PASSION

279. Passion is a sort of Fever in the Mind, which ever leaves us weaker than it found us.

280. But being, intermitting to be sure, 't is curable with care.

281. It more than any thing deprives us of the use of our Judgment; for it raises a Dust very hard to see through.

282. Like Wine, whose Lees fly by being jogg'd, it is too muddy to Drink.

283. It may not unfitly be termed, the Mob of the Man, that commits a Riot upon his Reason.

284. I have sometimes thought, that a Passionate Man is like a weak Spring that cannot stand long lock'd.

285. And as true, that those things are unfit for use, that can't bear small Knocks, without breaking.

286. He that won't hear can't Judge, and he that can't bear Contradiction, may, with all his Wit, miss the Mark.

287. Objection and Debate Sift out Truth, which needs Temper as well as Judgment.

288. But above all, observe it in Resentments, for their Passion is most Extravagant.

289. Never chide for Anger, but Instruction.

290. He that corrects out of Passion, raises Revenge sooner than Repentance.

291. It has more of Wantonness than Wisdom, and resembles those that Eat to please their Pallate, rather than their Appetite.

292. It is the difference between a Wise and a Weak Man; This Judges by the Lump, that by Parts and their Connection.

293. The Greeks use to say, all Cases are governed by their Circumstances. The same thing may be well and ill as they change or vary the Matter.

294. A Man's Strength is shewn by his Bearing. *Bonum Agere, & Male Pati, Regis est.*[9]

PERSONAL CAUTIONS

295. Reflect without Malice but never without Need.

296. Despise no Body, nor no Condition; lest it come to be thine own.

297. Never Rail nor Taunt. The one is Rude, the other Scornful, and both Evil.

[9] To do good and ill to endure is the part of a king.

298. Be not provoked by Injuries, to commit them.

299. Upbraid only Ingratitude.

300. Haste makes Work which Caution prevents.

301. Tempt no Man; lest thou fall for it.

302. Have a care of presuming upon After-Games:[10] For if that miss, all is gone.

303. Opportunities should never be lost, because they can hardly be regained.

304. It is well to cure, but better to prevent a Distemper. The first shows more Skill, but the last more Wisdom.

305. Never make a Tryal of Skill in difficult or hazardous Cases.

306. Refuse not to be informed: For that shews Pride or Stupidity.

307. Humility and Knowledge in poor Cloaths, excel Pride and Ignorance in costly attire.

308. Neither despise, nor oppose, what thou dost not understand.

BALLANCE

309. We must not be concern'd above the Value of the thing that engages us; nor raised above Reason, in maintaining what we think reasonable.

310. It is too common an Error, to invert the Order of Things; by making an End of that which is a Means, and a Means of that which is an End.

311. Religion and Government escape not this Mischief: The first is too often made a Means instead of an End; the other an End instead of a Means.

312. Thus Men seek Wealth rather than Subsistence; and the End of Cloaths is the least Reason of their Use. Nor is the satisfying of our Appetite our End in Eating, so much as the pleasing of our Pallate. The like may also be said of Building, Furniture, &c. where the Man rules not the Beast, and Appetite submits not to Reason.

313. It is great Wisdom to proportion our Esteem to the Nature of the Thing: For as that way things will not be undervalued, so neither will they engage as above their intrinsick worth.

314. If we suffer little Things to have great hold upon us, we shall be as much transported for them, as if they deserv'd it.

10 A second game played to reverse the issue of the first.

315. It is an old Proverb, *Maxima bella ex levissimis causis:* The greatest Feuds have had the smallest Beginnings.

316. No matter what the Subject of the Dispute be, but what place we give it in our Minds: For that governs our Concern and Resentment.

317. It is one of the fatalest Errors of our Lives, when we spoil a good Cause by an ill Management: And it is not impossible but we may mean well in an ill Business; but that will not defend it.

318. If we are but sure the End is Right, we are too apt to gallop over all Bounds to compass it; not considering that lawful Ends may be very unlawfully attained.

319. Let us be careful to take just ways to compass just Things; that they may last in their Benefits to us.

320. There is a troublesome Humor some Men have, that if they may not lead, they will not follow; but had rather a thing were never done, than not done their own way, tho' other ways very desirable.

321. This comes of an over-fulness of our selves; and shows we are more concern'd for Praise, than the Success of what we think a good Thing.

POPULARITY

322. Affect not to be seen, and Men will less see thy Weakness.

323. They that shew more than they are, raise an Expectation they cannot answer; and so lose their Credit, as soon as they are found out.

324. Avoid Popularity. It has many Snares, and no real Benefit to thy self; and Uncertainty to others.

PRIVACY

325. Remember the Proverb, *Bene qui latuit, bene vixit.* They are happy that live Retiredly.

326. If this be true, Princes and their Grandees, of all Men, are the unhappiest: For they live least alone: And they that must be enjoyed by every Body, can never enjoy themselves as they should.

327. It is the Advantage little Men have upon them; they can

be Private, and have leisure for Family Comforts, which are the greatest worldly Contents Men can enjoy.

328. But they that place Pleasure in Greediness, seek it there: And we see Rule is as much the Ambition of some Natures, as Privacy is the Choice of others.

GOVERNMENT

329. Government has many Shapes: But 't is Sovereignty, tho' not Freedom, in all of them.

330. *Rex & Tyrannus* are very different Characters: One Rules his People by Laws, to which they consent; the other by his absolute Will and Power. That is call'd Freedom, This Tyranny.

331. The first is endanger'd by the Ambition of the Popular, which shakes the Constitution: The other by an ill Administration, which hazards the Tyrant and his Family.

332. It is great Wisdom in Princes of both sorts, not to strain Points too high with their People: For whether the People have a Right to oppose them or not, they are ever sure to attempt it, when things are carried too far; though the Remedy oftentimes proves worse than the Disease.

333. Happy that King who is great by Justice, and that People who are free by Obedience.

334. Where the Ruler is Just, he may be strict; else it is two to one it turns upon him: And tho' he should prevail, he can be no Gainer, where his People are the Losers.

335. Princes must not have Passions in Government, nor Resent beyond Interest and Religion.

336. Where Example keeps pace with Authority, Power hardly fails to be obey'd, and Magistrates to be honor'd.

337. Let the People think they Govern and they will be Govern'd.

338. This cannot fail, if Those they Trust, are Trusted.

339. That Prince that is Just to them in great things, and Humors them sometimes in small ones, is sure to have and keep them from all the World.

340. For the People is the Politick Wife of the Prince, that may be better managed by Wisdom, than ruled by Force.

341. But where the Magistrate is partial and serves ill turns, he

loses his Authority with the People; and gives the Populace opportunity to gratifie their Ambition: And to lay a Stumbling-block for his People to fall.

342. It is true, that where a Subject is more Popular than the Prince, the Prince is in Danger: But it is as true, that it is his own Fault: For no Body has the like Means, Interest or Reason, to be popular as He.

343. It is an unaccountable thing, that some Princes incline rather to be fear'd than lov'd; when they see, that Fear does not oftener secure a Prince against the Dissatisfaction of his People, than Love makes a Subject too many for such a Prince.

344. Certainly Service upon Inclination is like to go farther than Obedience upon Compulsion.

345. The Romans had a just Sense of this, when they plac'd Optimus before Maximus, to their most Illustrious Captains and Cesars.

346. Besides, Experience tells us, That Goodness raises a nobler Passion in the Soul, and gives a better Sense of Duty than Severity.

347. What did Pharaoh get by increasing the Israelites Task? Ruine to himself in the End.

348. Kings, chiefly in this, should imitate God: Their Mercy should be above all their Works.

349. The Difference between the Prince and the Peasant, is in this World: But a Temper ought to be observ'd by him that has the Advantage here, because of the Judgment in the next.

350. The End of every thing should direct the Means: Now that of Government being the Good of the whole, nothing less should be the Aim of the Prince.

351. As often as Rulers endeavor to attain just Ends by just Mediums, they are sure of a quiet and easy Government; and as sure of Convulsions, where the Nature of things are violated, and their Order overrul'd.

352. It is certain, Princes ought to have great Allowances made them for Faults in Government; since they see by other People's Eyes, and hear by their Ears. But Ministers of State, their immediate Confidents and Instruments, have much to answer for, if to gratifie private Passions, they misguide the Prince to do publick Injury.

353. Ministers of State should undertake their Posts at their

Peril. If Princes overrule them, let them shew the Law, and humbly resign: If Fear, Gain or Flattery prevail, let them answer it to the Law.

354. The Prince cannot be preserv'd, but where the Minister is punishable: For People, as well as Princes, will not endure *Imperium in Imperio.*[11]

355. If Ministers are weak or ill Men, and so spoil their Places, it is the Prince's Fault that chose them: But if their Places spoil them, it is their own Fault to be made worse by them.

356. It is but just that those that reign by their Princes, should suffer for their Princes: For it is a safe and necessary Maxim, not to shift Heads in Government, while the Hands are in being that should answer for them.

357. And yet it were intolerable to be a Minister of State, if every Body may be Accuser and Judge.

358. Let therefore the false Accuser no more escape an exemplary Punishment, than the Guilty Minister.

359. For it profanes Government to have the Credit of the leading Men in it, subject to vulgar Censure; which is often ill grounded.

360. The Safety of a Prince, therefore consists in a well-chosen Council: And that only can be said to be so, where the Persons that compose it are qualified for the Business that comes before them.

361. Who would send to a Taylor to make a Lock, or to a Smith to make a Suit of Cloaths?

362. Let there be Merchants for Trade, Seamen for the Admiralty, Travellers for Foreign Affairs, some of the Leading Men of the Country for Home-Business, and Common and Civil Lawyers to advise of Legality and Right: Who should always keep to the strict Rules of Law.

363. Three Things contribute much to ruin Governments; Looseness, Oppression and Envy.

364. Where the Reins of Government are too slack, there the Manners of the People are corrupted: And that destroys Industry, begets Effeminacy, and provokes Heaven against it.

365. Oppression makes a Poor Country, and a Desperate People, who always wait an Opportunity to change.

[11] An empire within an empire.

366. He that ruleth over Men, must be just, ruling in the Fear of God, said an old and a wise King.

367. Envy disturbs and distracts Government, clogs the Wheels, and perplexes the Administration: And nothing contributes more to the Disorder, than a partial distribution of Rewards, and Punishments in the Sovereign.

368. As it is not reasonable that Men should be compell'd to serve; so those that have Employments should not be endured to leave them humorously.

369. Where the State intends a Man no Affront, he should not Affront the State.

A PRIVATE LIFE

370. Private Life is to be preferr'd; the Honor and Gain of publick Posts, bearing no proportion with the Comfort of it. The one is free and quiet, the other servile and noisy.

371. It was a great Answer of the Shunamite Woman, I dwell among my own People.

372. They that live of their own, neither need, nor often list to wear the Livery of the Publick.

373. Their Subsistance is not during Pleasure; nor have they patrons to please or present.

374. If they are not advanced, neither can they be disgraced. And as they know not the Smiles of Majesty, so they feel not the Frowns of Greatness; or the Effects of Envy.

375. If they want the Pleasures of a Court, they also escape the Temptations of it.

376. Private Men, in fine, are so much their own, that paying common Dues, they are Sovereigns of all the rest.

A PUBLICK LIFE

377. Yet the Publick must and will be served; and they that do it well, deserve publick Marks of Honor and Profit.

378. To do so, Men must have publick Minds, as well as Salaries; or they will serve private Ends at the Publick Cost.

379. Governments can never be well administered, but where those entrusted make Conscience of well discharging their Place.

QUALIFICATIONS

380. Five Things are requisite to a good Officer; Ability, Clean Hands, Dispatch, Patience and Impartiality.

CAPACITY

381. He that understands not his Employment, whatever else he knows, must be unfit for it, and the Publick suffers by his Inexpertness.

382. They that are able, should be just too; or the Government may be the worse for their Capacity.

CLEAN HANDS

383. Covetousness in such Men prompts them to prostitute the Publick for Gain.

384. The taking of a Bribe or Gratuity, should be punished with as severe Penalties, as the defrauding of the State.

385. Let Men have sufficient Salaries, and exceed them at their Peril.

386. It is a Dishonor to Government, that its Officers should live of Benevolence; as it ought to be Infamous for Officers to dishonor the Publick, by being twice paid for the same Business.

387. But to be paid, and not to do Business, is rank Oppression.

DISPATCH

388. Dispatch is a great and good Quality in an Officer; where Duty, not Gain, excites it. But of this, too many make their private Market and Over-plus to their Wages. Thus the Salary is for doing, and the Bribe, for dispatching the Business: As if Business could be done before it were dispatched: Or what ought to be done, ought not to be dispatch'd: Or they were to be paid apart, one by the Government, t'other by the Party.

389. Dispatch is as much the Duty of an Officer, as doing; and very much the Honor of the Government he serves.

390. Delays have been more injurious than direct Injustice.

391. They too often starve those they dare not deny.

392. The very Winner is made a Loser, because he pays twice for his own; like those that purchase Estates Mortgaged before to the full Value.

393. Our Law says well, to delay Justice is Injustice.

394. Not to have a Right, and not to come at it, differs little.

395. Refuse or Dispatch is the Duty and Wisdom of a good Officer.

PATIENCE

396. Patience is a Virtue every where; but it shines with great Lustre in the Men of Government.

397. Some are so Proud or Testy, they won't hear what they should redress.

398. Others so weak, they sink or burst under the weight of their Office, though they can lightly run away with the Salary of it.

399. Business can never be well done, that is not well understood: Which cannot be without Patience.

400. It is Cruelty indeed not to give the Unhappy an Hearing, whom we ought to help: But it is the top of Oppression to Browbeat the humble and modest Miserable, when they seek Relief.

401. Some, it is true, are unreasonable in their Desires and Hopes: But then we should inform, not rail at and reject them.

402. It is therefore as great an Instance of Wisdom as a Man in Business can give, to be Patient under the Impertinencies and Contradictions that attend it.

403. Method goes far to prevent Trouble in Business: For it makes the Task easy, hinders Confusion, saves abundance of Time, and instructs those that have Business depending, both what to do and what to hope.

IMPARTIALITY

404. Impartiality, though it be the last, is not the least Part of the Character of a good Magistrate.

405. It is noted as a Fault, in Holy Writ, even to regard the Poor: How much more the Rich in Judgment?

406. If our Compassions must not sway us; less should our Fears, Profits or Prejudices.

407. Justice is justly represented Blind, because she sees no Difference in the Parties concerned.

408. She has but one Scale and Weight, for Rich and Poor, Great and Small.

409. Her Sentence is not guided by the Person, but the Cause.

410. The Impartial Judge in Judgment, knows nothing but the Law: The Prince no more than the Peasant, his Kindred than a Stranger. Nay, his Enemy is sure to be upon equal Terms with his Friend, when he is upon the Bench.

411. Impartiality is the Life of Justice, as that is of Government.

412. Nor is it only a Benefit to the State, for private Families cannot subsist comfortably without it.

413. Parents that are partial, are ill obeyed by their Children; and partial Masters not better served by their Servants.

414. Partiality is always Indirect, if not Dishonest: For it shews a Byass where Reason would have none; if not an Injury, which Justice every where forbids.

415. As it makes Favorites without Reason, so it uses no Reason in judging of Actions: Confirming the Proverb, The Crow thinks her own Bird the fairest.

416. What some see to be no Fault in one, they will have Criminal in another.

417. Nay, how ugly do our own Failings look to us in the Persons of others, which yet we see not in our selves.

418. And but too common it is for some People, not to know their own Maxims and Principles in the Mouths of other Men, when they give occasion to use them.

419. Partiality corrupts our Judgment of Persons and Things, of our selves and others.

420. It contributes more than any thing to Factions in Government, and Fewds in Families.

421. It is prodigal Passion, that seldom returns 'till it is Hunger-bit, and Disappointments bring it within bounds.

422. And yet we may be indifferent, to a Fault.

INDIFFERENCY

423. Indifference is good in Judgment, but bad in Relation, and stark nought in Religion.

424. And even in Judgment, our Indifferency must be to the Persons, not Causes: For one, to be sure, is right.

NEUTRALITY

425. Neutrality is something else than Indifferency; and yet of kin to it too.

426. A Judge ought to be Indifferent, and yet he cannot be said to be Neutral.

427. The one being to be Even in Judgment, and the other not to meddle at all.

428. And where it is Lawful, to be sure, it is best to be Neutral.

429. He that espouses Parties, can hardly divorce himself from their Fate; and more fall with their Party than rise with it.

430. A wise Neuter joins with neither; but uses both, as his honest Interest leads him.

431. A Neuter only has room to be a Peace-maker: For being of neither side, he has the Means of mediating a Reconciliation of both.

A PARTY

432. And yet, where Right or Religion gives a Call, a Neuter must be a Coward or an Hypocrite.

433. In such Cases we should never be backward: nor yet mistaken.

434. When our Right or Religion is in question, then is the fittest time to assert it.

435. Nor must we always be Neutral where our Neighbors are concerned: For tho' Medling is a Fault, Helping is a Duty.

436. We have a Call to do good, as often as we have the Power and Occasion.

437. If Heathens could say, We are not born for our selves; surely Christians should practise it.

438. They are taught so by his Example, as well as Doctrine, from whom they have borrowed their Name.

OSTENTATION

439. Do what good thou canst unknown; and be not vain of what ought rather to be felt, than seen.

440. The Humble, in the Parable of the Day of Judgment, forgot their good Works; Lord, when did we do so and so?

441. He that does Good, for Good's sake, seeks neither Praise nor Reward; tho' sure of both at last.

COMPLEAT VIRTUE

442. Content not thy self that thou art Virtuous in the general: For one Link being wanting, the Chain is defective.

443. Perhaps thou art rather Innocent than Virtuous, and owest more to thy Constitution, than thy Religion.

444. Innocent, is not to be Guilty: But Virtuous is to overcome our evil Inclinations.

445. If thou hast not conquer'd thy self in that which is thy own particular Weakness, thou hast no Title to Virtue, tho' thou art free of other Men's.

446. For a Covetous Man to inveigh against Prodigality, an Atheist against Idolatry, a Tyrant against Rebellion, or a Lyer against Forgery, and a Drunkard against Intemperance, is for the Pot to call the Kettle black.

447. Such Reproof would have but little Success; because it would carry but little Authority with it.

448. If thou wouldest conquer thy Weakness, thou must never gratify it.

449. No Man is compelled to Evil; his Consent only makes it his.

450. 'T is no Sin to be tempted, but to be overcome.

451. What Man in his right Mind, would conspire his own hurt? Men are beside themselves, when they transgress their Convictions.

452. If thou would'st not Sin, don't Desire; and if thou would'st not Lust, don't Embrace the Temptation: No, not look at it, nor think of it.

453. Thou would'st take much Pains to save thy Body: Take some, prithee, to save thy Soul.

RELIGION

454. Religion is the Fear of God, and its Demonstration on good Works; and Faith is the Root of both: For without Faith we cannot please God, nor can we fear what we do not believe.

455. The Devils also believe and know abundance: But in this is the Difference, their Faith works not by Love, nor their Knowledge by Obedience; and therefore they are never the better for them. And if ours be such, we shall be of their Church, not of Christ's: For as the Head is, so must the Body be.

456. He was Holy, Humble, Harmless, Meek, Merciful, &c. when among us; to teach us what we should be, when he was gone. And yet he is among us still, and in us too, a living and perpetual Preacher of the same Grace, by his Spirit in our Consciences.

457. A Minister of the Gospel ought to be one of Christ's making, if he would pass for one of Christ's Ministers.

458. And if he be one of his making, he Knows and Does as well as Believes.

459. That Minister whose Life is not the Model of his Doctrine, is a Babler rather than a Preacher; a Quack rather than a Physician of Value.

460. Of old Time they were made Ministers by the Holy Ghost: And the more that is an Ingredient now, the fitter they are for that Work.

461. Running Streams are not so apt to corrupt; nor Itinerant, as settled Preachers: But they are not to run before they are sent.

462. As they freely receive from Christ, so they give.

463. They will not make that a Trade, which they know ought not, in Conscience, to be one.

464. Yet there is no fear of their Living that design not to live by it.

465. The humble and true Teacher meets with more than he expects.

466. He accounts Content with Godliness great Gain, and therefore seeks not to make a Gain of Godliness.

467. As the Ministers of Christ are made by him, and are like him, so they beget People into the same Likeness.

468. To be like Christ then, is to be a Christian. And Regeneration is the only way to the Kingdom of God, which we pray for.

469. Let us to Day, therefore, hear his Voice, and not harden our Hearts; who speaks to us many ways. In the Scriptures, in our Hearts, by his Servants and his Providences: And the Sum of all is HOLINESS and CHARITY.

470. St. James gives a short Draught of this Matter, but very full and reaching, Pure Religion and undefiled before God the Father, is this, to visit the Fatherless and the Widows in their Affliction, and to keep our selves unspotted from the World. Which is compriz'd in these Two Words, CHARITY and PIETY.

471. They that truly make these their Aim, will find them their Attainment; and with them, the Peace that follows so excellent a Condition.

472. Amuse not thy self therefore with the numerous Opinions of the World, nor value thy self upon verbal Orthodoxy, Philosophy, or thy Skill in Tongues, or Knowledge of the Fathers: (too much the Business and Vanity of the World). But in this rejoyce, That thou knowest God, that is the Lord, who exerciseth loving Kindness, and Judgment, and Righteousness in the Earth.

473. Publick Worship is very commendable, if well performed. We owe it to God and good Example. But we must know, that God is not tyed to Time or Place, who is every where at the same Time: And this we shall know, as far as we are capable, if where ever we are, our Desires are to be with him.

474. Serving God, People generally confine to the Acts of Publick and Private Worship: And those, the more zealous do oftener repeat, in hopes of Acceptance.

475. But if we consider that God is an Infinite Spirit, and, as such, every where; and that our Saviour has taught us, That he will be worshipped in Spirit and in Truth; we shall see the shortness of such a Notion.

476. For serving God concerns the Frame of our Spirits, in the whole Course of our Lives; in every Occasion we have, in which we may shew our Love to his Law.

477. For as Men in Battle are continually in the way of shot, so we, in this World, are ever within the Reach of Temptation. And

herein do we serve God, if we avoid what we are forbid, as well as do what he commands.

478. God is better served in resisting a Temptation to Evil, than in many formal Prayers.

479. This is but Twice or Thrice a Day; but That every Hour and Moment of the Day. So much more is our continual Watch, than our Evening and Morning Devotion.

480. Wouldst thou then serve God? Do not that alone, which thou wouldest not that another should see thee do.

481. Don't take God's Name in vain, or disobey thy Parents, or wrong thy Neighbor, or commit Adultery even in thine Heart.

482. Neither be vain, Lascivious, Proud, Drunken, Revengeful or Angry: Nor Lye, Detract, Backbite, Overreach, Oppress, Deceive or Betray: But watch vigorously against all Temptations to these Things; as knowing that God is present, the Overseer of all thy Ways and most inward Thoughts, and the Avenger of his own Law upon the Disobedient, and thou wilt acceptably serve God.

483. Is it not reason, if we expect the Acknowledgments of those to whom we are bountiful, that we should reverently pay ours to God, our most magnificent and constant Benefactor?

484. The World represents a Rare and Sumptuous Palace, Mankind the great Family in it, and God the mighty Lord and Master of it.

485. We are all sensible what a stately Seat it is: The Heavens adorned with so many glorious Luminaries; and the Earth with Groves, Plains, Valleys, Hills, Fountains, Ponds, Lakes and Rivers; and Variety of Fruits, and Creatures for Food, Pleasure and Profit. In short, how Noble an House he keeps, and the Plenty and Variety and Excellency of his Table; his Orders, Seasons and Suitableness of every Time and Thing. But we must be as sensible, or at least ought to be, what Careless and Idle Servants we are, and how short and disproportionable our Behavior is to his Bounty and Goodness: How long he bears, and often he reprieves and forgives us: Who, notwithstanding our Breach of Promises, and repeated Neglects, has not yet been provok'd to break up House, and send us to shift for our selves. Should not this great Goodness raise a due Sense in us of our Undutifulness, and a Resolution to alter our Course and

mend our Manners; that we may be for the future more worthy Communicants at our Master's good and great Table? Especially since it is not more certain that we deserve his Displeasure than that we should feel it, if we continue to be unprofitable Servants.

486. But tho' God has replenisht this World with abundance of good Things for Man's Life and Comfort, yet they are all but Imperfect Goods. He only is the Perfect Good to whom they point. But alas! Men cannot see him for them; tho' they should always see him In them.

487. I have often wondered at the unaccountableness of Man in this, among other things; that tho' he loves Changes so well, he should care so little to hear or think of his last, great, and best Change too, if he pleases.

488. Being, as to our Bodies, composed of changeable Elements, we with the World, are made up of, and subsist by Revolution: But our Souls being of another and nobler Nature, we should seek our Rest in a more induring Habitation.

489. The truest end of Life, is, to know the Life that never ends.

490. He that makes this his Care, will find it his Crown at last.

491. Life else, were a Misery rather than a Pleasure, a Judgment, not a Blessing.

492. For to Know, Regret and Resent; to Desire, Hope and Fear, more than a Beast, and not live beyond him, is to make a Man less than a Beast.

493. It is the Amends of a short and troublesome Life, that Doing well, and Suffering ill, Entitles Man to One Longer and Better.

494. This ever raises the Good Man's Hope, and gives him Tastes beyond the other World.

495. As 't is his Aim, so none else can hit the Mark.

496. Many make it their Speculation, but 't is the Good Man's Practice.

497. His Work keeps Pace with his Life, and so leaves nothing to be done when he Dies.

498. And he that lives to live ever, never fears dying.

499. Nor can the Means be terrible to him that heartily believes the End.

500. For tho' Death be a Dark Passage, it leads to Immortality, and that 's Recompence enough for Suffering of it.

501. And yet Faith Lights us, even through the Grave, being the Evidence of Things not seen.

502. And this is the Comfort of the Good, that the Grave cannot hold them, and that they live as soon as they die.

503. For Death is no more than a Turning of us over from Time to Eternity.

504. Nor can there be a Revolution without it; for it supposes the Dissolution of one form, in order to the Succession of another.

505. Death then, being the Way and Condition of Life, we cannot love to live, if we cannot bear to die.

506. Let us then not cozen our selves with the Shells and Husks of things; nor prefer Form to Power, nor Shadows to Substance: Pictures of Bread will not satisfie Hunger, nor those of Devotion please God.

507. This World is a Form; our Bodies are Forms; and no visible Acts of Devotion can be without Forms. But yet the less Form in Religion the better, since God is a Spirit: For the more mental our Worship, the more adequate to the Nature of God; the more silent, the more suitable to the Language of a Spirit.

508. Words are for others, not for our selves: Nor for God, who hears not as Bodies do; but as Spirits should.

509. If we would know this Dialect; we must learn of the Divine Principle in us. As we hear the Dictates of that, so God hears us.

510. There we may see him too in all his Attributes; Tho' but in little, yet as much as we can apprehend or bear: for as he is in himself, he is incomprehensible, and dwelleth in that Light which no Eye can approach. But in his Image we may behold his Glory; enough to exalt our Apprehensions of God, and to instruct us in that Worship which pleaseth him.

511. Men may Tire themselves in a Labyrinth of Search, and talk of God: But if we would know him indeed, it must be from the Impressions we receive of him; and the softer our Hearts are, the deeper and livelier those will be upon us.

512. If he has made us sensible of his Justice, by his Reproof; of

his Patience, by his Forbearance; of his Mercy, by his Forgiveness; of his Holiness, by the Sanctification of our Hearts through his Spirit; we have a grounded Knowledge of God. This is Experience, that Speculation; This Enjoyment, that Report. In short, this is undeniable Evidence, with the realities of Religion, and will stand all Winds and Weathers.

513. As our Faith, so our Devotion should be lively. Cold Meat won't serve at those Repasts.

514. It 's a Coal from God's Altar must kindle our Fire: And without Fire, true Fire, no acceptable Sacrifice.

515. Open thou my Lips, and then, said the Royal Prophet, My Mouth shall praise God. But not 'till then.

516. The Preparation of the Heart, as well as Answer of the Tongue, is of the Lord: And to have it, our Prayers must be powerful, and our Worship grateful.

517. Let us chuse, therefore, to commune where there is the warmest Sense of Religion; where Devotion exceeds Formality, and Practice most corresponds with Profession; and where there is at least as much Charity as Zeal: For where this Society is to be found, there shall we find the Church of God.

518. As Good, so Ill Men are all of a Church; and every Body knows who must be Head of it.

519. The Humble, Meek, Merciful, Just, Pious and Devout Souls, are everywhere of one Religion; and when Death has taken off the Mask, they will know one another, tho' the divers Liveries they wear here make them Strangers.

520. Great Allowances are to be made of Education, and personal Weaknesses: But 't is a Rule with me, that Man is truly Religious, that loves the Persuasion he is of, for the Piety rather than Ceremony of it.

521. They that have one End, can hardly disagree when they meet. At least their concern is in the Greater, moderates the value and difference about the lesser things.

522. It is a sad Reflection, that many Men hardly have any Religion at all; and most Men have none of their own: For that which is the Religion of their Education, and not of their Judgment, is the Religion of Another, and not Theirs.

523. To have Religion upon Authority, and not upon Conviction, is like a Finger Watch, to be set forwards or backwards, as he pleases that has it in keeping.

524. It is a Preposterous thing, that Men can venture their Souls where they will not venture their Money: For they will take their Religion upon trust, but not trust a Synod about the Goodness of Half a Crown.

525. They will follow their own Judgment when their Money is concerned, whatever they do for their Souls.

526. But to be sure, that Religion cannot be right, that a Man is the worse for having.

527. No Religion is better than an Unnatural One.

528. Grace perfects, but never sours or spoils Nature.

529. To be Unnatural in Defence of Grace, is a Contradiction.

530. Hardly any thing looks worse, than to defend Religion by ways that shew it has no Credit with us.

531. A Devout Man is one thing, a Stickler is quite another.

532. When our Minds exceed their just Bounds, we must needs discredit what we would recommend.

533. To be Furious in Religion, is to be Irreligiously Religious.

534. If he that is without Bowels, is not a Man; How then can he be a Christian?

535. It were better to be of no Church, than to be bitter for any.

536. Bitterness comes very near to Enmity, and that is Beelzebub; because the Perfection of Wickedness.

537. A good End cannot sanctifie evil Means; nor must we ever do Evil, that Good may come of it.

538. Some Folks think they may Scold, Rail, Hate, Rob and Kill too; so it be but for God's sake.

539. But nothing in us unlike him, can please him.

540. It is as great Presumption to send our Passions upon God's Errands, as it is to palliate them with God's Name.

541. Zeal dropped in Charity, is good, without it good for nothing: For it devours all it comes near.

542. They must first judge themselves, that presume to censure others: And such will not be apt to overshoot the Mark.

543. We are too ready to retaliate, rather than forgive, or gain by Love and Information.

544. And yet we could hurt no Man that we believe loves us.

545. Let us then try what Love will do: For if Men did once see we Love them, we should soon find they would not harm us.

546. Force may subdue, but Love gains: And he that forgives first, wins the Lawrel.

547. If I am even with my Enemy, the Debt is paid; but if I forgive it, I oblige him for ever.

548. Love is the hardest Lesson in Christianity; but, for that reason, it should be most our care to learn it. *Difficilia quæ Pulchra.*[12]

549. It is a severe Rebuke upon us, that God makes us so many Allowances, and we make so few to our Neighbor: As if Charity had nothing to do with Religion; Or Love with Faith, that ought to work by it.

550. I find all sorts of People agree, whatsoever were their Animosities, when humbled by the Approaches of Death: Then they forgive, then they pray for, and love one another: Which shews us, that it is not our Reason, but our Passion, that makes and holds up the Feuds that reign among men in their Health and Fulness. They, therefore, that live nearest to that which they should die, must certainly live best.

551. Did we believe a final Reckoning and Judgment; or did we think enough of what we do believe, we would allow more Love in Religion than we do; since Religion it self is nothing else but Love to God and Man.

552. He that lives in Love lives in God, says the Beloved Disciple: And to be sure a Man can live no where better.

553. It is most reasonable Men should value that Benefit, which is most durable. Now Tongues shall cease, and Prophecy fail, and Faith shall be consummated in Sight, and Hope in Enjoyment; but Love remains.

554. Love is indeed Heaven upon Earth; since Heaven above would not be Heaven without it: For where there is not Love; there is Fear: But perfect Love casts out Fear. And yet we naturally fear most to offend what we most Love.

[12] Those things are difficult which are beautiful.

555. What we Love, we 'll Hear; what we Love, we 'll Trust; and what we Love, we 'll serve, ay, and suffer for too. If you love me (says our Blessed Redeemer) keep my Commandments. Why? Why then he 'll Love us; then we shall be his Friends; then he 'll send us the Comforter; then whatsoever we ask, we shall receive; and then where he is we shall be also, and that for ever. Behold the Fruits of Love; the Power, Vertue, Benefit and Beauty of Love!

556. Love is above all; and when it prevails in us all, we shall all be Lovely, and in Love with God and one with another.

Amen.

END OF PART I

MORE FRUITS OF SOLITUDE

BEING THE SECOND PART
OF
REFLECTIONS AND MAXIMS, RELATING
TO THE CONDUCT OF HUMAN LIFE

CONTENTS

PART II

THE INTRODUCTION TO THE READER

THE Title of this Treatise shows, there was a former of the same Nature; and the Author hope he runs no Hazard in recommending both to his Reader's Perusal. He is well aware of the low Reckoning the Labors of indifferent Authors are under, at a Time when hardly any Thing passes for current, that is not calculated to flatter the Sharpness of contending Parties. He is also sensible, that Books grow a very Drug, where they cannot raise and support their Credit, by their own Usefulness; and how far this will be able to do it, he knows not; yet he thinks himself tollerably safe in making it publick, in three Respects.

First, That the Purchase is small, and the Time but little, that is requisite to read it.

Next, Though some Men should not find it relish'd high enough for their finer Wits, or warmer Pallats, it will not perhaps be useless to those of lower Flights, and who are less engaged in publick Heats.

Lastly, The Author honestly aims at as general a Benefit as the Thing will bear; to Youth especially, whether he hits the Mark or not: And that without the least Ostentation, or any private Regards.

Let not Envy misinterpret his Intention, and he will be accountable for all other Faults.

VALE.

MORE FRUITS OF SOLITUDE
BEING THE SECOND PART OF
REFLECTIONS & MAXIMS

THE RIGHT MORALIST

A RIGHT Moralist, is a Great and Good Man, but for that Reason he is rarely to be found.

2. There are a Sort of People, that are fond of the Character, who, in my Opinion, have but little Title to it.

3. They think it enough, not to defraud a Man of his Pay, or betray his Friend; but never consider, That the Law forbids the one at his Peril, and that Virtue is seldom the Reason of the other.

4. But certainly he that Covets, can no more be a Moral Man, than he that Steals; since he does so in his Mind. Nor can he be one that Robs his Neighbor of his Credit, or that craftily undermines him of his Trade or Office.

5. If a Man pays his Taylor, but Debauches his Wife; Is he a current Moralist?

6. But what shall we say of the Man that Rebels against his Father, is an Ill Husband, or an Abusive Neighbor; one that 's Lavish of his Time, of his Health, and of his Estate, in which his Family is so nearly concerned? Must he go for a Right Moralist, because he pays his Rent well?

7. I would ask some of those Men of Morals, Whether he that Robs God and Himself too, tho' he should not defraud his Neighbor, be the Moral Man?

8. Do I owe my self Nothing? And do I not owe All to God? And if paying what we owe, makes the Moral Man, is it not fit we should begin to render our Dues, where we owe our very Beginning; ay, our All?

9. The Compleat Moralist begins with God; he gives him his Due,

his Heart, his Love, his Service; the Bountiful Giver of his Well-Being, as well as Being.

10. He that lives without a Sense of this Dependency and Obligation, cannot be a Moral Man, because he does not make his Returns of Love and Obedience; as becomes an honest and a sensible Creature: Which very Term Implies he is not his own; and it cannot be very honest to misimploy another's Goods.

11. But can there be no Debt, but to a fellow Creature? Or, will our Exactness in paying those Dribling ones, while we neglect our weightier Obligations, Cancel the Bonds we lie under, and render us right and thorough Moralists?

12. As Judgments are paid before Bonds, and Bonds before Bills or Book-Debts, so the Moralist considers his Obligations according to their several Dignities.

In the first Place, Him to whom he owes himself. Next, himself, in his Health and Livelihood. Lastly, His other Obligations, whether Rational or Pecuniary; doing to others, to the Extent of his Ability, as he would have them do unto him.

13. In short, The Moral Man is he that Loves God above All, and his Neighbor as himself, which fulfils both Tables at once.

THE WORLD'S ABLE MAN

14. It is by some thought, the Character of an Able Man, to be Dark and not Understood. But I am sure that is not fair Play.

15. If he be so by Silence, 't is better; but if by Disguises, 't is insincere and hateful.

16. Secrecy is one Thing, false Lights is another.

17. The honest Man, that is rather free, than open, is ever to be preferr'd; especially when Sense is at Helm.

18. The Glorying of the other Humor is in a Vice: For it is not Humane to be Cold, Dark, and Unconversable. I was a going to say, they are like Pick-Pockets in a Crowd, where a Man must ever have his Hand on his Purse; or as Spies in a Garrison, that if not prevented betrays it.

19. They are the Reverse of Human Nature, and yet this is the present World's Wise Man and Politician: Excellent Qualities for

Lapland, where, they say, Witches, though not many Conjurors, dwell.

20. Like Highway-Men, that rarely Rob without Vizards, or in the same Wigs and Cloaths, but have a Dress for every Enterprize.

21. At best, he may be a Cunning Man, which is a sort of Lurcher in the Politicks.

22. He is never too hard for the Wise Man upon the Square, for that is out of his Element, and puts him quite by his Skill.

Nor are Wise Men ever catch'd by him, but when they trust him.

23. But as Cold and Close as he seems, he can and will please all, if he gets by it, though it should neither please God nor himself at bottom.

24. He is for every Cause that brings him Gain, but Implacable if disappointed of Success.

25. And what he cannot hinder, he will be sure to Spoil, by over-doing it.

26. None so Zealous then as he, for that which he cannot abide.

27. What is it he will not, or cannot do, to hide his true Sentiments.

28. For his Interest, he refuses no Side or Party; and will take the Wrong by the Hand, when t'other won't do, with as good a Grace as the Right.

29. Nay, he commonly chooses the Worst, because that brings the best Bribe: His Cause being ever Money.

30. He Sails with all Winds, and is never out of his Way, where any Thing is to be had.

31. A Privateer indeed, and everywhere a very Bird of Prey.

32. True to nothing but himself, and false to all Persons and Parties, to serve his own Turn.

33. Talk with him as often as you please, he will never pay you in good Coin; for 't is either False or Clipt.

34. But to give a False Reason for any Thing, let my Reader never learn of him, no more than to give a Brass Half-Crown for a good one: Not only because it is not true, but because it Deceives the Person to whom it is given; which I take to be an Immorality.

35. Silence is much more preferable, for it saves the Secret, as well as the Person's Honor.

36. Such as give themselves the Latitude of saying what they do not mean, come to be errant Jockeys at more Things than one; but in Religion and Politicks, 't is most pernicious.

37. To hear two Men talk the Reverse of their own Sentiments, with all the good Breeding and Appearance of Friendship imaginable, on purpose to Cozen or Pump each other, is to a Man of Virtue and Honor, one of the Melancholiest, as well as most Nauseous Thing in the World.

38. But that it should be the Character of an Able Man, is to Disinherit Wisdom, and Paint out our Degeneracy to the Life, by setting up Fraud, an errant Impostor, in her Room.

39. The Tryal of Skill between these two is, who shall believe least of what t'other says; and he that has the Weakness, or good Nature to give out first, (viz. to believe any Thing t'other says) is look'd upon to be Trick'd.

40. I cannot see the Policy, any more than the Necessity, of a Man's Mind always giving the Lye to his Mouth, or his Mouth ever giving the false Alarms of his Mind: For no Man can be long believed, that teaches all Men to distrust him; and since the Ablest have sometimes need of Credit, where lies the Advantage of their Politick Cant or Banter upon Mankind?

41. I remember a Passage of one of Queen Elizabeth's Great Men, as Advice to his Friend; The Advantage, says he, I had upon others at Court, was, that I always spoke as I thought, which being not believed by them, I both preserv'd a good Conscience, and suffered no Damage from that Freedom: Which, as it shows the Vice to be Older than our Times, so that Gallant Man's Integrity, to be the best Way of avoiding it.

42. To be sure it is wise as well as Honest, neither to flatter other Men's Sentiments, nor Dissemble and less Contradict our own.

43. To hold ones Tongue, or speak Truth, or talk only of indifferent Things, is the Fairest Conversation.

44. Women that rarely go Abroad without Vizard-Masks, have none of the best Reputation. But when we consider what all this Art and Disguise are for, it equally heightens the Wise Man's Wonder and Aversion: Perhaps it is to betray a Father, a Brother, a Master, a Friend, a Neighbor, or ones own Party.

45. A fine Conquest! what Noble Grecians and Romans abhorr'd: As if Government could not subsist without Knavery, and that Knaves were the Usefullest Props to it; tho' the basest, as well as greatest, Perversion of the Ends of it.

46. But that it should become a Maxim, shows but too grossly the Corruption of the Times.

47. I confess I have heard the Stile of a Useful Knave, but ever took it to be a silly or a knavish Saying; at least an Excuse for Knavery.

48. It is as reasonable to think a Whore makes the best Wife, as a Knave the best Officer.

49. Besides, Employing Knaves, Encourages Knavery instead of punishing it; and Alienates the Reward of Virtue. Or, at least, must make the World believe, the Country yields not honest Men enough, able to serve her.

50. Art thou a Magistrate? Prefer such as have clean Characters where they live, and of Estates to secure a just Discharge of their Trusts; that are under no Temptation to strain Points for a Fortune: For sometimes such may be found, sooner than they are Employed.

51. Art thou a Private Man? Contract thy Acquaintance in a narrow Compass, and chuse Those for the Subjects of it, that are Men of Principles; such as will make full Stops, where Honor will not lead them on; and that had rather bear the disgrace of not being thorow Paced Men, than forfeit their Peace and Reputation by a base Compliance.

THE WISE MAN

52. The Wise Man Governs himself by the Reason of his Case, and because what he does is Best: Best, in a Moral and Prudent, not a Sinister Sense.

53. He proposes just Ends, and employs the fairest and probablest Means and Methods to attain them.

54. Though you cannot always penetrate his Design, or his Reasons for it, yet you shall ever see his Actions of a Piece, and his Performances like a Workman: They will bear the Touch of Wisdom and Honor, as often as they are tryed.

55. He scorns to serve himself by Indirect Means, or be an Inter-

loper in Government, since just Enterprises never want any Just Ways to succeed them.

56. To do Evil, that Good may come of it, is for Bunglers in Politicks, as well as Morals.

57. Like those Surgeons, that will cut off an Arm they can't cure, to hide their Ignorance and save their Credit.

58. The Wise Man is Cautious, but not cunning; Judicious, but not Crafty; making Virtue the Measure of using his Excellent Understanding in the Conduct of his Life.

59. The Wise Man is equal, ready, but not officious; has in every Thing an Eye to Sure Footing: He offends no Body, nor easily is offended, and always willing to Compound for Wrongs, if not forgive them.

60. He is never Captious, nor Critical; hates Banter and Jests: He may be Pleasant, but not Light; he never deals but in Substantial Ware, and leaves the rest for the Toy Pates (or Shops) of the World; which are so far from being his Business, that they are not so much as his Diversion.

61. He is always for some solid Good, Civil or Moral; as, to make his Country more Virtuous, Preserve her Peace and Liberty, Imploy her Poor, Improve Land, Advance Trade, Suppress Vice, Incourage Industry, and all Mechanick Knowledge; and that they should be the Care of the Government, and the Blessing and Praise of the People.

62. To conclude: He is Just, and fears God, hates Covetousness, and eschews Evil, and loves his Neighbor as himself.

OF THE GOVERNMENT OF THOUGHTS

63. Man being made a Reasonable, and so a Thinking Creature, there is nothing more Worthy of his Being, than the Right Direction and Employment of his Thoughts; since upon This, depends both his Usefulness to the Publick, and his own present and future Benefit in all Respects.

64. The Consideration of this, has often obliged me to Lament the Unhappiness of Mankind, that through too great a Mixture and Confusion of Thoughts, have been hardly able to make a Right or Mature Judgment of Things.

65. To this is owing the various Uncertainty and Confusion we see in the World, and the Intemperate Zeal that occasions them.

66. To this also is to be attributed the imperfect Knowledge we have of Things, and the slow Progress we make in attaining to a Better; like the Children of Israel that were forty Years upon their Journey, from Egypt to Canaan, which might have been performed in Less than One.

67. In fine, 't is to this that we ought to ascribe, if not all, at least most of the Infelicities we Labor under.

68. Clear therefore thy Head, and Rally and Manage thy Thoughts Rightly, and thou wilt Save Time, and See and Do thy Business Well; for thy Judgment will be Distinct, thy Mind Free, and the Faculties Strong and Regular.

69. Always remember to bound thy Thoughts to the present Occasion.

70. If it be thy Religious Duty, suffer nothing else to Share in them. And if any Civil or Temporal Affair, observe the same Caution, and thou wilt be a whole Man to every Thing, and do twice the Business in the same Time.

71. If any Point over-Labors thy Mind, divert and relieve it, by some other Subject, of a more Sensible, or Manual Nature, rather than what may affect the Understanding; for this were to write one Thing upon another, which blots out our former Impressions, or renders them illegible.

72. They that are least divided in their Care, always give the best Account of their Business.

73. As therefore thou art always to pursue the present Subject, till thou hast master'd it, so if it fall out that thou hast more Affairs than one upon thy Hand, be sure to prefer that which is of most Moment, and will least wait thy Leisure.

74. He that Judges not well of the Importance of his Affairs, though he may be always Busy, he must make but a small Progress.

75. But make not more Business necessary than is so; and rather lessen than augment Work for thy self.

76. Nor yet be over-eager in pursuit of any Thing; for the Mercurial too often happen to leave Judgment behind them, and sometimes make Work for Repentance.

77. He that over-runs his Business, leaves it for him that follows more leisurely to take it up; which has often proved a profitable Harvest to them that never Sow'd.

78. 'T is the Advantage that slower Tempers have upon the Men of lively Parts, that tho' they don't lead, they will Follow well, and Glean Clean.

79. Upon the whole Matter, Employ thy Thoughts as thy Business requires, and let that have a Place according to Merit and Urgency; giving every Thing a Review and due Digestion, and thou wilt prevent many Errors and Vexations, as well as save much Time to thy self in the Course of thy Life.

OF ENVY

80. It is the Mark of an ill Nature, to lessen good Actions, and aggravate ill Ones.

81. Some men do as much begrutch others a good Name, as they want one themselves; and perhaps that is the Reason of it.

82. But certainly they are in the Wrong, that can think they are lessened, because others have their Due.

83. Such People generally have less Merit than Ambition, that Covet the Reward of other Men's; and to be sure a very ill Nature, that will rather Rob others of their Due, than allow them their Praise.

84. It is more an Error of our Will, than our Judgment: For we know it to be an Effect of our Passion, not our Reason; and therefore we are the more culpable in our Partial Estimates.

85. It is as Envious as Unjust, to underrate another's Actions where their intrinsick Worth recommends them to disengaged Minds.

86. Nothing shews more the Folly, as well as Fraud of Man, than Clipping of Merit and Reputation.

87. And as some Men think it an Allay to themselves, that others have their Right; so they know no End of Pilfering to raise their own Credit.

88. This Envy is the Child of Pride and Misgives, rather than Mistakes.

89. It will have Charity, to be Ostentation; Sobriety, Covetous-

ness; Humility, Craft; Bounty, Popularity: In short, Virtue must be Design, and Religion, only Interest. Nay, the best of Qualities must not pass without a But to allay their Merit and abate their Praise. Basest of Tempers! and they that have them, the Worst of Men!

90. But Just and Noble Minds Rejoice in other Men's Success, and help to augment their Praise.

91. And indeed they are not without a Love to Virtue, that take a Satisfaction in seeing her Rewarded, and such deserve to share her Character that do abhor to lessen it.

OF MAN'S LIFE

92. Why is Man less durable than the Works of his Hands, but because This is not the Place of his Rest?

93. And it is a Great and Just Reproach upon him, that he should fix his Mind where he cannot stay himself.

94. Were it not more his Wisdom to be concerned about those Works that will go with him, and erect a Mansion for him where Time has Power neither over him nor it?

95. 'T is a sad Thing for Man so often to miss his Way to his Best, as well as most Lasting Home.

OF AMBITION

96. They that soar too high, often fall hard; which makes a low and level Dwelling preferrable.

97. The tallest Trees are most in the Power of the Winds, and Ambitious Men of the Blasts of Fortune.

98. They are most seen and observed, and most envyed: Least Quiet, but most talk'd of, and not often to their Advantage.

99. Those Buildings had need of a good Foundation, that lie so much exposed to Weather.

100. Good Works are a Rock, that will support their Credit; but Ill Ones a Sandy Foundation that Yields to Calamities.

101. And truly they ought to expect no Pity in their Fall, that when in Power had no Bowels for the Unhappy.

102. The worst of Distempers; always Craving and Thirsty, Restless and Hated: A perfect Delirium in the Mind: Insufferable in Success, and in Disappointments most Revengeful.

OF PRAISE OR APPLAUSE

103. We are too apt to love Praise, but not to Deserve it.

104. But if we would Deserve it, we must love Virtue more than That.

105. As there is no Passion in us sooner moved, or more deceivable, so for that Reason there is none over which we ought to be more Watchful, whether we give or receive it: For if we give it, we must be sure to mean it, and measure it too.

106. If we are Penurious, it shows Emulation; if we exceed, Flattery.

107. Good Measure belongs to Good Actions; more looks Nauseous, as well as Insincere; besides, 't is a Persecuting of the Meritorious, who are out of Countenance to hear, what they deserve.

108. It is much easier for him to merit Applause, than hear of it: And he never doubts himself more, or the Person that gives it, than when he hears so much of it.

109. But to say true, there needs not many Cautions on this Hand, since the World is rarely just enough to the Deserving.

110. However, we cannot be too Circumspect how we receive Praise: For if we contemplate our selves in a false Glass, we are sure to be mistaken about our Dues; and because we are too apt to believe what is Pleasing, rather than what is True, we may be too easily swell'd, beyond our just Proportion, by the Windy Compliments of Men.

111. Make ever therefore Allowances for what is said on such Occasions, or thou Exposest, as well as Deceivest thy self.

112. For an Over-value of our selves, gives us but a dangerous Security in many Respects.

113. We expect more than belongs to us; take all that's given us though never meant us; and fall out with those that are not as full of us as we are of our selves.

114. In short, 't is a Passion that abuses our Judgment, and makes us both Unsafe and Ridiculous.

115. Be not fond therefore of Praise, but seek Virtue that leads to it.

116. And yet no more lessen or dissemble thy Merit, than over-rate it: For tho' Humility be a Virtue, an affected one is none.

OF CONDUCT IN SPEECH

117. Enquire often, but Judge rarely, and thou wilt not often be mistaken.

118. It is safer to Learn, than teach; and who conceals his Opinion, has nothing to Answer for.

119. Vanity or Resentment often engage us, and 't is two to one but we come off Losers; for one shews a Want of Judgment and Humility, as the other does of Temper and Discretion.

120. Not that I admire the Reserved; for they are next to Unnatural that are not Communicable. But if Reservedness be at any Time a Virtue, 't is in Throngs or ill Company.

121. Beware also of Affectation in Speech; it often wrongs Matter, and ever shows a blind Side.

122. Speak properly, and in as few Words as you can, but always plainly; for the End of Speech is not Ostentation, but to be understood.

123. They that affect Words more than Matter, will dry up that little they have.

124. Sense never fails to give them that have it, Words enough to make them understood.

125. But it too often happens in some Conversations, as in Apothecary-Shops, that those Pots that are Empty, or have Things of Small Value in them, are as gaudily Dress'd and Flourish'd, as those that are full of precious Drugs.

126. This Laboring of slight Matter with flourish'd Turns of Expression, is fulsome, and worse than the Modern Imitation of Tapestry, and East-India Goods, in Stuffs and Linnens. In short, 't is but Taudry Talk, and next to very Trash.

UNION OF FRIENDS

127. They that love beyond the World, cannot be separated by it.

128. Death cannot kill, what never dies.

129. Nor can Spirits ever be divided that love and live in the same Divine Principle; the Root and Record of their Friendship.

130. If Absence be not death, neither is theirs.

131. Death is but Crossing the World, as Friends do the Seas; They live in one another still.

132. For they must needs be present, that love and live in that which is Omnipresent.

133. In this Divine Glass, they see Face to Face; and their Converse is Free, as well as Pure.

134. This is the Comfort of Friends, that though they may be said to Die, yet their Friendship and Society are, in the best Sense, ever present, because Immortal.

OF BEING EASY IN LIVING

135. 'T is a Happiness to be delivered from a Curious Mind, as well as from a Dainty Palate.

136. For it is not only a Troublesome but Slavish Thing to be Nice.

137. They narrow their own Freedom and Comforts, that make so much requisite to enjoy them.

138. To be Easy in Living, is much of the Pleasure of Life: But Difficult Tempers will always want it.

139. A Careless and Homely Breeding is therefore preferable to one Nice and Delicate.

140. And he that is taught to live upon a little, owes more to his Father's Wisdom, than he that has a great deal left him, does to his Father's Care.

141. Children can't well be too hardly Bred: For besides that it fits them to bear the Roughest Providences, it is more Masculine, Active and Healthy.

142. Nay, 't is certain, that Liberty of the Mind is mightily preserved by it: For so 't is served, instead of being a Servant, indeed a Slave to sensual Delicacies.

143. As Nature is soon answered, so are such satisfied.

144. The Memory of the Ancients is hardly in any Thing more to be celebrated, than in a Strict and Useful Institution of Youth.

145. By Labor they prevented Luxury in their young People, till Wisdom and Philosophy had taught them to Resist and Despise it.

146. It must be therefore a gross Fault to strive so hard for the Pleasure of our Bodies, and be so insensible and careless of the Freedom of our Souls.

OF MAN'S INCONSIDERATENESS AND PARTIALITY

147. 'T is very observable, if our Civil Rights are invaded or in-croach'd upon, we are mightily touch'd, and fill every Place with our Resentment and Complaint; while we suffer our selves, our Better and Nobler Selves, to be the Property and Vassals of Sin, the worst of Invaders.

148. In vain do we expect to be delivered from such Troubles, till we are delivered from the Cause of them, our Disobedience to God.

149. When he has his Dues from us, it will be time enough for Him to give us ours out of one another.

150. 'T is our great Happiness, if we could understand it, that we meet with such Checks in the Career of our worldly Enjoyments, lest we should Forget the Giver, adore the Gift, and terminate our Felicity here, which is not Man's ultimate Bliss.

151. Our Losses are often made Judgments by our Guilt, and Mercies by our Repentance.

152. Besides, it argues great Folly in Men to let their Satisfaction exceed the true Value of any Temporal Matter: For Disappoint-ments are not always to be measured by the Loss of the Thing, but the Over-value we put upon it.

153. And thus Men improve their own Miseries, for want of an Equal and Just Estimate of what they Enjoy or Lose.

154. There lies a Proviso upon every Thing in this World, and we must observe it at our own Peril, viz. To love God above all, and Act for Judgment, the Last I mean.

OF THE RULE OF JUDGING

155. In all Things Reason should prevail: 'T is quite another Thing to be stiff than steady in an Opinion.

156. This May be Reasonable, but that is ever Wilful.

157. In such Cases it always happens, that the clearer the Argu-ment, the greater the Obstinacy, where the Design is not to be con-vinced.

158. This is to value Humor more than Truth, and prefer a sullen Pride to a reasonable Submission.

159. 'T is the Glory of a Man to vail to Truth; as it is the Mark of a good Nature to be Easily entreated.

160. Beasts Act by Sense, Man should by Reason; else he is a greater Beast than ever God made: And the Proverb is verified, The Corruption of the best Things is the worst and most offensive.

161. A reasonable Opinion must ever be in Danger, where Reason is not Judge.

162. Though there is a Regard due to Education, and the Tradition of our Fathers, Truth will ever deserve, as well as claim the Preference.

163. If like Theophilus and Timothy, we have been brought up in the Knowledge of the best Things, 't is our Advantage: But neither they nor we lose by trying their Truth; for so we learn their, as well as its intrinsick Worth.

164. Truth never lost Ground by Enquiry, because she is most of all Reasonable.

165. Nor can that need another Authority, that is Self-evident.

166. If my own Reason be on the Side of a Principle, with what can I Dispute or withstand it?

167. And if Men would once consider one another reasonably, they would either reconcile their Differences, or more Amicably maintain them.

168. Let That therefore be the Standard, that has most to say for itself; Tho' of that let every Man be Judge for himself.

169. Reason, like the Sun, is Common to All; And 't is for want of examining all by the same Light and Measure, that we are not all of the same Mind: For all have it to that End, though all do not use it So.

OF FORMALITY

170. Form is Good, but not Formality.

171. In the Use of the best of Forms there is too much of that I fear.

172. 'T is absolutely necessary, that this Distinction should go along with People in their Devotion; for too many are apter to rest upon What they do, than How they do their Duty.

173. If it were considered, that it is the Frame of the Mind that gives our Performances Acceptance, we would lay more Stress on our Inward Preparation than our Outward Action.

OF THE MEAN NOTION WE HAVE OF GOD

174. Nothing more shews the low Condition Man is fallen into, than the unsuitable Notion we must have of God, by the Ways we take to please him.

175. As if it availed any Thing to him that we performed so many Ceremonies and external Forms of Devotion, who never meant more by them, than to try our Obedience, and, through them, to shew us something more Excellent and Durable beyond them.

176. Doing, while we are Undoing, is good for nothing.

177. Of what Benefit is it to say our Prayers regularly, go to Church, receive the Sacraments, and may be go to Confessions too; ay, Feast the Priest, and give Alms to the Poor, and yet Lye, Swear, Curse, be Drunk, Covetous, Unclean, Proud, Revengeful, Vain and Idle at the same Time?

178. Can one excuse or ballance the other? Or will God think himself well served, where his Law is Violated? Or well used, where there is so much more Shew than Substance?

179. 'T is a most dangerous Error for a Man to think to excuse himself in the Breach of a Moral Duty, by a Formal Performance of Positive Worship; and less when of Human Invention.

180. Our Blessed Saviour most rightly and clearly distinguished and determined this Case, when he told the Jews, that they were his Mother, his Brethren and Sisters, who did the Will of his Father.

OF THE BENEFIT OF JUSTICE

181. Justice is a great Support of Society, because an Insurance to all Men of their Property: This violated, there 's no Security, which throws all into Confusion to recover it.

182. An Honest Man is a fast Pledge in Dealing. A Man is Sure to have it if it be to be had.

183. Many are so, merely of Necessity: Others not so only for the same Reason: But such an honest Man is not to be thanked, and such a dishonest Man is to be pity'd.

184. But he that is dishonest for Gain, is next to a Robber, and to be punish'd for Example.

185. And indeed there are few Dealers, but what are Faulty, which makes Trade Difficult, and a great Temptation to Men of Virtue.

186. 'T is not what they should, but what they can get: Faults or Decays must be concealed: Big Words given, where they are not deserved, and the Ignorance or Necessity of the Buyer imposed upon for unjust Profit.

187. These are the Men that keep their Words for their own Ends, and are only Just for Fear of the Magistrate.

188. A Politick rather than a Moral Honesty; a constrained, not a chosen Justice: According to the Proverb, Patience per Force, and thank you for nothing.

189. But of all Justice, that is the greatest, that passes under the Name of Law. A Cut-Purse in Westminster-Hall exceeds; for that advances Injustice to Oppression, where Law is alledged for that which it should punish.

OF JEALOUSY

190. The Jealous are Troublesome to others, but a Torment to themselves.

191. Jealousy is a kind of Civil War in the Soul, where Judgment and Imagination are at perpetual Jars.

192. This Civil Dissension in the Mind, like that of the Body Politick, commits great Disorders, and lays all waste.

193. Nothing stands safe in its Way: Nature, Interest, Religion, must Yield to its Fury.

194. It violates Contracts, Dissolves Society, Breaks Wedlock, Betrays Friends and Neighbors. No Body is Good, and every one is either doing or designing them a Mischief.

195. It has a Venome that more or less rankles wherever it bites: And as it reports Fancies for Facts, so it disturbs its own House as often as other Folks.

196. Its Rise is Guilt or Ill Nature, and by Reflection thinks its own Faults to be other Men's; as he that 's overrun with the Jaundice takes others to be Yellow.

197. A Jealous Man only sees his own Spectrum, when he looks upon other Men, and gives his Character in theirs.

OF STATE

198. I love Service, but not State; One is Useful, the other is Superfluous.

199. The Trouble of this, as well as Charge, is Real; but the Advantage only Imaginary.

200. Besides, it helps to set us up above our selves, and Augments our Temptation to Disorder.

201. The Least Thing out of Joint, or omitted, make us uneasy: and we are ready to think our selves ill served, about that which is of no real Service at all: Or so much better than other Men, as we have the Means of greater State.

202. But this is all for want of Wisdom, which carries the truest and most forceable State along with it.

203. He that makes not himself Cheap by indiscreet Conversation, puts Value enough upon himself every where.

204. The other is rather Pageantry than State.

OF A GOOD SERVANT

205. A True, and a Good Servant, are the same Thing.

206. But no Servant is True to his Master, that Defrauds him.

207. Now there are many Ways of Defrauding a Master, as, of Time, Care, Pains, Respect, and Reputation, as well as Money.

208. He that Neglects his Work, Robs his Master, since he is Fed and Paid as if he did his Best; and he that is not as Diligent in the Absence, as in the Presence of his Master, cannot be a true Servant.

209. Nor is he a true Servant, that buys dear to share in the Profit with the Seller.

210. Nor yet he that tells Tales without Doors; or deals basely in his Master's Name with other People; or Connives at others Loyterings, Wasteings, or dishonorable Reflections.

211. So that a true Servant is Diligent, Secret, and Respectful: More Tender of his Master's Honor and Interest, than of his own Profit.

212. Such a Servant deserves well, and if Modest under his Merit, should liberally feel it at his Master's Hand.

OF AN IMMEDIATE PURSUIT OF THE WORLD

213. It shews a Depraved State of Mind, to Cark and Care for that which one does not need.

214. Some are as eager to be Rich, as ever they were to Live: For Superfluity, as for Subsistence.

215. But that Plenty should augment Covetousness, is a Perversion of Providence; and yet the Generality are the worse for their Riches.

216. But it is strange, that Old Men should excel: For generally Money lies nearest them that are nearest their Graves; As if they would augment their Love in Proportion to the little Time they have left to enjoy it: And yet their Pleasure is without Enjoyment, since none enjoy what they do not use.

217. So that instead of learning to leave their greath Wealth easily, they hold the Faster, because they must leave it: So Sordid is the Temper of some Men.

218. Where Charity keeps Pace with Gain, Industry is blessed: But to slave to get, and keep it Sordidly, is a Sin against Providence, a Vice in Government, and an Injury to their Neighbors.

219. Such are they as spend not one Fifth of their Income, and, it may be, give not one Tenth of what they spend to the Needy.

220. This is the worst Sort of Idolatry, because there can be no Religion in it, nor Ignorance pleaded in Excuse of it; and that it wrongs other Folks that ought to have a Share therein.

OF THE INTEREST OF THE PUBLICK IN OUR ESTATES

221. Hardly any Thing is given us for our Selves, but the Publick may claim a Share with us. But of all we call ours, we are most accountable to God and the Publick for our Estates: In this we are but Stewards, and to Hord up all to ourselves is great Injustice as well as Ingratitude.

222. If all Men were so far Tenants to the Publick, that the Superfluities of Gain and Expence were applied to the Exigencies thereof, it would put an End to Taxes, leave never a Beggar, and make the greatest Bank for National Trade in Europe.

223. It is a Judgment upon us, as well as Weakness, tho' we wont't see it, to begin at the wrong End.

224. If the Taxes we give are not to maintain Pride, I am sure there would be less, if Pride were made a Tax to the Government.

225. I confess I have wondered that so many Lawful and Useful

Things are excised by Laws, and Pride left to Reign Free over them and the Publick.

226. But since People are more afraid of the Laws of Man than of God, because their Punishment seems to be nearest: I know not how magistrates can be excused in their suffering such Excess with Impunity.

227. Our Noble English Patriarchs as well as Patriots, were so sensible of this Evil, that they made several excellent Laws, commonly called Sumptuary, to Forbid, at least Limit the Pride of the People; which because the Execution of them would be our Interest and Honor, their Neglect must be our just Reproach and Loss.

228. 'T is but Reasonable that the Punishment of Pride and Excess should help to support the Government, since it must otherwise inevitably be ruined by them.

229. But some say, It ruins Trade, and will make the Poor Burthensome to the Publick; But if such Trade in Consequence ruins the Kingdom, is it not Time to ruin that Trade? Is Moderation no Part of our Duty, and Temperance an Enemy to Government?

230. He is a Judas that will get Money by any Thing.

231. To wink at a Trade that effeminates the People, and invades the Ancient Discipline of the Kingdom, is a Crime Capital, and to be severely punish'd instead of being excused by the Magistrate.

232. Is there no better Employment for the Poor than Luxury? Miserable Nation!

233. What did they before they fell into these forbidden Methods? Is there not Land enough in England to Cultivate, and more and better Manufactures to be Made?

234. Have we no Room for them in our Plantations, about Things that may augment Trade, without Luxury?

235. In short, let Pride pay, and Excess be well Excised: And if that will Cure the People, it will help to Keep the Kingdom.

THE VAIN MAN

236. But a Vain Man is a Nauseous Creature: He is so full of himself that he has no Room for any Thing else, be it never so Good or Deserving.

237. 'T is I at every turn that does this, or can do that. And as he

abounds in his Comparisons, so he is sure to give himself the better of every Body else; according to the Proverb, All his Geese are Swans.

238. They are certainly to be pity'd that can be so much mistaken at Home.

239. And yet I have sometimes thought that such People are in a sort Happy, that nothing can put out of Countenance with themselves, though they neither have nor merit other Peoples.

240. But at the same Time one would wonder they should not feel the Blows they give themselves, or get from others, for this intolerable and ridiculous Temper; nor shew any Concern at that which makes others blush for, as well as at them, (viz.) their unreasonable Assurance.

241. To be a Man's own Fool is bad enough, but the Vain Man is Every Body's.

242. This silly Disposition comes of a Mixture of Ignorance, Confidence, and Pride; and as there is more or less of the last, so it is more or less offensive or Entertaining.

243. And yet perhaps the worst Part of this Vanity is it's Unteachableness. Tell it any Thing, and it has known it long ago; and outruns Information and Instruction, or else proudly puffs at it.

244. Whereas the greatest Understandings doubt most, are readiest to learn, and least pleas'd with themselves; this, with no Body else.

245. For tho' they stand on higher Ground, and so see farther than their Neighbors, they are yet humbled by their Prospect, since it shews them something, so much higher and above their Reach.

246. And truly then it is, that Sense shines with the greatest Beauty when it is set in Humility.

247. An humble able Man is a Jewel worth a Kingdom: It is often saved by him, as Solomon's Poor Wise Man did the City.

248. May we have more of them, or less Need of them.

THE CONFORMIST

249. It is reasonable to concur where Conscience does not forbid a Compliance; for Conformity is at least a Civil Virtue.

250. But we should only press it in Necessaries, the rest may prove a Snare and Temptation to break Society.

251. But above all, it is a Weakness in Religion and Government,

where it is carried to Things of an Indifferent Nature, since besides that it makes Way for Scruples, Liberty is always the Price of it.

252. Such Conformists have little to boast of, and therefore the less Reason to Reproach others that have more Latitude.

253. And yet the Latitudinarian that I love, is one that is only so in Charity; for the Freedom I recommend is no Scepticism in Judgment, and much less so in Practice.

THE OBLIGATIONS OF GREAT MEN TO ALMIGHTY GOD

254. It seems but reasonable, that those whom God has Distinguish'd from others; by his Goodness, should distinguish themselves to him by their Gratitude.

255. For tho' he has made of One Blood all Nations, he has not rang'd or dignified them upon the Level, but in a sort of Subordination and Dependency.

256. If we look upwards, we find it in the Heavens, where the Planets have their several Degrees of Glory, and so the other Stars of Magnitude and Lustre.

257. If we look upon the Earth, we see it among the Trees of the Wood, from the Cedar to the Bramble; in the Waters among the Fish, from the Leviathan to the Sprat; in the Air among the Birds, from the Eagle to the Sparrow; among the Beasts, from the Lyon to the Cat; and among Mankind it self, from the King to the Scavenger.

258. Our Great Men, doubtless, were designed by the Wise Framer of the World for our Religious, Moral and Politick Planets; for Lights and Directions to the lower Ranks of the numerous Company of their own Kind, both in Precepts and Examples; and they are well paid for their Pains too, who have the Honor and Service of their fellow Creatures, and the Marrow and Fat of the Earth for their Share.

259. But is it not a most unaccountable Folly, that Men should be Proud of the Providences that should Humble them? Or think the Better of themselves, instead of Him that raised them so much above the Level; or in being so in their Lives, in Return of his Extraordinary Favors.

260. But it is but too near a-kin to us, to think no further than our

selves, either in the Acquisition, or Use of our Wealth and Greatness; when, alas, they are the Preferments of Heaven, to try our Wisdom, Bounty and Gratitude.

261. 'T is a dangerous Perversion of the End of Providence to Consume the Time, Power and Wealth he has given us above other Men, to gratify our Sordid Passions, instead of playing the good Stewards, to the Honor of our great Benefactor, and the Good of our Fellow-Creatures.

262. But it is an Injustice too; since those Higher Ranks of Men are but the Trustees of Heaven for the Benefit of lesser Mortals, who, as Minors, are intituled to all their Care and Provision.

263. For though God has dignified some Men above their Brethren, it never was to serve their Pleasures, but that they might take Pleasure to serve the Publick.

264. For this Cause doubtless it was, that they were raised above Necessity or any Trouble to Live, that they might have more Time and Ability to Care for Others: And 't is certain, where that Use is not made of the Bounties of Providence, they are Imbezzell'd and Wasted.

265. It has often struck me with a serious Reflection, when I have observed the great Inequality of the World; that one Man should have such Numbers of his fellow Creatures to Wait upon him, who have Souls to be saved as well as he; and this not for Business, but State. Certainly a poor Employment of his Money, and a worse of their Time.

266. But that any one Man should make Work for so many; or rather keep them from Work, to make up a Train, has a Levity and Luxury in it very reprovable, both in Religion and Government.

267. But even in allowable Services it has an humbling Consideration, and what should raise the Thankfulness of the Great Men to him that has so much better'd their Circumstances, and Moderated the Use of their Dominion over those of their own Kind.

268. When the poor Indians hear us call any of our Family by the Name of Servants, they cry out, What, call Brethren Servants! We call our Dogs Servants, but never Men. The Moral certainly can do us no Harm, but may Instruct us to abate our Height, and narrow our State and Attendance.

269. And what has been said of their Excess, may in some measure be apply'd to other Branches of Luxury, that set ill Examples to the lesser World, and Rob the Needy of their Pensions.

270. GOD Almighty Touch the Hearts of our Grandees with a Sense of his Distinguish'd Goodness, and that true End of it; that they may better distinguish themselves in their Conduct, to the Glory of Him that has thus liberally Preferr'd them, and the Benefit of their fellow Creatures.

OF REFINING UPON OTHER MEN'S ACTIONS OR INTERESTS

271. This seems to be the Master-Piece of our Politicians; But nc Body shoots more at Random, than those Refiners.

272. A perfect Lottery, and meer Hap-Hazard. Since the true Spring of the Actions of Men is as Invisible as their Hearts; and so are their Thoughts too of their several Interests.

273. He that judges of other Men by himself, does not always hit the Mark, because all Men have not the same Capacity, nor Passions in Interest.

274. If an able Man refines upon the Proceedings of an ordinary Capacity, according to his own, he must ever miss it: But much more the ordinary Man, when he shall pretend to speculate the Motives to the able Man's Actions: For the Able Man deceives himself by making t'other wiser than he is in the Reason of his Conduct; and the ordinary Man makes himself so, in presuming to judge of the Reasons of the Abler Man's Actions.

275. 'T is in short a Wood, a Maze, and of nothing are we more uncertain, nor in anything do we oftener befool ourselves.

276. The Mischiefs are many that follow this Humor, and dangerous: For Men Misguide themselves, act upon false Measures, and meet frequently with mischievous Disappointments.

277. It excludes all Confidence in Commerce; allows of no such Thing as a Principle in Practice; supposes every Man to act upon other Reasons than what appears, and that there is no such Thing as a Straightness or Sincerity among Mankind: A Trick instead of Truth.

278. Neither, allowing Nature or Religion; but some Worldly

Fetch or Advantage: The true, the hidden Motive to all Men to act or do.

279. 'T is hard to express its Uncharitableness, as well as Uncertainty; and has more of Vanity than Benefit in it.

280. This Foolish Quality gives a large Field, but let what I have said serve for this Time.

OF CHARITY

281. Charity has various Senses, but is Excellent in all of them.

282. It imports; first, the Commiseration of the Poor, and Unhappy of Mankind, and extends an Helping-Hand to mend their Condition.

283. They that feel nothing of this, are at best not above half of Kin to Human Race; since they must have no Bowels, which makes such an Essential Part thereof, who have no more Nature.

284. A Man, and yet not have the Feeling of the Wants or Needs of his own Flesh and Blood! A Monster rather! And may he never be suffer'd to propagate such an unnatural Stock in the World.

285. Such an Uncharitableness spoils the best Gains, and two to one but it entails a Curse upon the Possessors.

286. Nor can we expect to be heard of God in our Prayers, that turn the deaf Ear to the Petitions of the Distressed amongst our fellow Creatures.

287. God sends the Poor to try us, as well as he tries them by being such: And he that refuses them a little out of the great deal that God has given him, Lays up Poverty in Store for his own Posterity.

288. I will not say these Works are Meritorious, but dare say they are Acceptable, and go not without their Reward: Tho' to Humble us in our Fulness and Liberality too, we only Give but what is given us to Give as well as use; for if we are not our own, less is that so which God has intrusted us with.

289. Next, CHARITY makes the best Construction of Things and Persons, and is so far from being an evil Spy, a Backbiter, or a Detractor, that it excuses Weakness, extenuates Miscarriages, makes the best of every Thing; forgives every Body, serves All, and hopes to the End.

290. It moderates Extreams, is always for Expediences, labors to accommodate Differences, and had rather suffer than Revenge: And

so far from Exacting the utmost Farthing, that it had rather lose than seek her Own Violently.

291. As it acts Freely, so, Zealously too; but 't is always to do Good, for it hurts no Body.

292. An Universal Remedy against Discord, and an Holy Cement for Mankind.

293. And lastly, 'T is Love to God and the Brethren, which raises the Soul above all worldly Considerations; and, as it gives a Taste of Heaven upon Earth, so 't is Heaven in the Fulness of it hereafter to the truly Charitable here.

294. This is the Noblest Sense Charity has, after which all should press, as that more Excellent Way.

295. Nay, *most* Excellent; for as Faith, Hope and Charity were the more Excellent Way that Great Apostle discovered to the Christians, (too apt to stick in Outward Gifts and Church Performances) so of that better Way he preferred Charity as the best Part, because it would out-last the rest, and abide for ever.

296. Wherefore a Man can never be a true and good Christian without Charity, even in the lowest Sense of it: And yet he may have that Part thereof, and still be none of the Apostle's true Christian, since he tells us, That tho' we should give all our Goods to the Poor, and want Charity (in her other and higher Senses) it would profit us nothing.

297. Nay, tho' we had All Tongues, All Knowledge, and even Gifts of Prophesy, and were Preachers to others; ay, and had Zeal enough to give our Bodies to be burned, yet if we wanted Charity, it would not avail us for Salvation.

298. It seems it was his (and indeed ought to be our) *Unum Necessarium,* or the One Thing Needful, which our Saviour attributed to Mary in Preference to her Sister Martha, that seems not to have wanted the lesser Parts of Charity.

299. Would God this Divine Virtue were more implanted and diffused among Mankind, the Pretenders to Christianity especially, and we should certainly mind Piety more than Controversy, and Exercise Love and Compassion instead of Censuring and Persecuting one another in any Manner whatsoever.

END OF PART II